An Illustrated History
of Trigger

An Illustrated History of Trigger

The Lives and Legend of Roy Rogers' Palomino

LEO PANDO

Foreword by CORKY RANDALL

McFarland & Company, Inc., Publishers
Jefferson, North Carolina, and London

The present work is a reprint of the illustrated case bound edition of An Illustrated History of Trigger: The Lives and Legend of Roy Rogers' Palomino *first published in 2008 by McFarland.*

Frontispiece: The one and only, Trigger.

LIBRARY OF CONGRESS CATALOGUING-IN-PUBLICATION DATA

Pando, Leo, 1947–
An illustrated history of Trigger : the lives and legend of Roy Rogers'
palomino / Leo Pando ; foreword by Corky Randall.
p.   cm.
Filmography : p.
Includes bibliographical references and index.

ISBN 978-0-7864-6111-0
softcover : 50# alkaline paper ∞

1. Trigger (Horse)   I. Title.
PN1995.9.A5P36   2011   791.4502'80929 [B]—dc22   2007034266

British Library cataloguing data are available

Front cover: Trigger. Back cover: Little Trigger and
Roy Rogers (Ray White collection); background © 2011 Shutterstock

Manufactured in the United States of America

*McFarland & Company, Inc., Publishers
Box 611, Jefferson, North Carolina 28640
www.mcfarlandpub.com*

For my father, Leo,
who gave me a respect for nature and love of horses.
For my mother, Emma,
who loves her family unconditionally
and gave her children an appreciation of art.
And to them both for that fall day in 1957
when they took Eva, Priscilla, and me
to the Albuquerque State Fairgrounds
in the old '48 Chevy to see the King of the Cowboys
and his very special palomino.

Acknowledgments: Trigger Pals

Much of the material in this book came from the hard work of amateur and professional researchers alike. I am indebted to them not only for their work, but their inspiration as well.

I believe that a shared experience is a better experience, and I share my interest in Trigger with a group of people I refer to as the Trigger Pals. They are fans with whom I can discuss the varied aspects of his story in depth. I reference many of them throughout this book.

Robert W. Phillips' *Roy Rogers* book, with its groundbreaking scholarship and research, was my main inspiration. It was met with some criticism and even animosity when it was first published in 1995. Phillips had detractors who thought he was being disrespectful, but even they could not deny his knowledge. By documenting the life and career of Roy Rogers honestly and thoroughly, he also celebrated it. The western genre is replete with articles and books; but Rawhide Bob, as he liked to be called, broke from the pack with his unique voice. He documented Roy Rogers, Dale Evans, and Trigger as no one had before. Phillips didn't just report the facts; he brought candor and detailed analysis to his work. Beyond his passion, he had the ability to see the big picture. He could connect seemingly different aspects of his subject into a coherent whole. "My research will continue indefinitely and I hope that others will be devoted enough to carry on," he once wrote me.

The foundation of this book was laid in the pages of George Coan's newsletter, *The Old Cowboy Picture Show*, which he continues to edit and publish. As a B-western advocate, collector, and expert, there was not much about the genre he didn't know. His posse of saddle pals refer to me as the Professor of Triggernometry, something I take a great deal of pride in.

While selecting photographs for this book I tried to stay away from those that had been reproduced over and over. However, there were exceptions, like the few existing solo shots of Trigger. I wanted a mix of the classic and the unique. Fortunately, I met collector Roy Dillow, who has an amazing Roy Rogers photograph library and was very generous. Ardent fan and astute observer of the King of the Cowboys, Dillow made me aware of Rogers' appearance in the obscure film *Jamboree* (Exploitation Productions, 1954). He also reminded me of the retirement celebration for Trigger on the old Roy Rogers and Dale Evans *Chevy Show* (NBC, 1960s) television variety hour.

Corky Randall was cordial, candid, generous with his time, and very forthcoming with information and rare photographs (scanned by his grandson John Randall Morrissey). My sister Eva Radford was a godsend. Not only was she a great moral support, but she helped shape this book with her suggestions and editing skills. Jerry Dean, loyal *The Old Cowboy Picture Show* contributor, is a serious student of the life of Roy Rogers. Like Robert W. Phillips, Dean is able to see the big picture and was one of my primary sounding boards. He also proofread the last drafts of this book, and I cannot thank him enough for his insights and fresh approach. Joel "Dutch" Dortch, with ties to the Rogers family through the Happy Trails Foundation, accessed valuable information and phone numbers, including a copy of the actual bill of sale drawn up between Roy Rogers and Hudkins Stables toward the purchase of Trigger. Bobby J. Copeland, author, historian, and archivist, with an encyclopedic knowledge and willingness to share, was my safety net. Steve Jensen was my ace when it came to the Lone Ranger. He maintains one of the best sites on the Web devoted to the legendary masked man, *Clayton Moore/The Lone Ranger*. The great solo shot of Silver that graces this book, Jensen got from Adam Mendoza of Massachusetts. Jensen fact-checked my section on Silver and also put me in contact with Dawn Moore. Tim Lasiuta possesses a comprehensive knowledge of western comic books and was a tremendous resource. Larry Roe, Trigger fan to the core, served as a great touchstone. Roe spent hours viewing Roy Rogers movies and collecting data for this project.

Never in my wildest childhood dreams would I have seen that one day I would be receiving correspondence and rare photographs from the children of my cowboy heroes. In July of 2006, Dawn Moore sent me rare photographs, including one of her father, Clayton, with Roy Rogers and Dale Evans. Cheryl Rogers-Barnett not only loaned me rare photographs of her with her father and Trigger, but was very generous with information. She was very supportive of my book and a joy to correspond with. Around the same time I was also trading e-mails with Karla Buhlman, vice president of Gene Autry Entertainment. She too was forthcoming with rare photographs and even fact-checked my section on Champion. She also put me in contact with Cheryl Rogers-Barnett.

Thanks to George Mudryj for important contact information from the Palomino Horse Association; Carolyn Martin for photographs of the beautiful Estes Tarter golden statues of Trigger; researcher Bart Kooker for his help with the Lone Ranger; my good friend Alana Coghland for information and photographs of Trigger Street and Trigger Place; breed and registry expert Pat Mefferd who had firsthand knowledge of many of Hollywood's legendary horses, including Trigger, Dice, and others; Lisabeth West, for her expertise on Stuart horses and the gorgeous photograph of the rearing Trigger figure; Malcolm Macfarlane of the International Club Crosby for information on Bing Crosby; Mark Governor, who came through with advice regarding the use of lyrics and Republic Pictures contacts; Hunter Hampton, with an expert eye and lifelong experience of horses; Faye Thompson, photograph department coordinator of the Margaret Herrick Archive in Beverly Hills, for being kind and gracious; my good friend and ace designer Jack Tom for his suggestions; Steven Rebuck, president of the Palomino Horse Association; Petrine Mitchum for rare photographs and important contact information; Mark Nakamura for his computer assistance and support; Janey Miller for hard-to-find articles and rare photographs; Cece Phillips, Margaret and Jim Pananen, Mike Johnson, Debbie Percival, Derwood Harris, Bette Orkin Savitt; and *Lone Ranger* and *Hi-Yo Silver* artist, the late-great Tom Gill.

For their love and support, I thank my twin sister Priscilla Marquez and especially my wife, Diane Bowen. I would have been lost without her.

For their constant words of wisdom and encouragement, I thank my friends: Jim Barrett, Gerry Boyle, Johnny Lee, Francis Lewis, Dan Quarnstrom, David Russell, and Nick Komis who is always close by.

For their inspiration, my best wishes and affection go to the gentle Daisy, the formidable Beauty, sad Lieutenant, kind-hearted Herman, impressive Pal, precious Mary, angry Annie, reliable Pip, breath-taking Butcher, high-strung Elle, magnificent Zeus, and my very own beautiful Navajo. There was a little bit of "Trigger" in each while I was riding them.

Leo Pando • China, Maine • Fall 2007

Table of Contents

Foreword

All I can say about old Trigger is that he was just a lovely, gentle and kind horse. He was a wonder horse in regards to making pictures. For the longest period of time there were no doubles for him. Roy would get off and a stunt man would get on. I don't think that any other picture horse that I know of served their rider the same as old Trigger.

Around strangers and the public or whatever, you had to watch Little Trigger. You know, somebody might reach out and try to touch him or something. If you didn't have your eye on him, he might give them a nip. He would give Roy a nip or two on the stage when Roy was working him.

You can't imagine, I can't imagine the thousands, the millions of people. I don't have a picture but I've seen them where Roy is among a crowd and all these hands reaching out, rubbing and touching that horse. An animal can't tolerate that so much. You can't imagine the thousands of miles that horse traveled. And he traveled by airplane, he traveled by boat, and he traveled by van. And when Roy and my dad started out, why, he traveled in a two-horse trailer behind a station wagon.

Trigger Jr. was the most elegant of the three horses in appearance. He was a nice horse. I showed him in rodeos as Golden Zephyr. Roy only used him for a short period of time. Zephyr came right at the end of Roy's riding career. Zephyr had tricks on him, he had everything on him. When Little Trigger couldn't travel anymore, he took Zephyr and the tricks were there. They just went at it. I don't think people ever noticed the difference, even though none of the three horses looked alike at all.

Of all the western stars that came up a little before Roy and after, there's never been a set of three horses like those Triggers. All at the same time — that's just a phenomenal thing. Three great horses that I had the privilege to ride and care for. I rode all of them; they were in the barn and had to be exercised. Those horses were almost like family. They were the foundation that I stand on today.

Corky Randall
Newhall, California

Preface

This book offers a detailed look at how the magic of a palomino wonder horse was put on screen and before live audiences by Roy Rogers and by Glenn Randall, one of the finest trainers to work in Hollywood.

I wrote this book for a number of reasons. Beyond a desire to organize Trigger's confusing history and celebrate it, this book also started as an ode to my father.[1] As a child I was fascinated by the stories he told about being raised around horses on a farm in the northern part of New Mexico and using them for transportation before he rode in automobiles. As his health started to fade in the mid–1990s, I renewed my childhood interest in horses and B-westerns. At first not realizing the connection, later I was struck by the irony of how, in the shadow of his mortality, I was reconnecting with things that had brought me not only pleasure as a child, but also a sense of security. To those who prefer I'd left the fantasy of Trigger alone I say that a fresh look at what inspired us when we were young can be just as inspiring now.

Writing this book took me to places I hadn't anticipated. I thought I'd just be writing a biography of a special horse I'd become infatuated with when I was a child. I did not expect the process to be so introspective. Our passions define who we are. They can even touch on the spiritual. They are often unobtainable, and that only adds to their mystique. Like the quest for the Holy Grail, passions take us on an outward and inward journey. They are a way of getting to the best part of ourselves. In my case, one of my great passions has been horses, and Roy Rogers' palomino Trigger is one of many who I've always found fascinating.

I had no first-hand knowledge of the original Trigger. The only times I was around him, or what's left of him, was during two visits to the Roy Rogers and Dale Evans Museum in Victorville, California. I witnessed what the taxidermist had done. Although I saw Roy Rogers in person four times, only on one of those occasions was he with a palomino. I've accumulated a great deal of research from books, magazines, and the Internet, and feedback from fans whom I consider credible and expert in the B-western genre. I have supplemented my findings with common sense, knowledge gained through observation and my own experience of horses (I have been around them for most of my adult life) and the movie-making process (although I could best be described as a film aficionado, I have worked as an assistant film editor and storyboard illustrator).

The K Circle B Show

B-western heroes, and especially their horses, meant a great deal to me growing up in Santa Fe, New Mexico, in the 1950s. I have vivid memories that go back to 1952, recollections from my grade school days, watching wrestling matches and local variety shows on a neighbor's television set, By the time my family got our own television, B-westerns were syndicated on all three Albuquerque channels. I saw only a few on movie screens (I remember watching Roy Rogers and Trigger in *The Bells of San Angelo* at a theatre with my dad). I would come home from Alvord Elementary School at 3:30, head straight for our old black and white GE television and watch the films of Kermit Maynard, Bob Steele, and Johnny Mack Brown. These were very early B-westerns, ones without music during the chase sequences. KOB-TV, the NBC affiliate, started an after-school program called the *K Circle B Show*. The host was a local cowboy celebrity, Dick Bills, the uncle of singer Glenn Campbell. On Monday, Wednesdays, and Fridays, Bills presented the films of Roy Rogers; Tuesdays and Thursdays he'd show Gene Autry movies. They were followed by comedy shorts featuring the Little Rascals.

When I wasn't watching B-westerns on television, I was acting out B-western scenarios, either with the latest Marx toy sets from Sears or in costume with my neighborhood pals Rey Montez and Charlie Lopez. We formed a fearsome trio, our own version of the Three Mesquiteers, fighting imaginary evildoers in the yard around my home. I still have a stick horse my father carved out of an old piece of pine. With attached leather ears and a lacquer finish, it looked palomino. I named it Goldie.

The simplistic world of the B-western where Roy Rogers and his peers thrived gave way to teenaged angst. The genre and players soon became passé in the wake of rock and roll and the turbulent 1960s. I drifted away from B-westerns by the time I was in junior high. In my thirties, however, my interest was renewed unexpectedly in, of all places, Brooklyn, New York. I was working as a freelance illustrator in Manhattan when a friend invited me to go horseback riding. It had been about 12 years since I'd last been in the saddle. Before I knew it we were at Culmit Stables in Prospect Park. The minute I got on a horse again, I was transfixed. I felt as if I'd come home. I asked myself, "Why haven't I done this sooner?" The horse I'd rented that fateful day was a little palomino with a white blaze named Trigger.

I rediscovered B-western movies during this same time, and bought my first VCR. The first tape I purchased included three episodes of the *Lone Ranger* television show, including the pilot, "Enter the Lone Ranger." Life is circular, not linear. While B-westerns still nurtured me as they had when I was a boy, I saw them through the eyes of a grown man. The simple B-western plots and one-dimensional characters did not sustain me anymore; however, they had personality, the music was still great, the action sequences remained thrilling, and they still resonated of honesty and fair play. I was reminded the B-westerns had heart. I had a renewed admiration for what the modest B-westerns accomplished on the edges of the Hollywood mainstream. The cowboy and horse connection was at their core. Remove horses and B-western films are not as engaging: no horse, no cowboy. With all Roy Rogers' charisma and talent, take Trigger away, and Rogers is not as compelling. Just as mustangs have become noble symbols of the West, with their free spirits and endurance, Trigger and his equine peers stood for all that was good in B-westerns: trust, bravery, loyalty, friendship, and grace.

Webster's defines *grace* by how it manifests itself outwardly and inwardly; beauty or charm of form, composition, movement, or expression. It has to do with a sense of what is right and proper; decency. Mother Teresa, Eleanor Roosevelt, and Jacqueline Bouvier Kennedy Onassis were the personifications of grace. Fred Astaire had it. So did Cary Grant, James Stewart, Katharine Hepburn, Olivia de Havilland, and Grace Kelly. Roy Rogers and, yes, Trigger had it.

While researching this book I screened every Roy Rogers B-western that Republic Pictures made and was just as captivated as when I saw them as a kid. I was entertained again by old friends in their prime. How could one not like great characters like Gabby Hayes, Andy Devine, and Raymond Hatton? B-western clothes, with their colorful designs, were wonderful, especially the shirts. "Tumbling Tumbleweeds" and "Don't Fence Me In" are classic songs. Yes, B-westerns are naïve; still, there's a generosity of spirit in the simple black and white films. Sure, the early producers and players wanted to make a buck, but they didn't hit their fans over the head with things like product placement. Marketing was not as blatant or as diabolically efficient as it is today. If a kid came away with lessons in fair play, honesty, and good conduct, what was the harm if he also had the desire to buy a comic book? Entertainment, for good or bad, has enormous influence and serves as a normal compass to children.

A cynic many be defined as a wounded idealist. I understand that all too well. I also understand how some parents may not want to raise their children with romantic notions of how the world should be. Whether they do or not, a price is paid. My passion for Trigger, and horses in general, represents an idealized view of life. As an adult, living in a world of terrorism, corporate power, and a diminishing natural environment, it's an uphill battle to be optimistic. Trigger and Roy Rogers brought a sweet innocence into my life that, unfortunately, cannot exist the same way any more. A part of me died when they passed away. Their loss is even sadder given the current state of the world with its strip malls, built-in obsolescence, spin doctors, fast food, political scandals, corporate crime, pornography, and so on. Where is grace?

In spite of my age, the cynicism of the times, and the discoveries I made regarding Trigger, I cherish the fantasy of this special horse and will be forever grateful for having lived at a time when I could believe it.

The "So What" Factor

One can't work on a subject like Trigger without being aware of how out of sync it is with the times (kids today know only Roy Rogers as the name of a restaurant chain). A friend refers to this as the "so what" factor, and part of my task is to make an argument for why Trigger is still compelling. My main audience consists of people for whom the "so what" factor, regarding Roy Rogers, Trigger, and B-westerns, never enters their minds.

The B-western era is anachronistic, and even this is relative. After all, it was only 50-some years ago! Honesty, courage, and justice form the foundation of every healthy society. While cynical indifference seems to be the fashion today, the subject of this book called upon me to wear my heart on my sleeve. If I succeed, even to a limited degree, in reopening the door that has closed on the values and aspirations that B-western movies stood for, that would be great. The values found in the hero epics on which baby boomers were nurtured serve as a kind of distillation of cherished American and humanist values, and such values have always been best presented (and absorbed) through the popular media.

I submit that the story of Trigger and Roy Rogers is of value because our interests nourish us and we should, in turn, nourish them. Movies, television, even comic books, can sometimes be more than just entertainment. They serve as touchstones and guides, like great literature or paintings. Most important, they give us a sense of being alive; they awaken us from our routines. They reaffirm and define our humanity.

Who Was Trigger?

I spent a great deal of time discussing Trigger with Roy Rogers expert Robert W. Phillips. In spite of hours spent scrutinizing photos, text, films, and television shows, in the end, there were things about the horse that eluded us and that made Phillips cautious. When it comes to Hollywood, believe none of what you hear and only part of what you see. He and I agreed that there were some things we would never prove conclusively related to "Trigger," certainly not to the satisfaction of every serious fan.

Phillips (who passed away in 2001) never had firsthand knowledge of any "Trigger." Still, he was a meticulous investigator. He had a natural curiosity and loved research. He believed it was important to present as complete a story as possible, warts and all. In spite of all his accumulated knowledge of Trigger, Phillips was frustrated, and the following paragraphs from his personal correspondence to me explain why. They reflect some of what I've been discussing. In spite of his misgivings, his writings are filled with enthusiasm for his subject.

How many "Triggers" are up there in the sky, that have helped keep the Roy Rogers legend alive? There are so many different accounts (regarding Trigger) both prior to my book and since then, that they all merge together. There is not one fiftieth of doubt in my mind that there are more Triggers, Champions, Silvers, Toppers (yes, Topper) as well, and many no-namers than we will ever see. And there is not one iota of doubt in my mind that Golden Cloud (aka Trigger) ran across the cameras in more films than we will ever determine.

Hollywood created a mythical "Trigger." The machine went to work, with some ace people in position, the illusion machine, the publicity machine. Everything they released was meant for instant and immediate consumption and dissemination. Nothing was ever released, be it a statement or a photograph, for the purpose of anyone collecting them and comparing them. No film was ever made, no editing ever performed for someone to look at it frame by frame. If you do, you will see a lot of stuff that was not intended to be seen. You will see that which the editor knew you would not see with the frames in fast motion. This is a fiction in motion. Fantasy.

And any magician is almost being a traitor to his profession, by dispelling the illusions of his trade, revealing the secrets of his proud profession, and contributing to the end of magic as entertainment, even in retirement. They spent a lifetime putting on shows, thrilling young and old alike, and they look back upon their work with pride, for they were damned good at what they did; they became a legend. Houdini, the great this or that, or "Roy Rogers," the great "King of the Cowboys." No way is this legend likely to ever sell out the happiness that he brought folks, who assumed that he brought the "Smartest Horse in the Movies," "Trigger," all the way from sunny California, to the state of Michigan, or Kentucky or Maine, to put on a show for their fans. All palominos with more or less identical markings, gold in color with a white mane and tail, and 1–4 white stockings. [Here Phillips imagines Roy Rogers providing details about his horses:] "And the one I rode in such and such parade belonged to so and so who has a palomino ranch nearby, and I've ridden that horse in the parades every time I went to Fort Worth, etc. And we had this horse in the trailer that did such and such tricks, and for the next show, that horse in the trailer that did so and so tricks; and between shows my trainer was putting the next horse I would use through his tricks, and I have no earthly idea 'who' all those horses were, or who some of them even belonged to. When it came time for me to ride into that arena on a horse, I was 'Roy Rogers,' and that beautiful palomino was 'Trigger.'" It ain't gonna happen.

There were trainers who knew. There were horseman/friends/contractors/connections scattered all over the country who knew. But by and large the secrets and business transactions have all gone to the graves with the cowboys. And whatever secrets Roy Rogers can recall, will go the same way with him.

I am never, I am convinced, going to "prove" anything related to all these "Triggers." I am only going to be able to render opinions. It is almost impossible to search for and find reality and truth in a media that is meant in every detail, to deceive.[2]

Robert W. Phillips was, bless him, somewhat of a perfectionist. With respect to the study of history, loose ends are inevitable. The researcher is at the mercy of available resources and the mood of the times. It is a lucky historian who can corroborate his or her sources. Phillips would have loved to check his findings with Rogers and Randall. However, he knew better than to ask them to explain a fantasy which took them decades to build. That would have been expecting too much.

One may wonder, why attempt to sort out the legend of "Trigger" when even an expert such as Phillips had his misgivings? Why publish anything that would be contrary to the publicity generated by Rogers and company regarding such a beautiful fantasy?

First of all, it's a lot of fun. The fact that history can be elusive only makes it more fascinating. Readers are free to draw their own conclusions. It's highly doubtful Rogers, the directors he worked with, and the screenwriters who provided him with stories thought in deep symbolic terms. Admittedly, Robert W. Phillips and I got pretty carried away and read more into "Trigger" than Rogers and Randall may have intended. As kids, we were supposed to—and how could we not? Director Federico Fellini wisely advised, "Never lose your childhood enthusiasm." Fiction requires a suspension of disbelief and a leap of faith. Nevertheless, no matter how outrageous, fiction should be credible within the parameters of its genre. The audience should at least be entertained and not insulted. If something is learned about the human condition, all the better. Art is like that. While one can learn from an artist's intent, it's what one brings to an artwork that makes it resonate.

In the end, Phillips was pretty philosophical: "I understand your fascination with the legend of Roy Rogers, the legend of Trigger, etc," he wrote me. "It's some story, decades long ... involving many horses. Art Rush created one of the most intricate spider webs of a legend over the years, using Leonard Sly, that Ohio farm boy as 'Roy Rogers,' that ever came out of Hollywood, and it was everyone's desire to leave this world with it all intact ... and they accomplished this. I cut through a lot of it, out of a natural curiosity, and a love for research ... and most misinterpreted my intentions, seeing me as a traitor to something of value in their lives. So, continue spinning the web, keeping it around ... for I enjoyed working on it for years."

Fiction, Magic, Fantasy and the Great Contradiction

When children watched B-western movies in the 1940s and 1950s, they were ignorant of the filmmaking process. B-westerns were never discussed technically during their heyday. Fans believed what they saw on screen. Not much was known about look-alikes, stuntmen, or special effects. It never occurred to most fans that Rogers was riding Trigger doubles, although there were clues beyond differences in markings and conformation from horse to horse. The fact that the movies were black and white also gave them a special aura; they were already removed from reality in their own context. The black and white movie-making process gave Roy Rogers and "Trigger" an iconic stature. Film critic Roger Ebert hit the nail on the head with an insightful comment: "What black and white is, is the essence of something, whereas color is a particular example of it."[3]

Magic can be very fragile, especially as it applies to movies. That's ironic, because we live in a time when we have the film technology to realize any scenario that a screenwriter or a director can imagine. However, it's now commonplace for motion pictures to be released not only with previously deleted footage but with extra features that explain production techniques and special effects. Magazines like *Cinefex* and *American Cinematographer* are devoted to such things. All this is a mixed blessing. While the extra features that come with DVDs are great fun as well as educational, there's something to be said for not knowing anything

Roy Rogers and the original Trigger at a rare personal appearance by the palomino, most likely taken in Southern California circa 1947 judging by the hat Rogers was using (he changed to a flat style around the time he appeared in *Apache Rose*) (*Janey Miller collection*).

about special effects. On the one hand, one's appreciation for the talent and hard work of movie makers is enhanced. On the other, magic and mystery are sacrificed in degrees. Movies today are spectacular and great eye-candy, but there's no mystery to them anymore and, consequently, they've lost some of their magic. After the 1968 movie *2001: A Space Odyssey* (MGM) was completed, director Stanley Kubrick ordered all production plans and models destroyed. Kubrick may have been doing fans a favor when he denied them access to the film techniques behind his science fiction masterpiece.

I am amazed by what Roy Rogers, his trainer Glenn Randall, and "Trigger" accomplished. If anything, I have more respect for them now than I had as a kid. Still, that doesn't mean I wasn't straddling both sides of the fence while writing this book.

Fantasy and magic are almost synonymous; both have mystery at their core. One has to be careful when analyzing them. Take away mystery and they may not be as compelling. There's a fine line to be considered; deconstructing a fantasy may enhance it and may disempower it. While it sounds like a contradiction, my goal is to celebrate the fantasy of "Trigger" via biography and analysis. The contradiction here is not as great as one might believe at first. Yes, there is something lost and something gained, but the scales are heavily weighted in favor of the gains.

People become bored with fantasy that no longer stands up to their sophistication. Their taste changes as they grow. All that said, there is much that one doesn't outgrow, that one returns to again and again. Some magic is so potent that the secrets behind it are equally compelling. Some characters continue to grow as we do, and we never lose the affection we experienced from the start. For some, the potent fantasy of Roy Rogers and "Trigger" has not lost its luster, because the magic is not in the fantasy but in oneself.

A partnership like that of Roy Rogers, Glenn Randall, and "Trigger" is formed almost by luck and great timing, but it does not survive that way. B-western players gave their fans magic with timeless music, classic characters, engaging stories, and impeccable horsemanship. This book is a tribute to people, horses, and a genre that was popular from the 1930s till the late 1950s and resonates with fans to this day. The magicians who worked with "Trigger" are a very interesting bunch and are part of what this book is about. No apology is necessary for fleshing out the story of "Trigger." It is a journey from wonder to appreciation. The "Trigger" fantasy is in no danger from this book. Many fans now have also been part way down this same path; my job is to take them the rest of the way. At the end of this book, the reader should have a clearer picture of how the fantasy of a wonder horse was accomplished, and the magic will still linger.[4]

This book is, finally, a personal acknowledgement of what "Trigger" meant. He was, after all, at the core of every little cowgirl's and cowboy's dreams. A special horse (especially a palomino in fancy show tack) set the tone of a scene by its presence and still symbolizes the romance of the West. Take note of how fan Jerry Dean feels after five decades:

> But, no matter what anyone ever says about Trigger, or what I think about the way he was farmed out to trainers and caretakers almost all of his life, I'm happiest about the fact that, in his films and TV shows, Roy was always riding him. You can't say that for any of the other western stars. Even sidekicks came and went, but, for as long as I watched them, and loved them, and pretended to be them with my plaster lathe horse and cap guns, I always saw Roy riding "Trigger." In my heart, and in my memory of those days ... riding "Trigger" down the canyon between the barn and the old Chevy truck where I suspected there might lurk my "bad guy" brother in ambush ... my "Trigger" never failed to warn me of the danger just in the nick of time and get us both to cover for the gun battle that followed. And, when it was my brother's turn to be "Roy" and I was the bad guy, no matter how carefully I hid my presence, "Trigger" managed to alert my brother, too. It's nice to know today that no matter which movie or TV show of theirs I watch, I still see the companionship I believed in then. It's always the two of them together, no matter who the supporting cast may be, and it always will be.[5]

"Trigger" was intelligent, beautiful, athletic, and charismatic. These qualities enabled him to add a great deal of ambience and mystique to a movie. "Trigger" transported Rogers and his fans to a West that never was, a place where horses could keep up with cars and trains, where guns fired more than six rounds, where people were shot but never bled. Most importantly, in the Roy Rogers version of the West, good always won over evil. B-western cowboys like Roy Rogers, Gene Autry, and the Lone Ranger communicated a generosity of spirit partially through their horses. A silver-throated cowboy on a gorgeous horse, triumphing over the evils of the world with a gun, a guitar, and a faithful sidekick was a wonderful child's fantasy of how things should be.

Robert W. Phillips expressed what many have felt when he wrote, "Yes, it was all an illusion. It is still an illusion. But we're all the richer for it. We have a real need for illusions such as these, in the world today."

The Land of Eternal Youth

In one way or another, I've been chasing "Trigger" all my life. He existed in a romanticized West that I loved, and he still remains a symbol of a simpler place and time. In spite of all I've learned about his life — the workings behind the fantasy, the shaping of a corporate logo — it's a chase I continue to enjoy. I've heard it said many times that the journey is more important than the destination. I am reminded of cowboys in fiction who were obsessed with catching, training, and owning some special wild horse they never caught. Remember the Byrds' classic tune "Chestnut Mare," about an elusive horse and a never-ending pursuit for her? I see Robert W. Phillips that way. I have visions of him riding his own palomino, Thunder, with his lasso out and ready. "Trigger" is galloping ahead in the distance. With every hill and arroyo the golden stallion continues to maintain his distance while remaining in view. For Phillips and the rest of us, "Trigger" and the B-westerns he represents are constantly inspiring and yet always elusive. That's a great trail to have ahead and, with any luck, one that never ends.

In the 1993 film *Into the West* (Miramax) a grandfather tells his grandsons the legend of the Irish horse Tír na nÓg (pronounced tear-knee-no). As long as a rider stays on its back he will never age; if he ever dismounts or is thrown off, he will get old and die. When asked what the name Tír na nÓg means, the old man replies, "the land of eternal youth."[6]

It would seem that I have my own particular white whale to chase.[7] It has taken the form of a palomino I first became infatuated with as a little boy and has resulted in this book. Nostalgia is a very powerful thing. I'm glad to say I'll never be a kid again, but all I have to do is look upon "Trigger" and the feelings of hope that so nourished me and were the best part of being a kid are mine once more. When I watch B-westerns, I see individuals at their best. There are those who see B-westerns as arcane and naive. Historian Bobby Copeland was right when he told me, "You cannot explain to the younger generation the fascination that we, who grew up in that era, have for B-western films." If you were there, no explanation is necessary, and if you weren't, no explanation will do. To anyone who cannot empathize with or has no time for a genre from days gone by, I say, "Tread softly because you tread on my dreams."[8] For the general public now, Trigger is, at the same time, a fond remembrance and a morbid artifact in a museum. For me he's much more than a corporate logo or marketing tool. I choose to see him as a symbol of hope and grace. He's Tír na nÓg, and as such, he'll always be the land of eternal youth.

Introduction:
The Horse Prances

"Far back, far back in our dark soul the horse prances." — D.H. Lawrence[1]

Background

Horses are one of the most important animals humans ever domesticated. It is hard to imagine how civilization, for better or worse, would have proceeded without them. Whether as beasts of burden or transportation, in military campaigns or exploration, the horse made forward motion possible; civilization would have taken longer to develop had it not been for the horse.

Countless books have been published about the bond between humans and horses. In our imagination, that bond is strongest when it binds horse to cowboy. Today the cowboy is seen at his best, as a symbol of rugged individualism, when he's on a horse. The romance of the cowboy and the allure of the horse — especially in our culture and with baby boomers in particular — is deeply seated and can be traced back to early humans.

As bonds were formed with horses, especially enlightened humans felt the connection between them was ultimately a connection to nature. Serious riders have experienced the harmony — and even spirituality — connecting them not only to their horse, but to a universe extending beyond their own human state. Horses are not simply dumb brutes. Many an experienced horse person can recount situations when an animal has gone beyond the norm, beyond the expectations of even experts. For examples just study the careers of Seabiscuit and Secretariat.

What exactly is the romance and the allure of the cowboy's horse, and how did it figure into the cowboy's appeal? As horses played such critical roles in everything from war to recreation, they became symbols around the world of such diverse concepts as fear and beauty. The human-to-horse connection has always been great inspiration for literature, painting, and music. It is no wonder Hollywood films have glorified horses and national magazines devote pages to them every month. Human history is a great narrative for western movies, and horses are a key element. Along with that, the story of how horses were used in films and live appearances, to the point where some became celebrities, is interesting in itself.

Dale Evans, Gabby Hayes, Little Trigger (with a dappled coat), and Roy Rogers in a tense scene from arguably Rogers' most beloved and best known movie, *My Pal Trigger* (1946) *(Roy Dillow collection)*.

B-Westerns

The "B" in B-western stands for "budget," which is a polite way of saying "produced for very little money." A-movies had A-list stars, well crafted stories, and top-notch production values; aside from that, the primary difference between A-westerns and B-westerns was that the latter, like *My Pal Trigger* (1946), were usually geared towards children and were more of a fantasy of the West than their more expensive counterparts, such as *The Searchers* (Warner Bros., 1956). And this is particularly true with regard to the representation of horses.

"Anthropomorphism" is the assignment of human characteristics to animals or inanimate objects. From the beginning, the B-western anthropomorphized horses to a degree far beyond their actual nature. Presented in almost magical terms, their connection to cowboys was amplified. B-western cowboys talked to their horses and considered them friends. Movie horses often rescued their masters from the clutches of evil by running for help, untying ropes, or even attacking villains. The net effect of anthropomorphism of horses is that it made them especially appealing to children, and that effect was long-lasting.

Horses were used in western films not only as transportation and as draft animals but as integral parts of the scenery and ambience. When a horse was a major element in an A-

Trigger gallops into a packed stadium with the King of the Cowboys in the saddle. No B-western rider and horse partnership looked better *(Roy Dillow collection)*.

western story line, it was presented, for the most part, realistically — sometimes almost as an inanimate object, and certainly never with the same reverence as horses received in B-westerns. This was more true to life perhaps, but not as much fun and certainly not as inspiring.

In a press release written for CBS in 1958 titled "No Trick Horses for Me," James Arness, who played Matt Dillon on the *Gunsmoke* television series, stated: "In the real old West, horses were cheap and a cowboy—or a U.S. marshal—seldom had a favorite. He didn't keep a horse that long. He'd swap him off on a long trip for a fresh horse, or sell him between jobs knowing he could buy another when he needed to avoid stable bills."[2]

Silver screen cowboys and their horses were a rage from the 1920s through the 1960s and reigned supreme on radio, in movie theaters, in comic books, and eventually on television. They thrilled countless fans at rodeos, on auditorium stages, and at fairgrounds. From the start, the first cowboy superstars, William S. Hart and Tom Mix, realized what assets their four-legged partners, Fritz and Tony, were for their show business careers. Gene Autry knew what he was talking about when he stated, "In those days the horse was virtually the co-star. The kids all knew that the Lone Ranger's mount was Silver and Roy Rogers rode Trigger. But who could tell you, years later, the name of James Arness' horse or Paladin's or what the Cartwrights called theirs? ... Not for nothing were they called 'horse operas.'"[3]

Equine stars like Trigger, Champion, and the Lone Ranger's horse Silver were at the heart of B-westerns. Although these films may have been conceived as cheap entertainment and simple morality plays, the major players and their screen mounts became much more than one-dimensional characters on a movie screen. They became icons through their convictions and deeds.

The first film directors quickly realized that the essence of the motion picture was action, and underlying that action were an individual's beliefs and the courage to back them up. The western lent itself very effectively to action and basic morals. The horse was not only a symbol of the West, it helped drive a motion picture plot, and a cowboy's skill on horseback was mandatory if he was to prevail. Not only were moviegoers entertained, they were shown basic codes of good conduct: fair play, honesty, the value of hard work, and a respect for nature and age. All this they got from the back of a horse. It's no wonder adolescents who grew up in the 1940s and 1950s still respect B-western cowboys and their mounts.

Roy Rogers' Trigger is arguably the most famous equine movie star. The description of the *My Pal Trigger* (1946) movie on the Westerns Channel's schedule simply states, "About how Roy Rogers acquired the palomino." No other information is necessary. (The movie, by the way, rates three stars of a possible four.)

How Trigger's legend was created and nurtured via trainer Glenn Randall, a corral-full of palomino doubles, and Rogers' own expert horsemanship is an interesting story. The public relations material that the Rogers camp has propagated for decades regarding "Trigger" is the proverbial tip of the iceberg.

Trigger's contribution to the King of the Cowboys' success was immeasurable. Rogers was well aware that many fans were more interested in his horse than they were in him. Until the release of Robert W. Phillips' compendium *Roy Rogers*, information on "Trigger" was generic, carefully crafted public relations. It usually went something like this: "The mold was broken after Trigger was made. He could turn on a dime and give you nine cents change. He was in all of the Roy Rogers movies and television shows." The mold may have been broken when Trigger was made, but that didn't stop Roy Rogers and company from gluing it back together in hopes they could make more copies to use over and over.

Ground Rules

"**Trigger**"—Before we begin a study of Trigger there are ground rules that need to be acknowledged. The first has to do with the use of quotation marks around the name "Trigger." I have adopted this method of reference from Robert W. Phillips, who used quotation marks when referring to a character played by the numerous palomino doubles Roy Rogers used throughout his career. The name Trigger without quotation marks denotes the original animal. This method for denoting a character may also apply to the names "Champion" and "Silver."

When Roy Rogers discussed his palomino, he was usually referring to it in quotation marks: "Trigger." Whichever horse a particular answer most readily applied to was the "Trigger" he was talking about.

Palomino— An American Spanish word derived from Latin *palumbinus* from *palumbes*, meaning ringdove. The Spanish word for pigeon or dove is *paloma*. The word, fairly common in Spain, was first used in California as a name for a golden horse with a white mane and tail. The Spanish term for a horse of milk-white color is *palomilla*, and as such there's a possibility that it could have been transformed to palomino to denote a darker color. "Yellow-stained shirt tail" is the colloquial meaning of palomino in Spanish.

Movie Titles—A movie title followed only by a date and not the name of a releasing studio may be assumed to be a product of Republic Pictures, where Roy Rogers and "Trigger" did the majority of their work.

Serious Fan— Serious fans are those with more than just a passing familiarity with Roy Rogers and Trigger. They have remained devoted and interested in these individuals and the B-western genre even though they have never published a book or written an article. Examples of serious fans would be those I've met through "the Roy Rogers grapevine" like Jerry Dean (Beloit, Kansas), Roy Dillow (Tazwell, Virginia), and Larry Roe (Knoxville, Tennessee). Each is cited where appropriate.

Horse Primer—A horse is led, saddled, and mounted from its left or *near* side as opposed to its *far* or *off* side. When a horse is referred to as *at liberty*, that means it's without restraint, without a rope connecting it to a human. *Tack* is the equipment used to ride or drive a horse, like a saddle, reins, harness, and so forth. *Tapaderos* are stirrup covers. (Roy Rogers' tapaderos usually sported the "RR" initials.) The *forelock* of a horse is the part of the mane which starts between the ears and drops over the forehead.

A horse's height is measured from the base of the front foot to the top of its *withers*, the bump between the back and neck. Height is measured in *hands*, each equal to four inches. If a horse is 15.3 hands, it's $4 \times 15 + 3 = 63$ inches at the withers.

Color in Horses—Color is very subjective and, consequently, confusing. Scholars in both science and art have produced serious studies on color. Dr. Ben K. Green wrote an authoritative book titled *The Color of Horses* in 1974 (Northland Press). With wonderful paintings by Darol Dickinson to support his text, Green tells his readers how to identify color methodically and scientifically.

Art school students learn early on that a color is affected by the colors that surround it and available light. Place identical one-inch squares of blue on a field of purple and a field of yellow and they will look different, because purple can bring out the red and yellow can bring out the green. Similarly, a one-inch square of blue under cool fluorescent lights looks different from the same square under warm incandescent light bulbs. The same goes for horses. Their color changes not only given the time of day, but by season, and age. Even the weather and nutrition have an effect on color.

As if color weren't subjective enough, different breed registries have their own systems and this, more than anything else, really makes things confusing. Consequently, color terminology is not standardized.

Trigger was palomino in color; Gene Autry's Champions came in various shades of chestnut and sorrel. A horse (also mules and jacks), regardless of breeding or type, that has a golden coat and a white or ivory mane and tail is considered a palomino. The name designates color only; there is no palomino breed and hence no typical conformation.

Many describe sorrel as too dark to be a palomino and too light to be a chestnut. According to Dr. Green there are light, blonde and bright sorrels, all very close to palomino. He describes palomino as the precise color of 22-carat gold. Dr. Green presents standard dark and chestnut sorrels that look chestnut. One could argue colors all day and never arrive at an absolute conclusion.

According to the Palomino Horse Association, a palomino coat ranges from a creamy buff to a deep copper. However, as Dr. Green states, the standard color of the ideal palomino resembles pure gold — a newly minted gold coin. When the hair grows long, the palomino coat usually lightens in the winter and also usually dulls with age. A palomino should have black, dark brown, or hazel eyes, and the two eyes should match. Foals are almost never born with true palomino coloring but are mostly cream or honey color. They are not registered as palominos at birth due to the instability of their color. Before the Palomino Horse Association or the Palomino Horse Breeders of America will register them, fillies must be at least yearlings and colts two years of age. The original Trigger was not registered till he was almost three.

Some horses go through a stage of dapples — dark spots all over the coat — during their early development. They can also be dappled depending on time of year, coat, and condition. Usually dapples are seen after the semi-annual shedding season. Greys are sometimes dappled year round. Horses that are in good health and "bloom" (physical peak) and never show dapples may not have the dapple gene. The age of the horse does not affect dapples.

Photo Choices — While I would have loved to publish twice as many photos, I am limited by space. My goal is a mixture of the unique, the rare, and the classic. Fortunately, some very generous collectors came forward and offered seldom-seen shots that, in some cases, were obtained at considerable expense. Serious fans may be surprised as much by what's been included as by what was not.

1

Remembering Trigger

"The true journey of discovery consists not in seeking new landscapes but in having fresh eyes." — Marcel Proust

To begin a study of "Trigger," a good place to start is to acknowledge what was said about him by two of Roy Rogers' children, Dusty and Cheryl; by Corky Randall, the son of "Trigger's" trainer Glenn Randall; and Roy Rogers himself. Glenn Randall's comments may be found throughout this book and mostly in the chapters titled "Glenn Randall" and "The Smartest Horse in the Movies."

Dusty and Cheryl

Of the Rogers children, Roy "Dusty" Rogers, Jr., and Cheryl Rogers-Barnett are the most public and the most responsible for promoting the image their famous father cultivated.[1] They have both written autobiographies, both of which discussed "Trigger." I may not agree with everything they wrote, but I certainly respect their intentions. It would be presumptuous to expect them to have dissected the "Trigger" fantasy their father spent a lifetime creating and maintaining. While neither was deliberately deceptive, neither, apparently, has had the need or inclination to study their father's movies or career to the degree many serious fans have. Neither demonstrated an expert command of "Trigger's" history with respect to his use in their father's movies or in personal appearances.

People often make the mistake of assuming children of the stars know all about their parents' careers. Admittedly, Dusty and Cheryl do not have to back up their claims about "Trigger"; their stories may be taken at face value. With all due respect, that doesn't mean they're completely accurate. While ordinary fans may not know intimate details about stars' personal lives, serious fans know a great deal about them as celebrities. The reason is that serious fans, from the time they were kids, absorbed all publicity and studied a star's body of work. The more discriminating ones eliminated the outrageous and drew their own conclusions. Some continue to learn all they can about their heroes. Fan speculation has a fair claim to the truth, more than the principals care to admit at times. With regards to "Trigger," the public relations that the Rogers camp has propagated for decades is only a small part of the whole story; it's been a small group of serious fans (and the press, to a very small degree) who has exposed most of the story.

If one accepts Dusty Rogers' book *Growing Up with Roy and Dale* as the truth with regards

Roy Rogers, Dale Evans, Cheryl, Linda Lou, and Dusty on the original Trigger *(Roy Dillow collection)*.

to his father's palomino, one is left to believe that there was only one Trigger and a few incidental doubles. The only significant anecdote Dusty added to the legend was his account of how his father kept Trigger's death from the family for twelve months: "When Trigger died in 1965 Dad was so broken up he never told anyone about it, not even us, for more than a year." He said the same thing on the *A&E's Biography* program during an episode on his father. The fact that Rogers was able to keep the news of Trigger's death from his children for a year demonstrates they were not particularly involved with the palomino.[2]

Dusty Rogers also wrote in his autobiography that Trigger sired a son who was later used on tour as a trick horse: "One Easter morning we got a call from the stables where Trigger and most of Dad's other horses were kept. Trigger had sired a colt, and the foal looked just like him. We all went out to the stable before church to look at him. The colt never got to be as big as Trigger, but he was smart." The two horses Rogers used in public were Little Trigger and Trigger Jr. (the latter was especially good at dance routines). Trigger Jr. was not sired by the original Trigger, and it's very doubtful Little Trigger was. In fact, towards the end of his career Roy Rogers himself stated that the original Trigger never sired a foal. (See the chapter titled, "Trigger's Story," the section on "Trigger's Offspring.")

Dusty Rogers also offered a humorous anecdote that's been cited many times since, having to do with how "Trigger" sometimes misbehaved in public. He would take off after playing dead, leaving Rogers alone in the middle of an arena. For reasons that will become apparent, the horse Dusty was referring to was clearly Little Trigger. (Refer to the chapter titled, "Little Trigger," the section on "Temperament and Personality.")

Dusty Rogers followed in his father's footsteps as a singing cowboy.[3] However, he has never publicly defined himself as a horseman and hasn't had to. There is no evidence he had any particular interest in horses. However, Rogers' daughter Cheryl Rogers-Barnett took after her father and liked to ride, even on occasion with Glenn Randall's daughter Dolores. Cheryl had a personal relationship with Trigger and has the pictures to prove it. She used him on trail rides. There's a charming picture of Cheryl with Allan Lane's stallion Blackjack in her book *Cowboy Princess*. She loves horses. Her anecdotes regarding Trigger are great fun and one never gets tired of them. She's the only member of the Rogers family who included a chapter on Trigger in an autobiography. Much to her credit, in that book she acknowledged Little Trigger as no one in her family had before:

> Old Trigger remained Dad's favorite, but there were actually other Triggers. Dad bought Little Trigger a couple of years after he bought old Trigger. He purchased the second horse primarily to spare wear and tear on old Trigger. He wanted a horse that he would take on the road; he only used old Trigger for the movies. Dad never publicly admitted that there was more than one Trigger. He always said that he didn't want to confuse the little kids who loved Trigger. The fans knew Trigger Jr. — the studio even had a contest to name him when Dad first got him — but Little Trigger was a "secret."

Even with Cheryl Rogers-Barnett's honest acknowledgment of Little Trigger, it would seem she (and her writing partner Frank Thompson) had only a partial knowledge of "Trigger." While she provided a fair background for the legendary palomino, it wasn't up to date. Rogers-Barnett erroneously claimed that the original Trigger appeared in every one of Rogers' films except *Mackintosh and TJ* (Penland Productions, 1975). Roy Rogers also made the same claim over and over again: "I think I'm the only cowboy in history who started and finished his career with the same horse."[4] Trigger was present in all of the feature movies Roy Rogers made for Republic Pictures and in all the television episodes produced over six years. Trigger also appeared in a multitude of magazine photos, on comic book covers, and in advertisements. But it was only Little Trigger who starred with Rogers and Bob Hope in *Son of Paleface* (Paramount, 1952). Rogers-Barnett seemed to be of the impression that Little Trigger was used only on the road and the original Trigger was used on film, when in fact Little Trigger was in most Roy Rogers films after 1943. (Refer to the chapter titled, "Little Trigger," the "Movie Debut" section).

Cheryl Rogers-Barnett also presented information about Roy Rogers' purchase of Trigger that did not square with official documentation. She never gave any real dates and assumed her father started buying Trigger almost immediately after he started using him, making payments which continued until the early 1940s. She didn't make clear when payments started, leaving the reader to supply a date. Her most erroneous statement was that part of the agreement with Clyde Hudkins, Trigger's owner at the time, stipulated that no other cowboy could use the palomino while Rogers was buying him (refer to the "Golden Stallion" chapter and the section on the movie *Silver City Raiders*). Only about three months elapsed between the agreement to buy Trigger in 1943 and the date when the final payment was made, which means that this statement is probably technically true. However, Cheryl Rogers-Barnett seems to have honestly thought the agreement was in place for years, not a few weeks.

The section on Trigger in Cheryl Rogers-Barnett's book *Cowboy Princess*, excerpted in *Cowboys and Indians* magazine,[5] for the most part stays within the public relations that Rogers' autobiography written with Carlton Stowers, *Happy Trails*, maintained. Of the five photos

Proud daddy Roy Rogers with his daughter Cheryl in her Sunday best and sitting on the one and only Trigger *(Cheryl Rogers-Barnett collection)*.

accompanying the text, only three are of the original Trigger, with no distinction made between him and Little Trigger. A full page shot of Trigger in the rearing position with Rogers in the saddle is printed in reverse changing the markings on his blaze. It's safe to assume none of these photo errors were Rogers-Barnett's doing.[6]

Cheryl Rogers-Barnett was born in 1940. Roy "Dusty" Rogers, Jr., was born in 1946.

Their father's career was at its peak between 1942 and 1954; 1948 was Roy Rogers' biggest year. Cheryl and Dusty were 13 and 7 respectively when Roy Rogers' career was starting to level out. They were school children when their father, Glenn Randall, and "Trigger" were making movies and touring. It's doubtful Cheryl and Dusty were fully aware of how Trigger and his doubles were being used. It also has to be noted that Rogers' palominos were boarded on the Randall Ranch. (Dusty Rogers stated in his book, "Because Trigger was not a pet, dad kept him and all of his entertainment horses on a separate ranch.") Only if Cheryl and Dusty were on movie sets daily, keeping diaries and asking Randall direct questions, would they have a solid idea of what he and their dad were up to with Trigger, Little Trigger, and all the palomino look-alikes.

Judging by Roy Rogers' Victorville museum, it seemed he saved everything. One would think official records, like horse registration papers, bills of sale, and travel logs, might still exist. They would answer many questions and shed new light on "Trigger." Records for the original Trigger and Trigger Jr. are available through the Palomino Horse Association and Stud Book Registry. Perhaps one day some historically minded third-generation Rogers family member who's far enough removed from the myths and has enough curiosity to use the information available to the family may try to tell a more complete story.

It could also be argued that the Rogers family is wasting its time trying to cater to children today who have no interest in a fantasy of a singing cowboy and his horse. While the Rogers family actually focuses mostly on older fans, there is still an expectation that longtime fans should be satisfied with the same incomplete stories they've read and heard hundreds of times. All this seems to be another example of the publicity becoming a hotly defended public stance long after many fans see the necessity for truth. Serious fans no longer want to hear from official sources that every time Roy Rogers was pictured with a palomino, it was the original Trigger. If Trigger had done all that we saw him do on film, and in person, he would have indeed been a super horse. It's been noted in later interviews that Roy Rogers was a little less interested in promoting the image of his horse and more prone to telling the real story as best he could remember it. Many fans have acknowledged that while on visits to the Roy Rogers and Dale Evans Museum in Victorville they were able to ask Rogers very candid questions about his palominos. He in turn was very forthcoming with information on Little Trigger and another double named Pal.

Buford "Corky" Randall

Everyone who worked at close quarters with Roy Rogers and his "Triggers" is gone: the trainers, directors, stunt doubles, sidekicks, and Dale Evans. Buford "Corky" Randall, Glenn Randall's son, is the last person living with a working knowledge and experience of Rogers' mounts. For Rogers' children, the different "Triggers" were just one aspect of their parents' lives. For Corky Randall, his family's main income depended on Rogers' horses.

With his busy schedule running an empire, Roy Rogers did not have time to maintain a string of horses, and it made sense to board them at the Randall Ranch. Glenn Randall had immediate access to Trigger and his doubles. As their primary caregiver he attended to their conditioning and training. In fact, Rogers' palomino remuda lived at the Randall ranch up until the time the King of the Cowboys retired from personal appearances. Cheryl Rogers-Barnett acknowledged in her biography that her father lived with the Randall family for a time around 1947 after his second wife, Arlene, died.

Corky Randall on Little Trigger in the classic rearing pose circa 1945 *(Corky Randall collection)*.

Corky Randall was born in 1929. He started riding at an early age and was breaking in colts when he was in grade school. He learned how to train horses from his dad, as he put it, "from the get-go."[7]

Corky Randall actually handled Roy Rogers' palominos to a point far beyond just going on trail rides. He was about 14 when his father started working for Rogers. By the time Corky

Corky Randall circa 1951, in top hat and tails, riding Golden Zephyr in an English saddle and double reins *(Petrine Day Mitchum collection)*.

was in high school, he was already working in the motion picture industry, wrangling horses. He was 19 during Rogers' heyday. Corky took care of the Randall stable when his dad was out of town touring with Roy Rogers. It was not till his last year in high school that a barn man was hired, freeing Corky from some of his responsibilities. The year Glenn Randall was in Europe filming *Ben-Hur* (MGM, 1959), Corky toured with Rogers and Dale Evans. Corky was in his mid-twenties by then. Besides caring for Rogers' palominos, one of his duties was to drive the Rogers children from their hotels to where their parents were performing. By the time the Roy Rogers television show was going, Glenn Randall was touring the country with his own horses. A very young Corky worked on *The Roy Rogers Show* on television under Johnny Brim, an old time wrangler who once worked at Hudkins Stables, Trigger's early home.

While Corky Randall learned how to train horses from his father, it was Bill Jones, head wrangler and ramrod at Republic in the 1940s, who was his mentor in the movie business. Jones was in charge of recruiting horses and men, working with budgets, transportation, feeding livestock, etc. He taught Corky how scenes with horses were shot with respect to set-ups, angles, and such. A horse trainer's job was to provide an appropriate mount to do the required work and cue him accordingly.

As one of his father's assistants, Corky Randall not only hauled "Trigger" to different locations on occasion but even rode Trigger Jr. in horse shows, rodeos, fairs, and circuses under the palomino's first registered name, Golden Zephyr. He did so in order to acclimate the horse to crowds and all the distractions that confront an animal while performing in public. Although the horse belonged to Rogers at the time, Rogers was never mentioned as owner. By the time Rogers started to use the horse as Trigger Jr., the palomino was well schooled in front of live audiences.

Like his legendary father, Corky Randall became a professional horse trainer for private clients and, most notably, worked in motion pictures and television. His credits as livestock coordinator and trainer include such movies as *The Black Stallion Returns* (MGM/United Artists, 1983), *Silverado* (Columbia Pictures, 1985), *The Three Amigos* (Orion, 1986), *Hot to Trot*, (Warner Brothers, 1988), *Indiana Jones and the Last Crusade* (Lucasfilm/Paramount, 1989), *Back to the Future III* (Amblin Entertainment/Universal, 1990), *Robin Hood, Men in Tights* (20th Century Fox, 1993), *Spy Hard* (Buena Vista, 1996), and *The Mask of Zorro* (Sony Pictures Entertainment, 1998). He worked on such television shows as *Spin and Marty* (Disney, 1955), *Walt Disney's Zorro* (Disney, 1957–1958), *The Fall Guy* (Glen A. Larson, 1981–1986), and *Return to Lonesome Dove* (de Passe Entertainment, 1993).

The high point of Corky Randall's career as a Hollywood horse trainer came in 1978 when director Caroll Ballard hired him and his father as wranglers on *The Black Stallion* (United Artists, 1979), arguably one of the best horse movies ever made. Often described as poetry in motion, its soul and magic are due not only to Ballard's mastery as a filmmaker, but most especially to the performance Corky Randall elicited from the four-legged star of the film, a gorgeous Arab stallion named Cass Olé. *The Black Stallion* belongs as much to the Randalls as it does to Ballard.

Corky Randall earned his living by what he could actually do with horses, not by self-promotion. He has nothing to gain by not telling the truth about what happened with his dad, Rogers, and "Trigger." Needless to say, he would like to have his father look good, but given his father's solid reputation, there is no danger of his father losing face no matter what Corky says.

Corky Randall was interviewed by telephone for this book on a number of occasions.[8] I tape-recorded him from his home in Newhall, California, where at 77 he is semi-retired. He was cordial, candid, generous with his time, and very forthcoming with information and rare photographs. Corky does not have a photographic memory and made no claims to knowing every detail. He was quick to say he did not intend that his recollections cast aspersions on anyone else's. From this writer's perspective, Corky's experience and knowledge of "Trigger" are not to be denied. Corky Randall is a man who can tell you what it was like to care for and ride Trigger and actually put him up on his hind legs in the classic rearing pose. As to credibility, that says it all.

Roy Rogers

In December of 1949, when his career was close to its zenith, Roy Rogers and writer Aaron Dudley produced an article for *Western Horseman* magazine titled "Trigger: First, Get a Good Horse." It appeared in volume 14, number 12, and ran five pages. Along with a cover portrait, four photographs were published, including three of Rogers grooming his beloved palomino. It's an important essay not only because it appeared in a prestigious and well-respected magazine, but because it's a time capsule of sorts and offered Rogers the opportunity to present his four-legged partner exactly how he wished. It's interesting to note that this article was published the same year the *Golden Stallion* movie was released. Rogers and Republic Pictures had a horse and movie to promote.

What follows is a synopsis of the major points in the article. For reasons that will become apparent in the chapters that follow, Roy Rogers' *Western Horseman* article is true if "Trigger" is viewed as a fictional character and a composite of several palominos.

1. Rogers implied that after he'd signed on as a movie cowboy and realized he needed a movie horse, he initiated a search. "It was as an obscure movie extra that I began visiting ranches, stables and hanging around rodeos looking for a horse." He went on to say that he finally heard about one from San Diego that Art Hudkins had just purchased.

2. Rogers gave the year he purchased Trigger and the palomino's age at the time: "It took a lot of doing, but I finally owned Trigger. That was in 1938, and it was the cheapest $2,500 I ever spent. He was a five-year-old then."

3. According to Rogers, trainer Glenn Randall appeared on the scene later. "About three years later after Trigger and I had worked several pictures, I met up with Glenn Randall." Rogers also stated that he'd already started training Trigger as a trick horse, leaving Randall to continue: "Over the years, Randall helped me add 50 tricks to the meager ten I was putting on Trigger through in those early days."

4. Little Trigger was not mentioned when Rogers went on to note "Trigger's" prowess as a trick horse. "In addition to being a good all-around cow horse, Trigger today is considered the most versatile horse star in the motion picture business."

5. Rogers portrayed Trigger as a wonder horse, with great stamina, and capable of numerous tasks. "In the early days of our movie career, I worked the whole picture from start to finish with Trigger, close-ups, trick shots, running shots and all." While Trigger stand-ins were mentioned, the implication was that they didn't do that much: "Every leading actor in Hollywood has one or more doubles, so we have a couple of other palominos to do those long shots."

6. Rogers also discussed Trigger on tour: "We take him in hotels and theaters while on personal appearance tours."

7. Rogers also noted Trigger as a breeding sire. "There are only two genuine Trigger colts. The younger, a two-year-old, I own. The only other one I raised especially for a little girl in New England and presented to her as winner of a nation-wide contest."

2

Chasing Trigger

"This is the west, sir. When the legend becomes fact, print the legend."[1]
— From *The Man Who Shot Liberty Valance*

During his long and illustrious career Roy Rogers' name was paired in three different combinations: Roy Rogers and Dale Evans, Roy Rogers and the Sons of the Pioneers, and Roy Rogers and Trigger. It would seem that a pairing with his wife or the musical group that first brought him fame would be more important, but that is not so. For proof of Trigger's significance and popularity, one need only consider who was photographed with Roy Rogers most often and who received second billing in his films, television shows, and personal appearances. Trigger was truly an equal half of a magical team. Both man and horse remain powerful symbols of a place, a time, and even a state of mind. If Leonard Slye's formation of the Sons of the Pioneers is one of "his most significant contributions to the myth of the romantic west," as author Raymond White so insightfully states in his book *King of the Cowboys and Queen of the West*, the fantasy of a magical palomino was another.

Beyond a great screen persona and the talent to match, what made Roy Rogers special was his proximity to a very special horse. This was especially evident in live performances. When I watched Roy Rogers movies as a youngster I believed in the fantasy of a singing cowboy hero on a beautiful horse. I accepted the simple stories where good won over evil. As an adult I still find joy in the exciting black and white movies even if I don't believe them any more. When I watch them now, I find myself analyzing what I see. Although elements like the stunts, horsemanship, music, clothes, scenery, and camaraderie retain their resonance, I'm now interested in how B-westerns were made. These days I'm inspired not so much by the adventures of a cowboy hero, but by the talent, hard work and creativity it took to put B-western magic on screen. To understand the full story of how the character of "Trigger, the Smartest Horse in the Movies" was created and perpetrated, one has to consider a number of components.

Surely there's no adult now, especially not one with a rudimentary knowledge of equines and filmmaking, who doesn't know that it takes a number of animals and expert handlers to pull off the illusion of a single wonder horse. The story of how "Trigger" was turned into "the Smartest Horse in the Movies" is not rocket science, but it is very confusing, for reasons that will become apparent.

Image

A Republic Pictures press release circa 1946 claimed, "Trigger, Roy Rogers' beautiful palomino, performs more than 70 tricks on cue. Rogers has trained the horse himself and

Trigger goes through his repertoire of amazing tricks at children's and veterans' hospitals, on the stages of theatres, and at rodeos as well as in motion pictures." While this made nice copy, it was show business propaganda from the get-go, and by definition a half-truth. The fact that "Trigger's" trainer, Glenn Randall, was not acknowledged does not mean Roy Rogers or the public relations department at Republic Pictures were liars. Plainly speaking, they were putting on a show.

In 2005, author Bob Spitz cited an interview in *The Beatles: The Biography* in which Paul McCartney explained how the fab four and their manager, Brian Epstein, agreed on a "version of the facts" that would serve as their public story. Once agreed on, the story was adhered to and embellished to suit their needs. Consequently, the Beatles' history was often laced with a lack of "reliable source material." Spitz went on to say, "Even in those remarkable cases where sources are offered, the accuracy remains suspect. Either memories were vague, tales

The original Trigger rearing solo and on cue *(Larry Roe collection)*.

were recycled, facts went unchecked, or circumstances were fabricated or obscured." Spitz even quoted Napoleon: "History is a set of lies agreed upon."

Public relations and its by-products are nothing new, of course. They've been a staple of entertainment and show business from the beginning of recorded history. The pharaohs were aware of the power of image, as were Julius Caesar and the popes. Politicians like Teddy Roosevelt, John F. Kennedy, and Ronald Reagan were quite masterful when it came to controlling their images. Buffalo Bill was augmenting his image and the history of the West decades before Rogers was a celebrity. Control over image is crucial whether one is trying to succeed in show business, rule a country, or run a corporation. Companies spend millions on advertising and promotion. As much as selling a product, they're selling a way of life. Roy Rogers was no different. He spent most of his career trying to control his image and that of his horse. However, the truth catches up to the image eventually.

Publicity is about bending the truth to fit a public image. Celebrity is born out of publicity and by its very nature is subjective. In effect, cowboy stars and their publicists were telling the truth under imaginary circumstances. Even a fictional character, like a wonder horse, needed a background. However, on occasion the subject of the publicity may blur the truth so much and for so long, he or she loses sight of it. Some fans were also culpable, seeing only what they wanted and buying into any and all publicity. There are adults who are still very dedicated to Roy Rogers and Trigger and are very ambivalent towards any one who might tarnish the image they've held on to since they were children. By the same token there are adult fans who still love the "Trigger" fantasy, even if they don't believe it anymore. There are those who don't care if Rogers wanted to call every palomino in the world "Trigger," as that was his choice. There were, after all, different "Champions" and "Lassies," and fans loved them all, not knowing the difference. For them it didn't matter which horse played "Trigger." The horse was a character in their eyes just like the rider was. Fans loved the show that Roy Rogers and his team of professionals put on. They absorbed it and asked for more. Thousands paid money to see "Trigger," something they would recall for the rest of their lives. And don't try and tell them they didn't see the original Trigger or you're liable to have a fight on your hands.

Roy Rogers fan Jerry Dean said it best: "Yep, I'm a fan of Roy Rogers and Trigger. He was my number one childhood hero, and you never get another one of those. When I watch his movies today (and yes I do have a lot of them) on the most special level, it's to touch, again, for a brief moment, the old, nearly forgotten thrill I felt watching his every move, how he mounted and rode Trigger, how he wore his guns, everything about him! I still do that now, but these days, it's partly to answer adult questions about how things like making the movies were done, and why they did them that way. I find these things interesting now, but they are not why I am a Roy Rogers fan. That's something I became years and years ago, and nothing I learn now will ever change that."

B-western movies were fiction and their goal was wholesome entertainment. If reality interfered with what they were trying to accomplish, it was eliminated. Gabby Hayes and his bay Eddie looked more like a genuine cowboy and his horse in the early days of the old west than Roy Rogers and Trigger. Have you ever seen an archival photo of a genuine cowboy who dressed like Roy Rogers, riding a horse who wore tack like Trigger? A working cowboy back then would have most likely been riding a smaller horse, almost pony size, like a mustang. It would have looked pretty mangy from work and hard riding outdoors in all sorts of weather. Roy Rogers, Art Rush, and Republic Pictures wanted to fill movie seats and sell merchandise. It's doubtful it occurred to them that fans would read more into Rogers' myth and that of his horse than the obvious. However, fans did that and more.

An image, which can be a symbol, is a point of reference, a selling tool, and at times, a lot of fun. That's why so many fans embrace images. With regard to entertainment and art, it's best to trust art, not artists. It's also wise to take the same tack with symbols. Embrace the image if it nourishes you, but be aware of what the owner's motive and message are. Remember that an image is not the same as the actual human being, or an actual horse.

Trigger was a real horse who was humanized, even mythologized, on screen and television to the point where he became larger than life. He's at once a beloved memory of a more innocent time and also a corporate logo. Just drive up to the Roy Rogers museum today where a 23½-foot statue of a palomino greets visitors and tell me that he's not. The image of a rearing palomino or one in fancy show tack is very much associated with Roy Rogers.

The palomino Roy Rogers selected as his screen mount one fateful day, from a group of horses offered by Hudkins Stables, was more than just beautiful; he was a cut above. Trigger added a great deal of ambience with his regal looks and the way he carried himself. This was his major strength and why he was critical for close-ups or running full out. Fans have a mental picture of Trigger running during the opening credits of *The Roy Rogers Show* on tel-

Roy Rogers and Trigger in the classic rearing pose. The original Trigger hardly ever made public appearances and parade shots such as this one are rare.

evision and the voice-over: "... Trigger, his golden Palomino!" Then there was his striking signature pose, rearing in an almost perpendicular position with Rogers on his back. The palomino did it countless times, effortlessly and with the slightest cue.

"He was beautiful with his flaxen mane and tail and proud arched neck. As I hit an easy lope, then a fast gallop, I could feel that this boy was an athlete with power to spare and a fine balance that would set him in good stead for chases over rocky grades and down steep mountain slopes."[2]

When Trigger was being ridden down a road with Rogers sing-

Left: Poetry in motion, Roy Rogers on Trigger in an easy lope along a country road. *Below:* This photograph of Trigger, Roy Rogers, and Trigger Jr. was used in official tour programs during the 1950s *(Roy Dillow collection).*

ing a tune, the palomino didn't just walk, he pranced, his mane and forelock flowing in the wind. Author Richard Adams could have just as well been referring to Trigger in his book *Traveller*, written from the point of view of General Robert E. Lee's great horse. In one section the animal tells a barn cat friend about how he liked to carry himself when he was being ridden by his famous master: "It takes a durned good man to ride me, and I've no use for any other sort. I've got a lot of go in me, and I jest can't abide hanging around. I will walk, mind you, if a man really wants it and insists, but I always keep it fast and springy."

Trigger Doubles

It became obvious right away to Roy Rogers that Trigger could not retain his magnificence on the steady diet of movie work and personal appearance tours required of him, which meant being cooped up in a trailer for weeks on end. Even with all his intelligence and athleticism, Trigger was still just a horse. So a horse referred to as "Little Trigger" took on the majority of the work. Much more than a mere double, he was literally a second Trigger. However, as fantastic as Little Trigger was, he alone could not hold up to sustain a career as long as Rogers.' Shows were being scheduled miles apart, time was tight, and physical endurance got pushed to the limit. A Roy Rogers tour in 1961 included 50 performances in 26 cities.[3]

During Roy Rogers' heyday the majority of his fans assumed Trigger was one horse, but it was common knowledge, and confirmed in interviews, that doubles were used for stunts and long shots. Rogers and trainer Glenn Randall chose not to reveal much publicly about Trigger. While they acknowledged the use of palomino look-alikes, they did so almost in passing and only because they had to. Saying nothing at all would have been silly because a few children and even horse-ignorant adults assumed that doubles were being used. So Trigger Jr.—*not* Little Trigger—was introduced and promoted as Trigger's replacement. Little Trigger was Rogers' big secret, his personal appearance and trick horse. Glenn Randall did not seem so dogged about keeping Little Trigger a secret but no one suspected enough to ask. The Roy Rogers public relations machine was pretty animated, with its coverage of Trigger satisfying both the press and fans.

When asked how many Triggers there were, B-western director Joseph Kane replied, "Quite a few. After it got going, he had two or three. One for close-ups and stills, one for riding, and an extra one."[4]

Glenn Randall actually discussed Little Trigger in 1992. He was quoted in *Cowboy Magazine* in an article titled "He Spoke Horse" by Phil Spangenberger: "Actually, due to the grueling schedule of a superstar like Roy Rogers, it was necessary to train a trio of Triggers for the various films, and personal appearance tours and shows, including several trips abroad." As Randall also recalled, "Little Trigger was our personal appearance horse and, by God, he could do some of the most remarkable things."

Republic Pictures also agreed with Rogers not to risk two valuable palomino horses on hazardous movie stunts. Just as Rogers had stunt doubles, so did Trigger and Little Trigger. Different palominos were switched from scene to scene and sometimes from shot to shot depending on the requirements of a given situation. The original Trigger earned his oats and star treatment, but not anywhere near to the degree most of his fans were led to believe. Over the years, more palominos than will ever be known were used to keep Rogers and "Trigger" number one in the hearts of fans. Doreen M. Norton, in her book *The Palomino Horse*, wrote that "Trigger got a double to go on personal appearance tours. Eventually more doubles were obtained, because the main 'picture' Trigger was a horse too well trained to waste on any but the most important scenes, and other similar Triggers were obtained for stand-ins. These stand-ins pose while lights and camera are being adjusted, and a 'chase' Trigger does all the running in pictures."[5]

Director William Witney's claim that the original Trigger was taken on Rogers' tour for *Under Western Stars* (1938) is highly doubtful. It was Rogers' first movie in a starring role and he made almost every major city in the United States in about three months. Corky Randall maintained that the original Trigger did not like to travel. It would seem the horse appeared at only a few outings around Rogers' home base of Los Angeles. "Any time they ever saw Roy Rogers up close in person, it was [with] Little Trigger. The old horse was never in anything but film and would have only been on a film company set."

On page 18 of William Witney's book *Trigger Remembered*, there's a photo of Roy Rogers with the original Trigger. According to the caption the shot was taken during a parade on Fifth Avenue in New York City where the duo was appearing at Madison Square Garden for the first time. Without any New York landmarks in view, this photo could have been taken in any big city. Until more definite proof that the original Trigger appeared in public outside of Southern California, this writer will defer to Corky Randall. With the original Trigger's limited bag of tricks, it's doubtful Rogers would have taken him clear across the country to perform, especially since Little Trigger could do so much more in front of a live audience. If you saw a personal appearance by "the King of the Cowboys" and "the smartest horse in the movies" outside of southern California, you probably did not see the original Trigger.[6]

However, for such high-profile events as the laying of hooves into wet cement at Hollywood's Grauman's Chinese Theater, the original Trigger was present in all his glory. Rogers was not going have any other palomino immortalized!

Roy Rogers and the Truth

Roy Rogers was not a liar. However, there is a difference between an individual's truth and an absolute truth. As entertainers and celebrities, aspects of Roy Rogers' and Trigger's public lives were shaped by the studio that represented them, by Rogers himself, by Rogers' own publicist, and by the press. Author Tim "Tumbleweed" Lasiuta was very insightful when he said, "If we consider the Trigger dilemma, we can conclude that the spirit of the truth is more important than the substance. We all loved Trigger, but which one becomes the question."

Roy Rogers' goal was entertainment and the shaping of a character, a wonder horse, "the Smartest Horse in the Movies." Rogers is not often thought of as a storyteller and mythmaker in the classic sense, but that is in fact a lot of what he was.

Many fans start with the premise that it was only authors and journalists who embellished or were just plain inaccurate about Roy Rogers and Trigger, twisting things to suit their stories. Anything of questionable accuracy was not Rogers' responsibility, but a writer's concoction.

How could any serious fan make the argument that Rogers was consistent and always accurate concerning "Trigger"? One would be hard pressed to find printed text or a video interview where Rogers discussed Little Trigger specifically. For that matter, just the example of the date of purchase of the original Trigger should prove the point. Rogers had a bill of sale in his possession, and it clearly contradicted what he said in public. The bill of sale states that Rogers purchased Trigger in 1943. Yet this writer has not come across one print or video interview where Roy Rogers said he bought Trigger that year. (I mention video because in such cases, it cannot be said a writer twisted Rogers' words.) There's a good chance Rogers was aware of Trigger's solo performances in other movies between 1938 and 1943 but did not acknowledge them because it would have meant explaining why other movie studios had access to a horse he was thought to own.

An interview is only as good as the questions that are asked and the willingness of the subject to answer. For the most part the press didn't know what to ask Rogers beyond the same obvious questions, asked over and over. Rogers was not foolish enough to divulge more than he was asked. Had a real expert or even a serious fan interviewed Rogers, there's no telling what might have been revealed about Trigger and his doubles.

Public Relations

During the height of the hippie movement in 1967 Jerry Garcia, the lead guitarist for the Grateful Dead, said something I will never forget. He was talking to a reporter about the quality of press coverage of the "Summer of Love." Garcia was somewhat of an expert; he and his band mates were at ground zero, living in the Haight-Ashbury section of San Francisco. He was amazed at how some very prestigious magazine and newspaper articles were misleading and did not truly represent the spirit of the movement or what it meant. It got him to thinking: if the press could not deliver an honest and truthful accounting of such a simple story, how could the general public trust stories about more important and complex topics like war, the economy, political scandals, and the environment?

I've thought about Garcia often as I've been researching this book. I'm amazed at all the contradictions and misleading statements regarding a horse who was a celebrity in B-western movies and television shows. I understand that in the beginning a fictional scenario was deemed necessary to promote a new star, but it's amazing how much misinformation has persisted decades after Trigger's death.

Just as Leonard Franklin Sly (aka Slye)[7] spent a lifetime nurturing the character of "Roy Rogers, King of the Cowboys," he also spent decades creating and embellishing the fantasy of "Trigger, the Smartest Horse in the Movies." Subsequently, he and Glenn Randall apparently had a mutual agreement not to say much about "Trigger" during his heyday. Rogers employed public relations by design throughout his career until it became second nature. After a while, at times unintentionally, he mixed up the facts. Rogers did not make any of Trigger's official records public, like his registration form or bill of sale, most likely so he could control the fantasy of one special horse. This will be addressed later in more detail.

When researching the lives of Roy Rogers, Trigger and his palomino doubles, one is easily overwhelmed by the number of interviews and other material from books, magazines, press releases, newsletters, and television documentaries. It's easy to see why the combined effect becomes confusing and at times contradictory. How could it not be, with Rogers using more than one palomino to play Trigger over his career? They were all "Trigger" when he rode them. He used a Tennessee walker, a quarter horse, and a horse with Thoroughbred blood. One was descended from a great race horse. Some topped out at 16 hands, most averaged 15.2, one was 15 hands. They came from different breeders and different places; most were born from the mid–1930s on. Rogers used palominos that he owned and some who were provided on special occasions. Most were well mannered; one disliked women and children. Yet, over time, fans assumed all "Trigger" stories and information applied to one horse.

While Roy Rogers knew a great deal about all the "Triggers" he used, there's no way even he could remember every detail with absolute certainty. After some 90 movies, 100 television shows, and even more live appearances, how could he be 100 percent accurate? That would have required a photographic memory or the keeping of detailed records in a daily journal. However, it will become evident that even Rogers' seemingly contradictory statements make sense when seen chronologically and in the context of an entire career. Rogers had an empire to run, not to mention a personal life. As important as "Trigger" was to him and his public persona, he had to delegate the palomino's care and training to others. While Glenn Randall was "Trigger's" primary caregiver, even he was not present in every situation. Regrettably, Randall never wrote an autobiography and he never discussed "Trigger" in detail as only he could have. "Trigger" was by all accounts a very smart horse and at least one magazine article is attributed to him, the tongue-in-cheek "My Life with Roy" published in 1950 (publisher unknown).[8] As charming as this was, Trigger didn't write a biography or give interviews. Unlike television's other palomino celebrity, Mr. Ed, Trigger couldn't talk.

If one is trying to document Trigger's life, one is going to run into not only contradictions but lots of dead ends. The information that Roy Rogers and Glenn Randall once possessed between them is now gone forever. In the final analysis, they made some very shrewd decisions when it came to how Trigger and his doubles were used. The best way to manage Trigger's story is to present as many different sides as are credible and make judgments tempered by experience and common sense. No one person knows the complete "Trigger" story. This book is not a definitive statement and by no means the last word. "Trigger" is show business sleight-of-hand. If you want the truth, you'll find some here, but what you really have is the speculation of a dedicated fan and an honest attempt to sort out and construct a credible history.

When B-westerns were in their heyday, no one — not Roy Rogers, Glenn Randall, or William Witney — could have predicted that in time advances in technology, like DVD players, would allow millions of fans to own copies of their films, much less have the power to study them in detail and distinguish one palomino from another.

When director William Witney first identified Little Trigger in his book *Trigger Remembered* as the most important Trigger double Rogers used, I was reminded of the cliché, "Where there's smoke there's fire." Since the publication of Witney's book in 1989, many articles and books have discussed Little Trigger. Just as the use of Trigger look-alikes and palomino stunt doubles is no secret anymore, the existence of Little Trigger has been very well known to serious fans for a long time now.

No one who has honestly tried to sort out which "Trigger" is which would be surprised at the difficulty of separating fact from legend with regard to Roy Rogers' life. Leonard Slye really lived his role as Roy Rogers, "King of the Cowboys." It's common knowledge, almost tradition, that many Hollywood actors changed their names, but not many went on to play the same character in every one of their films as well as in, television, radio and public appearances. As Robert W. Phillips noted, "Gene Autry initiated the practice of portraying himself on screen. Going a step further, Roy was now patterning his life as close as possible in every aspect to that of his film character." This second layer of publicity protection to Roy Rogers may be unique in the world of show business.[9] This also extended to his horse.

When Rogers played a rowdy young upstart in *Dark Command* (1940) to John Wayne's heroic lead, fans wouldn't accept him. He wasn't as engaging. Fans didn't want Rogers as

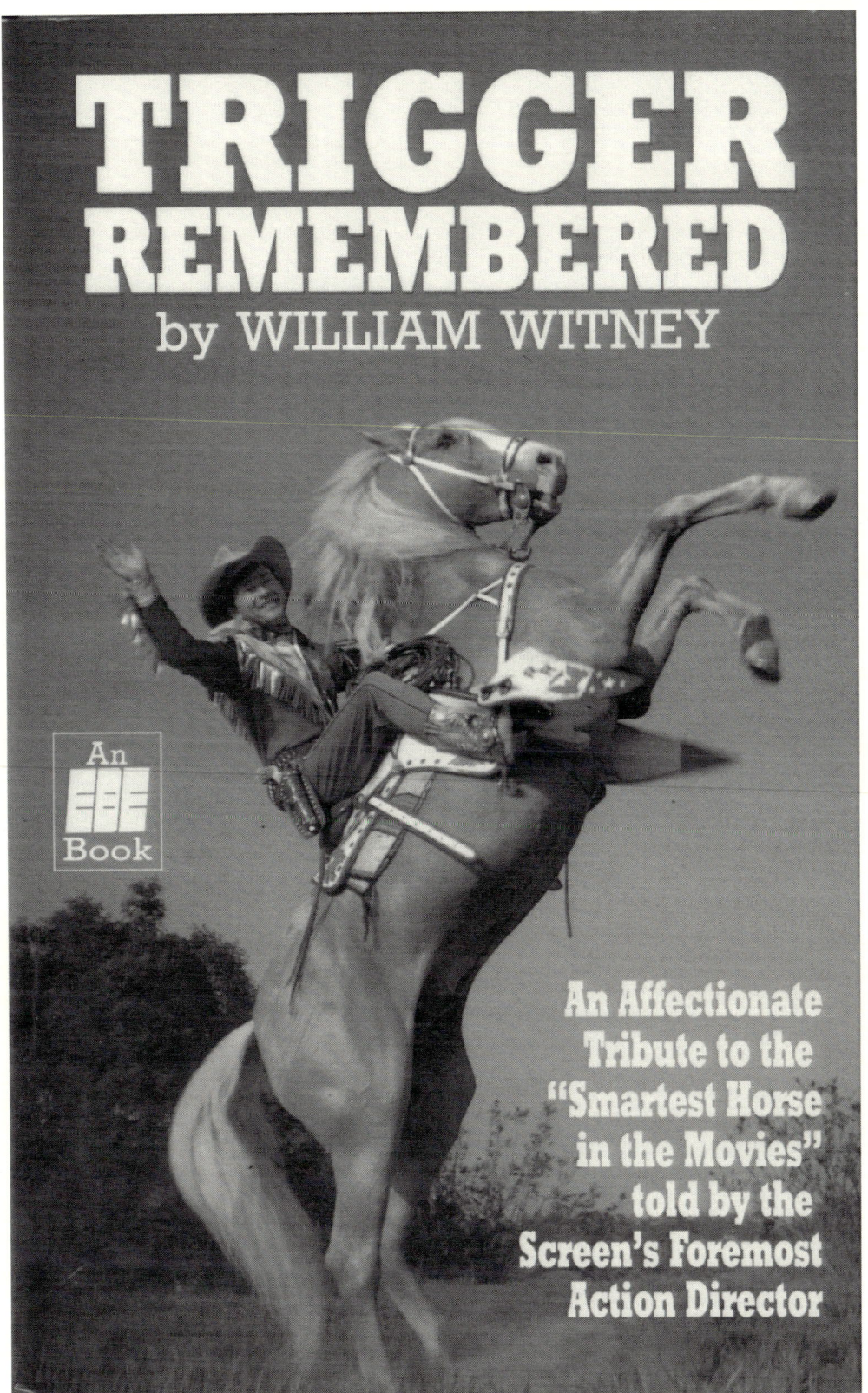

Trigger Remembered by William Witney (Earl Blair Enterprises, 1989).

some supporting character; they wanted him to be "the King of the Cowboys" in all his screen outings. They wanted to see him riding a palomino. In interviews Rogers stated categorically that he did not care for his role in *Dark Command* either and refused to be cast in similar productions.

An example of how sensitive Rogers was to his public persona was noted in the 2005 book *My Brush with History* by famed portraitist Everett Raymond Kinstler. He wrote about his experiences painting famous people, including Roy Rogers and Dale Evans. Every time he asked them to pose, Rogers would move to his wife's right side, which put him first if one was "reading" left to right. When Kinstler asked him why he kept doing that, Rogers replied, "Well. It does read Roy and Dale."

Photos of Roy Rogers on a rearing Trigger are almost always taken from the same side, the horse's right. Here again is another example of Rogers' acute awareness of image. Reading left to right, it's "Roy Rogers and Trigger."

Even Roy Rogers' romantic feelings towards his leading ladies had to be held in check for the sake of his image. "Cowboys weren't allowed to kiss girls in pictures, so one time I gave Dale a little peck on the forehead and we got a ton of letters to leave that mushy stuff out. So I had to kiss Trigger instead."[10]

3

Trigger's Story

"Any cowboy worth his stuff owes half of what he gets to his horse." — Roy Rogers

Watching the original Trigger on film, noting all that's been said by those who knew him, and even making allowances for palomino look-alikes who stood in for him, it's easy to conclude that he was a very special horse. "Trigger was the best and I'll probably never find another like him," said Rogers on *The Merv Griffin Show* in 1982.[1] It's no wonder he was held in such high regard as a movie star that only Roy Rogers himself got higher billing on marquees and movie screens. Baby boomers cannot think on Roy Rogers without remembering

Golden Cloud, aka Trigger, aka the Old Man.

"Trigger." Well over a quarter century after the palomino died, the King of the Cowboys was still signing autographs "Roy Rogers and Trigger." Even the president of the United States remembered the palomino the morning after Roy Rogers passed away. In a press conference Bill Clinton said, "Like most people my age, I grew up on Roy Rogers and Dale Evans and Trigger."[2]

Even though it took many palominos to build the legend of "the Smartest Horse in the Movies" and even though the original Trigger didn't perform a great variety of tricks, he made up for it in charisma, screen presence, and beauty. But he was much more than a mere glamour boy. He could also rear up astonishingly high and run like the wind. He was every inch the movie star he was billed as. Rogers and Glenn Randall would have been foolish to endanger Trigger unnecessarily or to wear him out. Little Trigger and Randall, along with many double horses and stunt riders, were a strong support system for Trigger and Roy. It took a great deal of work to pull off the illusion of a wonder horse, but no amount of work would have mattered without a great horse at the top.

But where did that great horse come from?

Roy F. Cloud, Jr.

Trigger was bred from stock owned by Captain Larry Good. Roy F. Cloud, a former U.S. border patrolman turned horse breeder from Nobelsville, Indiana, was the foal's second owner and registered him as the Golden Cloud in 1937. Neither Palomino registry existed at the time of Trigger's birth on July 4, 1934. Although it's been rumored that the Golden Cloud was born on a stock ranch near San Diego partially owned by singer Bing Crosby, that has never been confirmed. According to Pat Mefferd, pedigree research expert, Crosby's ranch was in Ventura County.

Mefferd also could not recall any palominos running on thoroughbred tracks in the U.S. at the time. Granted there could have been some match races pitting one horse against another in Mexico at Caliente, but chances are the horses were not a registered. According to Robert W. Phillips, Trigger actually raced at the Caliente Race Track.

Golden Cloud Registration Form

Roy Rogers gave 1932 as the date of Trigger's birth in interviews from 1957 and 1965. That would have meant he was 33 when he died in 1965, something Rogers maintained throughout his career.

Author David Rothel, in his book *Singing Cowboys*, stated that Trigger was three when actress Olivia de Havilland rode him in the Warner Bros. film *The Adventures of Robin Hood* (1938). Director William Witney indicated that the palomino was three or four during the filming of his first movie as Trigger *Under Western Stars* (1938). Those dates made Trigger's birth year 1934.

According to the Golden Cloud registration form provided by the president of the Palomino Horse Association and Stud Book Registry, Steve Rebuck, 1934 is the correct date of Trigger's birth. The form (registry number 214) carries two dates: "March 25, 1937" in the upper right-hand corner and "April 1, 1937" on a second date line. It reads:

I, Roy F. Cloud, Jr., *apply for registration for* Golden Cloud. *Sex* Stallion. *Bred by* Captain Larry Good. *Sired by* Tarzan. *Dam* Apac. Light Ch. [This is the color of the dam, "light chestnut," apparently accidentally entered on this line; it is entered again below.] *Color of sire* Golden Palomino. *And dam, if known* Light ch. *Foaled* July 4, 1934. *Now aged* 2 yrs. 8 mo. 27 d. *Body color* Golden Palomino. *Color of mane and tail* White. *All markings* White blaze extending from above eyes to

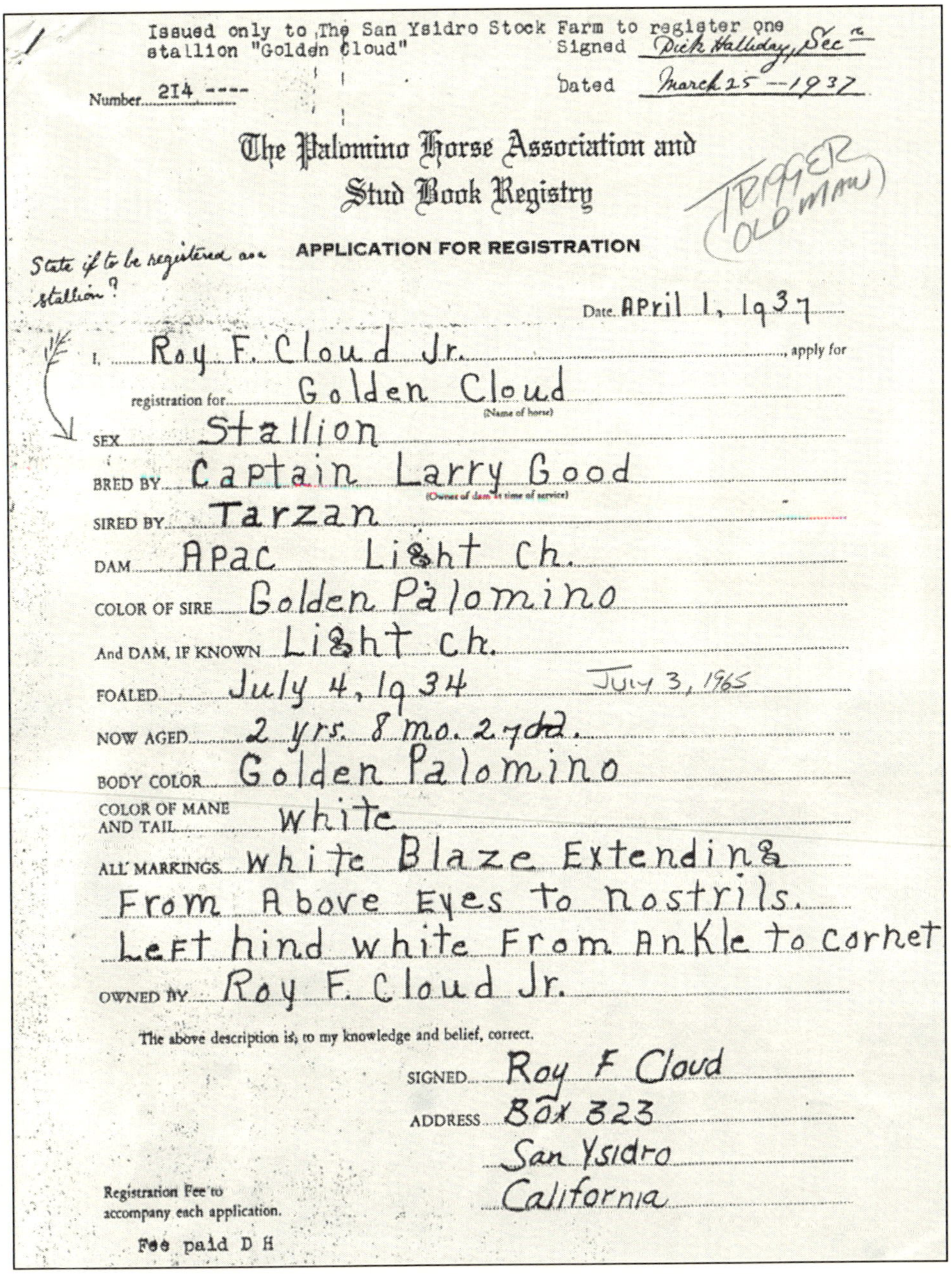

Issued only to The San Ysidro Stock Farm to register one
stallion "Golden Cloud"   Signed *Dick Halliday, Sec*

Number 214 ----   Dated *March 25 --1937*

The Palomino Horse Association and
Stud Book Registry

State if to be registered as a   **APPLICATION FOR REGISTRATION**
stallion?

Date APril 1, 1937

I, Roy F. Cloud Jr. , apply for

registration for Golden Cloud
(Name of horse)

SEX Stallion

BRED BY Captain Larry Good
(Owner of dam at time of service)

SIRED BY Tarzan

DAM Apac Light ch.

COLOR OF SIRE Golden Palomino

And DAM, IF KNOWN Light ch.

FOALED July 4, 1934   *July 3, 1965*

NOW AGED 2 yrs. 8 mo. 27 da.

BODY COLOR Golden Palomino

COLOR OF MANE AND TAIL white

ALL' MARKINGS White Blaze Extending
From Above Eyes to nostrils.
Left hind white From Ankle to cornet

OWNED BY Roy F. Cloud Jr.

The above description is, to my knowledge and belief, correct.

SIGNED Roy F Cloud

ADDRESS Box 323
San Ysidro
California

Registration Fee to
accompany each application.

Fee paid D H

Trigger registration form (*the Palomino Horse Association courtesy of Steven Rebuck and Patricia Rebuck*).

nostrils. Left hind white from ankle to cornet [coronet, i.e., an area just above the hoof]. *Owned by Roy F. Cloud Jr.*[4]

The lavish coffee table book *Roy Rogers: King of the Cowboys* by Georgia Morris and Mark Pollard quoted Rogers as saying, "Trigger made every picture. He was four and I was 26 when we made our first picture."[5] In this instance Rogers was right with regards to Trigger's age during the filming in 1938 of *Under Western Stars*. It means the palomino was born in 1934 and was 31 when he died in 1965. It remains a mystery as to why Rogers usually said Trigger died at age 33, which would have made the year of his death 1967, not 1965.

Bloodlines and Conformation

Trigger's bloodlines are not confirmed in his registration form and have always been a source of some confusion due to the various descriptions of him, his sire, and dam. When discussing Trigger's origin in interviews, Rogers usually claimed that he was "half Thoroughbred and half cold-blooded; his sire was a race horse at Caliente, and his dam was a cold-blooded palomino. He took the good parts from both of them."[6] It seems Rogers was incorrect with regards to the dam's color. The original Trigger inherited his color (as well as his speed) from his sire, and his fine conformation from his dam. Trigger's wide chest, short back, and powerful legs allowed him to rear safely straight up in his signature pose, with Roy Rogers in the saddle, waving with his right hand.

According to registry expert Pat Mefferd, stepdaughter of stunt man Fred Kennedy, who was around the original Trigger numerous times, "he was not half Thoroughbred, maybe one quarter. His half-bred sire could have been from the stock owned by Bing Crosby. His brother Bob Crosby had a Thoroughbred farm in Hemet for many years, so this is entirely possible."

Some have claimed Trigger was a grandson of the great Sir Barton, the first Triple Crown

Bing Crosby, an avid horseman, dressed in his best cowboy attire in a scene from *Rhythm on the Range* (Paramount Pictures, 1935). Coincidentally, the Sons of the Pioneers (with Roy Rogers, aka Leonard Slye) also appeared in the same movie, which was released a year after Trigger was born.

Trigger conformation pose. While ideal equine proportion varies from breed to breed, a square look to the body from a side view is often preferred. The original Trigger was nicely proportioned, and that had everything to do with his athleticism and endurance.

winner. After Sir Barton's race career was over, he was purchased by the U.S. Remount Association in 1933 and sent to Wyoming Remount Station, where he was bred to many unregistered mares.[7] That is where he stayed until his death in 1937. In actual fact, it was Pal, a palomino look-alike Rogers and Dale Evans both rode, who was a descendent of Sir Barton. This was according to Wyoming veterinarian Dr. Jack Ketcham and confirmed by trainer Orval Robinson, both who worked for Pal's former owner, Walt Rymill.

At one time the Tennessee Walking Horse Breeders Association ran national magazine ads stating that Trigger was indeed a Tennessee walking horse. They were supported in an article by a horse expert who made the same assertion.[8] The problem with that claim, as is often the case when Trigger is discussed, is determining which horse they were referring to. This inconsistency may stem from the fact that Trigger Jr. was a registered Tennessee walking horse. It also needs to be noted that Trigger, Little Trigger, and Trigger Jr. were not related.

Early Movie Stables

When Hollywood was still just a spot on the map, and studios were called "camps" or "colonies" operating out of makeshift locations like abandoned barns, an enterprising

Roy F. Cloud, Jr. (left), on his beautiful palomino Golden Cloud. (Second rider and horse are unknown.) This is the earliest known photograph of Trigger; it was taken circa 1936, probably in San Diego, California, when the horse was just over two.

individual named Fat Jones realized he could make money renting horses to the fledgling movie industry. This was circa 1912, when a company called Pathé began filming two-reeler westerns outside of Los Angeles. Jones was sure movies would develop into a major industry in California, and he built a stable with barns, corrals, and a blacksmith shop.[9] He purchased land in North Hollywood and started scouting the Southwest for all types of horse-related transport.[10] The Fat Jones stable became a magnet for real cowboys who came to Hollywood for jobs in pictures during the winter months when work was slow in ranch country. While the majority did not find permanent employment, a few stayed. Two of the most famous were the legendary western author Will James and character actor Ben Johnson.[11]

Hudkins Brothers Stable

At the same time Jones was starting his business, four brothers, Ace, Art, Clyde and Ode Hudkins, ran a riding academy in the Los Angeles area. Ace and Art owned the stable. Ace, Ode and Clyde handled the day to day operations. At first they even assisted Jones, but soon they broadened their academy to a sales and rental business. They gained a reputation in the film industry for their stock company, which could furnish horses, cattle, western gear and horse-drawn vehicles, and eventually became second only to Jones. Even with all that, their real claim to fame would be one special palomino they acquired from Bing Crosby's San Diego stock farm.

William Witney wrote that Clyde Hudkins, while on a horse buying trip in San Diego, first laid eyes on Trigger in the pasture on the Crosby ranch where he was foaled. Clyde saw that the colt would be perfect in movies with his great looks. Horses with the best breeding and classiest markings were leased for the benefit of the star of a motion picture. They were called "cast horses."[12] Apparently Trigger was part of a herd Ace Hudkins purchased all at once.[13]

As is common practice, Trigger would have been just over two when he was started under saddle. The earliest known picture of Trigger shows him being ridden by his then owner Roy F. Cloud, Jr. It is safe to assume that the animal was still on the San Ysidro ranch in 1936. Although the date is undocumented, it was around 1937 that Trigger was moved from the San Diego ranch to the Hudkins stables in Los Angeles. Once there, he got movie work right away. With his golden color, great proportions and intelligence, he was a natural movie horse. By 1937 he was on the sets of *Cowboy from Brooklyn* (Warner Bros.) and *The Adventures of Robin Hood* (Warner Bros.). Trigger was some times referred to as the "Barrymore of horses"—a reference to John "the great profile" Barrymore, an actor from the silent movie days, noted not only for his skills as a thespian but for his classic looks.

The Hudkins Brothers stable was originally located in Burbank where Forest Lawn Cemetery now stands. It was later relocated to North Hollywood and finally Coldwater Canyon. At one time, the Hudkins' and Glenn Randall's ranches

Stuntman Fred Kennedy and the original Trigger (left) at the Hudkins Brothers Ranch on the Los Angeles River bed. The facility was there for many years before it was moved to the Valley. Kennedy's stepdaughter Pat Mefford of Cottonwood, California, stated that her mother took the photograph, "and in the photo album, the date shows, in her hand, 'Fred and Trigger 1940.'" Kennedy was a stuntman, bit player and 1982 Stuntmen's Hall of Fame inductee. The mount on the right was a Hudkins movie horse named Smokey, described by actress Peggy Stewart as part Arabian *(Pat Mefford collection)*.

were within a couple of blocks of each other in North Hollywood near Sherman Way. Both concerns were removed from that area due to zoning changes in the mid–1960s.

Typically the Hudkins brothers would begin work at about five in the morning. The wranglers arrived and checked a booking sheet for the day's rentals and locations. There would be a number of studios requiring the use of Hudkins stock. Horses were grained, cleaned up, and tacked accordingly. Horses and vintage wagons were loaded onto long Pullman trucks and driven to three possible destinations: a studio for interior shooting; a movie ranch location in north Hollywood; or on an extended trip that might cross state lines. Republic Studios was located at 4024 Redford Avenue in North Hollywood.[14]

Ace Hudkins would have had a hard time listing all the films for which he supplied horses. It was all in a day's work, whether supplying a cast horse, a dozen horse extras, or any combination a movie studio required. On any given day there might have been a request for a gentle mare for a star who wasn't much of a rider, or perhaps for a fancy, highly schooled palomino who could make a movie star stand out.

Work was steady at the Hudkins stable. Wranglers and craftspeople were busy with any number of jobs, from training saddle horses to repairing and cleaning tack. With all the horses that needed to be shod and wagons needing maintenance and repair, the blacksmith shop was constantly busy. On top of all that activity, teaching actors how to ride properly was one of the most important functions of the stable.

Horses were a business for the Hudkins brothers. They didn't care which motion picture production company rented their stock, just so long as their animals were on location. Studios paid from $5 to $10 a day for extra or chase horses, and these animals made money consistently. Cast horses, who did not work as often, commanded from fifty to one hundred dollars a day.[15] For every week Trigger was a Hudkins rental horse, there was the probability he was on a film set. It cost more to rent Trigger for a week than what Roy Rogers was being paid initially as a star.

From Sly to Weston to Rogers

Born Leonard Frank Sly[16] in 1911 in Cincinnati, Ohio, the future King of the Cowboys grew up on farm near Duck Run. After a move to Southern California in 1930, he teamed with Tim Spencer and Bob Nolan and formed the Pioneer Trio. They added fiddler Hugh Farr and his brother, guitarist Karl Marx Farr, and became the Sons of the Pioneers in 1934, the same year Trigger was born in San Diego. Slye and the Sons of the Pioneers would go on to appear in the films of Dick Foran (*Song of the Saddle*, Warner Bros., 1936, and *California Mail*, Warner Bros., 1936), Gene Autry (*The Big Show*, 1936; *The Old Corral*, 1936; *The Old Barn Dance*, 1938), Charles Starrett (*Gallant Defender*, Columbia, 1935; *The Mysterious Avenger*, Columbia, 1936; and *The Old Wyoming Trail*, Columbia, 1937) and even Bing Crosby (*Rhythm on the Range*, Paramount, 1936).

Slye signed with Republic as a solo in 1937 and with that came a name change to Dick Weston. In October of the same year Slye heard that Republic Pictures was conducting auditions for a new singing cowboy because Gene Autry had walked out on his contract after completing work on *The Old Barn Dance* (ironically, "Dick Weston" had a small role in the movie as a square dance caller). Weston's screen test led to a contract and another name change to Roy Rogers. He was given the starring role in what would have been Autry's next film, *Under Western Stars*, originally titled *Washington Cowboy*.[17] The publicity department

1937 b.t. (Before Trigger): Roy Rogers (left), aka Leonard Slye, in the Charles Starrett western *The Old Wyoming Trail* (Columbia, 1937). (Starrett is at right on white horse; other actors not identified.) Just a few years later, the image of Rogers and Trigger would become so ingrained in the hearts and minds of fans that he would never look quite right when not riding a palomino.

at Republic Pictures came up with a fictional biography for the newly christened Rogers. He "was a true-blue son of the West, born in Cody, Wyoming, and raised on a sprawling cattle ranch." He was even supposed to have labored as a ranch hand in New Mexico for a while "before finally making his way to the bright lights of Hollywood."[18]

Just as movie studios had casting directors for actors, they had casting directors for animals. Filmmakers depended on them to find not only photogenic animals but those with even temperaments, able to perform well on movie sets. Bill Jones was head livestock man at

Roy Rogers and the original Trigger on location with a Republic Pictures movie crew. Like all animal actors, Trigger was accustomed to film equipment and, despite a natural flight instinct, did not feel threatened.

Republic; he had also worked at Hudkins Stables.[19] When Roy Rogers began to work on *Under Western Stars*, all the stables that leased livestock to the studios were asked to send their cast horses. According to Rogers, about a half-dozen mounts were brought in for the equine casting call. He actually rode a couple down the street and back. The third horse he tried was Trigger, and he never looked at the rest. Unfortunately the wrangler who was handling the Hudkins stock that fateful day has never been identified. When he handed Golden Cloud's reins to Roy Rogers, he made one of the most important introductions in western film history.

In a 1976 interview, Rogers recalled, "I knew I wanted a palomino to start with. The third horse they showed me was Trigger. I hadn't liked the first two, but when I took O' Trigger for a test ride, I told 'em he was the one I wanted. I didn't even look at any of the others."[20] Circa 1995 Rogers said the same thing on the *Horseworld* television show in a nine minute segment on Trigger) to host Larry Mahan. A champion rodeo rider, Mahan questioned Rogers about first acquiring Trigger, and the King of the Cowboys answered, "So I'll never forget the day they called me up to go over to pick out a horse. They had seven or eight of them there and I believe Trigger was the third one I got on. I never looked at the rest of them."

Under Western Stars, the first B-western to premiere on Broadway,[21] was a hit. According to William Witney, everywhere Rogers toured, audiences would ask for Trigger. Rogers realized that he was not in a position to take the palomino on personal appearances because he didn't own him. He had to make some kind of commitment to owning the horse (or a look-alike horse).

Bill of Sale

As with Trigger's date of birth and bloodlines, sources differ regarding the year when Rogers purchased him. Several different years have appeared in different sources. They range from as early as 1937 to as late as 1941. The official tale was that Rogers bought Trigger right after he rode him in *Under Western Stars*, released in 1938. Numerous published articles even stated that Rogers used a guitar as part of the down payment. One of the earliest biographies of Roy Rogers and Dale Evans, *The Answer is God*, gives 1940 as the year Trigger was purchased.[22] Another popular story is that Rogers bought Trigger right after he came back from the first tour for *Under Western Stars*. In *Liberty* magazine (December 1946) Rogers was quoted as saying he bought Trigger in 1937 on the installment plan. "About the second or third picture, I went to Hudkins Stables and bought him from them." Rogers and Hudkins apparently worked out some kind of deal, part of which was the exclusive use of Hudkins stock in all his films. He reportedly told Clyde Hudkins, "Sell him to me and if I'm lucky and hit the jackpot, I'll see that Hudkins' horses are on my set."[22] This was of major importance and would serve Rogers well in future negotiations with Republic, who was unaware of the transaction.

Writer Sam Henderson stated, "Roy raised Trigger from a colt, and scrimped and saved to buy him, feed him and train him." In his autobiography *Happy Trails*, Rogers claimed, "We rented my palomino from Hudkins, one of the stables Republic did considerable business with. So I drove out there one day and, after quite a bit of horse trading, bought him for twenty-five hundred dollars."

In her autobiography *Cowboy Princess*, Cheryl Rogers-Barnett claimed that her father bought Trigger in 1938 for two thousand dollars on time payments after their third film together: "Dad and Ace Hudkins had struck up a deal for Dad to make payments while Ace continued to rent Trigger to Republic — but he wouldn't let them put another cowboy on him — until the last payment had been made. However, according to the official bill of sale, Rogers made a down payment to Hudkins Stables in September of 1943 and paid the balance on Trigger the following December.

Roy Rogers never threw anything out and his son Dusty eventually made Trigger's actual bill of sale public.[23] It revealed that Rogers purchased Trigger from the Hudkins Brothers for $2,500. Trigger's bill of sale is dated September 18, 1943, and reads, "Sold to Roy Rogers, one palomino stallion named "Trigger" for the sum of Twenty-five Hundred Dollars. ($2500.00) Five Hundred Dollars has been paid down and the balance, $2000.00 to be paid on Roy Rogers return from New York."

HUDKINS STABLES
MOTION PICTURE EQUIPMENT
3744 Barham Blvd.
Hollywood, Calif.
Phone HOllywood 9078

DATE Sept. 15, 1943
INVOICE NO.
ORDER NO.
PICTURE NO.

TERMS: NET CASH, NO DISCOUNT monthly account payable on or before 10th of following month

Sold to Roy Rogers, one palomino stallion named "Trigger" for the sum of Twenty-five Hundred Dollars. ($2500.00) Five Hundred Dollars has been paid down and the balance, $2000.00 to be paid on Roy Rogers return from New York.

HUDKINS STABLES
MOTION PICTURE EQUIPMENT
3744 Barham Blvd.
Hollywood, Calif.
Phone HOllywood 9078

DATE Dec. 6, 1943
INVOICE NO.
ORDER NO.
PICTURE NO.

TERMS: NET CASH, NO DISCOUNT monthly account payable on or before 10th of following month

Received of Roy Rogers Two Thousand Dollars, ($2000.00.)
Payment in full for one palomino stallion named "Trigger".

Art Hudkins
(By) Helen Meyers

Top: Trigger bill of sale *(copy courtesy of Joel "Dutch" Dortch). Bottom:* Receipt from Hudkins Stables for payment of the balance on the purchase of Trigger.

Ray White was one of the first who noted the bill of sale and 1943 as the purchase date for Trigger in the June 2001 issue of *Western Horseman* magazine in an article titled "B-western Horses." Trigger's bill of sale was eventually acknowledged by others and the details became well known via the Internet.

Of course the record of Trigger's purchase in 1943 dispels the myth that Roy Rogers bought him when he was making only $75 a week. By 1943 Republic was paying him around $1000 a week and he was making big money with personal appearances and rodeos.[24] The bill of sale does not say who transacted the deal. It is not known for sure if it was between Rogers and Ace Hudkins, or between Hudkins and Glenn Randall acting on Rogers' behalf.

The purchase date on the bill of sale is remarkable because it means Roy Rogers was riding a horse he did not own for five full years after appearing with Trigger in *Under Western Stars*! Trigger also appeared in six other films that we know in that same period: *Cowboy from Brooklyn* (Warner Bros., 1938), *The Adventures of Robin Hood* (Warner Bros., 1938), *Juarez* (Warner Bros., 1939), *Shut My Big Mouth* (Columbia, 1942), *Bad Men of the Hills* (Columbia, 1942), and *Silver City Raiders* (Columbia, 1943). Obviously Rogers did not have exclusive use of the palomino; Hudkins Stables was controlling where and when Trigger worked. It's safe to assume that Rogers was rightfully concerned that Trigger was up for grabs to anyone who could afford to rent him. It's understandable that in later biographies and interviews, the publicity-conscious Rogers avoided making it known that he was ever riding someone else's horse. This was not how Rogers or his family wanted the public to picture the relationship between Trigger and Roy.

No hard-copy, documented evidence has ever surfaced regarding any arrangements between Hudkins and Republic or Rogers for Trigger's services between the time that Rogers first started riding him and the time he actually bought him. Did Rogers strike a deal with Hudkins promising that he would buy Trigger eventually? Was there an understanding between both parties that Trigger could be rented but not sold to anyone else? William Witney claimed that Rogers asked Clyde Hudkins directly if he would sell Trigger to him. Hudkins, seeing potential in Rogers and Trigger, made a counter-offer: he would take care of the horse until Rogers was in a position where he could pay him a little at a time.

Why didn't anyone else buy Trigger? It doesn't seem to have occurred to Herb Yates, president of Republic Pictures. Fans just assumed Rogers owned the horse. Perhaps there were offers made to Hudkins but turned down because of the agreement with Rogers? If he didn't have the resources to buy the palomino, there were many cowboy stars who did. Rogers' regular use of Trigger during his filming period may have limited the palomino's availability for rental to other studios for big chunks of the year, to the point where there was no chance another western movie star would use the horse enough to become established with him in the public's mind.

While no record of any arrangement has come to light, one could reasonably accept that Roy and Hudkins reached an oral agreement — as often described by Rogers — which was then sealed with a handshake. We kids did our part too, by accepting every palomino Rogers rode as "Trigger." At the time, there likely seemed no pressing need for Rogers to own the original Trigger.

There's much to consider regarding the timing and reasons (some not so obvious and perhaps a little controversial) behind when Rogers purchased Trigger. With what we know so far, some reasonable conclusions may be drawn.

Roy Rogers wasn't being paid a lot by Republic Pictures and was under a Term Players Contract from October 13, 1937, through December 3, 1948.[25] His initial weekly salary of $75.00 (by 1940 it had been doubled to $150) was certainly not enough to buy, transport, outfit and maintain an expensive horse. Although his first movies were successful, the young Rogers was probably not sure if he could sustain a career as a singing cowboy. A movie cowboy's fortune back then could change at the drop of a Stetson, and if Rogers felt he was constantly just shy of having to rejoin the Sons of the Pioneers, it was not without reason. After an eight-year run, even the popular Hopalong Cassidy films had begun to wane. Some of the older cowboy stars were taking lesser roles as heavies and supporting characters. Some had moved on to unrelated businesses. Roy Rogers would have noticed all that going on around him and undoubtedly wondered if he really should buy an expensive horse.

We now have the benefit of hindsight and know what a huge star Roy Rogers became, but back then he could only have hoped for the best. What he had was a dream, a plan, and lots of talent. He also had great timing and luck. He was sharp enough to take ownership of his image and his new name from shortsighted studio head Herb Yates. This would serve him well as Rogers would eventually make most of his income from personal appearances and merchandising. Still, he had to gamble on a business that was fickle at best and that alone was reason not to buy Trigger at first, though he surely wanted to.

When Gene Autry, Rogers' only real singing cowboy rival, went into the army and Herb Yates started putting more money and promotion behind Rogers and his movies, his career went into high gear. He soon had become the number one box office western star. That certainly gave him the confidence to think that there might be a sustained future in being Roy Rogers, and he knew darn well that Roy Rogers wasn't Roy Rogers without Trigger! In *The Weekly Reader* (April 1954), Rogers was quoted as saying, "Some children like Trigger more than they do me. They write letters to Trigger. I am glad that they like my horse."

Roy Rogers and Trigger were so closely linked that Rogers did not look right on a horse if it wasn't a palomino. On those rare occasions when a script put him on another mount—for example, when Trigger was stolen in *Under California Stars* (1948) and Rogers was forced to ride a chestnut—he looked out of place. Roy Rogers was not complete without Trigger—but it was a two-way street. Had Herb Yates or some other movie person purchased Trigger, the horse might have had only a short career as attractive equine transportation.

Rogers' draft status also may have been a factor in when he bought Trigger. America was at war from 1941 to 1945. According to Robert W. Phillips' book *Roy Rogers*, Rogers' status jumped around during that time—at first he was enlisting, then he wasn't. In 1943 Rogers' draft status was 3-A (sole surviving son, married with children). During the war, as things got hotter and manpower scarcer, men were being reclassified. With no immediate end in sight, Rogers received notice that he had been reclassified 1-A. Republic nervously began grooming Monte Hale to take his place.[26] That changed as the war drew to a close. In 1945 Rogers was reclassified 3-A because of a change in the deferment age. Furthermore, as it turned out, the war ended before Rogers' number ever came up.

Like John Wayne and so many others who never actually saw combat or active duty, Rogers did a tremendous amount for the war effort, giving freely of his time. According to publicity, he could flat outsell most entertainers when it came to war bond drives. Wrote Joel Dortch, "Roy was a patriot who loved his flag and country. He sold millions of dollars worth of War Bonds during World War II and made numerous USO tours of military bases with 'Trigger,' performing for the men and women in uniform. During one record setting tour of Texas bases, Roy and Trigger made 136 performances in just 20 days! Years later he made a tour of Vietnam to cheer up the troops fighting there."[27]

Gene Autry said that Herb Yates offered to call in some favors and keep him out of military service. Autry refused, which added more tension between him and Yates during their second contract dispute. Yates made good on his threat to Autry to throw Republic Pictures resources into building up Rogers. Did Yates make the same offer to Rogers that he made to Autry—to pull some strings to keep him out of the military? Would he have done so without Rogers' knowledge in order to protect his studio's one remaining singing cowboy star? All this would have certainly had an influence on Rogers' decision to buy Trigger. Would he have made a major purchase that would only be useful to him as a civilian if he were going off to war, perhaps never to return? It does not make sense that he would unless he was darn sure he was going to be around. It seems safe to assume Rogers did not believe he was going

Although Roy Rogers never served in the military like his singing cowboy rival Gene Autry, the King of the Cowboys was patriotic to the core and appeared at many war bond drives with his palominos.

to serve in the military when he decided to buy Trigger. Why and how he got out of military service — whether it resulted from his having kids, or being 31 years old at the time, or some other reason — is unknown. At any rate, Rogers wouldn't have spent $2,500 on a horse if he wasn't fairly certain of his future as a movie cowboy.

Finally there's Rogers' contract status with Republic Pictures, which was coming up for renewal in 1944. Rogers always claimed that his dispute with Yates was not over his contract, but over money for secretaries needed to help deal with the tons of fan mail he was receiving. He had to hire help out of his own pocket to handle bags of letters arriving weekly. Perhaps he could have reasoned that buying Trigger in 1943 would give him better leverage in contract talks between his agent Art Rush and Yates. Rogers wanted his negotiating bases covered. If Rogers owned Trigger, Rush could offer Republic Pictures a package deal. If things didn't work out with Republic, he could take his package deal to other studios, and Yates would know it. Since Rogers owned his name and likeness, he could shop around.[28]

Rogers said in his book *Happy Trails*, "Republic was planning to shoot a movie entitled *Front Page*, and Yates wanted me to play the part of a cocky newspaper reporter. It just didn't make sense to me to suddenly switch my image just after I had begun to establish myself in Westerns. So we got into a pretty heated argument which resulted in me telling him in no uncertain terms that I wasn't going to do the part. 'In that case,' he said, 'maybe we'll just have to put some other cowboy on Trigger and let him do your next movie.' 'You may get someone to do the next picture,' I told him, 'but he won't be riding Trigger. I bought him.' Once aware that the horse belonged to me, Mr. Yates signed Lloyd Nolan for the part in *Front Page*, and I went on about my business of being a singing cowboy."[29]

Fortunately Yates was slow to recognize how important Trigger was to Rogers' career; otherwise he might have even pressured Hudkins to sell and then teamed the animal with anyone he wished. Rogers was honest about the reason for buying Trigger; he just altered the time frame to fit his public image. Rogers didn't want it known that he waited five years. It makes sense that he bought Trigger when he did. Underscoring all of this was the fact that Rogers may have gone for a few years at first not knowing whether he would actually get to own Trigger in the end.

When considering the circumstances surrounding the timing of Rogers' purchase of Trigger, his contractual relationship with Republic must be taken into account. Beyond the signing of his first contract in 1937, we must speculate about the length and specifics of his contract with the studio. Contracts did not run only seven years, as has been often assumed. According to *Republic Confidential — the Players*, "Security — the primary personal inducement in these alliances — was fleeting for most players, with nearly 60% contracted for one year or less before they were terminated while only 26 endured for more than three years. Of the top 11 whose options were repeatedly renewed, Roy Rogers was extended for over 11 years.... Termination did not necessarily spell an end to Republic appearances, however, since many of the 146 either converted to multiple-picture arrangements as did Rogers and Gene Autry or returned in single films as free-lancers."[30]

On page three of the same book, there's a box showing Rogers' term contract ran from October 13, 1937, to December 3, 1948. The exact terms and conditions obviously underwent changes during this period. Unless the Rogers family chooses to make that information public, we simply cannot know the details of those changes. It can be assumed that the purchase of Trigger would have been an advantage to Rogers' position with the studio, whenever it happened. The impression from reading Rogers' many biographies was that he made very few financial moves without consulting his managers, and the business aspects of purchasing Trigger would have had to be a driving force in the decision. As Dusty Rogers has pointed out, Trigger was not a pet. Rogers and his team surely realized that losing the association of "Roy Rogers and Trigger" was not a wise business decision. Trigger was sharing top billing with Rogers in all the films, and it wouldn't have looked good to splash the horse's name all over the place and then have some other cowboy ride off on him!

Trigger expert Larry Roe theorized that Roy Rogers probably knew the palomino was being used in 1943 for Columbia's movie *Silver City Raiders* and that knowledge really motivated him to buy the horse. While it will never be proven conclusively, consider the following. It's obvious Rogers loved Trigger, he knew how popular the horse was with fans, and he had even bought a silver saddle. Rogers' agreement with Hudkins Stables could have continued status quo; it wasn't absolutely imperative that he buy Trigger then. Republic Studios was renting the horse for him, and he'd already bought Little Trigger. However, the bottom line was that he had no control over how Trigger was used or what star could ride him. Republic Pictures may not have cared as long as they could get the palomino for Rogers' movies. Trigger's conspicuous appearance in *Silver City Raiders* was the last straw.

"Trigger was still owned by the Hudkins Stables, which meant that I couldn't take him out on a personal appearance tour if I wanted to; it also meant they could lease him to another cowboy actor if they wanted to."[31]

In 1938 Trigger appeared in six movies. Warner Bros.' *The Adventures of Robin Hood* was probably his first. A review exists dated May 7, 1938, which means the film had just hit theatres. Republic Pictures was promoting Rogers as its next singing cowboy star, and publicity shots of him riding a dark bay had already been printed. *Under Western Stars*, Rogers' first movie for Republic as the lead, was released on April 7, 1938. What those dates indicate is that both films were probably in production at the same time. They were followed by *Cowboy from Brooklyn*, another Warner Bros. production, on July 16 with Trigger in a cameo appearance. Three Roy Rogers Republic films filled out the year: *Billy the Kid Returns*, released September 4; *Come On Rangers*, released November 25; and *Shine On Harvest Moon*, released December 30.

Trigger appeared in Warner Bros.' *Juarez* in 1939. While Trigger's Republic movies are well known from 1940 to 1941, it's hard to believe he wasn't used in other sans–Roy Rogers movies, although none have been discovered at this time. In 1942 he was used in 10 movies, including two for Columbia: *Shut My Big Mouth*, released February 19, and *Bad Men of the Hills*, released August 13.

Roy Rogers' movie *South of Santa Fe*, released February 17, 1942, was shot around the same time as *Shut My Big Mouth*. Columbia did not bother changing the saddle and used the same tack that Rogers had. In Charles Starrett's *Bad Men of the Hills*, Trigger's mane was combed to the left side of his neck; his mane naturally flowed to the right side.

Trigger was in six movies in 1943, one that we know of with Russell Hayden, *Silver City Raiders*, and five with Roy Rogers. By the time the palomino made this appearance with Hayden, 39 Roy Rogers movies had been released. Rogers' last movie with Trigger in 1943 was made in October, *The Man from Music Mountain*, and released on the 30th of that month. Columbia most likely was using Trigger as Hayden's mount during the latter part of October; *Silver City Raiders* was released on November 4.[32]

If Larry Roe is correct about Roy Rogers knowing that Columbia and Russell Hayden were using Trigger in *Silver City Raiders*, it's a safe bet that it was at this point in time when the King of the Cowboys made up his mind to buy the palomino outright. Trigger's bill of sale date is dated September 18, 1943. Rogers went to Hudkins and finalized the deal. After that, nobody had control over Trigger but Roy Rogers. Trigger could even be seen as an early Christmas present Rogers gave himself in 1943.

Contract

Trigger was never under contract with Republic, in spite of early reports to the contrary. Doreen M. Norton, in her 1949 book *The Palomino Horse*, wrote, "Trigger's contract stipulates that he be given equal billing with Roy Rogers, and that in each picture he have at least three close-ups." Rogers is quoted in Elise Miller Davis's 1955 biography *The Answer Is God*: "Trigger shares top billing with me. And he has a contract that calls for three close ups and a direct part in motivating the plot in each picture. He gets his own fan mail and his own salary." Nevertheless, when author David Rothel asked Rogers in the 1980s whether Trigger's contract called for three close-ups in each film, equal billing, and scripts showing him helping to motivate the story, Rogers replied that was nonsense, some publicity guy's daydream.

Trigger did not get a salary, not even scale. He was part of a package deal with Rogers.

Tag Lines and Screen Billing

Trigger didn't start to get billing alongside Rogers on movie posters and screens till the early 1940s. Posters from 1938 and 1939 do not bear his name. But by the time Dale Evans starred in *The Cowboy and the Senorita* (1944), Trigger was well established, and his name appeared right below Rogers' and above everyone else's in the cast for the remainder of his career at Republic Pictures. What's more, Trigger's name was printed in the same size as Rogers' and larger than the names of the other cast members.

What about screen billing? Trigger was not the first horse to be so honored. Rogers was still one of the Sons of the Pioneers when the group appeared in the Dick Foran western *The California Mail* in 1936. Foran's beautiful palomino Smoke, in classic western show tack, received star billing and the tag line "the wonder

Roy Rogers' long time agent Art Rush jokingly offers the original Trigger a contact to sign. In reality the horse was not under any contract with Republic Pictures *(Roy Dillow collection)*.

horse." In *The California Mail* Smoke was instrumental in driving the plot; he even killed two of the villains. Years later, when Rogers became a star and finally had his own palomino, he may have thought back on Smoke.[33]

Many horses were dubbed "the wonder horse," beginning with the temperamental black Morgan stallion Rex who achieved stardom in the early days of film. Tom Mix was the first cowboy to use the tag line "the King of the Cowboys." Mix's horse, Tony, was called "the wonder horse"; so was Ken Maynard's horse, Tarzan. Autry's horse, Champion, was referred to as "the world's wonder horse." A popular comic book produced by Charleton in the 1950s and 1960s titled *Black Fury* used the "wonder horse" tag on its covers. Even Trigger was referred to as "the wonder horse" on toys occasionally, and one of the three versions of the National Safety Council statuettes awarded annually by Rogers read, "Official Roy Rogers' Trigger The Wonder Horse."

Rogers and Republic started using the tag line "King of the Cowboys" shortly after the film of the same title. In the last scene of that movie, Rogers was referred to as "King of Cowboys." In the film that follows, *Song of Texas*, Rogers is introduced in a scene at a rodeo as "the King of the Cowboys." The posters seem to be different; Rogers and Trigger may have gotten their tag lines on posters before they got them on screen. Trigger received no screen billing up through *Song of Texas*, released by Republic in June of 1943. However, in the film that followed in August of that same year, *Silver Spurs*, the line "Trigger, the Smartest Horse in the Movies" appeared right under Rogers' name. Perhaps after Republic, Rogers and Art Rush decided to use the "King of the Cowboys" title, giving Trigger his own tag line was a natural next step. In *Shine On Harvest Moon* (1938), Rogers refers to Trigger not only by name but describes him as "the smartest horse I've ever had." Trigger even got billing along with Rogers in his cameo appearance in *Hit Parade of 1947*, the Republic musical extravaganza, along with stars Eddie Albert and Constance Moore. Trigger got fourth billing under Bob Hope, Jane Russell, and Roy Rogers in *Son of Paleface* (Paramount, 1952). During the film's opening credits, when Trigger's name appears, the sound of a horse neighing is heard.

While Roy Rogers was billed as "King of the Cowboys" on movie marquees, posters and publicity materials, he was not billed that way on movie screens. However, after awhile, Trigger was billed as "the Smartest Horse in the Movies" everywhere including movie screens.

According to *Variety*, in order to make Rogers "king," a publicity campaign in 1944 placed 192 billboards across the country carrying 24-sheet movie posters featuring Rogers and Trigger and announcing that he was "King of the Cowboys" and Trigger was "the Smartest Horse in the Movies." The budget for the campaign has been estimated from $100,000 to $500,000. Nothing like this was ever done for another B-western cowboy, but Republic was determined to make Rogers number one. While there may have been resentment from the other cowboys after Rogers was christened "King of the Cowboys," it was not of his doing. He never referred to himself as king.

When *Time* magazine acknowledged Dale Evans' death in February of 2001, it was noted that despite her popularity, Trigger out-billed her in Roy Rogers' films. Said Bill Whitaker of the *Abilene Reporter News*, "When I interviewed her 15 years ago, she recalled with humor how Trigger — Rogers' famous horse —'used to get billing over me.' Eventually the Uvalde native graduated to the point she got billing over Gabby Hayes, Rogers' wizened, bearded, ever-cantankerous sidekick. But more often than not, Trigger still got more attention than she did, both in film credits and in the film itself. 'It never bothered me that much,' she said, 'but it bothered my agent.'"

Trigger's Name

Rogers claimed that sidekick Smiley "Frog Milhouse" Burnette first suggested the name "Trigger" on the set of *Under Western Stars* after someone commented, "As fast as that horse is, you ought to call him Trigger. You know, quick-on-the-trigger?" This scenario was sort of appropriated in the film *My Pal Trigger* (1946). After Trigger's dam, Lady, gives birth to him, Rogers notes that the colt was delivered quickly, saying, "You're kinda quick on the trigger, son." Then he's asked, "What are you going to name him, Roy?" To which he replies, "I just did: Trigger."

In point of fact, the palomino Roy Rogers rode to fame underwent a couple of name changes before he was called Trigger. He'd already been given the name Golden Cloud as a colt in San Diego and kept it for a time after Hudkins Stables bought him. On the fateful day Rogers discovered him among the string of horses Hudkins Stables brought for him to audition, the wrangler in charge referred to the palomino as "Pistol."[34] According to William Witney in his book *Trigger Remembered*, the horse was renamed "Trigger" the same day in 1937 that Leonard Slye's name was changed to "Roy Rogers."[35] Rogers, an avid hunter and outdoorsman, liked naming his animals after parts of firearms. Remember his dog Bullet?

It has been suggested that Ace Hudkins may have named Trigger. E.J. Fleming wrote in an International Movie Database biography that Roy Rogers went to Hudkins Stables looking for a horse to use in his first starring vehicle *Under the Western Stars*. "After the lengthy ride Rogers and the horse had become instantly attached, and although Rogers was only making $75 a week at the time, he agreed to pay Ace $2,500 for the horse. It took him several years to pay for his new partner, whom Ace had named 'Trigger.'" It's unclear by this text whether Ace Hudkins made the claim himself or if Fleming made it for him. Roy Rogers mostly recalled that a number of rental stables took horses to Republic Pictures for him to try out, not that he went to any place in particular looking for one.

It is uncertain who really named Trigger. It's a bit of the Trigger legend that has been lost to time. B-western historian Bobby Copeland stated, "I'm going along with Joe Kane on the naming of Trigger. Roy always said, I 'believe' or I 'think' it was Smiley. Kane said, without reservation, that it was he who named the horse."

Many prefer to believe it was indeed Smiley Burnette who named Trigger. Burnette was very creative and wrote hundreds of songs. With his gift for clever lyrics, he may well have come up with an appropriate name for the beautiful palomino.

It will never be known whether Rogers and the script writer for the movie *Come On, Rangers* (1938) were having fun and making a veiled reference to Trigger's first name, but in that film, when the King of the Cowboys is asked by sidekick Raymond Hatton how he's going to get out of jail, Rogers replies, "I'm going to ride out on a cloud."

William Witney in *Trigger Remembered* claimed that Trigger was nicknamed the "Old Man" on movie sets. Apparently this was for two reasons: to distinguish Trigger from his doubles and to denote the horse's age and wisdom. Wrote Witney, "It has been shown that Trigger was relied upon for years to get Roy and the producers out of tough filming situations. They would have the doubles on the scenes for certain stunts, but there were some stunts they just couldn't film, despite numerous attempts, because the horses were afraid. They could always depend on the 'Old Man,' as they called him, to bail them out, however. The horse had quite a reputation with everyone on the set for being fearless. How much of this is fact and how much publicity, we will probably never know, but it's a beautiful story." Here Witney is referring to a chase sequence in *Far Frontier* (1948), where Trigger narrowly avoids barrels thrown from a truck by bad guy Roy Barcroft. Dodging those barrels was a stunt the horses on the set refused to do.

Another source for the origin of Trigger's name comes from the book *King of the Bs* by Todd McCarthy and Charles Flynn. They quote Joe Kane, who directed many of Rogers' films: "While we were on location on that picture [*Under Western Stars*, 1938], they sent word up that he was going to be called Roy Rogers, and they wanted a name for his horse. We were getting ready to shoot a scene with a revolver, so I said, "Why don't we call him Trigger? They took the name, and he became Trigger."[36]

Yet another story of the origin for Trigger's name came from a Roy Rogers comic book special section titled "My Pal Trigger" (reprinted in *Roy Rogers Western Classics*, number 3 [AC Collector Classics, 1990]: "The day I found Trigger was just about the luckiest day of my life. He was only a romping colt then, but, today, he is one of the greatest trick horses in the world. I started right away to train him, and he learned so many tricks so fast that I named him Trigger, because he could think 'quick on the trigger.'"

In one instance, Trigger was referred to as Comanche when he appeared with Russell Hayden in *Silver City Raiders* at Columbia in 1943.

Trigger's Offspring

Rogers referred to "Trigger" as a stallion and that's the image fans wanted to believe. Rogers also always described "Trigger" as well mannered and gentle in spite of being a stallion. On a few occasions, he claimed that he had a number of his children on "Trigger" all at the same time. "Trigger has a different personality," he said. "He was a stallion, but you'd never know it, he was so gentle and kind. And he had a great rein on him as a cow pony. I've had several of my kids on him at one time, from his ears back to his tail and would just ... aw, he was a fabulous horse."[37]

There are many photos of Rogers and "Trigger" in their signature rearing pose where the horse looks gelded. However, in some pictures the horse is complete. A number of conclusions can be drawn from this: Rogers was riding different palominos; Trigger was gelded at a later time; or photos were doctored.[38]

As to any offspring of the "real" Trigger, the most famous horse in the world, it's very doubtful whether Rogers would have allowed anyone but himself to have kept the foal. Perhaps he wanted to breed Trigger to maintain his bloodline but didn't for fear it would change the palomino's disposition; in that case, he surely wouldn't have bred Trigger for someone else. Promoter that he was, he would have made the biggest deal in the world had Trigger really sired a foal. Fans would have known about it. A foal might have been a secret for a little while, but not for long.

In *My Pal Trigger*, Trigger sired two identical colts at the end of the film.[39] In the *Golden Stallion*, he sired Trigger, Jr. These are fictional scenarios, of course, but children, understandably, wanted to believe them. The Rogers publicity machine got carried away on occasion with regard to Buttermilk's gender. It was once reported that the gelding was a mare and gave birth to one of Trigger's offsprings.

A multitude of conflicting stories about Trigger's offspring have appeared in print through the years. Rogers himself related many stories in radio interviews and television guest appearances. A mythical Trigger foal appeared in advertising from time to time, sometimes in contests under such headlines as "name the son of Trigger." In some instances, actual

P1856-1

Trigger's birthday was often used as a publicity gimmick, especially while on tour, and it didn't matter which "Trigger" was on hand. In this photograph, the original Trigger eyes what must be a carrot cake *(Roy Dillow collection)*.

winners were identified or alluded to as having received an offspring or descendant of Trigger. Quaker Oats sponsored a "Name the Son of Trigger" contest; first prize for the youngster with the winning entry was a week with Roy Rogers.

Trigger's alleged offspring were offered to fans in contests advertised in national magazines. In November of 1947 *Movie Star Parade* magazine devoted a couple of pages to such a contest. The headline read, "Win a Wee Trigger!" The tag went on to exclaim, "Hurry, Hurry, Hurry, Here's your last chance to win a real live colt, sired by Trigger, Smartest Horse in the Movies." The copy went on, "Roy Rogers has offered two live colts, sired by the one and only

Trigger, to two alert MSP readers." Showing four still photos from a Rogers film, the contest ad instructed readers to identify the film and to finish a Roy and Trigger limerick.

An April 16, 1952, issue of the *Dispatch News Services* featured a picture of Roy Rogers standing next to "Trigger" and a newborn colt who had been named Easter. The caption read that Trigger "has just become the father of a little colt and Trigger looks down admiring at his offspring."

In 1946 a number of articles placed Rogers in the horse breeding business with the slogan "Colts By Trigger." Published reports claimed that Mr. J. B. Ferguson, a wealthy Texas oilman, tried but failed to purchase Trigger in 1951 and had to accept one of his specially bred colts. In a televised interview it was claimed that a Pennsylvania girl was the recipient of the only colt Trigger ever sired. In 1990 country singer Randy Travis allegedly purchased the "grandson" of Trigger. All these stories delighted fans and were great public relations.[40]

Palomino Horse Breeding Business

Around the time *My Pal Trigger* was released in 1946, it was reported in a number of fan magazines that Roy Rogers tried to get into the palomino horse breeding business. Writer Len Simpson reported that Rogers had decided to breed palominos "on a large scale." According to Simpson the King of the Cowboys went so far as to purchase five palomino stallions and twenty-five chestnut brood mares. Rogers supposedly had a 560-acre ranch located seven and a half miles west of Las Vegas.

The inspiration for the palomino horse breeding venture was supposed to have come to Roy Rogers on the *My Pal Trigger* set during the filming of the last scene when the title character is about to become a father. Simpson even made the farfetched claim, "For the first time, the actual birth of a palomino colt was recorded for the screen." Apparently this article was written before the movie was released. While there is a birth scene in the movie, the actual act is not shown. The colt's name was Golden Hours, and the article includes a photo of him with Rogers. It's from the scene where Rogers has to shoot Trigger's mother, Lady, after she has been attacked by a mountain lion.[41]

An article by Don Allen makes many of the same claims Simpson's article does: "Horse lovers wrote to Roy asking how they could buy Trigger colts. Rogers was glad to oblige. Soon, however, the demands began to pile up and Roy saw the possibilities of a good business in breeding palomino colts. Today Rogers' ranch in Van Nuys, California, proves Roy had a profitable idea. His farm has 24 brood mares, with 17 of them in foal. Each Trigger colt's value is from $1,000 to $2,000, proof that Roy can make money either riding or selling horses."[42]

Allen even wrote about breeding for the golden palomino color: "For breeding purposes, sorrel mares are used entirely. This is because a palomino foal usually is the result of a union between a palomino stallion and a sorrel mare. An albino colt result from palomino stallion and a palomino mare."[43] This differs from Simpson's article, which claims, "For his breeding farm, Roy largely is giving the break to the method he feels is most successful — breeding of chestnut mares to palomino stallions. Statistics point out that in such cases approximately seventy per cent of the colts are palominos."

Rogers finally came clean about breeding Trigger and had the last word on the subject. According to entertainment industry writer John Chadwell, Roy Rogers said in an interview, "Not so." Chadwell went on to state, "He [Rogers] felt that since Trigger was so unusually

Dale Evans on Pal and Roy Rogers on Little Trigger, probably taken after a performance (judging from the sweat on the King of the Cowboys and his palomino) *(Roy Dillow collection)*.

gentle for a stallion, he didn't want to take the risk that he [Trigger] might change if he were put out to stud."[44]

When asked by Sam Henderson for an article in *Western Horse* magazine why he never bred Trigger, Rogers noted that for him, the best palomino horse coloring came when he bred his all-white, quarter-type (but nevertheless "grade") stallion to quality dark bay quarter horse mares. When it came time for a replacement, Roy Rogers' famous horse bowed once again to a stand-in — a quiet-mannered grade stallion named Whitey.[45]

Champion rodeo rider Larry Mahan, host of the *Horseworld* television show (circa 1995), asked Rogers about breeding Trigger. Rogers answered: "Some horses, if you breed them they get mean and so old Trigger was so gentle. I've got pictures of all my kids on him, I had seven of them at this time, clear from his ears back to his tail, you know. He was so gentle, he'd just stand there. He knew he had to be responsible, you know."

"Today there are no descendants of Trigger. Roy believed that fatherhood might make Trigger less gentle to people. 'My kids could walk right under his belly and it wouldn't bother him.' Roy explained. 'He was real gentle, and I wanted to keep him that way.'"[46]

According to Corky Randall, Trigger, Little Trigger, and Trigger Jr. were all stallions. Only Trigger Jr. was ever used to breed. Trigger doubles California and Pal were both gelded. All the equine prizes for "name Trigger's colt" contests were from other sources, not the real thing.[47]

Coda

"Trigger" achieved such fame that while on tour he was often on exhibit in full tack in front of an arena. Not only was this great publicity and an incentive to go into the show, but it was done so that kids who couldn't afford tickets could at least see the beautiful palomino.

"Boys and girls like Trigger so much that I tried to station him and his fancy trailer outside each auditorium for a few hours before a performance. I figured that this was a way for those who didn't have enough money for a ticket to get a chance to see him."[48]

A favorite story among Trigger fans had to do with the way Roy Rogers proposed to Dale Evans. In 1947 the couple were headlining a rodeo at the Chicago Stadium. As they were waiting on horseback to be introduced, Rogers popped the question. While that story has been refuted for another with a more pedestrian breakfast setting, it's the story most fans prefer. For a cowboy proposing to his lady love, what better place than on his horse?

"There was one other part of that bargain Dale had to learn to love: my horse. Maybe it sounds odd that I proposed marriage to her on horseback — not too romantic. He was my partner and my pal, and part of nearly everything I did."[49]

4

Little Trigger: The Horse Behind the Horse

"That horse probably had more tricks on him than any other horse in the world." — Corky Randall describing Little Trigger.[1]

The original Trigger seemed to have had it all. According to Roy Rogers, "He was an iron horse. And smart! He just would do anything, and he had a rein on him as good as any cow pony you've ever seen. He would stop on a dime and give you nine cents change."[2]

Trigger was blessed with great looks, an even disposition, fine conformation, athleticism, and perfect timing. When Roy Rogers selected him from a string of rental horses as his movie co-star, the palomino was more than ready to make his mark in show business. Beyond his assets, all Trigger needed for the challenge that lay ahead was a first-rate support team: a great trainer and a very special double horse to perform a variety of tricks on movie sets and on tour. Rogers found Glenn Randall to handle training duties and an extraordinary palomino look-alike who would be referred to as Little Trigger.

Glenn Randall's son Corky claimed the only traveling the original Trigger did was to movie locations in states neighboring California like Utah, Nevada, and Arizona. The palomino was too much of an asset to be used touring across the country. He was groomed like a Hollywood starlet, and his main jobs were to be seen and photographed; to run at full speed with Rogers on his back; and to rear up. For just about everything else, he had doubles.

Rogers needed not only a second "Trigger" with similar looks, but a horse with intelligence and endurance because the demands on him would be great. While Little Trigger was not as beautiful as the original Trigger, he could do things like dance, count, pull sheets off a bed, and sign an "x" on a hotel registry. According to Cheryl Barnett-Rogers, Little Trigger was extremely smart, a quick study and did not forget tricks. Little Trigger would eventually go on to double not only the original Trigger, but Trigger Jr. as well. It was Little Trigger who secured the title "the Smartest Horse in the Movies" for the original Trigger.

Little Trigger was not a stunt horse but a trick horse. When he performed in rodeo arenas, fair grounds, parades, hospital rooms, and hotel lobbies, he had to endure public adulation to the point where parts of his mane and tail were clipped by enthusiastic fans as souvenirs. Rogers even used soldiers and policemen to guard him. He claimed that the pilfering became such a problem that "Trigger" was sometimes forced to wear a "toupee" till his mane and tail grew out.

Although Little Trigger was seen in public by more people than any other palomino Roy Rogers used, much more is known about Trigger Jr. and even Dale Evans' palomino, Pal. When researching Little Trigger one mostly encounters theories, hearsay, and colorful anecdotes. The best one can expect is to corroborate an occasional story. What one doesn't run across are official documents. Corky Randall said Little Trigger was not papered. Little Trig-

Little Trigger prancing. The palomino could do many dressage steps without a rider in the saddle cuing him.

Little Trigger on tour with Roy Rogers circa 1947. Author Robert W. Phillips found this photograph hanging in the Longhorn Bar-B-Q Restaurant in Tulsa, Oklahoma, and bought it on the spot from owners Tom and Carol Nimmo. Phillips tore a wall loose with a borrowed hammer and saw because the photo was glued directly to the surface.

ger's place of birth, date of birth, breed, and breeder are all unknown. Sadly, even the date of Little Trigger's death was never acknowledged. When asked by Joel "Dutch" Dortch of the Happy Trails Foundation in May of 2006, Dave Koch, the Internet administrator for the Roy Rogers and Dale Evans Museum and Dusty Rogers' son-in-law, replied, "Little Trigger was purchased after Trigger for stunt purposes to protect Trigger. We have no information on when or where Roy purchased him, or his birth and death dates."[3]

Even if papers did exist, it's doubtful he would be referred to as "Little Trigger" officially. One would have to rely on the description of the animal on the registration form for identification and hope that Rogers didn't own more than one small stocky palomino. It's a shame Roy Rogers didn't keep better records for Little Trigger — and it's strange, really, because of his tendency to hang on to things.[4]

As one would expect, stories regarding Little Trigger are laced with contradictions. Roy Rogers and Glenn Randall covered their tracks, and, with very rare exceptions, neither acknowledged the horse as an individual to the press. One exception was when Glenn Randall was quoted in an article titled "He Spoke Horse" which appeared in the summer of 1992 in *Cowboy Magazine*: "Little Trigger was our personal appearance horse and, by God, he could do some of the most remarkable things."

During Roger's career, however, Little Trigger's name was not used publicly and was kept out of most all published matter. Little Trigger was never recognized as a character in his own right, like Trigger Jr., Buttermilk, Bullet, or even sidekick Pat Brady's jeep, Nellybelle. Little Trigger was never the subject of any of Rogers' films like Trigger and Trigger Jr. were. He existed only as a double for the original Trigger.

It's never been known exactly how many "Trigger" doubles Roy Rogers used, much less from where and from whom he got them. One 1946 article claimed, "So valuable is Trigger that he has four stand-ins who also double for him in hazardous shots. Trigger is capable of performing any spectacular stunt, but Rogers and Republic Pictures prefer to use the other four horses, each a specialist in running, jumping, or talking falls for any trick action scenes. Trigger is there for the human interest, devotion-of-master-to-horse scenes. The stand-ins are raised on the Rogers ranch."[5] Corky Randall claimed that Rogers didn't own that many Trigger doubles and further claimed that during many personal appearances anonymous palominos were provided by either Republic or whoever was sponsoring a particular event.[6] Rogers occasionally rode horses that were on loan. This happened at the beginning of his career and especially at the end.

Breeder

Although official papers have never surfaced, it's very possible that Roy Rogers might have purchased at least one, maybe two palominos from cowboy star Ray "Crash" Corrigan, and Little Trigger may have been one of them.

Ray Corrigan maintained a living by promoting himself. Many fans thought he was just being a publicity hound when he claimed to have sold "Trigger" to Roy Rogers. No matter how shaky the underlying facts were, Corrigan did not draw a distinction between the original Trigger and Little Trigger. However, there are ear witness accounts to what Roy Rogers said when asked from whom he got Little Trigger. In 1993 longtime Rogers fan Carol Johnson noted, "I asked him where he bought Little Trigger. He said, 'as a matter of fact from Ray Corrigan.'"

Roy Rogers, Dale Evans, and Little Trigger arrive in England for a tour. As a publicity gimmick, the palomino presented a traveling passport.

I asked him where he bought Little Trigger. He said, "As a matter of fact from Ray Corrigan." I think both are telling the truth but talking about different Triggers. I then asked him if he purchased another horse at the same time and he said, "No, that was later but that one didn't turn out as good as Little Trigger." Then I asked him about the one time that Trigger was used as a stud and what happened to the foal. He told me about the close friend of his trainers that talked him into using Trigger and how the owner of the mare couldn't wait to go on tour with the offspring. He whispered to me that he wasn't very happy about that. Roy did also say on one of the *Happy Trails Theater* shows that Trigger was used once at stud. I have that on tape.[7]

This may also be corroborated in the Frank Rasky biography *Roy Rogers: King of the Cowboys*. Rasky goes into detail about how Rogers bought "Trigger" from Crash Corrigan.[8] There are diehard Roy Rogers fans who believe it was Little Trigger who Rasky, unknowingly, was referencing.

Ray Corrigan also claimed he sold Trigger to Rogers for $250. "I sold Roy two palominos for $500 — that's for both of them —$250 apiece. A millionaire from Texas later offered $50,000 for the one with the four white stockings, the horse you know as Trigger. The second horse had only three white stockings so when it doubled the other palomino they painted his leg with white paint. Roy named both of the horses Trigger — and folks, until this day he still owes me $250!"[9]

During the 1975 Nashville Film Festival, Ray Corrigan recalled the following conversation with Roy Rogers: "'Ray, if I ever get a horse I want to call him Trigger.' At that time, I

Little Trigger in a stall provided for him while on tour (*Jerry Dean collection*).

had thirty-one horses. Among those were three beautiful palominos. Two of the palominos looked almost exactly alike. One of them had four white stocking feet, and the other had three white stocking feet."[10]

The Rasky biography of Rogers was clearly written for the youth market, and it made a number of outrageous claims, even though it seemed to have had Roy Rogers' blessing. While it still remains within reason that Rogers could have indeed purchased Little Trigger from Ray Corrigan, if one is going to trust the Rasky book, one has to consider the following inconsistencies. Rasky noted (page 98) that Roy Rogers bought a palomino at one and a half years of age from Corrigan in 1938 for $360. This was not the original Trigger because the palomino's first film as Trigger, *Under Western Stars*, was shot the same year. On page 102 Rasky wrote that trainer Glenn Randall worked Trigger "between twelve and fourteen hours a day, alternating between twenty minutes of training and twenty minutes of rest." Horses do not have a long attention span, and that much training would be not only counter-productive but ultimately very stressful. Rasky also claimed it was Rogers who originally named Trigger, foregoing the Smiley Burnette claim. Rasky does not mention Jimmy Griffin, Rogers' first trainer. Rasky also stated the palomino Rogers bought from Corrigan was "fifteen and a half hands" (15.2). It is generally agreed that Little Trigger was about 15 hands, and he may have looked bigger because he was more of a bulldog-type quarter horse, very stocky compared to the original Trigger.

There are clearly timeline issues with the Rasky book. Rasky had Rogers going out on his personal appearance tour and looking high and low for a horse, then buying "Trigger" from Corrigan. If Rogers didn't have Trigger until after the personal appearance tour, what horse he was riding in *Under Western Stars*? But if one draws a distinction between Trigger and Little Trigger, then the story works.

In all probability Roy Rogers realized that he needed a horse for touring, bought one from Ray Corrigan and used the horse in movies too. Absent a bill of sale, this is a good theory, and the scenario fits the pattern of the Rogers public relations machine, i.e., changing the facts just enough to release the best-sounding story.

The palomino Rasky mentioned was bought in 1938. Roy Rogers biographer Robert W. Phillips gave 1940 as the year Little Trigger was bought at age 18 months.[11] If one goes by the timeline provided by Roy Rogers spokespersons, Little Trigger died in 1965 at around age 25. This would mean he was born in 1940 and the Phillips date is incorrect. However, it is very

Roy Rogers and Little Trigger circa 1939–1940, in what is believed to be one of the earliest known photographs of this palomino. For serious fans the saddle looks like tack Ray "Crash" Corrigan used. The future King of the Cowboy's gun holster, still nice and new in this photo, would soon show wear and tear from use (*Jerry Dean collection*).

unlikely Little Trigger was born in 1940, because he would have been too young to have been doubling Trigger and performing fancy tricks in front of cameras at age three. Little Trigger appeared for the first time in a Roy Rogers movie in 1943. Horses, by rule, are started under saddle at two and are performing more complicated tricks at four and five years. The Lippizaner stallions from the Spanish Riding School of Vienna are started at four or five and aren't put into advanced training until they are eight or nine!

In February of 1944 "How I Trained Trigger" by Roy Rogers (as told to Adrienne Ames) was published in *Motion Picture* magazine. Rogers said, "I bought Trigger in Santa Susanna, California, for $350, and that was on-time, no money down.... He was only a year and a half old." It sounds like Rogers is talking about Little Trigger in this case, and it may well corroborate the Corrigan connection.

A very likely scenario is that Rogers may have tried to nip the Corrigan–Little Trigger connection in the bud because he wanted to maintain the fantasy of Trigger as one horse, discovered through Hudkins Stables. In later years, after William Witney first mentioned Little Trigger in his *Trigger Remembered* book and fans started to ask questions about him, Rogers may have decided to acknowledge the Corrigan connection to Little Trigger. Once

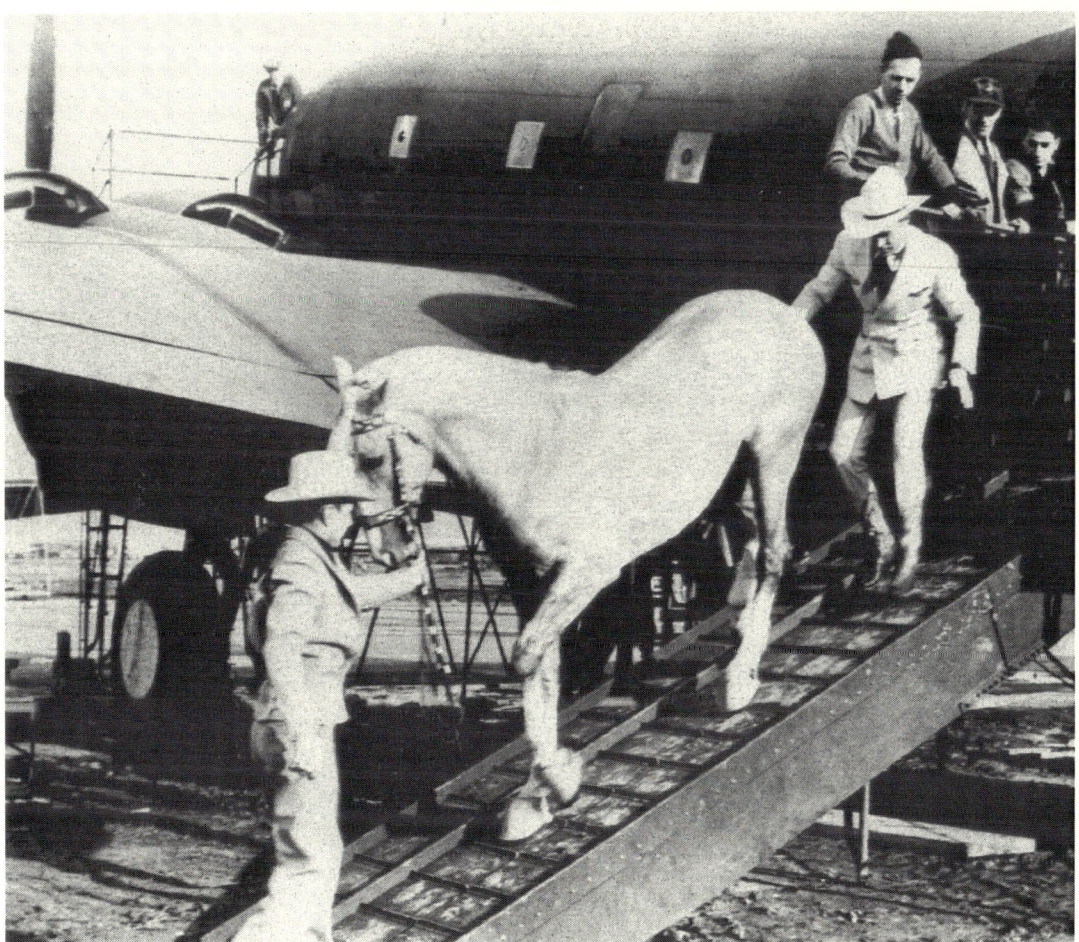

Little Trigger being led down a ramp after an airplane flight. Roy Rogers was literally bringing up the rear *(Corky Randall collection)*.

again Roy Rogers and his family may have been spinning facts for best effect. Rogers may have thought it was good public relations, like Trigger's appearance in *The Adventures of Robin Hood* movie, to associate Little Trigger with an action hero like Ray "Crash" Corrigan—one of the Three Mesquiteers, no less.[12]

Bob Livingston

According to author Merrill T. McCord in his book *Brothers of the West*, Ray Corrigan claimed that he'd helped Roy Rogers with his career. This took his *Three Mesquiteers* co-star Bob Livingston by surprise. It's well known that there was no love lost between Corrigan and Livingston. When told of Corrigan's claim that he had a hand in Rogers being signed by Republic Pictures, Livingston categorically stated, "That's a lot of bunk.... Corrigan at that time couldn't help anybody do anything. He was having too much trouble holding his own job."[13]

Like Corrigan, Livingston also claimed to have had a hand in the uniting of Roy Rogers and Trigger. He stated: "I was walking from the back lot up to the front office one day. This was the beginning of Roy Rogers' career. He said, 'Hey Bob, do me a favor will you?' He said, 'They want me to pick a horse out of this bunch (they had about five horses there) to ride in the picture. I wish you'd help me pick one out.' So I'm in a big hurry. I'm not much interested in this routine anyway because I know the background of it.... I said (sarcastically), 'Oh, that's a beauty! That palomino there. That's the one!' And I went on my merry way."[14]

Birth Date

On page 10 of *Roy Rogers: King of the Cowboys* by Georgia Morris and Mark Pollard, a book produced in conjunction with an AMC cable television biography, there is a picture of Rogers on tour with Little Trigger. The photo was dated 1941. It is one of the earliest known photos of Rogers with Little Trigger. The horse was probably around four.

Roy Rogers collector and expert Roy Dillow says there is another shot of Rogers on Little Trigger and claims it's the earliest shot to his knowledge, circa 1939 or 1940. He dates the picture by the style of hat Rogers is wearing and by the fact that Little Trigger appears to be using a Ray Corrigan saddle. The future King of the Cowboy's clothes left a little to be desired. On the other hand, his gun belt is nice and new in the photo; it would show wear and tear from use in future pictures.

A few news releases from the mid–1940s may offer a clue to Little Trigger's birth year. *The New York Times* published a short press release on October 7, 1943. It reported that a celebration for "Trigger" was being held in the Plantation Room of the Hotel Dixie in Manhattan: "Smartest Horse in the Movies will be seven years old today."[15] It's safe to assume it was Little Trigger touring with Rogers at the time. *The New York Times* date would make Little Trigger's birth year 1936. (As previously stated, the original Trigger's registration gave July 4, 1934, as his date of birth.) A similar story published in May of 1943 in the *Junior Rodeo Fans* newsletter claimed that a "rodeo tour 'Trigger' was not at home for his sixth birthday but was honored with his own party in the main dining room of a Boston hotel." This would mean the horse mentioned was born in 1937. Again, most likely it was Little Trigger who was

Roy Rogers and Little Trigger on tour. This photograph is dated 1941, which supports a case for placing the palomino's birth year in the mid–1930s.

being referenced. It also needs to be understood, with regards to the New York celebration especially, that a phony birth date may have been concocted as a publicity stunt to promote Rogers' appearance at Madison Square Garden.[16]

A Roy Rogers comic book special section titled "My Pal Trigger" stated, "Trigger, a Palomino stallion, weighs 1,100 pounds and stands 15 hands. His birthday is March 17." This description matches Little Trigger's, in which case March 17 might be his date of birth. However, the same paragraph also contains the erroneous claim, "He has sired numerous colts, but one in particular, Trigger Junior, is almost a perfect likeness of his father."[17]

In the 1944 *Motion Picture* article "How I Trained Trigger," credited to Roy Rogers ("as told to Adrienne Ames"), it was reported that "Trigger" "made his 'stage' debut about three years ago in Tulare, California, when Roy made a personal appearance there, and [Trigger] was very bad in the first show. But after a few performances, he began to like it." That would put the debut in 1941. If Little Trigger is the horse being mentioned, and he's around three or four, that too would put his year of birth at 1936 or 1937.

In an article titled "That Horse, Trigger" which appeared in *Pageant* magazine (February 1947), Stephen Strassberg wrote, "Tricks, however, are Trigger's main claim to fame. Since buying him for $350 in 1935, Rogers has taught him more than 50." Given the price

Candid shot of Roy Rogers on Little Trigger. The palomino was rarely photographed in plain tack, the exception being his appearance at the end of the *Golden Stallion* in 1949 *(Roy Dillow collection)*.

paid, this again sounds like a reference to Little Trigger, but the date would mean he was born before the original Trigger.

If we accept Robert W. Phillips' claim that Little Trigger was purchased in 1940 at age 18 months, then the palomino was born in 1937. Little Trigger's first appearance was in *Song of Texas*, released in 1943. Prior to 1943, "Trigger's" tricks on film were limited. Trigger was hardly seen in *King of the Cowboys*, the movie released right before *Song of Texas*. When Little Trigger arrived on the scene, all of a sudden there was dancing, bowing, and more. We know that a horse is started under saddle at two, and that by three or four a trick horse is moved along to more complicated tricks. Using 1943 as a point to count back from, it's reasonable to say that Little Trigger was born between 1936 and 1939. It's doubtful Roy Rogers and Glenn Randall needed to wait till Little Trigger was six before he was ready to appear in a film. This writer will split the difference and place his likely birth year at 1938.

Movie Debut

In *Song of Texas* Roy Rogers, playing a rodeo star, visited the Texas Springs Hospital and took Little Trigger into a children's ward packed with recovering patients, most of them lying in beds. The first time Little Trigger appeared on camera in a movie was when he was walking down a corridor with Rogers and the Sons of the Pioneers right before they entered the children's ward. Apparently the palomino had been given a full beauty treatment in order to pass as the original Trigger. His forelock was teased and he was immaculate. While the Sons of the Pioneers played "Git Along Little Dogies," Rogers hopped up on Little Trigger and they performed a short dance. Rogers even cued the horse to rear up, which he did quickly and in a very confined space. Little Trigger also threw a kiss to the adoring children.

This sequence — in which Little Trigger truly shone — was typical of how he was to be used to enhance the "Trigger" legend. The sequence was more or less an abbreviated version of the show Rogers, Little Trigger, and the Sons of the Pioneers put on a year later in *The Hollywood Canteen* (Warner Bros., 1944).

Purchase Time Line

We know that Rogers bought the original Trigger in 1943. The question becomes, why did he buy Little Trigger before the original? Probably because he had first priority use of Trigger with Hudkins Stables and also a probable first option to buy. Rogers either came to this conclusion on his own or was advised that having Little Trigger as a touring trick horse was more important than owning the original Trigger. Little Trigger, as a double with a bag full of tricks, may have been viewed as more of a necessity, a higher priority. The ever practical Rogers saw "Trigger" as a prop as much as a partner. He obviously wanted a personal appearance "Trigger" of his own, and most likely was able to get Little Trigger for less money than the original Trigger.

Little Trigger was probably assigned to Jimmy Griffin, Rogers' first trainer. Corky Randall remembered that Little Trigger was already being ridden when his father first started working for Rogers. Since Jimmy Griffin was Little Trigger's first trainer, that eliminates the idea that Glenn Randall may have found Little Trigger for Rogers as some have thought.

Temperament and Personality

For those who have made an effort to learn about Little Trigger, his reputation for being unpleasant is common knowledge. According to Corky Randall, Little Trigger eventually became quite impatient with fans while on tour and could be aggressive if they got near him. One couldn't blame the horse. Any animal who's overstimulated by too much hands-on attention, especially from strangers, has a breaking point. Little Trigger had to tolerate an enormous amount of traveling and attention. Early on, he was sometimes put on display in front of an arena on show days so children who couldn't go inside could at least see the palomino.

Roy Rogers and Little Trigger on tour in Texas. The palomino was provided with a stall built just for him in the lobby of a San Antonio hotel.

A 1943 *Song of Texas* press release claimed that Rogers and "Trigger" gave 136 performances in 20 days. With a schedule like that, it's astonishing that Little Trigger actually behaved most of the time. One is amazed not only by what tricks the palomino mastered, but also by the many different situations in which he was able to perform them.

Along with his reputation for being impatient with strangers, Little Trigger was by nature temperamental. Cheryl Rogers-Barnett described him as being like an ornery little kid: "Little Trigger hated women, and he didn't much care for kids except for when dad had him under saddle and bridle. He wasn't one you would let out in the paddock for little kids to go and pat."[18]

The following anecdotes cannot be connected to Little Trigger absolutely, but they sound very much like him. After all, when it came to personal appearances and touring, he was on the front line, and these stories depict a horse with a bad disposition.

There were occasions when Roy Rogers was in the center of an arena singing a hymn and "Trigger" came up behind him and grabbed a piece of his shirt in his mouth along with a good chunk of his shoulder. The audience thought the palomino was giving his master an affectionate nuzzle, but in reality it hurt like crazy. "Trigger" seemed to know Rogers could not acknowledge his pain in the middle of the hymn. During rehearsals when there was no audience the horse never attempted the same stunt. Little Trigger sometimes left teeth marks along Roger's forearms. In her *Cowboy Princess* book, Cheryl Rogers-Barnett even recounts a time when her dad mockingly threatened to discipline the diminutive palomino with a baseball bat.

In the 1944 article "How I Trained Trigger," Rogers admitted to author Adrience Ames, "'And sometimes he even goes so far as to give me a nip. If you don't believe me, I'll show you.' And with that he rolled up his sleeve and showed me his arm, with some 'gentle' reminders of Trigger's temperament."

It was noted in the pages of *Esquire* magazine (December 1975) that fans were shocked by

Roy Rogers and Little Trigger. Here the dark area around the palomino's muzzle is evident (*Janey Miller collection*).

a certain exchange between Roy Rogers and his four-legged partner: "He [Trigger] and his master had more than one set-to over his penchant for scene stealing. After one such episode at the Earle Theater in Washington, Roy stormed off the stage and announced, "Someday I'm going to shoot that god damn horse right between the eyes."

In August of 1956 Roy Rogers, Dale Evans, and the Sons of the Pioneers were appearing at the Iowa State Fair in Des Moines. A local newspaper published a photo of Rogers and a handler (probably Glenn Randall) moving clear of "Trigger" as he rolled on the ground. In all fairness, even the most highly trained horse can spook, but this roll appears to be deliberate misbehavior. A horse should not just roll on the ground when he's being handled, especially when he's wearing a saddle. The accompanying caption read:

Des Moines, Aug. 31 — Roy and Trigger part company — Dale Evans (mounted, background) holds a hand over her mouth in apprehension as her husband Roy Rogers (left) and a handler (right) fall clear of Rogers' sprawling horse Trigger at the Iowa State Fair yesterday. Trigger, for reasons unknown, reared, twisted and fell as Rogers started to mount him on the muddy infield in front of the fair grandstand. The western movie star moments later mounted without trouble and rode away.

In 1952, in Los Angeles, actress Mabel Smeyne (aka Mable Smaney) filed a lawsuit against Roy Rogers Enterprises seeking $186,000 plus court costs and general relief. She alleged that Rogers and others recklessly failed to control "Trigger" on the movie set of *Son of Paleface*,

Top: Glenn Randall and Little Trigger (with fans and flight crew) about to depart for yet another personal appearance. *Bottom:* "Trigger" misbehaving during a performance at the Iowa State Fair.

allowing him to kick her. She claimed permanent internal and external injuries to the head, chest, and breast. The trial did not begin till October of 1954. Rogers spoke for himself and "Trigger." On October 29 the jury was out only 39 minutes and rendered a verdict in favor of Rogers and "Trigger." To win the case, Smeyne was required to prove the accident happened because Rogers was negligent. She was unable to do so. The Mabel Smeyne case was finally dismissed on appeal in 1955.

Touring with Little Trigger

It is hard to imagine any room for negligence in the touring routine described by Corky Randall. Both animal and tack, Randall said, were kept immaculate and in top condition. He also confirmed that he and his dad actually drove "Trigger's" touring trailer. Roy Rogers was not involved in the day-to-day care of his horse while on the road because he was too busy attending to miscellaneous business and promotion. Corky also claimed that if Rogers had checked in on his mount after hours, he would have been mobbed. The Randalls handed "Trigger" to the King of the Cowboys right outside a performance arena. When the show was over, the palomino was returned and Rogers was either off to his hotel or involved in more promotion and tour business. Corky Randall also insisted that it was only Little Trigger who went on the road. Taking along a double was not an option. There was simply no other palomino as highly trained.

Picture Proof

Not surprisingly, there are few existing photos that show the original Trigger with his doubles. Professional publicity shots showing the two together would not have fostered the image of Trigger as a single horse. Nor are there many amateur shots; the cast and crew on movie sets were sure to have seen Randall and Rogers off camera with two or three palominos in fancy show tack, but Republic probably had rules against taking pictures behind the scenes. Nevertheless, Rogers did allow shots of Trigger with Trigger Jr. when he was promoting the latter. Even shots of "Little Trigger" with Trigger Jr. exist. In one of the last scenes of *The Golden Stallion* fans get a very rare look at Little Trigger and the original Trigger together (refer to the "Golden Stallion" chapter).

Rarest of all are photos showing the original Trigger with Little Trigger. Only one such photo is known. Published in *Pic* magazine in July 1946 over the caption "Trigger and His Doubles," it shows Trigger, Monarch, California, Pal, and Little Trigger.

In *Pals of the Golden West* (1951), the last movie Roy Rogers made for Republic Pictures, Little Trigger did a small comedy bit with Dale Evans. The palomino was tied up in, of all places, a freight office. Evans, who played an ambitious reporter, took a seat next to him. As she concocted a story about Rogers, Little Trigger swished her with his tail.

Little Trigger was the cast horse in the movie *Son of Paleface*, making him the last "Trigger" to star in a motion picture. The original Trigger was nowhere to be found in the production despite the King of the Cowboy's claims that he was in every Roy Rogers film. While most serious fans know this, they fail to ask why. Corky Randall's simple and obvious explanation was that the script called for a trick horse who would be called upon to perform in most every scene he was in. Only Little Trigger was up to the task. *My Pal Trigger* and *The*

Extremely rare shot of Roy Rogers and Dale Evans with the original Trigger and four of his palomino doubles. From left to right: Monarch (featured in such films as *Pals of the Golden West*); the original Trigger; California (ridden in running insert shots by stuntman Joe Yrigoyen in such movies as *North of the Great Divide*); Pal; and Little Trigger standing next to Evans. This photograph, with the caption "Trigger and his doubles," appeared in *PIC*, "a magazine for young men," in July 1946 *(Roy Dillow collection)*.

Golden Stallion included, no other Roy Rogers movie required more tricks of "Trigger" than *Son of Paleface*.

Markings and Color

There were a number of palominos featured in Western movies from the 1930s to the 1950s. Johnny Mack Brown, Eddie Dean, Hoot Gibson, Russell Hayden, and Ken Maynard all rode them at one time or another. From time to time some well-meaning fan claims to have made a Trigger sighting in a non–Roy Rogers movie; however, most of the time the palomino in question doesn't hold up to close scrutiny. Horses may resemble each other closely, but individuals have their own unique markings and conformation.

Original Trigger

Two important things to keep in mind about the original Trigger were that he had a very wide blaze (white marking on his face) and only one white half-stocking, on his left hind leg (some published photos are reversed). His blaze extended from the left side of his face, jutting out over his left eye with a notch cut out, to the right side, covering his entire right nostril and the top part of the mouth. Above his left eye, the blaze returned, with a jagged edge, to

Little Trigger, Roy Rogers, and Trigger Jr. posing in front of their touring van. Trigger Jr. was taller, darker, and more slender than Little Trigger *(Roy Dillow collection)*.

the center of his face, resulting in a very large white area on his forehead. One of the best unobstructed frontal views of Trigger's blaze can be seen during the horseback square dance in *My Pal Trigger* (1946). Because of the English tack Trigger carries, the top of his blaze is exposed; one can see how it ends in a pyramid shape at the top of his forehead and how at that location it covers more of his left side (over his eye) than his right side. Viewed from his right side, the blaze ran straight up, considerably away from his eye, to the high part of his forehead, where it turned in. The white area well below the right nostril, made a 90-degree right turn and, with a jagged edge, continued toward the mouth. It is really this formation that most prominently distinguishes the original Trigger from his doubles.

In 1952 Trigger weighed 1100 pounds according to *Western Horseman* (April 1961) and *Movie Fan* (March 1953). David Rothel's *Roy Rogers Book*[19] gives Trigger's height as 15.3 hands. Bobby Copeland wrote in his book *Silent Hoofbeats*[20] that the original Trigger was 16 hands and weighed 1150 lbs. Corky Randall claimed the original Trigger was 16 hands.

Almost every artist's rendition of Trigger shows him with four white stockings—flashier than the single stocking he actually had. This was Rogers' reason for requesting that four white stockings be painted on the 23.5' fiberglass statue of Trigger for the front of his museum. According to the Tennessee Walking Horse Association, as with any breed of horse, a palomino's coat can bleach out under lots of sun. But true socks are white and permanent, making them a useful aid to identification. They are not considered socks if they are simply a lightening of the hair from exposure to the sun and are not visible year round.

In some photos even the original Trigger's front legs look white. It is entirely possible

Roy Rogers with the stocky Little Trigger, who was 15 hands at best. Note the light coat and four white feet *(Roy Dillow collection).*

that photos may have been doctored and makeup used to lighten Trigger's legs in some instances. There are even those who claim that Trigger sometimes appeared with four white stockings because his legs were intentionally bleached. This is absurd; however, it is likely that peroxide was used on "Trigger's" mane and tail to keep them white. It has also been reported that makeup artists polished "Trigger's" hoofs and used extra long lashes on his eyes.[21]

On a horse's stifle joint (analogous to the human knee), the flesh covering the area makes a bulge with a slight indent below. Trigger's stifle on his off side was more pronounced than on his near side, and some use it as a way to identify him.[22]

One of the problems in finding a good "copy" of Trigger was that he had brown eyes. Most palominos have blue eyes. When looking for palomino doubles, Glenn Randall had to get around that little quirk. For example, Loco, the palomino Leo Carillo used in the *Cisco Kid* television show, could not double Trigger because of his blue eyes. In some running scenes, however, he would have been a pretty close match.

Little Trigger and Trigger Jr.

The Encyclopedia of TV Pets describes Little Trigger as a quarter horse. Corky Randall thought he looked like a Morgan.

Little Trigger had four nearly matching white stockings and a black line across his back.

The original Trigger and Roy Rogers posed for a Schwinn Bike advertisement. Pictures from this sequence were touched up to make it look like the palomino had four white stockings. However, high quality versions indicate Trigger's legs had bleached out from exposure to the sun. According to Corky Randall, this shot was taken at the Randall stables in Long Ridge, the same year Roy Rogers lived on the property in quarters close to the barn in the background (*Joel "Dutch" Dortch collection*).

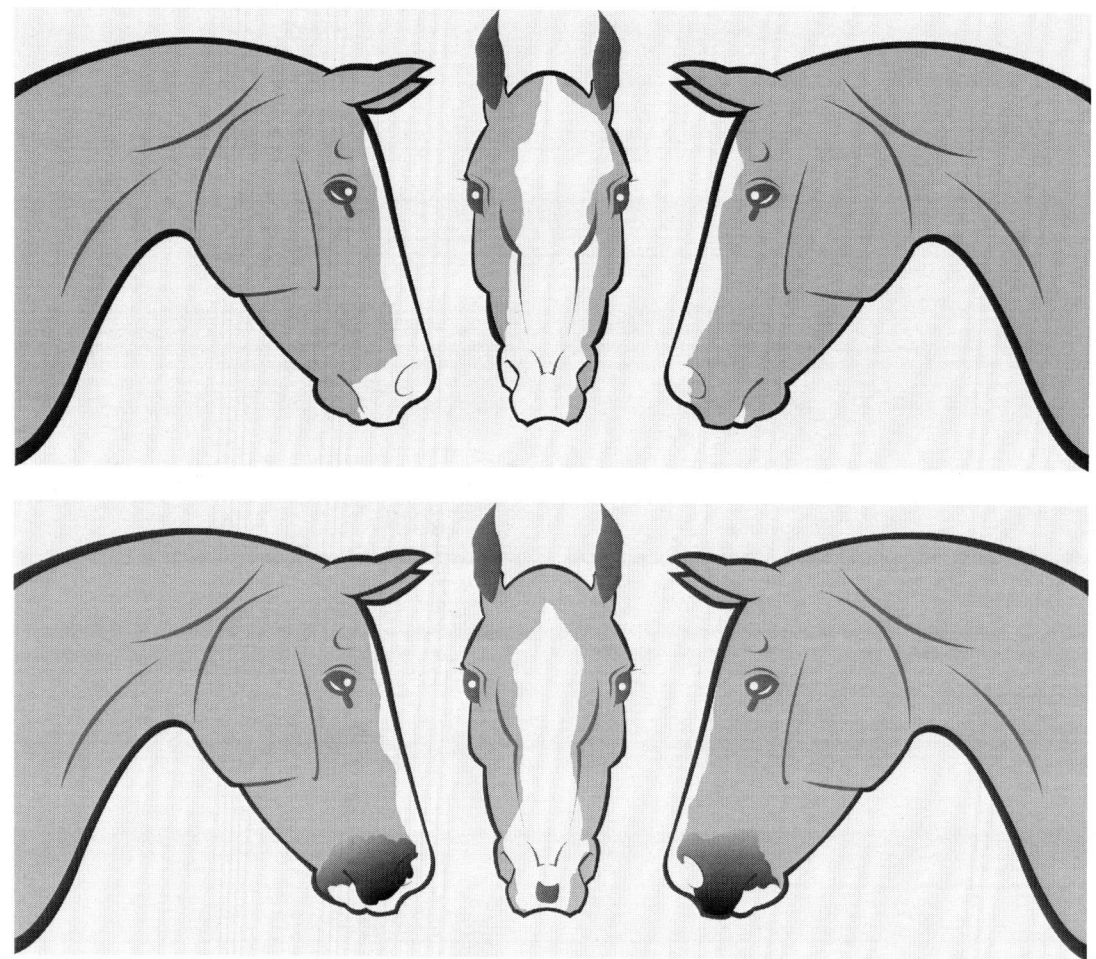

Top: Trigger blaze diagram. *Bottom:* Little Trigger blaze diagram *(Illustrations by the author)*.

He had a very narrow blaze at top of the forehead, which gradually widened to approximately 2–3" as it ran downward, along the center of his face. The blaze widened to approximately 3–4" at the bridle, where it began to angle towards his right nostril. Only the top part of the right nostril was covered as the blaze worked its way toward the center of his mouth. Even with the area just below the top part of the nostril, there was a noticeable quarter-sized dark spot. The white area under his nose, near the top center of his mouth, had a large notch, which was very visible. Little Trigger's blaze ran narrow and straight up the left center of his face. Only the top part of the left nostril was covered. Little Trigger was also very dark around his nostrils and mouth.

In the *Son of Paleface* (Paramount, 1952) sequence where Little Trigger chased Bob Hope into a hotel and up a flight of stairs, the palomino stuck his head out a window, eyeing Hope as the comedian tried to shimmy down a drainpipe. As the horse wasn't wearing a bridle, his blaze was very visible. The window curtains parted his forelock, and one can see his blaze peak at the top of his forehead. In a later sequence when Little Trigger is sharing a bed with Bob Hope, one can see all his facial markings quite well.[23]

The drawings of Trigger and Little Trigger shown on these pages are intended to help the reader attempt to distinguish their facial markings—which are only one aspect of identification. At best the drawings are simple diagrams. The horse heads are generic, just like the ones horse owners would find on an equine registration form; they do not address conformation or head type. Those are entirely different subjects. Determining a horse's conformation is a science and is possible only with complete access to a particular horse and full cooperation of the owner for specific measurements. No two horses have the same exact conformation; just as with the human fingerprint, no two are identical.

The illustrations here do not address the subtleties of color or hue. There are various shades of palomino, often having to do with age and season. Palominos come with either light skin or dark skin. Most have dark skin, which makes for the most beautiful golden color. Whatever their skin color, their fine hair may catch the light, making the color appear different in alternate shots. (Light-skinned palominos can have freckles on their skin, which are more apt to show during the summer when they don't have thick coats; unlike the dark-skinned ones, light-skinned palominos can be darker in the winter than the summer. They have lighter eye color, too.)

Little Trigger was not only smaller than the original Trigger but was also lighter in color. Trigger Jr. was the darkest of Rogers' three main palominos.

Trigger Jr. had four white stockings to the knees. He had a blaze, but it was not nearly as wide as the original Trigger's. He was perfect in body color and was sometimes dappled. The ideal palomino is the color of a newly minted penny, dark with a pure white mane and tail. It's not easy to find the perfect color, but Trigger and Trigger Jr. were nearly perfect.

In the movie *Trigger Jr.* there is a scene where the original Trigger appears with some dapple spots. Rogers and company have just arrived at the Harkrider ranch in the wind storm and the horses are being led into the tent. Rogers is standing beside Trigger, ready to blanket the horse. Looking closely, one may notice that there are some dapple spots around Trigger's stomach area. In *My Pal Trigger* Little Trigger displays dappling in the scene where Rogers returned him to Gabby Hayes. The animal is tied to a stall door.[24]

Serafix and "Trigger"

In December of 1984 an article appeared in *Arabian Horse World* magazine on a British stallion named Serafix, legendary in Arabian horse circles and named the Leading Sire of Champions. In 1954 he was purchased by an American breeder named John Rogers for more money than had ever been paid for a stallion imported to the states at the time. As it happened, on the flight back to America, Serafix shared an airplane with Roy Rogers' horse "Trigger" and a double. It is not known which of Rogers' palominos these were, but it's a good bet one was Little Trigger.

Serafix was described as massive in structure and, at 15 hands tall, a good size for an Arab. He was a rich copper chestnut with a very satiny coat. His head was slightly dished (concave) in profile, with large eyes and a broad forehead, giving him a very intelligent look. It was said that quality radiated from him, with charisma "up to the gills." He had structure and balance — an overall look that gave Arabian horse experts chills.

Comparing different horse breeds is like comparing apples to oranges, and when Arabian fans in the *Arabian Horse World* article compared Serafix to "Trigger" and his double, the two palominos got shortchanged. While "Trigger" was acknowledged as a well-balanced and handsome animal, alongside Serafix both he and his double were described as "coarse and clumsy."

Arabians have a reputation for being much more slight and delicate than quarter horses and Tennessee walkers. If Little Trigger was indeed the palomino who shared an airplane with Serafix, it's to be expected that, with his stocky build, he would not come off well. He probably looked like a draft horse in comparison. Corky Randall, an expert horseman, described Little Trigger as "a chubby little horse." It's reasonable to think that the original Trigger and Trigger Jr. could have won some legitimate beauty contests. One would not say the same for Little Trigger. Nevertheless, although he did not have show-quality looks, he was a nice-looking animal. After all, he had enough eye appeal to stand in for one of the most beautiful horses in Hollywood history, and he fooled fans for decades. This sleight of hand was accomplished by shifting fans' attention from Little Trigger's looks to his talent and athleticism.

Obit

Corky Randall stated categorically that although he could not recall the exact date, Little Trigger died years before the original Trigger, sometime before the Rogers family moved to Hidden Valley in 1963.

In e-mail correspondence, Cheryl Rogers-Barnett maintained that Little Trigger actually died at her father's ranch in Hidden Valley, which was between Malibu and Thousand Oaks. "Dad and Mom never lived at that ranch as it only had a one bedroom house while Dad owned it," she wrote. "He planned on adding on to it but Debbie [another daughter] died and Dad wanted to move away. Anyway, he had the horses out there (that is where the Old Man [the original Trigger] died as well) when Little Trigger died and he had a pit dug and buried him there. With the old horse, Dad and Mom had already moved to Apple Valley but Dad didn't have a barn and worked a deal with the new owner of the Hidden Valley ranch to keep Old Trigger and his thoroughbreds there until Dad had a place for them."

Corky could not recall if Little Trigger died of old age or was put down. It's no wonder he did not live as long as the original Trigger; he worked harder and in

Little Trigger at liberty (*Roy Dillow collection*).

more stressful situations. Corky said the horse developed severe problems with his knees when he got old as a result of all the traveling he did in trailers. "His knees bucked. Now you know how a bow-legged guy's knees buck out? His bucked forward." This happened because of all the stopping and starting during the trailer rides. (Horse trailers are now designed to haul horses sideways, not straight on, to avoid such problems.)

Little Trigger was also ridden in a number of situations, like parades, where he had to walk on hard surfaces. This probably also contributed to the problems he eventually developed with his legs.

Little Trigger Summary

He was probably born a few years after the original Trigger, in the mid to late 1930s.

He was not related to Trigger or Trigger Jr.

He topped out at about 15 hands.

He looked like a quarter horse or Morgan, very chunky in build, described as "bulldog" in type.

There's a very good chance he was purchased from cowboy star Ray Corrigan.

He was the most highly trained horse in the Rogers remuda and was one of the first equines on record to be house-broken.

He appeared in most of Roy Rogers' movies after 1943.

He was the primary horse with which Rogers toured the United States and parts of Europe. If you saw Roy Rogers in person, you most likely saw him with Little Trigger, especially outside of southern California.

When needed, he also appeared in *The Roy Rogers Show* on television. Little Trigger was also used almost exclusively when Roy Rogers made a guest star appearances on television rodeos or variety shows.

He was the star of the movie *Son of Paleface* and appeared on the cover of *Life* magazine.

After years of touring and public appearances, he became temperamental from overexposure to adoring fans.

Although a stallion, it's very doubtful he was ever used as a breeding stud.

He died in the early 1960s, a few years before the original Trigger passed away.

Roy Rogers and the original Trigger built their careers on Little Trigger's back. Corky Randall's claim that his dad and Rogers didn't use very many trick horse doubles means Little Trigger worked harder than most people have ever imagined. As well cared for as Little Trigger was and as glamorous as his job seemed to be, he was a work horse. On days when he and Roy Rogers weren't in the mood to perform, they were still out there. Fans just saw the glory; they did not see the blood, sweat, or tears.

The more one researches Little Trigger and makes a conscious effort to locate him in movies and personal appearance footage, the more one understands his importance and how he was as critical to Rogers' career as the original Trigger. Little Trigger was truly a wonder horse, and he earned the honor of being photographed with Rogers on the cover of *Life* magazine. A more accurate billing on movie marquees and posters should have been, "Roy Rogers, Trigger and Little Trigger."

While a great deal is known about the original Trigger, there's much that remains unresolved about the most important horse who doubled him. By not discussing Little Trigger,

Roy Rogers and Glenn Randall added to his mystery, and that's ultimately what makes him so compelling. Not being able to tie up important facts leaves Trigger's story open-ended. Little Trigger continues to give the Trigger fantasy resonance. For that reason, the desire to sort out the fantasy continues, and there are many fans wouldn't have it any other way. This book is as much about Little Trigger as it is about the original Trigger. One cannot say enough for Little Trigger. For all his shenanigans and notorious temperament, he was, in a word, extraordinary.

5

Trigger Jr., the Roy Rogers Remuda, and Other Doubles

"When he visited a horse farm during this quest the horseman would nearly always ask him: 'Well, sir, just what kind of horse are you looking for?' Roy would explain that he wanted a fine western stock horse, with a good rein and preferably a palomino."— William Roper[1]

Apart from Little Trigger, Trigger Jr. was the most-used double. Corky Randall could confirm only three others: Pal, California, and Monarch. He also stated that many of the palominos that doubled Trigger were not owned by Roy Rogers but were provided by Hudkins Stables.[2]

Trigger Jr. and Paul K. Fisher

"During the shooting of the picture *My Pal Trigger*, one scene called for the birth of a colt. The studio arranged to rent one from a California horse breeder, and the rancher was so pleased with the deal that he gave the colt to Roy when the picture was completed. Roy began training the young horse to become Trigger's understudy. He named him Trigger Junior. Later Roy and Glenn Randall took over the training, and Trigger Junior appeared in two pictures as Trigger's son."

This charming account of Trigger Jr.'s origin from the book *Roy Rogers — King of the Cowboys* by William Roper made a nice story for young fans. Unfortunately, like the two foals who were sired by Trigger in *My Pal Trigger*, the story is a fantasy.

Rogers purchased Trigger Jr. much later in his career. Trigger Jr. was born in 1941 and died 28 years later in 1969.[3]

Trigger Jr. was originally owned by breeder O.C. Barker of Readyville, Tennessee. When Paul K. Fisher of Souderton, Pennsylvania, owned the gorgeous palomino, the animal was registered with the Palomino Horse Breeders Association (PHBA) as Allen's Gold Zephyr. Glenn Randall purchased the horse as Rogers' agent. The original registration was later canceled and the palomino was re-registered as Trigger Jr. by Roy Rogers of Hollywood, California. The horse was also registered with the Palomino Horse Association [PHA] and the Tennessee Walking Horse Association (TWHA).

Allen's Gold Zephyr was sired by Barker's Moonbeam (registered with the Tennessee

Trigger Jr., with dappling on his coat, circa 1950 on the set of the movie that bore his name. The Tennessee walker had wonderful conformation and great looks. It's no wonder that his original owner, Paul Fisher, and Roy Rogers wanted to use the palomino as a breeding sire *(Roy Dillow collection)*.

Walking Horse Breeders Association [TWHBA], color: yellow) and he by foundation Tennessee walking stallion Golden Sunshine. Zephyr's dam was Fisher's Gray Maud (registered TWHBA, color: gray) and she by Curlee's Spotted Allen out of Susie Hill. At five years of age Allen's Gold Zephyr stood 15.3 hands tall and weighed about 1050 lbs. He was described as dark golden in body color with four evenly matched white stocking legs, blaze face, and white mane and tail.

Trigger Jr. received billing on personal appearance tours. Marquees read, "Roy Rogers, Trigger, and Trigger, Jr." Glenn Randall taught Trigger Jr. a full range of crowd-pleasing tricks including how to dance. Beyond the movie that bears his name in the title, Trigger Jr. was not used in films but extensively in personal appearances throughout the 1950s and 1960s. On certain occasions he was used as a double for Trigger. Copies of an old Perry Como television show are in circulation with an appearance by Roy Rogers, Dale Evans, and "Trigger." It's in fact Trigger Jr. standing in. When author David Rothel asked Rogers about using Trigger Jr. in movies, he replied, "Very little, we used him for personal appearances. He wasn't worth a nickel as a cowboy horse, but he could do a beautiful dance routine."[4]

At one time Fisher Farms was considered one of the largest palomino breeding farms in the United States. Before Roy Rogers, Hoot Gibson and Tom Mix were customers of Fisher's. Paul Fisher often took his horses to Madison Square Garden Rodeo to show and sell them. Fisher's palominos were in great demand, as Roy Rogers found out when he tried to buy Allen's Gold Zephyr. Rogers stated that it took him six years to buy Trigger Jr. Fisher had

Roy Rogers riding a Hudkins Trigger double in a scene from *Under Western Stars* (1938) *(Roy Dillow collection).*

many offers besides the one from Rogers. At first Fisher refused because the horse was so important to his breeding program.[5] Rogers really fell in love with Trigger Jr. during the filming of the movie that bears the palomino's name, but Fisher had still not agreed to sell him. Fisher allowed Rogers to use Trigger Jr. in personal appearances, according to Corky Randall.

It has been rumored that Trigger Jr. and Buttermilk had stalls in the first Roy Rogers and Dale Evans Museum when it opened in 1966 in Apple Valley, California, and lucky visitors during the first three or four years got to see them in the flesh.[6]

Rogers used Trigger Jr. as a stud and raised some good palomino foals on his Happy Trails Ranch in Oro Grande, California. The horse that actor Val Kilmer led on stage as a tribute to Rogers and his B-western cowboy peers during the Academy Awards show in March 1999 was reportedly a descendent of "Trigger." Since Trigger was never bred, this horse — if descended from any of Rogers' horses — was most likely a descendant of Trigger Jr.[7]

For many years, Rogers also raised and trained Thoroughbred race horses at his Happy Trails Ranch. Run Trigger Run took first place in his maiden race. Another Rogers race horse was called Triggero. In October 1993, he auctioned the last of his herd, which included grandsons and granddaughters of Trigger Jr. The palomino sired several foals that were registered with TWHBA, and his bloodline continues today.[8]

Pal O' Mine

In the *Bells of San Angelo* (1946) and the *Golden Stallion* (1949), Dale Evans rode a brown and white pinto. It seemed she and Rogers decided she needed a regular horse and had started looking. It's no surprise they tried to match Evans at first with another palomino. Around 1950 she was using one named Pal for personal appearances. Evans rode him in the pilot episode of her television series, *Queen of the West*. The show never aired (it is included in the DVD release *The Rogers Family Presents: TV Collection, Pilots & Rarities*) because Evans joined her husband in the highly successful and long-running *The Roy Rogers Show* in 1951. She didn't use Pal in that particular show because he looked too much like Trigger. It was felt that the audience would get the two horses confused. In *Rainbow Over Texas* (1946) Rogers rode Pal in a Pony Express race where one rider used a string of horses. Pal was the first mount

Roy Rogers and Trigger Jr. with their custom-made touring van. It's easy to see by this photograph why Corky Randall described the dappled palomino as "elegant" (*Janey Miller collection*).

Pal standing in for Trigger and posing with Roy Rogers. Note how the palomino's blaze explodes slightly halfway down his face and cuts through his nostril on his far side.

Rogers rode to compete in the event. Pal also doubled as Trigger on occasion during personal appearances.

Dale Evans rode a very young Pal during a brief sequence in *My Pal Trigger*. In the scene, after Rogers discovers Trigger's sire, the Golden Sovereign, dead in a corral, Evans rides up on Pal.

Pal's original name was Pal O' Mine and he was foaled on a ranch owned by Joe and Mary Reynolds in Douglas, Wyoming. Pal O' Mine's dam was a buckskin mare named Steel-

Dust. His sire was a bay stallion named Temple Boy, the son of Sir Barton and Temple Girl. As noted earlier, this has led some to believe it was the original Trigger who was a descendant of the famous Sir Barton.[9]

Pal O' Mine was first sold to a rancher named Walt Rymill, who employed Orval Robinson, a trainer and former jockey, on his ranch. Glenn Randall, a native of the Lusk-Torrington area, was acquainted with Rymill. In the 1940s, when Randall was looking for horse to double Trigger, he called Rymill and was invited to see Pal O' Mine at the Rymill Ranch. Robinson happened to be riding the horse when Randall arrived. Immediately Randall was struck by Pal O' Mine's resemblance to Trigger, except that he had white stockings on both hind legs and the front left. Randall bought the horse for $2,500.[10]

The Lusk Herald dated May 25, 1944, printed the statement: "It is understood Rogers gave $2000 for the horse. He intends to train him to take the place of Trigger, who is getting a little too old to follow the strenuous life of a movie actor." At first it was assumed that Pal O' Mine became Trigger Jr. but this was not the case. Darryl Manring of Lusk, while visiting

Dale Evans on Pal and Roy Rogers on the original Trigger. Each horse is using a plastic saddle with double R logos on the tapaderos. Rogers is holding a riding crop to cue Trigger *(Roy Dillow collection).*

the Roy Rogers Museum in Victorville in May of 1993, was able to speak to Rogers about Pal O' Mine. The King of the Cowboys was very candid about the horse. He verified that Pal O' Mine became a star in certain ways. He called the horse versatile and talented. He acknowledged that Pal O' Mine was in some of his movies, was Dale Evans' mount during public appearances for a time, and was Rogers' favorite trail horse.[11]

Corky Randall said that his father maintained ownership of Pal and that the horse never belonged to either Dale Evans or Roy Rogers. Pal was eventually sold to a local dressage rider.[12]

California

Corky Randall recalled another Trigger double named California that Rogers bought at a California horse show. The palomino had a narrow blaze, shaped almost like a diamond up on his forehead, then narrowed down to his muzzle. As with many of the more anonymous doubles, records on this particular horse have not surfaced. When he was still in junior college, Corky used the horse. Rogers loaned him the palomino to compete in a college rodeo in San Francisco to rope calves. California doubled Trigger a lot in *The Roy Rogers Show* on television.

Roy Rogers roping a calf on Trigger double California (*Roy Dollow collection*).

Fight sequence from the color movie *Trigger Jr.* (1950). Stunt double California stood in for the title character during this confrontation with a wild stallion named Phantom.

In the second fight sequence from *Trigger Jr.*, California was the stunt "Trigger." Director William Witney said that the horses were not injured doing these scenes because wires were used to pull and guide them off one another.[13]

Monarch

The last Trigger double Corky Randall was able to identify was a tall palomino named Monarch. Larry Roe identified the horse in William Witney's book *Trigger Remembered*.[14] According to Roe, Monarch was ridden by Dale Evans (along with Trigger) during a dressage sequence in *My Pal Trigger* (1946). She also rode him shortly afterward in an equine square dance scene. Monarch acted up when Roy Rogers rode up on his mare Lady. Rogers also rode Monarch in some of the climactic racing footage at the end of *My Pal Trigger*. Monarch was used sometimes as a stunt double. He appeared in *Home in Oklahoma* (1946) and was ridden by stuntman Joe Yrigoyen in *North of The Great Divide* (1950).

Monarch may be seen in a couple of photographs in this book, the most notable being the "Trigger and His Doubles" photo from *Pic* magazine and a still from *Pals of the Golden West* (1951). Monarch was a very close match to the original Trigger in head type and size,

Roy Rogers converses with border patrolman Pat Brady in *Pals of the Golden West* (1951). The palomino standing behind Rogers was named Monarch. Visible in a high quality copy of this photo are string hobbles on the animal's two front feet at the cannon bones *(Roy Dillow collection)*.

but with white socks in the rear and pale socks in front. His wide blaze was similar to Trigger's but came down through his right nostril, where Trigger's dropped behind.

Larry Roe also spotted both California and Monarch in two Spade Cooley low-budget westerns, *The Silver Bandit* (Friedgen, 1947) and *The Kid from Gower Gulch* (Friedgen/Aster, 1950).

In *The Silver Bandit*, California (all decked out in fancy parade tack) was ridden by the title character. Monarch was ridden by Spade Cooley when he chased the Silver Bandit, who was trying to escape in a wagon.

In *The Kid from Gower Gulch*, protagonist Craig Morgan and female lead Peggy Andrews both rode California. Shorty, a little cowboy, rode Monarch during a calf roping demonstration. Spade Cooley climbed on board the palomino in a brief sequence right before three cowboys pursued him in a long chase sequence.

Liberty Palomino Act

At one time Roy Rogers performed on tour with a string of eight highly trained palominos in a ring without halters or reins, the kind of act one would see at a circus. The horses were owned by Glenn Randall and referred to as the Roy Rogers Liberty Horse act. On occasion

The Roy Rogers Liberty Horse act, owned and trained by Glenn Randall (*Joel "Dutch" Dortch collection*).

the King of the Cowboys used the act on personal appearances at rodeos and state fairs for a couple of summers. Individual horses came and went. Corky Randall recalled a particular palomino named Tiger, who was out of an Oklahoma stallion named Phillips 66, as being very difficult. Satin was the first lead horse. Tiger later became lead and was followed by Murphy, Chalk Eye, Dick, Sonny, and Elmer. When Glenn Randall was putting the act together, he purchased horses in groups. Koko, the stallion who was eventually teamed with singing cowboy Rex Allen, was bought as part of such a group, because of his chocolate color, he was never considered for the Liberty Horse act.

Buttermilk

Trigger had a number of four-legged sidekicks. Frog Milhouse's mare, Ring-Eyed Nellie, and Raymond Hatton's little mule, Dinah, were the first. Gabby Hayes' bay, Eddie, was probably his most regular sidekick. Rogers' German shepherd, Bullet, was probably his best known, along with Dale Evans' light buckskin, Buttermilk.

According to Ken Beck and Jim Clark's *Encyclopedia of TV Pets*, Buttermilk was born in 1941. It was trainer Glenn Randall who found Buttermilk, a buckskin quarter horse gelding with dark points. That Buttermilk survived his early life and made it to Hollywood is a story in itself. He was bought as a colt from a horse trader as he was being taken to slaughter.

Buttermilk had been severely abused and was very mean. The cattle farmer who rescued him gave him the name Taffy and began training him as a cutting and roping competition horse. With patience and kindness, Taffy eventually came around to assume a friendly disposition. Glenn Randall, always looking for animals to train, noticed Taffy in a competition at the miniature rodeo in Nebraska and purchased the little buckskin, originally for Corky. Later he thought the horse would make a good mount for Dale Evans. Buddy Sherwood, a wrangler on the set of *The Roy Rogers Show*, suggested the name "Soda."[15] Evans named the gelding "Buttermilk" from a line in a Hoagie Carmichael tune, "buttermilk skies."

Dale Evans first rode Buttermilk on screen in 1950 in *Twilight in the Sierras*. Actress Penny Edwards rode Buttermilk when she co-starred with Rogers in *Spoilers of the Plains* and *Heart of the Rockies*, both released in 1951. Evans was on maternity leave at the time, having just given birth to her baby Robin.

Buttermilk was even noted in Dale Evans' comic book. While Evans was switching her publisher from DC to Dell, her horse was given the name Soda for the last few issues. So Pal was in the DC series at first, then Soda came next for a brief stint, then Buttermilk in the Dell series.

Buttermilk appeared in all but six *Roy Rogers Show* episodes that aired from 1951 to 1957. Many people associated with Rogers and Evans have commented that Buttermilk was a hard ride; it was rumored that the diminutive horse even managed to unseat Glenn Randall one time. Roy Rogers referred to Trigger as a good "using" horse for chases and such. He claimed that Trigger never had any ankles, hocks, or knees go wrong in all the chases through the rocks, over the mountains, down steep grades, and so forth. Rogers claimed that he did running mounts and dismounts and never had any problem with Trigger. The palomino could outrun any horse on the set. But you had to be "with him" whenever you gave him a cue to go left or right or he'd spin right out from under you. However, quarter horses are bred for a fast takeoff and Buttermilk was actually faster in short distances than Trigger. This irritated Rogers and often required retakes of scenes when Evans broke away faster. Rogers had to ask Evans to slow Buttermilk down when they were shooting chase sequences for their television show.

According to Corky Randall, the light buckskin Buttermilk did

Dale Evans with Buttermilk.

not have a double per se. Although he appeared on most of the episodes of *The Roy Rogers Show*, he wasn't ridden hard. On rare occasions, when a double was necessary, a grey horse was used for long shots.

Corky Randall also claimed that his father, Glenn, eventually gave Buttermilk to Dale Evans after *The Roy Rogers Show* had been canceled on television. Buttermilk died in 1972. Like the original Trigger, he lived to 31 years of age.

6

The Golden Stallion

"About nineteen years ago, Trigger was a colt romping around on a San Diego ranch, when a movie talent scout saw him and brought him to the Ace Hudkins Stables in North Hollywood for training. He had appeared in quite a few movies and was six years old when we met." — Roy Rogers[1]

Regrettably, uncut copies of Roy Rogers' movies are rare. The films were trimmed down for syndication on television from around 70 minutes to just over 50 in order to fill a one-hour slot with room for commercials. It's possible special scenes with "Trigger" were lost in the process.

Roy Rogers and Republic Pictures capitalized on the original Trigger's great looks, camera presence, and intelligence, using him to maximum effect. This was a gradual process, of course; first Rogers himself had to become established with the moviegoing public. As "Trigger's" popularity increased, more attention was given to him. At first the original Trigger was primarily used as decoration and transportation (if most kids were like yours truly, their eyes were focused on "Trigger" no matter what was going on during a scene). However, whenever the opportunity arose, the "Trigger" character was referred to by name or at least acknowledged even when he did not have a significant role in a scene. In time, movie plots were influenced by "Trigger," as when he ran for help as in *Spoilers of the Plains* (1951) or *Bells of San Angelo* (1947). Rogers, a diligent promoter, even referred to "Trigger" in songs.

Eventually "Trigger" was held in such high esteem that not only was he billed just below Rogers, but six movies were produced around him, more than any other B-western horse including Ken Maynard's Tarzan and Gene Autry's Champion.

"Trigger's" Movie Persona

"Trigger's" role changed from film to film and, as with any other character, was at the service of the plot. In some movies he actively protected his master; on other occasions, he was like any other horse and was just transportation. In *Utah* (1945) he actually saved Gabby Hayes from bad guy Wally Wales (Hal Taliaferro). At the end of *San Fernando Valley* (1944) Rogers ran down bad guys Kenne Duncan and Leroy Mason. Forced to fight both men, Rogers lost the upper hand and was knocked out. Duncan grabbed a large dead branch to finish him off. "Trigger" (actually Little Trigger) came to the rescue and attacked Duncan as Rogers regained consciousness. In *Sunset in the West* (1950), however, "Trigger" stood by as a bound

Roy Rogers and Trigger in an outtake from the *Golden Stallion* (1949). Trigger was so well trained and accustomed to movie sets that even when at liberty he required no hobbles *(George Coan collection)*.

and blindfolded Rogers was nearly thrown off a cliff by a couple of crooks. In *South of Caliente* (1951) "Trigger" also stood passively as Rogers fought two gypsies. After they overpowered him and departed, "Trigger" nuzzled Rogers as he lay in the dirt.

"Trigger" seems to have been able to run at a full gallop without ever tiring. After many long chases Rogers never once changed him for a fresh mount. One would be hard pressed to find an instance in any Rogers movies where he ever said that his horse needed a rest. In *Heart of the Golden West* (1942), after Rogers and the Sons of the Pioneers lost the trail of a gang of cattle thieves, Rogers suggested that they get fresh horses and resume the search in the morning. The next day, however, he was on "Trigger" again. In *The Gay Ranchero* (1948), Rogers mounted up and rode off to rendezvous with, of all things, an airplane. At a full gallop over miles, horse and rider reached an appointed rendezvous spot only to find that the pilot and passengers had been attacked after landing near a gang of bad guys on horseback. Rogers put "Trigger" into high gear again and proceeded to chase the crooks. "Trigger" was fresh as a daisy, never breaking a sweat, catching up to horses who hadn't been running all afternoon.[2]

"Trigger" also never seemed to make any mistakes. In contrast, in the 1936 Gene Autry movie *Red River Valley*, Champion neighed and inadvertently alerted a couple of bad guys to a trap his master had set.

Top: Little Trigger being interviewed by a Hollywood reporter who may be Hedda Hopper in September of 1943 (*The San Francisco Examiner Archives*). *Bottom:* Trigger, the Golden Stallion *(Roy Dillow collection).*

Trigger as Shield

Realism aside, some fans were surprised and a little disappointed when Rogers hid behind "Trigger" to avoid gunfire. Many a time Rogers was seen ducking behind the palomino as they pursued bad guys who were returning fire as they fled. Rogers did it in chase sequences in *On the Old Spanish Trail* (1947), *The Gay Ranchero*, *The Far Frontier* (1948), and *Sunset in the West*. "Trigger" is used the same way in the last movie Rogers made for Republic Pictures, *Pals of the Golden West* (1951). Rogers was not, however, the last cowboy to use this tactic. Augustus McCrea (Robert Duvall) in *Lonesome Dove* (Motown Productions, 1989) stabbed his horse in the neck, killing it instantly, to create a barrier to hide behind as a gang of thugs was closing in on him. Shocking, but close to how it must have been in the Old West.

Not only did Rogers use "Trigger" as a shield, but he also gambled that the palomino wouldn't get shot during many a difficult situation. At the end of *The Gay Ranchero*, Rogers cornered bad guy Leroy Mason in a cabin. Rogers approached on foot and then tried to draw Mason out by stomping on the front porch. Mason shot through the front door and Rogers ducked for cover. He then whistled for "Trigger," who approached, turned around and started mule-kicking the front door to break it down. Luckily for the palomino, instead of shooting through the door again, Mason panicked and hid.

Much to the chagrin of some fans, the King of the Cowboys sometimes used his palomino as a shield against bullets.

In *Home in Oklahoma* (1946), Rogers and Gabby Hayes used their mounts as shields when they charged through a line of riflemen. In today's westerns, that stunt wouldn't work because marksmen would simply shoot the horses. In the 1994 Warner Bros. motion picture *Wyatt Earp*, actor Kevin Costner told his partner to shoot the horses being ridden by a gang of outlaws who were pursuing them. "Shoot the horse. Shoot the lead horse. You can shoot a horse, can't ya?" No self-respecting B-western cowboy would have ever uttered such a line, and he would have been deserted by his fans if he had.

Considering all the gun fights "Trigger" was exposed to on screen, it's a wonder he wasn't shot more often. In *Frontier Pony Express*

(1939) Rogers was cautioned by sidekick Raymond Hatton not to take "Trigger" into a gunfight. The palomino finally took a bullet in *Twilight in the Sierras* (1950). Veterinarian Sparrow Biffle, played by Pat Brady, attended to his wound while Rogers calmed the horse down.

Golden Cloud Roles: 1938

The original Trigger was already in the Hollywood area earning his oats as a cast horse for Hudkins Stables by 1937. With his striking looks, it hadn't taken the palomino long to find work in motion pictures. It is unknown exactly which movie he appeared in first. In 1938 he was in six that are known, and of those, only four were made with Roy Rogers at Republic Pictures. The other two were made for Warner Bros.: *Cowboy from Brooklyn* and *The Adventures of Robin Hood.*

The Adventures of Robin Hood

Trigger's first appearance in a movie may have been in *The Adventures of Robin Hood*, which was based on the well-known English legend of Robin of Locksley, a nobleman forced to become

an outlaw when evil Prince John took the throne from his absent brother Richard I, who was off fighting in the crusades. Locksley fled to Sherwood Forest, where he gathered his famous band of "merry men" and became Robin Hood. He defended the townsfolk, who were being heavily taxed by Prince John and the Sheriff of Nottingham. Along the way Robin Hood defended the throne for Richard I and won his childhood love, Maid Marian.

Much press has been devoted to Trigger and his role as actress Olivia De Havilland's mount in *The Adventures of Robin Hood*. This is undoubtedly the most famous of his film appearances without Roy Rogers and the only one ever officially acknowledged by the King of the Cowboys.

From a production standpoint, *The Adventures of Robin Hood* is arguably the best film Trigger ever appeared in. It was

Olivia de Havilland (as Maid Marian) on the Golden Cloud, standing next to Errol Flynn (as Robin Hood) on the set of ***The Adventures of Robin Hood*** (Warner Bros., 1938).

a big budget motion picture, shot in glorious Technicolor, and featured Errol Flynn at the head of an A-list cast. It is generally considered a classic, and in 2003 Warner Bros. issued a special edition DVD.

Along with a restored version of the film, the special edition included a documentary titled *Welcome to Sherwood Forest*. During the section on casting, Rogers fan and film historian Leonard Maltin points out that although many of the cast members were movie veterans at the time the film, there was one rookie: Trigger. He goes on to say that the palomino was at the beginning of "a long and distinguished career" and describes Trigger as "one of the greatest horses in the history of movies, and apparently, from all accounts, an exceptionally smart horse." He noted that the palomino was then called Golden Cloud. There are even a couple of behind-the-scenes shots of De Havilland on Trigger.

It has never been revealed how Rogers learned of Trigger's appearance in *The Adventures of Robin Hood*. Some business associate or friend may have spotted the horse and told him. Glenn Randall or Rogers may have been told by one of the Hudkins brothers as the palomino was being used at the same time in the film *Under Western Stars*.

Rogers obviously liked the story of Trigger's appearance in *The Adventures of Robin Hood* and repeated it often. When the publicity folks followed suit, it became part of the "Trigger" story. Trigger's appearance in *The Adventures of Robin Hood* is so well known that when the film is shown on the Turner Movie Classics Channel, host Robert Osborne acknowledges Trigger.

The golden palomino appeared for the first time about 35 minutes into *The Adventures of Robin Hood*. Robin Hood (Errol Flynn) and his men overpowered and captured the Sheriff of Nottingham (Basil Rathbone) and his company of soldiers, who were escorting a royal treasure of gold and Maid Marian (De Havilland), riding Trigger. As Robin Hood and his men led the royal company back to their secret camp, Trigger was in full view briefly in the same frame as De Havilland, Flynn and Rathbone. Flynn was on foot leading the palomino. The Sherwood Forest sequence ended when De Havilland and company were released, at which point Flynn once again led Trigger, carrying De Havilland, to a clearing at the edge of his secret camp. The palomino is last seen from behind as he gallops off.

The Golden Cloud was ridden by an anonymous stuntwoman doubling for actress Priscilla Lane in this very brief sequence from the Warner Bros. western musical comedy *Cowboy from Brooklyn* (Warner Bros., 1938).

Cowboy from Brooklyn

The musical comedy titled *Cowboy from Brooklyn* featured an all-star cast of Hollywood celebrities including Dick Powell, Pat O'Brien and future U.S. president Ronald Reagan.[3] Dick Foran appeared as the heavy; later he would go on to make a few singing cowboy westerns with his own palomino, Smoke.

A typical fish-out-of-water story, *Cowboy from Brooklyn* concerned a Brooklynite (Dick Powell) who became a cowboy in spite of himself. After drifting into a small western town, he met a cowgirl (Priscilla Lane), who offered him a ranch job. He was a gifted singer and attracted the attention of a talent scout (Pat O'Brien). Before long, he became America's favorite singing cowboy but was hard pressed to prove his western skills. He was especially afraid of horses.

Trigger appeared very briefly in the first five minutes of *Cowboy from Brooklyn* when actress Priscilla Lane rode him while leading a posse of cowgirls. They approached a house, where Lane dismounted and handed Trigger over to a wrangler, who led him away. The blaze across Trigger's nose (dropping on his far side and ending at his lip) is obvious with a frame-by-frame inspection.

Later, Lane mounted Trigger quickly to pursue star Dick Powell who'd been running away from an angry donkey. Here Trigger's appearance was even briefer than before.

Later Roles

Juarez

Juarez (Warner Bros., 1939) is a weighty costume epic about the 19th-century Mexican revolutionary Benito Juarez. It's sizeable, not only for a running time of 132 minutes, but with 1,000 extras and 54 massive sets. *Juarez* was as ambitious a production as *The Adventures of Robin Hood,* but it never attained the same status as a classic. The legendary Bette Davis played Carlota von Habsburg, the wife of Emperor Maximilian; John Garfield portrayed General Porfirio Diaz, and Claude Rains played Emperor Louis Napoleon III. Paul Muni starred as the title character, Don Benito Pablo Juarez. As president of Mexico, Juarez led his beloved country in its fight for independence in the 1860s when France was trying to colonize it.

In the film, the newly named emperor Maximilian (Brian Aherne) and his wife Carlota arrived in Mexico to clash head on with the popular sentiment that favored Benito Juarez and democracy. It was at this point, in the first part of the film, when actor Gilbert Roland, as Colonel Miguel Lopez, may be seen riding Trigger. Lopez and his men were escorting the royal couple from their docked ship to the emperor's castle. Emperor Maximilian and Lopez engaged in a brief dialogue, Maximilian from the window of the royal coach and Lopez riding Trigger alongside. It's a brief sequence but long enough to get a good look at Trigger's distinctive blaze.

Shut My Big Mouth

Shut My Big Mouth (Columbia, 1942) is the story of a timid horticulturist named Wellington Holmes, played by comedian Joe E. Brown, and his adventures in the small western town of Big Bluff. About two minutes into the western comedy Trigger appeared in a brief sequence with villain Buckskin Bill (Victor Jory) riding him, fancy show saddle and all. Jory and his men dismounted under a stand of trees to wait for the coach carrying Wellington Holmes. Trigger may be seen in close up waiting next to Jory. The remaining shots are of the palomino in motion, usually from a distance.[4]

In a scene approximately 17 minutes later, Wellington Holmes escaped Big Bluff disguised as a woman, when his stage was again held up by Buckskin Bill. Trigger was very striking in this brief sequence among the other horses, which were all bays. Trigger is not on screen again after the first 20 minutes of *Shut My Big Mouth*— a pity, because his cameo appearance is the only redeeming thing in this silly movie.

Bad Men of the Hills

While *The Adventures of Robin Hood* may have been the most prestigious film Trigger appeared in without Roy Rogers,

Trigger with villain Victor Jory in a scene from the Joe E. Brown comedy *Shut My Big Mouth* (Columbia, 1942). Jory was best known to serial fans as *The Shadow* (Columbia, 1940).

one of the palomino's most important non–"Trigger" roles was in an obscure Charles Starrett western titled *Bad Men of the Hills* (Columbia, 1942).[5] The 58 minute, black and white B-western was released one a month after Republic released its thirtieth Roy Rogers movie, *Sons of the Pioneers*. Consequently, it's reasonable to assume people at Columbia knew the beautiful palomino they'd leased from Hudkins Stables for the *Bad Men of the Hills* production was Trigger. Columbia was probably not allowed to give him a screen credit or refer to him as Trigger, but director William A. Berke certainly used him for more than just beautiful transportation. The palomino figured into the plot of *Bad Men of the Hills* from the beginning. Trigger played the part of a nameless horse first owned by Marshal Dave Upjohn (played by John Shay). He was later given to Lucky Shelton (Russell Hayden). Ironically, neither man actually rode Trigger on screen in *Bad Men of the Hills*; he was ridden only by an unidentified stuntman, briefly, in an early sequence.[6]

Charles Starrett played Marshal Steve Carlton, who'd been sent to investigate after Upjohn was murdered. Carlton ended up in Chimney Hole, where he ran into Harmony Haines (Cliff "Ukulele Ike" Edwards) and Lucky Shelton. Shelton was now the owner of Marshal Upjohn's palomino (Trigger), who was found roaming the hills. Shelton tied Trigger up and asked Haines to look after him. Apparently Trigger had an attitude problem and misbehaved by stamping on the ground when Haines approached him. Carlton offered to help settle him. (At this point) Trigger turns toward the camera and, because his forelock is parted to one side, we get a great look at how his wide blaze ends at the top of his forehead and goes straight up on his far side and makes an arrow shape on his near side). Carlton even cradled Trigger's head affectionately in his arms, causing his own horse, Raider, to let out a jealous neigh.

Trigger's third appearance took place at night. When Carlton returned to the barn after

Opposite: Actor Gilbert Roland, as Colonel Miguel Lopez, on the Golden Cloud on the set of the Warner Bros. motion picture *Juarez* in 1939. Roland, on the Golden Cloud, leads an honor guard for Emperor Maxmillian (Brian Aherne).

Charles Starrett (left) and Cliff "Ukulele Ike" Edwards share a scene with Trigger in *Bad Men of the Hills* (Columbia, 1942). Edwards' considerable vocal talents were featured in the Disney animated classic *Pinocchio* (1940) as the voice of Jiminy Cricket.

some late night investigating, the palomino started stomping again and woke Haines, who was asleep in a bunk. Carlton went to the horse to calm him. Haines described the horse as "one of the meanest critters I've ever seen." Carlton questioned Haines as to the palomino's origins, trying to find out what a horse that belonged to his murdered friend Marshal Upjohn was doing in Lucky Shelton's possession.

In a scene taking place the next morning, Trigger appeared for one last time. He was still in his stall; Carlton was tacking Raider up next to him. Before Carlton left he asked Haines to watch his horse and stepped out. Haines looked at Trigger, pointed to the well-behaved Raider, and asked, "Why don't you act like him?" Trigger began to misbehave again and stomped on the ground. Haines threatened the horse but the palomino continued to stomp.

Why Trigger's mane was combed to the left side of his neck is a puzzlement. Why would the good folks at Columbia want to disguise the most famous horse in movies unless Hudkins made a conscious effort?

Silver City Raiders

Silver City Raiders (1943) was the first in a series of movies featuring Russell Hayden as the star at Columbia. He played Lucky Harlan, the same type of character he'd played in the

Hopalong Cassidy movies.[7] The plot revolved around Hayden attempting to prove that a crooked land baron, played by Paul Sutton, didn't have prior claim on an entire territory. After legal methods failed to produce conclusive results, Hayden and his pals, Dub "Cannonball" Taylor and Bob Wills (both veterans from Charles Starrett's series of movies), used more effective methods to deal with Sutton and his thugs.

As he had in *Bad Men of the Hills*, director William A. Berke used Trigger to maximum effect. It's obvious the cast and crew knew they had a very special celebrity horse on the set and featured him for all he was worth, taking every opportunity to show him off. Trigger seemed to play a more pivotal role in *Silver City Raiders* than he did in many of Rogers' own movies. Almost all the running shots, from close up to medium, were actually done by Trigger. It could be argued that the folks at Columbia were having fun at Rogers' expense. It was one thing to rent Trigger for use in period pieces like *The Adventures of Robin Hood* and *Juarez* when Rogers was new to the movies, but it was

Trigger as Comanche, Russ Hayden's mount in *Silver City Raiders* (Columbia Pictures, 1943) *(Bobby Copeland collection)*.

something else again to rent him to another cowboy star of a B-western when Rogers was the number one western movie cowboy. Hayden started the movie in a dark hat but was then given a white hat to wear. One could speculate that this was intentional and meant as a visual cue to Rogers.

Seeing Hayden riding Trigger — and he did plenty of it — is astonishing because Rogers' family maintained that no other cowboy was allowed on him. Hayden was taller than Rogers, but not too big for Trigger.

Trigger did not make an appearance till about 30 minutes into *Silver City Raiders*, when Lucky Harlan decided to go to Santa Fe for the official records that would save all the ranches in the valley. For his ride to the train station he changed mounts. As he dismounted from the dark sorrel he'd been riding since the movie started, he removed the saddle and ordered one of his saddle pals, "Bring me Comanche." Out came Trigger. Harlan saddled him up and rode off.

In a later sequence Harlan was riding fast over a hill on "Comanche" when three bad guys started shooting. Harlan pulled up, evaluated the situation and cued the horse to move on. He spun to one side to shoot, then spun to the other side to take off running. It was here that the palomino was featured in a nice profile shot. Trigger never looked better.

Harlan eventually pulled up behind some rocks and started returning fire with the horse looking over his shoulder. This is the same shot used on a lobby card. It's a comic book cover shot if ever there was one.[8]

When Lucky Harlan returned from Santa Fe, his enemies were waiting at the train station and got the drop on him. They forced him at gunpoint into a barn where "Comanche" was stabled. As they commenced to threaten Harlan, the palomino backed out of his stall, knocking down one of the thugs and giving Harlan the opportunity to relieve him of his gun. Finally in control, Harlan ordered his adversaries to bring his horse out of his stall and saddle him up. The palomino was placed center stage.

In the next scene, Harland was on his horse, riding down a road with a bad guy on each side. Trigger was prancing like he was leading a parade! Bob Wills caught up to them and they all continued. By the time Harlan and company reached town, Russell Hayden was back on the sorrel he began the movie on. It was odd for a B-western cowboy star to begin a movie with one horse and end it with another.

As B-westerns go, *Silver City Raiders* is pretty good. Bob Wills and the Texas Playboys provide great musical interludes and there's plenty of action. It's certainly on a par with some of the King of the Cowboy's movies, except that even riding Trigger, Russell Hayden was no Roy Rogers.[9]

About Russell Hayden

Hayden first appeared in the Hopalong Cassidy film *Bar 20 Rides Again* in 1936. A year later he appeared as sidekick Lucky Jenkins in the movie *Hills of Old Wyoming*. During his tenure as Jenkins, he rode some palominos, but Trigger was nowhere to be seen in a Hopalong Cassidy movie. Russell Hayden went on to star in his own series at Columbia filmed after 1943, the same year Rogers bought Trigger.[10] Trigger could have appeared in other Russell Hayden Columbia movies.[11]

Halfway through Hayden's movie *Knights of the Range*, released by Paramount years earlier in 1940, one gets a good look at his palomino. The animal had more than one white stocking and the blaze on the far side of his head did not match Trigger's. This horse might well be the same palomino Victor Jory rode in *Lights of Western Stars*, also released by Paramount in 1940. Hayden and leading lady Jo Ann Sayers shared a beautiful palomino named Pal who was featured prominently. Pal had four white socks. The blaze running down his nose did not match Trigger's.

Russell Hayden was unique in being associated with the two most famous horses in B-westerns. Not only was he the only other cowboy to star in a western using Trigger as his horse; he also (briefly) rode Gene Autry's television Champion. In a *Gene Autry Show* episode titled "The Peacemaker," Hayden played a heavy who stole the sorrel and tried to ride away. Champion refused to leave Autry and bucked the Hayden character off, killing him in the fall.

Movies About Trigger

Six motion pictures were produced around "Trigger": *Hands Across the Border, My Pal Trigger, The Lights of Old Santa Fe, Under California Stars, The Golden Stallion,* and *Trigger, Jr.*

Duncan Renaldo (left), before his role as the Cisco Kid, aided Roy Rogers (center) and sidekick Guinn "Big Boy" Williams in their quest to save Trigger after a price was put on his head (*Hands Across the Border*, 1943).

In *Hands Across the Border* (1943) Rogers played a wrangler looking for a job when he first met "Trigger" on a ranch owned by entertainer Kim Adams (Ruth Terry). She was the daughter of a rancher, Jeff Adams (Joseph Crehan), who raised prize horses for the army. The palomino was part of a herd Adams caught and was hoping to train and sell as army remounts. Kim's dad loved "Trigger" but got thrown and killed when he tried to ride him. It fell on Rogers to befriend the palomino and save him from being destroyed by the villainous Brock Danvers (Onslow Stevens) who wished to marry Kim, take over her ranch, and monopolize the horse business in the area.

"Trigger" escaped back into the wild, but Rogers captured him with the help of sidekick Guinn "Big Boy" Williams and ranch foreman Duncan "the Cisco Kid" Renaldo. The three friends hid "Trigger" and Rogers set to work training him. Rogers was eventually able to show Kim how valuable the palomino would be to her horse business. After she was convinced, she realized she could carry on her dad's work with horses and win a valuable contract supplying the army remounts (the palomino even got to kiss her on the cheek). "Trigger" redeemed himself by winning a race for the army remount contract against Danvers' horses.

Roy Rogers acknowledged *My Pal Trigger* (1946) as his favorite of his own movies. ("Roy, commenting later on his own role in the picture featuring Trigger, said that while he was virtually playing 'a supporting role to a horse,' it was one of his favorites."[12]) It is certainly one of his best known and ranks as a fan favorite too. Serious Roy Rogers fans remember the first time they saw it as children, sitting enthralled as the opening film credits crawled over a shot of Trigger in the back of a horse trailer. The movie began as Rogers drove under a sign which reads "Golden Horse Ranch — Home of Golden Sovereign." Rogers was heard in a voice-over saying, "Golden horse: that's what they call the palomino. And palominos have quite a history. You know, the history of my palomino begins right here at this ranch. If I hadn't gone through that gate a few years back, I'd never have gotten my pal Trigger."

My Pal Trigger featured a top-notch cast headed by Rogers, Gabby Hayes, and Dale Evans. They were followed by the best gang of villains in B-westerns: Roy Barcroft, Leroy Mason, Kenne Duncan, William Haade, Fred Graham, and Jack Holt. For musical support the Sons of the Pioneers were on board featuring Bob Nolan.

The story of how Rogers first got "Trigger" had been touched on before, not only in *Hands Across the Border*, but also in *Come On Rangers* (1938), which included a sequence where Rogers got "Trigger" after his first owner (Rogers' brother) was slain. However, there is no

Left to right: Gabby Hayes, Dale Evans, and Roy Rogers in *My Pal Trigger* (1946). Evans is riding Trigger in English tack. The palomino was playing his own sire, the Golden Sovereign. Lady, who also played the Belle Mare in *The Golden Stallion* (1949) *(Roy Dillow collection)*.

argument that *My Pal Trigger* is the definitive (fictional) origin story. Rogers was cast as a traveling horse trader who wanted to breed his mare, Lady, to the Golden Sovereign, a prize palomino stud on Gabby Hayes' Golden Horse Ranch. Gambling house operator Jack Holt had similar plans for his brood mares. Hayes made it known that the Sovereign wasn't for stud at any price, even a million dollars. Holt, with the help of heavies LeRoy Mason and Roy Barcroft, stole the Golden Sovereign. The stallion escaped and, in turn, ran off with Rogers' Lady. After a romantic equine interlude on the open range, the Golden Sovereign was shot by Holt. Rogers got blamed and, with his beloved Lady, who was carrying the Golden Sovereign's foal, became a fugitive. While on the run Lady gave birth to "Trigger"; then, months later, she died after she was attacked by a cougar.

Rogers raised "Trigger," the only son of the Golden Sovereign. (The name of the colt playing "Trigger" as a yearling was Golden Hours). He returned him to Hayes, who refused to acknowledge the animal. Rogers was sent to jail, then lost "Trigger" in an auction to cover his debts. Holt bought "Trigger" secretly to race him against Hayes' prized Golden Empress. Upon his release from prison, Rogers learned that Holt owned the palomino and signed on as his trainer. The movie climaxed in a race between "Trigger" and the Golden Empress. Holt was revealed as the killer of the Golden Sovereign and Rogers was exonerated.

A number of unusual elements make *My Pal Trigger* atypical of the Roy Rogers movies.

The original Trigger, Roy Rogers, and Dale Evans in the closing scene from *My Pal Trigger* (1946). The beautiful palomino was about to become a father in this charming sequence *(Roy Dillow collection).*

First of all, Roy had no real sidekick; only the ever-loyal Bob Nolan came close. He defended Rogers against the false accusation that he stole and killed the Golden Sovereign. Rogers was a loner, with only a good horse for companionship. Second, the original Trigger, playing the Golden Sovereign in an early sequence, could be seen for the first and only time on film in English tack during a dressage demonstration with Evans. (In the first shot, Evans appeared to be on the palomino double Monarch.)[13] As Evans approached Rogers on the sideline, she was on the original Trigger. In an equine square dance that followed, one may note the original Trigger throughout.

Third, although Evans and Rogers clearly had eyes for each other — they even sang a duet — there was no romance between them. The love story in this outing was between Rogers and Lady, then Rogers and "Trigger."

Fourth, Gabby Hayes, as Evans' father, played an especially sour individual and a man who gambled too much. "Your hatred of Roy has become an obsession, it's dominating your whole life...," Evans lectured him. Through most of the movie, Hayes was an enemy of Rogers and referred to him as "a hoss killer and a skunk." He called "Trigger" a "half-breed."

Fifth, Rogers rode two other horses in *My Pal Trigger*, the chestnut mare (and Champion look-alike) Lady and a dark bay horse in a sequence while he was searching for Lady.

Sixth, two lead horses died violently in this movie: Lady and the Golden Sovereign.

A final unusual element was Rogers' voice-over. He narrated the introduction and the sequences before and after Lady's death.

In spite of being one of the best of Roy Rogers' movies, *My Pal Trigger* has a number of holes in the plot. It isn't *High Noon*, after all. As it was made for children, such holes may be forgiven. But consider: First, Rogers was accused of killing the Golden Sovereign, when it was villain Jack Holt who shot the animal with a rifle. By simply digging out the bullet it would have been easily determined that the slug did not come from Rogers' six-shooter. Second, Bob Nolan and the Sons of the Pioneers beat confessions out of Jack Holt's henchmen, LeRoy Mason and Roy Barcroft. How legal could that have been. Third, palomino couplings rarely produce a palomino. Palominos may be bred from chestnuts and grays, grays and palominos and (preferably) from chestnut and palominos — although none of these couplings guarantees a palomino either. However, breeding a palomino to a palomino makes a cremello.[14]

During most of his career, Rogers followed in Gene Autry's footsteps. With *My Pal Trigger*, the tables were reversed. Years later Autry filmed *Strawberry Roan* (Columbia Pictures, 1948), a fictional account of how he got Champion. While not an exact copy of *My Pal Trigger*, *Strawberry Roan* was clearly in the same vein. Here the Rogers film is far superior to Autry's. Rogers was in his prime with all his supporting players still in place and Republic Pictures solidly behind him.

Gene Autry got the jump on Rogers, however, with the song "Ole Faithful," a tune Gene Autry sang to Champion in *The Big Show* (1937). Rogers sang it to his beloved Lady later in *My Pal Trigger*.

It's fitting that the best stuntman in the movie business, Yakima Canutt, was called in as second unit director for *My Pal Trigger*. His hand was clearly visible in a staged fight sequence between the Golden Sovereign and a wild black stallion, and later in a race between Rogers on "Trigger" versus Evans on the Golden Empress. Evans did her own riding, much to the displeasure of Republic Pictures executives.

Like most Roy Rogers movies, *My Pal Trigger* was a showcase for Little Trigger's talents. The film could not have been made without him. There's no better example of this than the training sequence staged after Rogers went to work for Holt. Trigger and Little Trigger were used flawlessly from shot to shot, giving the illusion of one horse. Little Trigger retrieved Rogers' hat; Trigger reared up on command; Trigger carried Rogers at a full-out gallop; Little Trigger reared up on command with Rogers on his back, then bowed after Rogers dismounted; Little Trigger walked on his hind legs and, after he stopped, kissed Rogers.

After Rogers raised "Trigger," he returned him to Hayes. It was Little Trigger that Hayes first saw in his barn and confused for the Golden Sovereign. Hayes refused the colt, untied him and sent him back to Rogers. Little Trigger also stood in for the original Trigger as he was being auctioned off to cover Rogers' legal expenses after he was falsely accused of killing the Golden Sovereign. It was Little Trigger again in the sequence when he escaped from Holt's ranch and headed into town looking for Rogers.

In the climactic race between "Trigger" and the Golden Empress, the original Trigger was seen in some cuts at a full-out gallop. In the closing scene, when Golden Empress gave birth to "Trigger's" twin sons, it was the original Trigger seen pacing in his stall. After the vet announced the birth of the second twin, it was Little Trigger who sat in astonishment (any time "Trigger" was in a seated pose it was more than likely Little Trigger performing the trick).

One of the last shots in *My Pal Trigger* was not what it seemed: The frame with Trigger's twin sons was a simple double exposure of the same palomino colt. (Note the foal on the left whose left rear leg fades into the hay bedding.) It was magic to children. If ever a film is from the heart, it's *My Pal Trigger*. It's fine entertainment and a great fantasy.

Although *The Lights of Old Santa Fe* (1944) was not built around "Trigger" per se, he was the focus of attention. As in other Roy Rogers movies, Rogers and Trigger played themselves. In the film, "Trigger" and Rogers were a star attraction rodeo act and a coup for anyone who could book them. They were a team, a package deal, and it was clear on screen as in real life that the palomino was instrumental to Rogers' celebrity.

Rogers decided to hire on with the Brooks International Rodeo show, which was owned by Dale Evans and managed by Gabby Hayes. Before he hired Rogers, "Trigger" and the Sons of the Pioneers, Hayes inspected "Trigger" closely. He checked his top line and his croup, picked up his feet, then stood back, smiled and sighed. Hayes then referred to the palomino as "that magnificent specimen of horse flesh."

In a later attempt to convince Evans to keep the rodeo going, Hayes took her to meet "Trigger." Hayes, his face aglow with pride and smiling from ear to ear, led the palomino in a couple of small circles to show him off. Evans too was transfixed and declared "Trigger" "a beautiful animal." As she and Hayes continued the scene, she stood next to the original Trigger, cheek to cheek. Fans were treated to a close look at the palomino's beautiful face and markings. He was indeed a breathtaking sight.

Later in *The Lights of Old Santa Fe* Dale Evans borrowed "Trigger" to go to a nearby lake with villain Tom Keene, the owner of a competing rodeo show. Rogers was upset when he found out that she was using "Trigger" and asked Bob Nolan to drive him out to retrieve "a valuable horse." Not only did he get "Trigger" back, but Rogers threw Keene in the lake. Evans was left on foot and had to walk home. With cues from Rogers, "Trigger" encouraged her to start walking with a nudge. This afforded Rogers the opportunity to sing the Tim Spencer tune "Trigger Doesn't Have a Purty Figure."

In a later sequence, henchman Roy Barcroft wreaked havoc at Hayes' rodeo campsite. He turned stock loose and set wagons on fire. He got his rawhide rope on "Trigger" (Little Trigger actually) but the palomino broke free. "Trigger" ran into camp with a cut rawhide

Formal portrait of three of the best-looking individuals in Hollywood movies of the 1940s: Roy Rogers, Dale Evans, and the original Trigger. All three were in their prime when they starred in the *Lights of Old Santa Fe* in 1944.

rope around his neck. A couple of scenes later, "Trigger" spotted Barcroft's horse in town and alerted Rogers, who found the rest of the rawhide rope still tied to the saddle. With "Trigger's" help, Rogers found the guilty man.

In the closing sequence of the film, Rogers and Evans shared a duet of the ethereal title song. Rogers lifted Evans onto the original Trigger. It is indeed glorious to see the three at their prime and in their full glory. The short sequence is sublime. *The Lights of Old Santa Fe* is a very satisfying movie and one of Rogers' best.

Under California Stars (1948) was released in Trucolor. The plot centered on the kidnapping of "Trigger." Rogers and Trigger again played themselves, a movie star cowboy with a famous and valuable horse. The implication was that Rogers was as much a hero and cowboy in real life as he was on movie screens. Art imitating life.

Trigger attacks one of his kidnappers in a scene from *Under California Stars* (1948). During this sequence the palomino reared up and fell over backwards. It wasn't a double horse and it had to have been an accident. Everyone on the set must have been relieved when the palomino stood up unharmed. Horses have at times broken their necks after such dangerous mishaps.

Under California Stars opened with a brief look at the Republic Pictures back lot in Studio City, California, where Rogers was completing a movie. He was anxious for a break and had made plans to drive to his Double R Ranch.[15] His friend Cookie Bullfincher, played by Andy Devine, managed the place with the help of the Sons of the Pioneers (in an early sequence Little Trigger helped Pat Brady play a hand of cards against the rest of the Pioneers). When Rogers and Trigger arrived they found Bullfincher had hired some of his relatives including his cousin Caroline (Jane Frazee) as a horse trainer.

Rogers, Devine and the Sons of the Pioneers soon found themselves forced to fight a gang of men who were hunting range horses. The brains behind these crooks was Pop Jordan (George Lloyd), who along with his muscle, Lige McFarland (Wade Crosby), changed their focus and decided there was money in kidnapping "Trigger." Young Ted Conover (Michael Chapin), McFarland's innocent stepson, and his dog Tramp ran away and were taken in by Rogers. Pop Jordan employed the young Conover as a spy at the Rogers homestead.

In order to kidnap "Trigger," the kidnappers coaxed him out of his stall with a mare. Once outside and on an open road, he was ambushed by a couple of wranglers who managed to rope him. One clubbed him with a rifle butt and, sadly, the palomino went down (in this heart-breaking sequence, "Trigger" was played by Little Trigger). "Trigger" was taken to a secret hideout. His abduction was headline news all over the country. The *Victorville Tribune* ran a front-page story titled "Movie Horse Abducted."[16] Pop Jordan demanded a $100,000 ransom.

"Trigger" was roughed up by his captors, but he got his revenge by crippling one (ironically named Glenn). Young Ted Conover, who would do anything to recover the imperiled "Trigger," went to the palomino's aid as McFarland was about to destroy him. Conover's dog Tramp saved the day by leading Rogers to Conover at the secret hideout. Pop Jordan, Lige McFarland, and the rest of the gang tried to escape during a fierce gun battle.

In a final chase, Rogers reunited with "Trigger" and rode him bareback in pursuit of villain McFarland. When they caught up, Rogers fought McFarland, and "Trigger" fought McFarland's horse. In the climactic shoot-out, villains Jordan and McFarland ended up betraying and killing each other.

This film had young fans on the edge of their seats, concerned over the fate of "Trigger." It made a deep impression and was a little traumatic.

The Golden Stallion (1949) was released in Trucolor. Directed by prolific B-movie and serial specialist William Witney, the *Golden Stallion* began as Roy Rogers and the Riders of the Purple Sage were trying to fill a contract with a large western stock company who supplied rodeo horses. Hoping to capture a fine wild herd that roamed back and forth across the Mexican border, Rogers leased the Circle B Ranch from Stormy Billings (Dale Evans) to use as his headquarters. The wild herd, led by a specially trained horse referred to as the Bell Mare,[17] was being used by a band of smugglers to transport diamonds from Mexico to their confederates in the U.S. They employed a specially made hollow shoe on the sorrel mare to conceal diamonds.

Rogers and his men rounded up the herd; then he unsaddled "Trigger" and let him loose among the frightened horses in the hope that he could settle them down. Just as the Bell Mare took a shine to "Trigger," the diamond smugglers scattered the herd, and all the horses, including Trigger, ran off. Later that night, "Trigger" drove the Bell Mare back to the Rogers ranch. "Trigger" put on a nice performance—at liberty, no less—when he first led the wild Bell Mare into a corral after Rogers cued him with a whistle. Still later, one of the smugglers sneaked on to the property to retrieve the mare. The mare killed him and ran away. The sheriff, believing that "Trigger" was the killer, demanded that he be destroyed. Rogers "confessed" to the murder to save his horse and was sentenced to prison.

Little Trigger (left, wearing bridle), playing Trigger Jr., face to face with the original Trigger in *The Golden Stallion* (1949). This is the only instance when both palominos appeared together on screen.

Trigger was put up for auction to cover Rogers' expenses. The smugglers won the palomino, thinking they could train him to drive the herd back and forth to Mexico since they could not find the Bell Mare. Awhile later she was caught outside of their secret hideout, but she and "Trigger" escaped once again. She went into hiding and "Trigger" returned to the wild herd. The Bell Mare gave birth to "Trigger's" son, "Trigger Jr.," but died in the process. Again "Trigger" put on a nice performance at liberty as he discovered the Bell Mare. "Trigger" led his son back to the Evans ranch for safekeeping and returned to the wild herd. The Bell Mare was never mentioned again.

After being auctioned off to a gang of smugglers, Trigger returns to Roy Rogers in this scene from *The Golden Stallion* (1949).

While Rogers was serving time in prison, "Trigger" was trained by the diamond smugglers as the new leader of the herd. Little Trigger stepped in to play "Trigger Jr." for the first time in a film in a brief dance sequence with Evans riding him. When Rogers was freed, he enlisted the sheriff to help set a trap to capture the smugglers.

"Trigger" remained wild and was still leading a herd of horses. Riding Little Trigger, who was again playing "Trigger Jr.," Rogers cornered "Trigger" (played by the original) among some rocks. He dismounted and let Little Trigger approach "Trigger." The two palominos acknowledged head to head and for a brief moment both were together in the same frame. Rogers approached and, standing between the two horses that made him a star, greeted "Trigger" after their long separation. For serious Trigger fans this brief scene is a treasure.

While the *Golden Stallion* is considered one of Rogers' more mature efforts, like all his movies, it bent horse behavior where necessary to tell a story. It's great fun and sets up the only Rogers movie that even comes close to being called a sequel, *Trigger, Jr.*, which was released just one year later.

Although *The Golden Stallion* wouldn't seem to hold much appeal for the maverick filmmaker of *Pulp Fiction* (Miramax, 1994), Quentin Tarantino, it is one of his favorite movies.

He referred to *The Golden Stallion* in *The New York Times'* celebrated "Watching Movies" series of 2000.[18] *The Golden Stallion* was a bold choice and helped to call attention to the long career of the film's director, Republic Pictures' veteran action specialist, William Witney. Tarantino praised Witney's direction and Roy Rogers' performance. Tarantino found the relationship between Rogers and "Trigger" particularly moving, "You know, in some movies, a cowboy might go to jail to save his best friend from being shot down dead. Well, Trigger is Roy's best friend. It's the easiest leap to have him do that here, yet it's so powerful and so unexpected. What's great is that you buy it, you absolutely buy it, and I don't know that I really would buy it from anybody else but Roy and Trigger."

Quentin Tarantino also acknowledges "Trigger" twice at the end in his opus *Kill Bill 2* (Miramax, 2004). David Carradine played the title character, leader of a group of assassins for hire. He was attracted to blondes, Uma Thurman in particular. He'd been obsessed with them all his life. Tarantino used footage from *The Golden Stallion*, a movie about a blonde horse, to accent this.[19] Thurman finally ended up in Carradine's home, which she'd been trying to find for two hours in this film and its prequel, *Kill Bill*. When she lay in bed with her daughter, a Breyer Trigger figure was standing on the night table close by. During a conversation between Carradine and Thurman there was a television in the room showing *The*

Roy Rogers takes the blame for a murder of which Trigger was falsely accused in this emotional scene from ***The Golden Stallion*** (1949). (Of course, Rogers didn't commit the murder, either; the culprit was another horse.) Left to right: Unidentified actor, Frank Fenton, Douglas Evans, Pat Brady, Roy Rogers, Trigger, Dale Evans, Al Sloey, Johnny Paul, Estelita Rodriguez, and Foy Willing *(Roy Dillon collection)*.

Golden Stallion. It's no coincidence that the sequence playing was the same one Tarantino discussed in the *New York Times* essay. While Carradine and Thurman discussed the chain of events that led to this moment, Rogers was sacrificing himself to save his beloved horse.

Trigger, Jr. (1950) is one of a handful of movies that was featured on the *Happy Trails Theatre* television show taped in Knoxville, Tennessee, in 1986. Hosts Roy Rogers and Dale Evans introduced it with great anecdotes and were pretty candid about the actual Trigger Jr. It was obvious Rogers was very attached to the palomino. He said that the stallion was three when he first saw him. Rogers was doing a show at Madison Square Garden when the horse was brought from Pennsylvania for him to look at. Rogers also noted that he had a difficult time buying him; he claimed that it took nine years before owner Paul Fischer would sell. Rogers went on to say that Trigger Jr. was a Tennessee walker and his original name was Allen's Gold Zephyr. Rogers also acknowledged trainer Glenn Randall and how he trained Trigger Jr. to do a number of dance routines.

Directed by William Witney, *Trigger, Jr.* was released in Trucolor and features Rogers, Trigger, Trigger Jr., sidekicks Gordon Jones and Pat Brady, Foy Willing and the Riders of the Purple Sage. In the film, Rogers' circus and wild west show was headed towards its winter quarters, a ranch owned by wheelchair-bound Colonel Harkrider (George Cleveland), his daughter Kay (Dale Evans), and grandson Larry (Peter Miles). Larry's mother, a circus bareback rider, was killed during a performance. Consequently, the boy had a paralyzing fear of horses.

On the set of *Trigger Jr.* (1950): Roy Rogers and Trigger (wearing protective goggles) with Trigger Jr. (the title character) and sidekick Gordon Jones.

Trigger Jr. is an odd film and plays pretty fast and loose with both human and horse behavior. At the time of its release it was considered one of Rogers' more sophisticated outings, but in retrospect, while it may be seen as a well-intended lesson in finding courage and growing up, by today's standards it is very naive. Nevertheless, it did attempt some serious character development. Both Colonel Harkrider and Larry were wrestling with problems. We learned that the Colonel's reliance on the wheelchair was psychosomatic and that he was verbally abusing Larry for being fearful and the no-account son of a drifter, consequently leaving the boy constantly afraid and miserable.

Villain Grant Withers and his so-called range patrol, which were supposed to keep rancher's horses from straying onto neighboring ranges and prevent wild horses from making off with their herds, had accomplished nothing yet charged the ranchers exorbitant fees. Withers used a vicious wild stallion, an equine killing machine named the Phantom, to terrorize the area's horse-breeders. Both "Trigger" and "Trigger Jr." lost a fight with the Phantom. A lucky blow the Phantom delivered to "Trigger's" head caused the palomino to go blind when the optic nerve was paralyzed. (Poor Trigger spent half the movie sidelined and wore a pair of protective goggles.) Rogers attempted to uncover the foul doings but was ambushed by the patrol. He and sidekick Jones kept the patrol at bay, hoping they'd get rescued.

Roy Rogers with child actor Peter Miles on the original Trigger on the set of *Trigger Jr.* (1950).

The Phantom was so mean and dangerous that he went on a killing rampage and eventually attacked Colonel Harkrider in his wheelchair. The rogue horse next went after "Trigger" who was confined in a corral. Once again he landed a couple of blows to "Trigger's" head and the blind palomino went down. "Trigger Jr." came to his father's rescue and went down as well. "Trigger's" sight was restored when his optic nerve was struck again. "Trigger" chased off the Phantom, and Larry had to ride "Trigger Jr." to rescue Rogers and Jones, who remained surrounded by bad guy Grant Withers and his men.

Larry found the courage to mount "Trigger Jr." and rode for Dale Evans and the Riders of the Purple Sage. He led them to Rogers and Jones and saved the day. In the meantime "Trigger" had chased the Phantom towards Rogers, who disposed of the Phantom with a bullet to the head — not a pleasant thing to see, and a sorry plot solution for a movie aimed at children. Larry overcame his fear of horses and was cured. Colonel Harkrider overcame his psychological attachment to his wheelchair.

Trigger Jr. is unique among Roy Rogers movies because the three major horses he used in his career were present: the original Trigger, Trigger Jr. and Little Trigger. Trigger Jr. is not hard to identify in the movie that bears his name; at the time his dappled coat was very distinctive. Trigger and Trigger Jr. first appeared side by side in a dramatic shot on top of a rocky hill. Trigger Jr. mischievously ran off, scattering a herd of horses. Rogers whistled for Trigger and mounted up bareback, and they took after Trigger Jr. Stuntman Joe Yrigoyen, substituting for Rogers, did some fancy riding among the herd of horses and got a rope around Trigger Jr. For a brief instance Rogers may be seen riding Trigger bareback at a gallop.

Even Little Trigger got into the action when he substituted for Trigger during his last fight with the Phantom. He was the palomino seen in close-up chasing the Phantom out of the corral where they were fighting. A few scenes later Little Trigger substituted for Trigger Jr. as he stopped a stampeding herd of horses. He cut across the foreground of the picture frame.

William Witney

Luckily for Roy Rogers, Republic Pictures had some excellent directors on its payroll, including Joseph Kane, John English, and Frank McDonald. At the end of his motion picture career he was teamed with one of the best action directors of all time, William Witney. Like Rogers, Witney loved the outdoors and was an experienced horseman, which made him especially adept at action and stunts. Of all the directors Rogers worked with, Witney was especially drawn to Trigger and it makes sense that he directed three movies with the palomino at the center of the plot: *Under California Stars*, *The Golden Stallion*, and *Trigger, Jr.*

Between 1937 and 1946, Witney directed or co-directed 23 of Republic Pictures' greatest cliffhanger serials, including *Adventures of Captain Marvel*, *Dick Tracy vs. Crime, Inc.*, *Drums of Fu Manchu*, *The Lone Ranger*, *Perils of Nyoka*, *Spy Smasher*, and *Zorro's Fighting Legion*. (Witney's serials inspired Steven Spielberg's Indiana Jones movies of the 1980s. From 1946 to 1951 Witney directed 27 Roy Rogers westerns that marked a dramatic change in content and style, cutting back on the musical aspects in favor of more serious stories.

William Witney was one of the first directors to choreograph fight scenes. He had never been satisfied with how movie fights were filmed, much less how they looked — a stuntman free-for-all in front of a camera. "The fights always seemed to be okay for the first punch. Then the stuntmen were always out of place for the next punch. By the time three or four minutes had passed, the stuntmen were out of breath, scattered all over the set and seemed to be staggering around waiting for someone to hit them."[20] After watching choreographer-turned-director Busby Berkeley rehearse a dance sequence with 40 dancers at Warner Bros., Witney learned a valuable lesson. He saw how Berkeley lined up the dancers to execute one tiny movement, over and over until it was perfect. He shot that movement, then went on the rehearse another. When that next movement was perfect, he shot again. Eventually he shot some close-ups to fill in between the dance shots.

Using Berkeley's method, Witney started staging and filming fight sequences, breaking them into fragments, mixing camera angles and even using close-ups. With good editing, this had a huge impact on movie audiences. Witney's technique has become an industry standard.

William Witney appeared on the *Happy Trails Theater Show* (Cintel) on August 22, 1987 (the "Far Frontier" episode), and promoted his book *Trigger Remembered*. Rogers praised him for the effort.

Trigger's Special Scenes

When one reviews Roy Rogers' movies, what's obvious is how important Trigger became, not only as ambience and transportation, but also as a supporting character. The palomino affected plots in a number of movies, sometimes in ways that were critical to the story line. Other times he was on screen simply to showcase his beauty.

Rogers called "Trigger" by name in his second film, *Billy the Kid Returns* (1938). "Trigger" didn't do any fancy tricks, just snorted in response when Rogers spoke to him. At one point he neighed to warn Rogers of trouble. The most spectacular horse stunt in this early film was performed by a palomino double and a stuntman when they jumped off a cliff into a lake and swam across to the other side. This footage was used a number of times in Republic movies.

In *Come On, Rangers* (1938), when Rogers was caught on foot spying on some renegades, one of the gang was ordered to retrieve "Trigger." The palomino was roped but did not submit; he pulled free and fled. A little later sidekick Raymond Hatton, who was out looking for his partner Rogers, saw "Trigger" running loose and proceeded to pick him up. Rogers' character didn't even own "Trigger" at the beginning of *Come On, Rangers*; his older brother, played by Lane Chandler, did. The two men and Raymond Hatton were Texas Rangers (in an early scene three actors who were in the first Lone Ranger serial may be seen around a campfire: Lee Powell, Lane Chandler, and George Montgomery). White men disguised as Indians attacked Chandler's farm. He's killed and his house and barn were set on fire. Rogers arrived in time to pull "Trigger" out of his burning stall. After Chandler was buried, Rogers rode off on his bay army mount leading "Trigger."

"Trigger" really started to shine in *Frontier Pony Express* (1939); he was the fastest horse working for the company. Rogers rode the dangerous California-to-Kansas-City route while the Civil War raged in the East. For the climax of the film, while carrying important Union vouchers, Rogers was ambushed and wounded by a gang of Confederate thugs and tried to make an escape. Weakened by a bullet in the arm, he fell from "Trigger." The faithful palomino returned for him but Rogers signaled the horse to keep running. The Confederates ignored Rogers and pursued "Trigger," hoping to take the vouchers. "Trigger" was forced to jump off a cliff into a lake and swim for the other side. This is likely one of the times that the cliff-jump scene from *Billy the Kid Returns* was used. (The original Trigger is easily identifiable in the chase sequences. As he was about to run off the cliff, an unidentified palomino double made the jump and swam across the lake.) It was at this point that Raymond Hatton caught "Trigger" with his speedy little mule, Dinah. She could run faster than "Trigger" and proved it a couple of times in the Roy Rogers films. Hatton made a transfer from mule to horse and continued on with the vouchers. He encountered a company of Union soldiers and sent them back to deal with the Confederate gang. As Hatton was about to separate from his Union allies, "Trigger" reared up, surprising his diminutive rider; but the B-western veteran stayed with the palomino and continued his escape. A running joke in *Frontier Pony Express* was that Hatton, a trader of goods, kept including "Trigger's" horseshoes as bonus items.

Rogers asked "Trigger" to buck him off as a ruse to speak to actress Pauline Moore in *Days of Jesse James* (1939). A stunt man and stunt horse completed the scene.

In *Rough Riders' Roundup* (1939), Raymond Hatton's mule Dinah again outran "Trigger" in a friendly race. She also wandered off and gave Rogers and Hatton away as they tried to sneak up on some banditos. Hatton used his catch phrase, "Hi Ho, Dinah,"[21] throughout the film. The little mule was clearly given much more attention than "Trigger" in this outing.

In *Ridin' Down the Canyon* (1942), young Bobby Blake (Buzzy Henry) got to experience every little saddle pal's fantasy: He rode "Trigger" surrounded by the Sons of the Pioneers with Rogers on Pat Brady's horse. Bobby idolized Rogers and even named his own pinto pony Trigger Jr.

The original Trigger was pretty much on his own in *Silver Spurs* (1943); Little Trigger was nowhere in sight. There were a couple of exciting stunt sequences in the film, including one where an unidentified stuntman and palomino slid down a hill into a river, then swam to the opposite shore. "Trigger" showed his cow horse training by standing firm after Rogers tied a rope to the pommel of his saddle then lowered himself down a hill. When Rogers wanted an assist, he yelled to "Trigger" to back up and Rogers, holding the rope, made the climb.

The closing musical number of *Don't Fence Me In* (1945), a reprise of the title track, began with dancers performing on a stage in front of a movie screen. As they parted, Rogers and "Trigger" appeared, riding full towards the camera, eventually bursting though the screen itself. Rogers was riding Trigger towards the camera in the outdoor footage; after they broke through the screen, he was on Little Trigger. The four white-stockinged feet were clearly visible as the animal reared up onstage. The palomino was wearing rubber boots on his feet to keep from slipping. In one of the last shots of the sequence, Little Trigger blew a kiss towards the camera, and the black spot on his muzzle was in plain view.

In *Utah* (1945) "Trigger" was pretty much a typical cowboy's horse till the climax of the movie. Rogers and Gabby Hayes chased bad guys Grant Withers and Hal Taliaferro (aka Wally Wales) from Utah to the Chicago stockyards. Rogers disposed of Withers after "Trigger" helped run him down. As Rogers put the final touches on Withers with his fists, from out of nowhere "Trigger" took it upon himself to look after Hayes, who had caught up to Taliaferro. Hayes was holding his own, but as the younger Taliaferro was about to get the upper hand, "Trigger" (Little Trigger) attacked. Taliaferro ended up cowering on the ground for fear of his life. Rogers arrived, called the palomino off and that was the end of that.

Heldorado (1946) is noteworthy for a number of reasons. Even though "Trigger" was mostly used as transportation, he was depicted as a local celebrity along with Rogers who worked for the state. (Fans were asked to believe that, on his state salary, he could afford a

Roy Rogers and Little Trigger in the classic rearing pose during the musical climax of *Don't Fence Me In* (1945). The rubber boots were used to give the palomino secure footing.

very expensive saddle and had a highly trained horse.) During the Heldorado Days celebration shown in the film, Rogers appeared in a parade on Little Trigger. He also used Little Trigger during a rodeo performance. He rode into an arena; Little Trigger reared up; Rogers dismounted and handed him over to Glenn Randall. After Rogers sang "My Saddle Pals and I" with the Sons of the Pioneers, Randall brought Little Trigger back for Rogers to use in a dance routine.

Rainbow Over Texas (1946) is very interesting from a horse-watcher's point of view. Three of the most well known palominos Roy Rogers used were present. The original Trigger was, of course, dominant and was mentioned by name throughout. Rogers was sort of playing himself, a famous western entertainer. Dale Evans played the rebellious daughter of a very rich easterner who owned ranch. At one point Evans stole "Trigger," leaving Rogers no choice but to chase her in a wagon. During the chase the cinch on "Trigger's" saddle came loose (it was never cinched up tightly). Evans panicked but could not slow the palomino down. Rogers cut her off and made a flying leap from the wagon, dismounting Evans from Trigger, saddle and all. After they dusted themselves off, they loaded the saddle onto the wagon, climbed aboard, and headed into town with "Trigger" following behind. After they got back to town, the palomino, still without his saddle, started following Rogers down a sidewalk until he was told not to.

Rainbow Over Texas includes a climactic Pony Express race. Riders were allowed a string of horses stationed over a long course. Rogers rode palominos from Evans' father's ranch. Before the race Rogers, Evans, and Gabby Hayes visited the ranch to inspect horses. Little Trigger was in the first stall they visited, and Pal was in the second. For the race itself, Pal was the first of the string of horses Rogers used. Before the riders mounted up, fiddler Hugh Farr walked Pal to the starting line and handed the horse to Rogers. Pal's three white stockings were easy to spot, as was his unique blaze, which exploded halfway down his face on his off side. One got a better look at Pal's facial markings when Rogers mounted up right before the race began. *Rainbow Over Texas* was to Pal what *My Pal Trigger* was to the original Trigger and *Son of Paleface* was to Little Trigger.

Roy Rogers on Pal. The palomino's leg marking were the opposite of Trigger's, three white stocking feet instead of one (*Roy Dillow collection*).

Trigger was a beautiful sight

when he ran for help in *Bells of San Angelo* (1947) and reared up amidst the Sons of the Pioneers, alerting them that Roy Rogers and Dale Evans were in trouble.

In *Springtime in the Sierras* (1947), Rogers and "Trigger" chased down villain Roy Barcroft. Both men used their empty rifles like clubs and struck at each other while still on horseback. Rogers was eventually knocked to the ground and Barcroft, hoping to finish off the King of the Cowboys, went after him while still mounted. Rogers yelled to "Trigger" to shield him, and the palomino reared up in front of Barcroft, giving Rogers the opportunity to go on the offensive.

In *Night Time in Nevada* (1948) two city gals bumped into "Trigger" and one referred to him as a "blonde horse." One even asked Rogers what he used to make "Trigger's" mane so white; then she leaned against the palomino and draped his mane over her head to simulate a wig. Rogers replied, "Not a thing, ma'am, he was born that way." Later, after Rogers stopped villain Grant Withers with a punch to the jaw, he asked "Trigger" to stand guard over him and not let him get away.

In *Eyes of Texas* (1948) villain Roy Barcroft tried to run "Trigger" out of his barn when the palomino wandered in to get a drink from a water trough. When Barcroft went after "Trigger" with a pitchfork, the horse attacked him. Rogers called "Trigger" off, but Barcroft came after the King of the Cowboys with a whip. As Rogers and Barcroft mixed it up with their fists, "Trigger" joined in. Twice he head-butted Barcroft into Rogers' fist.

The plot of *Eyes of Texas* centered on a pack of dogs trained to kill on command by villain Nana Bryant. Eventually one was wounded and left for dead. Rogers later found him, but the half starved and half wild animal wouldn't let him come near. It was "Trigger" who was able to break through to the frightened dog.

In another sequence Rogers was kidnapped by Barcroft and his gang. They threw Rogers on the ground, bound his feet, tied the rope to the saddle of another horse and whipped the horse into a run. It dragged Rogers down a dirt road. "Trigger," seeing his master in trouble, followed and intercepted the horse, stopping him long enough for Rogers to untie his feet. He hopped up on "Trigger" and eluded Barcroft and his gang.

In *The Far Frontier* (1948), "Trigger" got Rogers in trouble with leading lady Gail Davis. The palomino accidentally bumped Rogers, knocking a package out of his hand. It fell into a puddle of mud and splashed all over Davis. "Trigger" was most impressive later on in a chase sequence where he actually jumped over and narrowly avoided a barrel thrown from a truck by bad guy Roy Barcroft.[22]

During the gunfight climax of *Down Dakota Way* (1949), Little Trigger attacked a bad guy and kept him at bay.

In *Susanna Pass* (1949) "Trigger" was noted for his speed. When the boss villain made a quick escape during the film's climax, Rogers was forced to take after him on another horse. Standing at a distance, "Trigger" noticed and took off after his master. As Rogers proceeded, he discovered the horse he'd borrowed was very slow. The King of the Cowboys yelled, "Is this all you've got, fella?" Shortly after he noticed "Trigger" coming on strong behind him. He shouted to his palomino and, a few seconds later, made a switch as "Trigger" caught up.

In *North of the Great Divide* (1950), "Trigger" (Little Trigger) saved Rogers and his Indian friend Dacona (Keith Richards) from a wolf attack. After killing the lupine with his teeth, the palomino backed off. In the nearby brush Rogers found a wolf pup, which he adopted and raised.

About forty minutes into *Twilight in the Sierras* (1950), "Trigger" got shot while a posse and a pack of hunting dogs were pursuing Rogers. The palomino ran till he eventually began to limp. Rogers dismounted and was forced to hide. After checking "Trigger" closely, Rogers saw that the horse had taken a bullet in the shoulder. Rogers removed the palomino's saddle to lessen the weight he was carrying and made for a stream to disguise his scent from the dogs that were tracking them. The original Trigger did a very convincing limp as Rogers led him to a marshy area. It was Little Trigger who stepped in when Rogers cued him to lie down. The cowboy and his horse lay motionless in tall grass while the posse and hunting dogs passed them by. After they were gone, Rogers cued Little Trigger to stand, and they departed for a drier hiding place. Rogers contacted the local veterinarian, Sparrow Biffle, played by Pat Brady. As Trigger lay alone and wounded, a mountain lion spotted him and started to close in, but retreated as Rogers and Brady approached. Rogers held Little Trigger by the head to calm him as Brady removed the slug. The dark spot on Little Trigger's muzzle was clearly visible. The bullet, fortunately, was not deep and only pinching a nerve. "Trigger" was fine and able to stand right after the bullet was removed.

The Trail of Robin Hood (1950) is significant because of guest appearances by several cowboy stars, including Monte Hale, Crash Corrigan, Tom Tyler, and Kermit Maynard. Rex Allen and Rocky Lane appeared as well with their famous horses Koko and Black Jack. Regrettably, a great opportunity was lost to film the three celebrity horses together. No publicity shot exists of the event, although there were some good group shots of the cowboys on foot. At one point, Trigger and Koko shared a scene. It's unfortunate the sequence wasn't blocked differently to show both horses. Still photos exist of the sequence, but Rogers and Trigger are in front, hiding Koko.

Dale Evans (a stuntwoman most likely) rode Trigger sidesaddle in *Bells of Colorado* (1950). Little Trigger bit and tossed a thug (a dummy actually) that Rogers was fighting with.

The plot of *South of Caliente* (1951) is built around horses, and "Trigger" drove the plot as much as any human in the cast. Rogers owned a horse transporting business. Sidekicks Pat Brady and Pinky Lee worked for him. Dale Evans played the owner of a Thoroughbred breeding ranch. She hired Rogers to take some very valuable horses down to Mexico, including her prized mare, Miss Glory. "Trigger" raced Miss Glory to a dead heat and clearly had eyes for her.

Roy Rogers, Trigger, Little Trigger, Joe Yrigoyen and a couple of Trigger doubles put on quite a show about 15 minutes into *South of Caliente* when the truck transporting horses (including Trigger) was hijacked, leaving the wranglers on foot in the Mexican desert. After thieves made their getaway, they stopped to unload the stolen horses. "Trigger" got loose, attacked a couple of rustlers and escaped. Once empty of its valuable equine cargo, Rogers' truck was put in neutral gear and was sent careening down a dirt road. "Trigger" ran back to Rogers, who was in pursuit on foot. Rogers mounted up and, riding bareback, continued the chase. Rogers and Trigger were actually filmed in this following sequence, riding at a full gallop without a saddle. As they approached the driverless truck, a stuntman and a palomino double closed in till the rider made a transfer into the cab and stopped the vehicle.

In *Spoilers of the Plains* (1951) Rogers was ambushed and shot in the shoulder. He tried to escape on "Trigger" but was too wounded to ride. He eventually slipped off, allowing his assailants to catch up, but it was his German shepherd, Bullet, who tried to protect him.[23] He too was shot and it was left to "Trigger" to run for help. He found Penny Edwards, who followed him (on Buttermilk) back to his fallen master and canine friend.

Later Rogers was captured by villain Grant Withers and his gang. While the gang was transporting Rogers by wagon with some stolen equipment, sidekick Gordon Jones and the Riders of the Purple Sage chased them down in a second wagon. "Trigger" also ran along at a distance, shadowing his master. What followed was a thrilling sequence, as dangerous as any Republic Pictures ever filmed. The two wagons, drawn by teams of six horses, started racing side by side down a dirt road. Men from both started jumping from wagon to wagon in a huge brawl. At one point Withers jumped onto his team of horses and Rogers followed. Rogers can actually be seen standing on the tongue of the wagon between the galloping team of horses. Withers freed his pair of horses and speeded up. Rogers did the same and stayed in pursuit. The riderless Trigger moved in, and Rogers switched to the palomino and continued the chase.[24]

Trigger was mostly beautiful transportation in the 1951 movie *In Old Amarillo*. It's only during the closing moments that he was featured in a special sequence. Stuntman Joe Yrigoyen stepped over four bay horses tied to a hitching rail and standing in a row. He mounted Trigger, who was standing at the opposite end, and rode off.

Little Trigger was the equine star of Rogers' last feature film, *Son of Paleface* (Paramount, 1952). "Trigger" got fourth billing under the names of his master, comedian Bob Hope and actress Jane Russell. Little Trigger was featured prominently throughout *Son of Paleface* and it's unique because it was the only A-western Roy Rogers and "Trigger" ever appeared in together.

In *Son of Paleface* Little Trigger performed a number of gags. He untied Rogers and Hope while they were bound together in a barber's chair. He chased Hope into a hotel, then popped his head out of a second story window to catch Hope trying to escape down a drainpipe.

Comedian Bob Hope and Little Trigger shared a bed in this funny and charming sequence from the *Son of Paleface* (Paramount, 1952) *(Roy Dillow collection)*.

Little Trigger ran back down the stairs, exited the building, ran to the pipe, and loosened it, dropping Hope into a barrel of water below.

Little Trigger was used in many sequences in *Son of Paleface*, but other doubles appeared as well. A stuntman (either Buddy Van Horn or Joe Yrigoyen) dropped from a tree on to a palomino double and galloped off. Rogers rode another double in an interior sequence that may have been shot on a treadmill. While on his galloping horse, he placed a wheel on Bob Hope's moving automobile.

The most famous sequence involving "Trigger" in *Son of Paleface* occurred midway through the movie after Hope, wishing to use "Trigger" (Little Trigger) for an escape, disguised himself as Rogers. He walked toward the animal carrying a guitar and singing "Four-legged Friend," then mounted up, only to have Little Trigger run him back into an abandoned hotel, trot up a series of stairs, and pitch him onto a bed. Later, Rogers, Hope, and "Trigger" were sleeping — Rogers in one bed, Hope and Little Trigger sharing the other. What commenced was a fight between the comedian and the palomino over the bedsheets. Here the blaze and black spot on Little Trigger's muzzle are plain to see, especially by freezing key frames on a DVD player.

The last scene of *Son of Paleface* featured Roy Rogers and "Trigger" in their signature pose: the palomino reared and the cowboy waved goodbye. This, appropriately, was the last shot of the last movie Roy Rogers and "Trigger" appeared in as themselves.

Little Trigger was about 14 years old when he performed in *Son of Paleface*. The original Trigger was 18 by that time.

Trigger, Beautiful Transportation

Trigger's first appearance with Roy Rogers in *Under Western Stars* (1938) was inauspicious at best. In point of fact, it was another horse that had a more important role: sidekick Frog Milhouse's white mare, Ring-eyed Nellie. It seems she was a former fire horse who was trained to follow the sound of a ringing bell. *Under Western Stars* closed with Milhouse helplessly aboard Ring-eyed Nellie, chasing after the sound of a bell from a passing truck.[25]

Although Trigger's appearance in *Under Western Stars* was pretty low key, it offered a hint of things to come. His first scene with Rogers opened as the cowboy was repairing a barbwire fence. Trigger was standing next to Milhouse, who was mounted on Ring-eyed Nellie. Distant gunfire drew their attention and they all decided to investigate. Rogers mounted up quickly. As he turned Trigger to move out, the palomino reared up ever so slightly.

In a later scene Trigger performed his first trick in a Roy Rogers film. While Rogers was rehearsing a speech he was planning to give to a political rival, Trigger, acting as his audience, gave a simple nod.

Trigger was not mentioned by name in *Under Western Stars* but fans got a very good look at him. In a short sequence after Rogers rescued starlet Carolyn Hughes, Rogers and Hughes ended up walking together with Trigger in between. It's safe to assume there were many fans who saw this film when it premiered in 1938 and gladly paid another nickel the next time a Roy Rogers film was in theaters just to look at Trigger again.

Many of Trigger's appearances were spent simply as beautiful transportation: *Wall Street Cowboy* (1939), *The Arizona Kid* (1939), *Southward Ho!* (1939), *Saga of Death Valley* (1939), *Young Buffalo Bill* (1940), *Young Bill Hickok* (1940), *Colorado* (1940), *The Border Legion* (aka *West of the Badlands*, 1940), *Nevada City* (1941), *Badman of Deadwood* (1941), *Jesse James at*

Trigger, Roy Rogers, and actress Carol Hughes in *Under Western Stars* (1938). Hughes went on to play Dale Arden in the *Flash Gordon Conquers the Universe* serial (Universal, 1940) *(Roy Dillow collection)*.

Bay (1941), *In Old Cheyenne (1941), Romance on the Range* (1942), *Sunset on the Desert* (1942), *South of Santa Fe* (1942), *Heart of the Golden West* (1942), *Sons of the Pioneers* (1942), *Idaho* (1943), *Man from Music Mountain* (aka *Texas Legionaires*, 1943), *The Yellow Rose of Texas* (1944), *Song of Nevada* (1944), *The Man from Oklahoma* (1945), *Roll On Texas Moon* (1946), *Grand Canyon Trail* (1948), *Heart of the Rockies* (1951), and *Pals of the Golden West* (1951). Beyond serving as any horse would, he did nothing out of the ordinary to affect the plot of a movie. In *Young Bill Hickok*, Trigger was never referred to by name, only as Rogers' horse. In *Sunset Serenade* (1942) Trigger functioned for the most part as transportation; however, during the climax of the film, Rogers tied a rope to Trigger's saddle horn, then lowered himself into a deep canyon to rescue an injured man. Rogers hoisted the man onto his back and whistled to Trigger. The palomino started backing up, helping Rogers walk back up the steep incline with the injured man in tow. Later, Rogers would film a very similar scene for *Silver Spurs*.

Caught on film in the 1939 movie *In Old Caliente* in a very rare scenario, the always surefooted Trigger tripped while he and Rogers were fleeing from a gang of outlaws.

Although Trigger was considered a one-man horse, many rode the famous palomino in Roy Rogers' movies: Gabby Hayes in *Robin Hood of the Pecos*, Lane Chandler in *Come On, Rangers*, Gale Storm in *Red River Valley*, Bob Nolan in *Utah*, Adele Mara in *Night Time in Nevada*, Raymond Hatton in *Frontier Pony Express*, Gordon Jones in *Trigger, Jr.*, Jane Frazee in *On the Old Spanish Trail*, Jack Rockwell in *Shine On Harvest Moon*, and Buzzy Henry in

Ridin' Down the Canyon (Rogers rides Daisy, Pat Brady's horse with the wide blaze). Even villains got to ride the palomino: Frank McDonald in *The Carson City Kid* and Bradley Page in *Sons of the Pioneers*. Dale Evans rode Trigger in three movies: *Rainbow Over Texas*, *Bells of San Angelo* and *Bells of Colorado*. She rode Little Trigger in *The Golden Stallion*. Bob Hope rode Little Trigger in *Son of Paleface*. Publicity shots exist of Roy Rogers, Bob Hope, and Jane Russell riding triple on Little Trigger. Sidekick Pat Brady and the young John Meek both ride Trigger in the television episode titled *Fighting Sire*. Don "Red" Barry rode double with Rogers on Trigger as they escaped a posse in *Days of Jesse James* and Rand Brooks rode double twice with Rogers on Trigger in *Heart of the Rockies*.

Trigger Cameo Appearances

Like Rogers, Trigger made cameo appearances as himself in other movies: *Hollywood Canteen* (Warner Bros., 1944), *Out California Way* (Republic, 1946), *Hit Parade of 1947* (Republic, 1947), and *Melody Time* (RKO Radio Pictures, 1948).[26]

Rogers and Little Trigger delivered a short and flawless cameo performance in *The Hollywood Canteen*. The sequence opened with the Sons of the Pioneers singing Bob Nolan's immortal "Tumbling Tumbleweeds." Next, Rogers entered the hall which was filled with G.I.s, a bevy of young ladies and dozens of motion picture celebrities (comedian Joe E. Brown [*Shut My Big Mouth*] and actress Betty Davis [*Juarez*] appeared in a movie with "Trigger" a second time). The crowd parted as the cowboy and the horse entered. Little Trigger reared up in the middle of the dance floor; then Rogers dismounted. He introduced the palomino who, took a bow, then blew a kiss to the crowd. When the Sons of the Pioneers started to play Cole Porter's classic "Don't Fence Me In," Rogers handed Little Trigger over to Tim Spencer and joined the Pioneers on stage and sang a couple of verses. When he got to the "on my cayuse" line, he turned towards Little Trigger and smiled. One can see the pride on Rogers' face as he serenades his palomino. As the instrumental break began, Rogers handed his guitar to Spencer and quickly mounted Little Trigger again. They went into a dance routine as the song played out. Right before they left the room, Little Trigger reared up. The entire sequence lasts about five minutes. One is amazed by how easily it all went down. Rogers was as smooth fronting a band as he was on horseback. Little Trigger wasn't even wearing rubber boots!

In the Monte Hale picture *Out California Way*, Rogers, Dale Evans and Trigger made a cameo appearance as themselves. Roger and Evans sang "Ridin' Down the Sunset Trail." Evans rode a jet-black horse during the sequence — not a good complement to Trigger's golden color or Evans' image.

In *Hit Parade of 1947* "Trigger" shared a scene with Roy Rogers, the Sons of the Pioneers, and star Eddie Albert who was giving friends a tour of Hyperion Studios. Rogers and company sang "Out California Way" while Little Trigger stood behind them, all decked out in his fancy show tack. Minutes later actor Gil Lamb shared a solo scene with the original Trigger. Lamb exclaimed, "What a horse! What a horse! Trigger, you look like a two year old! How old are you?" Trigger counted by pawing on the ground, to which Lamb replied, "Look, a talking horse!"

In the "Pecos Bill" sequence of *Melody Time*, the original Trigger stood calmly next to a campfire and added so much ambience with his beauty and regal countenance. Roy Rogers and the Sons of the Pioneers recounted in song the ballad of Pecos Bill, animated brilliantly

Trigger (and a rider believed by serious fans to be Roy Rogers) in a sequence from the Spade Cooley B-western *The Kid from Gower Gulch* (Friedgen/Aster, 1950) *(Roy Dillow collection)*

by the Walt Disney studios. Trigger even got screen credit and added his two cents by neighing, reminding Rogers about Pecos Bill's horse, Widow Maker, another palomino with a white blaze.

Roy Rogers expert Roy Dillow found Trigger in a secret cameo appearance in a very obscure B-western titled *The Kid from Gower Gulch* (Friedgen/Aster, 1950). Director Oliver Drake filmed the minor musical on a shoestring budget at his own ranch near Pearblossom, California. The star of the movie was one of the "Kings of Western Swing," Spade Cooley. Dillow claims the original Trigger was used in a long chase sequence midway through the film. Freezing the DVD frame by frame, it's impossible to see the blaze clearly; there's simply too much motion blur. However, the palomino in question bears a striking resemblance to the original Trigger, and Larry Roe, another serious Roy Rogers fan, supports Dillow's view.

Dillow further claims that Roy Rogers actually did some of the riding in the chase sequence. Despite the rider's attempt to look like an amateur, the riding style was classic Roy Rogers. Larry Roe stated, "There was no one who ad-libbed on a horse like Rogers, the way he looked back, the way he moved from side to side of Trigger's head and neck. Running inserts were Rogers' forte, no one did them better. There wasn't a horse in the world who looked as good running full out as the original Trigger, the way he held his head back and close to his neck."

The Kid from Gower Gulch was produced by Raymond Friedgen in 1947 and released in 1950. As has already been established, Roy Rogers made the final payments on Trigger in 1943. The question becomes, why would he loan a major asset like Trigger to a professional bandleader making an obscure budget western? Rogers and Spade Cooley were friends and worked together on occasion. *The Kid from Gower Gulch* was as low budget a movie as was ever produced and it's possible that Rogers, still under contract to Republic Pictures, may have loaned his horse and even his own services simply as a favor for a friend.

Jamboree is described as a pleasant, high-gloss rock and roll musical about two singing hopefuls trying to succeed in show business. It includes musical interludes throughout by such talents as Fats Domino, Jerry Lee Lewis, Carl Perkins, Connie Francis, Frankie Avalon, and Roy Rogers and "Trigger." Directed by Roy Lockwood for Warner Bros., it was released in 1957 with a running time of 86 minutes.

In 1976 Paul Heller and Fred Weintraub produced an 86-minute color documentary for United Artists titled *It's Showtime.* The tagline on posters was, "Not all the great movie stars were people. Some of the greatest stars were animals!" Animal movie stars were the focus. Among the performances were those of Asta, the dog from *The Thin Man* series, and Cheetah, the chimpanzee from the Tarzan movies. Little Trigger was in a great company, which included Champion, Silver, Tony, and Topper. The dogs featured included Lassie, Rin Tin Tin, and Pete (Little Rascals). Even Flipper the dolphin and Francis the talking mule were showcased.

Trigger's Movie Reviews

Trigger always fared well with the critics as one can see in quotes from reviews:

Trigger, Jr.: "Trigger and Trigger Jr. display their fine training in amazingly good performances." *The Hollywood Reporter*, 6/29/50.

Under California Stars: "Golden palomino, incidentally, shows up beautifully in Trucolor." "... the shots of Trigger in full pursuit of a mare and of his fights with the men who are trying to pacify him are quite exciting." "... the device of giving Trigger, a truly gifted and photogenic horse, considerably more to do than in the past, will bring this film home the same winner as the others in the series." *Variety*, 5/6/48.

Son of Paleface: "Parody often makes for strange bedfellows but whoever thought of putting Bob Hope in the sack with Roy Rogers' famed mount Trigger deserves the iconoclasm award of 1952! In a thorough milking of the Hollywood western, Trigger has all the finest anthropomorphized attributes — like brains — while our boy Roy appears as a wooden figure of a sheriff ..." *Pacific Film Archive*, 9/87.

The Golden Stallion: "Trigger shines as his master's co-star with every trick in the book." "... members of the cast are all excellent, but it is Trigger and the other four-footed actors who steal many of the honors." *The Hollywood Reporter*, 10/25/49.

B-western cowboys were honored during the 1999 Oscar awards broadcast. The deaths the year before of Roy Rogers and Gene Autry were the catalysts for an acknowledgment, and it was long overdue. The movie industry owed a great deal to western movies as the lowly B-western made significant contributions, especially with respect to action sequences and stunts. The Roy Rogers song "Cowboy Heaven" was played over film clips of those who were mentioned in its lyrics. Actor Val Kilmer was on hand with a Trigger look-alike to introduce the song. Unlike Rogers, who made many public appearances mounted on Trigger in front of huge crowds, the broadcast producers probably insisted Kilmer not ride the animal on stage.

The palomino Val Kilmer was paired with was meant as a symbol for the B-western. A Trigger look-alike was the obvious first choice.

Palomino Pal of Mine

Much of Roy Rogers' appeal was musical. Along with the Sons of the Pioneers and the Riders of the Purple Sage, he left a legacy of great western songs, and he acknowledged Trigger in quite a few. Rogers recorded "A Lonely Ranger Am I" in 1938 for ARC.[27] He mentioned Trigger in the tune, possibly for the first time in any song. An accomplished singer and yodeler, Rogers also tried his hand at composing and came up with a few pretty nice songs, notably "My Saddle Pals and I," "I've Sold My Saddle for an Old Guitar" (with Fleming Allan), "Heldorado," "The Man in the Moon Is a Cowhand," "My Heart Went That-a-way" (with Dale Evans), and "May the Good Lord Take a Likin' to You" (with Peter Tinturin). He never wrote anything on a par with fellow Pioneer Bob Nolan, such as "Cool Water," "Cowboy," "When Payday Rolls Around," or the immortal "Tumbling Tumbleweeds." Dale Evans eclipsed Rogers as a songwriter when she came up with "Happy Trails." That one song guaranteed her a place in western music history. Ironically it was Evans, not Rogers, who wrote a song about Trigger: "Don't Ever Fall in Love with a Cowboy" (*Happy Trails: The Roy Rogers Collection* [1937–1990], Rhino Entertainment Company, 1999). With tongue in cheek, Evans dealt with Trigger being higher on the pecking order than she, both on movie posters and in her husband's heart. Ironically, it was released around the time they announced their engagement to be married.

When Rogers made a cameo appearance in *Hollywood Canteen*, he sang "Don't Fence Me In" and at the end of the tune mentioned his palomino by name. He did the same in "Four-Legged Friend" (Jack "That's Amore" Brooks and Lyn Murray) from *Son of Paleface* (Paramount, 1952). (Little Trigger was at his peak as he danced to the tune in an early sequence). Found on *Roy Rogers and the Sons of the Pioneers: King of the Cowboys* (Bear Family Records; RCA, 1983) and *Happy Trails: The Roy Rogers Collection* (1937–1990) (Rhino Entertainment Company, 1999), the tune was a hit for Rogers in England.

Rogers also shouted "Whoa, Trigger" during the long "Lore of the West" title track number he did with Gabby Hayes. Dale Evans got into the act by mentioning her horse, Buttermilk, twice on the track "Texas for Me" from the same compilation (*Lore of the West* released on CD in 1996 by ESX Entertainment, Inc.).

Roy Rogers had a minor hit on the ARC label titled "Hi Yo Silver." In June of 1938 it reached number 13 on the popular charts. "Hi Yo Silver" was a tribute to the Lone Ranger's gallant mount, of course. The Lone Ranger was never mentioned by name in the song, and Tonto makes only a brief appearance in the last verse. "Hi Yo Silver" was credited to De Leath and Erickson as co-writers and may be found on a recording titled *Roy Rogers: King of the Cowboys* (Living Era; ASV Ltd.; England, 1998).

Trigger was mentioned in "Who Taught You Everything?" (Ghost Town, RR 181) and in the tune "Singing Down the Road" by Charles Tobias and Raymond Scott from *Bells of Rosarita* (1945).

Ironically, Rogers did not mention Trigger in any of the songs in *My Pal Trigger* (1946), but he sang the classic "Ole Faithful" by Michael Carr and Hamilton Kennedy to Trigger's movie mother, Lady.

Bob Nolan never lent his skills as a songsmith to writing a tune about Trigger, but his fellow Pioneer Tim Spencer composed "Trigger Hasn't Got a Purty Figure" for the film *The Lights of Old Santa Fe* (1947). Rogers sang it to Dale Evans, hoping to coax her into riding double.

Oddly enough, a song perfectly suited for Trigger, "That Palomino Pal of Mine," was not performed by Roy Rogers in any of his movies. The Kingsley and Kenwood song was recorded by Rogers for RCA Victor on December 1, 1947. It is available on a CD, *Lore of the West* (released on CD in 1996 by ESX Entertainment, Inc.). It is also found on *The Best of Roy Rogers* LP (RCA Camden).

There are two different songs with similar titles. The first, "Palamino Pal of Mine" (Fleming Allan/Dick Foran) is from *Dick Foran's Song Folio No. 1: 20 Original West Songs* (Cross Music, 1943). Foran's publisher spelled it as "palamino." The song makes a reference to Smoke, the horse Foran rode in his westerns. Circa 1950 Wilf Carter (Montana Slim) recorded "Palomino Pal of Mine" (Canadian Victor). At about the same time Eddie Dean recorded the song on Standard Transcriptions. Dean rode a palomino named White Cloud and a sorrel named Copper in his films.

The title track from the *Golden Stallion* movie of 1949, with ethereal lyrics written by Foy Willing and Sid Robin, was about Trigger and tailor-made to promote him as a magical animal. Trigger was also mentioned in the tune from the same movie titled "Night on the Prairie" by Nathan Gluck and Anne Parentean.

In the song "Roy Rogers, King of the Cowboys" by Jack Elliot from *Under California Stars* (1948), Andy Devine sang a line that referred to Trigger. In a later sequence, Rogers tucked young Michael Chapin into bed with a lullaby titled "Little Saddle Pal" (Jack Elliot), which also referred to his golden palomino.

Spade Cooley added a sweet violin during the original recording session for "Make Believe Cowboy" (Carroll Lucas), a lullaby for Rogers' son Dusty. (78 rpm recording reissued on *Roy Rogers: King of the Cowboys*, Living Era; ASV LTD; 1998). Roger referenced his horse in the last verse.

The closest Rogers ever got to singing a song about Trigger Jr. was when he recorded "Tennessee Stud" (*Happy Trails to You: Roy Rogers*, 20th Century Records; 1973). The tune was, in all likelihood, chosen on its own merits, but it's safe to assume that Rogers must have been pleased by the coincidence, as Trigger Jr. was a Tennessee walker stallion.

Even British rocker Elton John honored Trigger in song. "Roy Rogers" was a tune he and songwriting partner Bernie Taupin wrote for the album *Goodbye Yellow Brick Road* (Polydor, 1973).

Trigger was mentioned in the "Cowboy Heaven" track written by singing cowboy Eddie Dean and his partner Hal Sothern (*Happy Trails to You*, LP; 20th Century Fox, 1975; Nostalgia Merchant Records).

Rogers wasn't going to complete the *Roy Rogers Tribute* CD without mentioning Trigger. He did so in the autobiographical tune titled "Alive and Kickin'" (RCA, 1991; also featured on the *Happy Trails: The Roy Rogers Collection* (1937–1990) (Rhino Entertainment Company, 1999).

Rogers' son Roy "Dusty" Rogers Jr. contributed the song "King of the Cowboys" (Roy Rogers Jr. and Larry Carney) to the *Roy Rogers Tribute* CD (BMG Music, 1991). Trigger was acknowledged in the line that refers to a golden palomino.

Rex Allen, Jr. mentioned Roy Rogers and Trigger in his own composition, "Last of the Silverscreen Cowboys," from his 1995 album *Singing Cowboys*.

In the comedy track "A Letter to Roy" by J. Nunnally and G. Nunnally (*Roy Rogers: A Musical Anthology*, A&E — Biography; 1998; Capitol Records Inc.), Rogers read a letter from a fan with questionable motives and a loose grasp of the facts. Trigger wasn't mentioned, but his main equine rival, Champion, was.

Country star Lyle Lovett tipped his hat to Trigger in the tune "If I Had a Boat" (*Live in Texas*, MCA, 1999 and *Anthology, Vol. 1: Cowboy Man*, MCA/ Nashville, 2001).

Roy Rogers wisely mentioned Trigger in song whenever there was an opportunity *(Roy Dillow collection).*

Roy Rogers and Dale Evans were also radio celebrities, of course. Sixty-five half-hour episodes were packaged onto an audio CD in 2004. Along with musical numbers, short dramatic stories were featured. In these "Trigger "was played by a number of anonymous sound technicians to full effect. One episode was titled "Trigger Has Been Stolen."

7

Trigger on Television

"In a barn on my Double R Bar Ranch in California is a horse named Trigger. He is my pride and joy and to a great extent shares all the success I have had in show business." — Roy Rogers[1]

The Roy Rogers Show

By 1945 Roy Rogers' best movies were behind him and the change was dramatic. The Sons of the Pioneers, who usually numbered around six members, were replaced by the Riders of the Purple Sage, who numbered four.[2] Great sidekicks such as Gabby Hayes, Smiley Burnette, and Raymond Hatton had been replaced by the sometimes irritating Gordon Jones, Pat Brady, and possibly the worst of all, Pinky Lee. The only sidekick Rogers teamed with in his later films worthy of Hayes and Burnette was Andy Devine. The Trucolor film process that Republic used in later Roy Rogers movies didn't help much; it looked dull and artificial. B-westerns began to wind down as budgets and fan interest started to wane. Hopalong Cassidy and Gene Autry made moves into television in 1949 and 1950 respectively. In 1951, Roy Rogers followed.

The Roy Rogers Show was produced by Rogers' own Frontier Productions, Inc. It was set on the Double R Bar ranch in Paradise Valley, not far from Mineral City, where Dale Evans owned the Eureka Cafe. The 30-minute, black-and-white show aired initially on Sunday evenings on NBC from 1951 to 1957. Between 1958 and 1961 it was syndicated on mostly NBC affiliate stations on Saturday mornings. Reruns were broadcast on CBS on Saturday mornings from 1961 until 1964.

The two main assets Rogers took with him when he made the move to television were his wife and his horse. Even with Dale and Trigger on board, however, his small screen adventures paled in comparison to those on the big screen. Unlike Autry, who understood that his television episodes were smaller versions of his movie features and spent money accordingly, Rogers and company worked within such tight budgets that only his charisma sustained them.

It is worth nothing, however, that the day of the movie Western was waning and that television Westerns, regardless of budget, lacked the punch and pizzazz of their film predecessors. Autry spent more money than Rogers, and consequently Autry's television episodes were better produced in every way, but they still had the feel of dinner theatre productions with small ensemble casts and sparse settings. That is to say, they were on a par with Autry's movies of the same time period. Even action sequences, once a Republic trademark, started to look generic. Running inserts, in particular, were not as exciting on television.

Roy Rogers on Trigger and Dale Evans riding Buttermilk. This formal portrait was taken during the height of their popularity on television. Evans had ridden both pintos and palominos before settling on this light buckskin — clearly a good choice and a fine complement to Trigger with his golden coat.

Nevertheless, broadcast on a weekly basis in the 1950s and coupled with the novelty of the new medium of television, the television Western succeeded. Today, watching daily reruns on Western movie cable channels, one can see that B-western television shows were extremely formulaic — but at the time, the formula worked. In all fairness, they were never meant to be seen back to back and it's unfair to subject them to a great deal of scrutiny. And in spite of everything, there were magic moments, though admittedly few and far between.

The greatest casualty of *The Roy Rogers Show* on television was "Trigger" himself. He was already so well established in the hearts and minds of fans (a television short titled *Trigger Tricks* was already in production) that the King of the Cowboys seems to have decided to focus more attention on his German shepherd, Bullet, and sidekick Pat Brady's jeep, Nellybelle. Bullet's importance may have had a little to do with the presence of *The Adventures of Rin Tin Tin* and *Lassie* television shows, which both came along in 1954. "Trigger" didn't get nearly the attention that he received in movies. Although he got second billing on *The Roy Rogers Show,* he was used primarily as transportation and ambience.

Synopses of every episode of *The Roy Rogers Show* are available in *The Roy Rogers Book* by David Rothel and *Roy Rogers, King of the Cowboys: A Film Guide* by Bob Carman and Dan Scapperotti. One may conclude from these two sources that none of the shows were built

The original Trigger taking it easy with his German shepherd pal, Bullet *(Larry Roe collection)*.

around "Trigger," and only a few ever featured him in any special way. Conversely, Gene Autry produced two of his television show episodes around his horse, Champion: "Six-Shooter Sweepstakes" and "Horse Sense." It's odd Rogers did not do the same for "Trigger." It may have been that the tighter budgets did not allow "Trigger" to have as many special scenes as he did in Rogers' movies. Scenes where animals perform special routines require more time to rehearse and shoot. Time, especially on television, is money. At any rate, "Trigger" was not allowed to be quite the magic horse on television that he was on movie screens. (And

Corky Randall, rather than his father, worked on *The Roy Rogers Show* under Hudkins wranglers Johnny Brim and Buddy Sherwood.)

When it came to television, Gene Autry's sorrel "Champion" was clearly ahead of "Trigger." A spin-off series from *The Gene Autry Show*, *The Adventures of Champion*, was a natural manifestation of the horse's popularity with fans. Produced by Gene Autry, 26 episodes ran from 1955 to 1956.

Meanwhile back on *The Roy Rogers Show*, "Trigger" did the best he could. Some episodes, like "Ghost Town Gold," open with Rogers on Little Trigger rearing up in front of the Double R Bar ranch sign. Rogers says, "Well riders, Trigger here is raring to go, so let's get started with today's story."[3] In a later sequence "Trigger" comes to Rogers's aid after he's roped by bad guy Marshal Reed. Little Trigger attacks Reed before he can drag Rogers down the road with his own horse. The sequence lasts only a few moments, with many cuts. Little Trigger and the original Trigger are switched from shot to shot.

In "Bullet for a Burro," one of the first of the television episodes, Rogers has almost come to a complete circle in his career. One of his first sidekicks, Raymond Hatton, is featured as an old prospector. "Trigger" and Bullet help Rogers escape jail. He whistles for his four-legged companions from inside his cell. They run to the back of the jail house. Bullet gets Rogers' rope off "Trigger's" saddle and takes it to his master. Rogers lassoes the horn on "Trigger's" saddle and ties the other end to the jail bars. He cues "Trigger" to pull, the bars give way and Rogers is freed.

"The Phantom Rustlers" is one of the most interesting television show episodes, thanks to Little Trigger. It opens with Rogers putting the palomino through a routine of tricks including lying down on his side and sitting down. Later, Rogers is shot as he's riding down a dirt road. Because he's too weak to get up, he cues Little Trigger to lie down beside him. Rogers slides over the saddle, and the horse rises back up and carries him back to his ranch.

Although Bullet had already appeared in a few of Roy Rogers' movies, it was on the television show that he really blossomed. In many episodes, Bullet either attacked a villain or tracked him down. Rogers even used a motorboat instead of "Trigger" during a chase sequence in "Mountain Pirates" (11/56).

It stands to reason Rogers would use what he had available to fill out story lines since he was producing his shows. Why not use things he wouldn't have to rent? Rogers may have also wanted to get Bullet and Nellybelle established with youngsters the way "Trigger" was, in order to add to their merchandising potential.

Trigger Jr. appeared in a commercial with Rogers for the chocolate drink Nestle's Quik, aired during *The Roy Rogers Show*. The palomino, in a red, white, and blue show saddle and matching bridle, did a short dance and bow.

Trigger Tricks

Just as Dale Evans filmed a pilot for a television series, *Dale Evans, Queen of the West*, "Trigger" was up for his own show as well. It was to be sponsored by Quaker Oats and titled *Trigger Tricks*. It seems to have been planned as a 15-minute show, common in the early days of television, to showcase "Trigger's" famous rodeo and personal appearance stunts. Perhaps it was because *Trigger Tricks* was in the works that special scenes with the palomino were not deemed necessary on *Roy Rogers Show* episodes.

Trigger Tricks may have also been an attempt by Rogers to establish a presence on television pending the outcome of a lawsuit with Republic Pictures at the time. If nothing else, it would have given him a chance to develop a relationship with a sponsor pending the start of his own television series.

Rogers was suing Republic Pictures to keep his movies off the air. He wanted a television show like Hopalong Cassidy's and Gene Autry's, but he couldn't get any sponsors. Republic didn't want a show that would compete against Rogers' old movies, which they were planning to syndicate on television. *Trigger Tricks* and the pilot for the Dale Evans television show (with Pat Brady as the comic relief) were ready to go if Republic had won the lawsuit. After Republic lost, "Trigger's" and Dale Evans' shows were scrapped. *The Roy Rogers Show* was put on the air quickly that same year, in the event that Republic might win on appeal. After about two years the appeal was successful, but that was enough time for *The Roy Rogers Show* to become well established.

It is unknown if the *Trigger Tricks* shows were actually aired. Allegedly a handful were made. They were mentioned in the Roy Rogers rodeo souvenir programs of the time: "'Trigger' made his debut on television in a series sponsored by Quaker Oats titled *Trigger Tricks* which shows all of his famous rodeo and personal appearance stunts. For once, he easily steals the show from Roy."

Dale Evans Queen of the West

In 1950 Dale Evans filmed a television pilot for the *Dale Evans, Queen of the West* show titled "Slip of the Gun." Pal was the horse she used. Fans got a very good look at the palomino

Formal portrait of Roy Rogers, Trigger, Pal, and Dale Evans. Even with Trigger's forelock in the way, the differences in the palominos' blazes are obvious.

with his three white stockings and unique blaze. Evans even mentioned the horse in the opening song, "Lo De, Lo Di." She rode him in pretty showy tack which included ridiculously large tapaderos.

Pal was used in the Dale Evans pilot just as Trigger and Little Trigger had been used in Rogers' movies before. At one point, while exchanging gunfire with a gang of thugs, Evans ducked behind Pal and used him as a shield as she rode off. As Evans was being pursued she dismounted and cued Pal to lie down and hide with her in some tall grass as the bad guys rode past.

There are also some beautiful shots of the palomino double California substituting for Pal in *Dale Evans, Queen of the West*. During one sequence where two bad guys were waiting for Evans, her horse acted up as a way of warning her; it was California she was riding.[4]

Miscellaneous Trigger Television Appearances

Beyond his appearances on *The Roy Rogers Show*, the original Trigger rarely if ever appeared on television. He was retired in 1957 at age 23 to Rogers' ranch in Chatsworth, California. Little Trigger and Trigger Jr. usually doubled for him on the small screen.

Over the course of their careers, Roy Rogers and Dale Evans made a number of guest appearances together and solo on television. In October of 1950 they appeared with "Trigger" and even Bullet on *The Gabby Hayes Show* on NBC. Rogers and Evans even hosted their own variety hours; some were taped performances at rodeo and fairs. It's regrettable the original Trigger was not on any of these shows.

Before *The Roy Rogers Show* premiered on NBC television on December 30, 1951, an introductory half-hour special with Bob Hope, Dale Evans, the Whippoorwills, Pat Brady, and "Trigger" was aired to promote the movie *Son of Paleface* (Paramount, 1952). NBC and Post Cereals aired the special and first episode in December of 1951 live from the El Capitan theater in downtown Hollywood. Little Trigger was showcased on the television special in a sequence playing cards around a table with Hope, Roy Rogers, and trainer Glenn Randall. Little Trigger's cards were held up on a wire stand. Said Rogers, "We did a sketch in which Bob, I, and Trigger were all supposed to be playing poker together. When Trigger spots Bob trying to pull an ace from his sleeve, he knocks over the table with his nose and pushes him offstage."[5] "Trigger" also appeared with Roy Rogers and Dale Evans on *The Bob Hope Show* in February of 1955.

Beyond their weekly adventure show, Rogers and Evans starred in a number of *Roy Rogers Rodeo* appearances. In an October 1948 show the King of the Cowboys appeared with the Roy Rogers' Liberty Horses act. In 1955 the *Roy Rogers Rodeo: TV Special* was broadcast from the San Antonio, Texas, Coliseum. The one-hour show featured "Trigger" and Trigger Jr.

In the fall of 1960 Roy Rogers and Dale Evans hosted the *Grand National Championship Rodeo* from the San Francisco Cow Palace. The show was broadcast on their *Chevy Show* on NBC. "Trigger's" trainer, Glenn Randall, was one of the guests. It was during one of these broadcasts that "Trigger" was officially retired at a rodeo performance. Trigger Jr. was present and introduced as the original Trigger's replacement. Little Trigger stood in for the original Trigger.

"Trigger" appeared with Roy Rogers and Dale Evans in the winter of 1961 at the Championship Rodeo at San Antonio, Texas. The program was also broadcast on the *Chevy Show*.

The original Trigger does not seem to have appeared in the televised *Roy Rogers and Dale*

Evans Show variety hour produced by ABC in 1962. "Trigger" appeared with Rogers and Dale Evans on the *Hollywood Palace* show on ABC in February of 1964 and February of 1965.

Little Trigger stood in for Trigger on the *This Is Your Life* episode dedicated to Roy Rogers in 1953. The program was hosted by Ralph Edwards, who introduced the palomino by saying, "No show on Roy Rogers would be complete without Trigger. We can't forget Trigger. We couldn't tell the story of your life without Trigger sharing the spotlight.... Trigger, thank you for the part you played in Roy's life." The palomino appeared from behind a curtain and gave Rogers a kiss before being led off stage.

Roy Rogers, Dale Evans, and Trigger Jr. appeared on *The Perry Como Show* in 1956. Trigger Jr., doubling for Trigger, got a good deal of screen time on the variety hour. Roy Rogers, Trigger Jr., and even Glenn Randall first appeared among the studio audience. Como called Rogers and Trigger Jr. on stage, where he asked the cowboy to introduce him to his horse. What followed was a little routine where Como offered the palomino a lump of sugar. One gets a close look at the animal in this sequence and can see that he is immaculately groomed. Rogers effortlessly did a step mount onto Trigger Jr. and cued him to extend his front leg to Como as a parting gesture. Later Trigger Jr. was featured in a western setting. Como, a former barber, offered to trim the palomino's forelock, but Rogers objected. In a closing sequence, Rogers brought the palomino out and performed a short dance routine. If anything the appearance demonstrated how ably Trigger Jr. filled in for his legendary predecessor. Not only was he well trained, but he was beautiful.

Roy Rogers and Dale Evans also rode in a number of parades across the country, many of which were televised, including the Tournament of Roses Parade held on New Year's Day in Pasadena (in 1977, they were selected as grand marshals). When they weren't riding Little Trigger, Pal, or Buttermilk, they rode on elaborate floats.

Actor John Ritter hosted a documentary salute to B-western cowboys titled *The Singing Cowboys Ride Again* which aired in October 1979 on HBO. "Trigger" and "Champion" were featured in clips from their movies. Also the same year, Rogers discussed Trigger on *The Phil Donahue Show*.

In 1982 on *The John Davidson Show* Roy Rogers talked about Trigger, and Dale Evans added anecdotes about her days at Republic Pictures trying to improve her horseback riding skills. Also in 1982, *The Merv Griffin Show* (NBC) was taped at record producer Snuff Garrett's ranch. Griffin devoted the entire show to B-westerns and interviewed Gene Autry, Rex Allen, Yakima Canutt, and Roy Rogers. The King of the Cowboys told Griffin that he first started teaching Trigger tricks but later hired Glenn Randall.

Sometime in 1989 or 1990, Roy Rogers and Dale Evans appeared on *The Pat Sajak Show* (CBS). Sajak asked a few questions about Trigger, which Rogers dealt with in the same fashion he did in countless interviews. He said Trigger was four when he first worked with him in *Under Western Stars*. When Sajak asked Rogers what he thought of current western movies, the King of the Cowboys responded as he had so many times before, saying there were some he wouldn't even let Trigger watch.

In 1994 on *The Late Late Show with Tom Snyder* (NBC), Roy Rogers and Dale Evans talked about Trigger and Buttermilk.

A nine-minute segment on Trigger for the *Horseworld* television show was broadcast circa 1995 and included a visit to the Roy Rogers and Dale Evans Museum in Victorville. It was hosted by champion rodeo rider Larry Mahan, who interviewed Rogers.

Roy Rogers' horse Trigger was featured on the Outdoor Life Channel program *Complete Rider*. The segment lasted about five minutes and began with a brief biography. Dusty Rogers

Jr. spoke about how his dad was hoping to find an equine partner with a more interesting color than black, bay, or white when he began at Republic Pictures.

Towards the end of his career, Rogers rode a palomino (in a standard western stock saddle) in a Randy Travis 60-minute television special for the Nashville Network (TNN) titled *Randy Travis — Happy Trails* (1990). Rogers made a dramatic entrance riding in at a full gallop. He accounted for himself pretty well considering his advanced age. As he slowed down and dismounted, he was holding on to the saddle horn, something he never did in his films or television shows.

Roy Rogers and "Trigger" first appeared on the television show *The Fall Guy* in January of 1983 in an episode titled "Happy Trails." The last appearance of "Trigger" on television occurred on *The Fall Guy* in 1984 in episode #65, titled "King of the Cowboys." Rogers and former television cowboy stars John Russell (*Lawman*), Peter Breck (*The Big Valley*), and Jock Mahoney (*Range Rider*) join series star Lee Majors and Roy "Dusty" Rogers Jr. to track a gang of diamond smugglers. Rogers rode a gorgeous Trigger look-alike for the occasion. The closing shot of the episode is of Rogers on "Trigger" riding towards the camera and performing his signature rearing pose.

In March of 1999 actor Val Kilmer appeared on the Academy Awards show with a "Trigger" double to introduce a B-western cowboy tribute commemorating the deaths of Roy Rogers and Gene Autry the previous year. Kilmer at one point referred to the palomino as "Trigger." One source claimed the horse was the grandson of Trigger Jr.[6]

The History Channel program *America's Lost and Found* featured a short segment on Trigger, following his life and career all the way up to when he was mounted and put on display at the Roy Rogers and Dale Evans Museum in Victorville.

In January of 2005 the Animal Planet cable show presented a two-hour program on the 50 greatest animal stars. Trigger was 39th on the list. Toto from *The Wizard of Oz* (MGM, 1939) was number one. This was obviously more an acknowledgment of the movie than the animal. When one accounts for the countless performances on film by Rin Tin Tin, Lassie, Rex, etc, Toto is pretty small potatoes in comparison.

In 2005, Trigger was mentioned in the "Taxidermy" episode of the History Channel's weekly program *Modern Marvels*.

Trigger Documentaries and Cameos

When Roy Rogers was the subject of documentaries, "Trigger" was mentioned, of course. However, unfortunately, he was discussed in the same way he had always been, in public relations terms. No mention was made of Little Trigger, and palomino doubles were acknowledged only in passing. Three documentaries of note are *A&E Biography Roy Rogers* (2001) and *Roy Rogers: King of the Cowboys* (Republic/AMC/Galen Films, 1992). The AMC network also produced a fabulous documentary titled *The Republic Pictures Story* in 1990 featuring interviews with Rogers.

Cowboys of the Saturday Matinee, a 76-minute documentary on "Hollywood legends of the old west," was produced in 1984. It was produced and written by Ken Shapiro, directed by Jerry Kramer, and narrated by James Coburn. Referring to Roy Rogers, Coburn states, "He was the King of the Cowboys. Now I don't know who named him that, but it was probably Trigger. After all, he was the smartest horse in the movies."

In 1992 Thys Ockersen, a fan from Holland, wrote and directed a documentary titled

Roy Rogers: King of the Cowboys. It was released through Scorpio Film Productions Ltd., Nos Television, Holland. Ockersen had incredible access to the Rogers family and the Republic movie archive. *Roy Rogers: King of the Cowboys* begins with an interview of Mindy Peterson, the granddaughter of Dale Evans from a previous marriage. As it happened she was living in Amsterdam in 1981 and working with the International Mission Organization. She told Ockersen about how she and her siblings often went out to the Rogers ranch and rode Trigger and Buttermilk. She recalled one instance when she was riding Trigger and inadvertently miscued him to rear up on his hind legs. Her grandfather rescued her from the predicament.

Certainly the most moving segment in Ockersen's documentary occurred while he was interviewing former Republic director William Witney. Witney talked about the stunts Trigger, "the Old Man," would do on movie sets that professional stunt horses would not. In the film *Far Frontier* barrels were thrown from a truck, Trigger narrowly avoids them without fear.

Witney got very emotional when he reminisced about the last time he saw the original Trigger. Witney happened to be directing an episode of the old *Sky King* (NBC, 1951—1962) television show near Roy Rogers' ranch in Chatsworth. During a lunch break he drove over to see the palomino, whose eyesight was failing. As he approached the stall, he called out. Trigger's ears perked up and he moved towards the director. Witney's eyes started to tear up as he described the aged palomino. That was the last time he saw the horse alive. One can see why Witney devoted a book to the horse; he was clearly very attached to him.

The Witney interview is the high point of the Ockersen documentary. For all the access he had, Ockersen asked the same tired questions that had been asked before. Rogers, Dale Evans, and Dusty Rogers gave the same generic responses they'd given time and time again. Nothing new was revealed. However, because it is one of the last glimpses into Roy Rogers' world during the final years of his life, the Ockersen documentary is worth viewing. There's even a sequence at the Roy Rogers celebration in Portsmouth and a visit to Rogers' boyhood home.

The History Channel presented a two-hour documentary on western movies titled *When Cowboys Were King* in 2004. Narrated by veteran character actor Eli Wallach, *When Cowboys Were King* not only explored the popularity of Westerns, but examined their impact on American culture. It won a 2004 Golden Boot Award for outstanding contribution to Western movie heritage. *When Cowboys Were King* was produced for the History Channel by Lou Reda Productions. The documentary featured extensive film clips and interviews with such Western film veterans as Tom Selleck, Ernest Borgnine, Stuart Whitman, Peggy Stewart, Rand Brooks, and Morgan Woodward. Even the children of cowboy stars were interviewed: John Ritter, Dusty Rogers, and Cheryl Rogers-Barnett. Trigger and Tom Mix's Tony were the only horses singled out in *When Cowboys Were King*. It was erroneously stated that Republic Studios owned Trigger at the time Rogers insisted on buying him.

William S. Hart's pinto Fritz was the only horse hero mentioned in the 90-minute documentary *Golden Saddles, Silver Spurs: The History of Movie Westerns* (2006), although other four-legged stars were featured, like Tony, Champion, and Trigger.

8

Glenn Randall Magician

"A bus load of fans drove out once to where they were filming an episode and some-body asked Roy, 'To what do you attribute your success?' Roy walked over to Trigger, and he took Glenn Randall's hand, and he said, 'These two right here.' He attributed his success to Trigger and Glenn Randall Sr." — Bill Catching[1]

Roy Rogers had many deep relationships in his life beyond those with his wife and family. Many extended to his celebrity and business life. He was very close to his manager, Art Rush; a few of the men who played his sidekicks (especially Gabby Hayes and Pat Brady); the original Sons of the Pioneers (especially Tim Spencer); and the man who cared for and trained his horses, Glenn Randall. When one studies how Rogers and Randall worked together, it's easy to conclude that their relationship transcended that of client and trainer to that of confidant and mentor. After speaking to Randall's son Corky, it's easy for this writer to conclude that they were almost family. When Corky Randall spoke about Roy Rogers, he said, "He was like a father to me." Cheryl Rogers-Barnett says that her father even lived at the Randall ranch for a while some time around 1947: "He stayed at the home of Glenn Randall, his good friend and Trigger's trainer, which was also practically right around the corner from Republic."[2]

Rogers entrusted Glenn Randall with what could arguably be his most precious celebrity assets, his horses. Both men spent hours together training and traveling all over the United States and parts of Europe.

Not only did Rogers give Randall control over his horses, the two men also shared their stock. Rogers and Dale Evans did not own Trigger look-alike Pal or the palomino Liberty Horse act remuda; these belonged to Randall. Conversely, Roy Rogers owned look-alike California but lent the palomino to Corky Randall during a college rodeo in San Francisco for a calf roping contest.

During the golden age of Hollywood, only movie headliners, and certain people in production working in areas such as special effects, set design, and wardrobe, were given screen credit. There was no screen credit for stuntmen, horse trainers, or wranglers—the people who had the most dangerous jobs. (Today, every crew member's name is in a film's credits, even drivers and caterers.) But, credited or not, great trainers are all-important for animals who spend as much time before the public as Trigger and his doubles. Glenn Randall's contribution to Roy Rogers' and Trigger's public personae was just as important as that of Dale Evans and agent Art Rush. According to Cheryl Rogers-Barnett, her dad was quick to point out that he owed his success to Trigger and his trainer, Glenn Randall.

Before Glenn Randall arrived on the scene, three men are known to have had a hand in

The legendary Glenn Randall poses in front of his rental stable in Newhall, California, circa 1960 (*Joel "Dutch" Dortch collection*).

training the original Trigger. His first owner, Roy Cloud, in all probability started the palomino under saddle when the horse was around two years of age. According to Corky Randall, a trainer named Johnny Goodwin was responsible for finishing horses at Hudkins Stables, and it's safe to assume that Goodwin probably continued Trigger's training, preparing him for work in motion pictures.[3] By the time the palomino was ready to become a cast horse, he was well prepared for work on a movie set. After Rogers started riding Trigger, he hired his first trainer, a cowboy named Jimmy Griffin who brought the palomino up another level and most likely taught him a first repertoire of simple tricks. According to Republic director William Witney, Griffin was not only responsible for care and training of Trigger and Little Trigger, but he transported them wherever necessary.

Jimmy Griffin left Rogers' employ sometime in 1941 to work in the defense industry. According to author David Rothel, Glenn Randall claimed to have started working with Trigger, replacing Jimmy Griffin, the same year. It was Glenn Randall who would work with Roy Rogers' horses for the next 24 years.

Corky Randall does not remember a Jimmy Griffin. According to Corky, Rogers was already in possession of Little Trigger when he started working with Glenn and needed the palomino trained for a forthcoming appearance at Madison Square Garden.

Trainer Glenn Randall allows a young fan on board Little Trigger backstage at a personal appearance *(Roy Dillow collection)*.

Randall's Early Years

Glenn Randall was born on Christmas Day, 1909, in western Nebraska. His family homesteaded in the area around Melbeta, and he grew up farming with his dad's team. He always loved horses and began training them at an early age. The very first horse Randall owned and trained was a little mustang named Rags.

When Randall was only nine years old, he trained and sold a black and white half–Shetland/American Saddlebred paint mare to the Sells-Floto Circus. "My people were horse people," he explained. "I used to go to all the circuses and horse shows and [watch the] stunts, and I'd always see a horse do something and go home and try it on my pony."[4]

In the early 1930s, Randall's first job away from home was breaking horses for the cavalry and artillery. After that he also worked for the mayor of Torrington, Wyoming, training his standardbred trotters and pacers. He also worked for movie cowboy Tim McCoy's Wild West show, handling 250 horses. Randall went on to train remount horses and mules for the cavalry at Ft. Robinson, Nebraska, and worked at the Oregon Trail Days celebrations near Gering. He trained horses for the government at Ft. Warren, Wyoming. Randall eventually left his military job and followed the professional rodeo circuit, where he rode bucking horses and even worked as a rodeo clown.

By the late 1930s, Randall moved to California, where he managed a thoroughbred breeding facility owned by Elmer Houchins outside Bakersfield in Arvin. It was here that Randall branched out and started his own training stable at the Arvin facility. He eventually ran across the Hudkins brothers, who introduced him to the horse and client who would change his life.

Randall Takes Over

Clyde Hudkins, brother to Ace and Art Hudkins, recommended Glenn Randall to Roy Rogers after Jimmy Griffin left. Clyde Hudkins told Rogers of a young man living in Weedpatch, California, who was naturally gifted with equines and who he thought could help with his palominos. According to Corky, Art Hudkins brought Roy Rogers to Bakersfield to meet Glenn Randall. This introduction gave Randall his start in the film industry and began one of the great partnerships in entertainment history.

"When I started working with Trigger," said Randall, "I discovered right away that Roy's claims about the horse sure weren't exaggerated. He was smart, full of action, and hungry to learn. I've worked with horses since I was a boy in Nebraska. But from that morning when I started working with Trigger, I knew he was the savviest horse I'd ever seen."[5]

Randall told Rogers biographer Elise Miller Davis how he wound up touring with Rogers: "About a week before he was scheduled to leave for Baltimore, Roy came up to my place for a sober-faced talk with me. 'Glenn, I'd like you to go on this trip with me,' he said. 'I'd feel better if you'd handle Trigger on the road.' Roy worried about Trigger all the way across country on that first trip. He wouldn't turn in himself until he saw that the horse had been stabled down properly."[6]

During training sessions at Hudkins Stables, Randall worked closely with Rogers. After the singing cowboy purchased Little Trigger, the palomino was moved to the Randall ranch. Randall began to work exclusively for Rogers, training and managing all the "Triggers" that were used on film and in personal appearances. Like Rogers, Randall was captivated by Trigger, and he made sure to stick closely to the horse and to Rogers. In Randall's mind, that might not have constituted being Trigger's "trainer," even though a part of his job, while working at Hudkins, would have included working with Rogers and Trigger part of the time. Not until he went to work exclusively for Rogers, and the singing cowboy was Trigger's owner, would Randall's job title have been Trigger's trainer.[7]

Cheryl Rogers-Barnett claimed that Trigger and all his doubles were trained by Glenn Randall and her dad.[8] Early Roy Rogers publicity maintained that Trigger had been trained by Rogers since the horse was five years of age.[9]

Rogers and Randall did not sign a formal contract; a handshake sealed their association. Rogers knew he needed a dependable and expert trainer to travel with his horse. In all probability one of the first major tasks he and Randall needed to work out was how to appear across the country in varied and unusual venues with "Trigger." "At first, it wasn't easy to find the right kind of quarters in every strange city we pulled into," said Glenn Randall. "It was on Roy's mind a lot in those days." Eventually, said Randall, they knew the "best stables in every city," and Randall booked Trigger's reservations in advance.[10]

Randall's most important assignment was to train "Trigger" to a point where he would secure the tag line "the Smartest Horse in the Movies." Fortunately, "Trigger" was up to the task. Anything a script or show called for, Trigger, Little Trigger, and Randall could handle. Smiling, dancing, you name it: The palominos and their trainer would deliver. Counting

Rogers and Trigger at a personal appearance. Standing behind Trigger and wearing a black hat is trainer Glenn Randall. When Corky Randall was shown this photo, he remarked, "I think this is their first tour. Glenn was staying close to Roy and Trigger, not knowing how each would react [to the crowd]."

(simple addition and subtraction, as well as counting to twenty) was one of their primary routines and used in more publicity stories than any other trick. "Trigger" could sign his name on a sheet of paper by making an X with a pencil. He could drink milk from a bottle. Not only could he rear when asked, but he could also walk 150 feet on his hind legs. All cues for the tricks were from subtle hand motions by Rogers.

Roy Rogers and Little Trigger entertain a group of extras on the set of Paramount Pictures' *Son of Pale-face* (1952).

At one point in time "Trigger" was credited with knowing fifty-two tricks. That number eventually grew to around one hundred, according to a *Western Horseman* article from April 1961. The public relations machine wasted no time reporting "Trigger's" tricks, offering every number imaginable.[11]

One might ask whether Trigger deserves the recognition he has achieved, considering that he gained his reputation on the skills of other horses. It's worthwhile to reiterate, however, that no one horse could have done all that was asked of the original Trigger. Rogers and Randall weren't going to compromise him through overuse. It would be like expecting Sean Connery to have performed all the stunts in his role as James Bond or Harrison Ford to have done the same in his role as Indiana Jones. Between movies, with all the action that scripts demanded, with all the traveling involved in personal appearances, one single horse would have broken down over time. Even though the original Trigger could perform a few specialties like rearing and nodding his head on cue, his most powerful assets were his beauty, charisma and camera presence. Most important, he ran full out with no accidents. Said Rogers, "He was just a flawless horse. He never made a mistake in his life. All those running shots down hills, up hills, side-ways and every ways. He never once fell with me, in all those pictures."[12]

As Roy Rogers' trainer, equine confidant, and advisor, Glenn Randall became the mid-dleman in one of the best horse deals in Hollywood history. As Randall claimed later, the

$2,500 paid for Trigger was the finest investment Rogers ever made. Considered a fortune in the 1940s, it was nevertheless pretty near a steal. According to one biography, Rogers talked over the matter with Randall and he, too, agreed that the singing cowboy should own Trigger.[13]

Since Rogers didn't buy Trigger until late in 1943, Randall could have been training the palomino for as long as two years and would, therefore, have been the person on hand to advise Rogers on the purchase. Randall had a huge influence later in the selection of horses Rogers bought to fill in for Trigger, except for Little Trigger, whom Rogers already owned. According to Corky Randall, his father was instrumental in every equine purchase Rogers made while they were working together.

Other Horse Students

Beyond Trigger, his doubles, and Dale Evans' horse, Buttermilk, Randall also trained the Roy Rogers Liberty Horse Act, a matched group of eight palominos who, minus lead lines, responded to voice commands and visual whip cues.

With "Trigger" being highly visible, Randall eventually earned a reputation as one of the finest horse trainers in motion pictures, and many wanted to use him. Rogers and Randall worked out an agreement whereby Randall could train horses for other western stars. Randall started a training and rental stable in North Hollywood where he schooled mounts and supplied them to the movie industry, rodeos, and other show business venues. His list of equine pupils included Rex Allen's chocolate stallion, Koko. After Gene Autry's trainer, Johnny Agee, passed away, Randall worked with the last Champion. Glenn Randall also trained White Flash for Tex Ritter, many of John Wayne's horses, and Slim Pickens' Appaloosa, Dear John. Glenn Randall and his son Corky trained horses for such television shows as Walt Disney's long-running *Zorro* series and James Garner's *Maverick*, and they trained the last palomino to play Mr. Ed in television commercials.

Eventually Glenn Randall toured with his own horse acts, leaving Corky to tour with Roy Rogers and Dale Evans. When Rogers gradually stopped touring with "Trigger," Glenn Randall continued to work with other clients. He helped Corky train Cass Ole and actor Kelly Reno for their roles in *The Black Stallion* (United Artists, 1979). It was Corky who went on location to manage the tricks during the actual filming.

Along with training Trigger and his doubles, one of the high points of Glenn Randall's career was his masterful work training the four whites (Altair, Rigel, Antares, and Aldebaran) that Charlton Heston drove in the mega-movie *Ben-Hur* (MGM, 1959). The heart-pounding chariot race sequence still thrills audiences today. It was filmed in real time, live and in person, with very limited special effects. Along with the second unit director, the legendary Yakima Canutt, Glenn Randall gave audiences one the most impressive action sequences ever put on film. In a dramatic contrast to the silent era production of *Ben-Hur,* horses were not injured or killed during filming.

Ironically, the most difficult task Randall faced in *Ben-Hur* was in the more benign sequence when Sheik Ildrim, owner of the Arabian horses, first introduced them to Judah Ben-Hur. After dinner in his tent, Ildrim clapped his hands and a curtain was pulled, revealing four white horses standing free, with no halters or reins. "If I had a song to sing, I would sing you the song of horses," the sheik says before he asks the horses to step inside to greet Ben-Hur. The horses' movements—entering the tent, playfully nuzzling and licking Ben-

Glenn Randall with Buttermilk, originally trained as a cutting and roping horse, before the gelding was used by Dale Evans *(Petrine Day Mitchum collection).*

Hur's hand, and eventually leaving — were controlled, on the set with the cameras rolling, with hand signals from Randall, who was lying on the floor out of camera range.

Randall Honored

The night Roy Rogers was the subject of *This Is Your Life*, the television biography show, "Trigger" was one of the surprise guests. The palomino (Little Trigger) appeared from behind a curtain to greet his surprised master. After "Trigger" gave Rogers a kiss, the horse was led off stage.

Glenn Randall with Trigger Jr. in a personal appearance performance. Like Little Trigger, Trigger Jr. was trained to sit down *(Corky Randall collection).*

Glenn Randall was not mentioned on *This Is Your Life*. While Rogers frequently acknowledged him in interviews, Randall's role was strictly behind the scenes. Glenn Randall's part in making Roy Rogers "the King of the Cowboys" and Trigger "the Smartest Horse in the Movies" was enormous, but he never received screen credit in a Roy Rogers movie. Randall did make one brief cameo appearance in *Heldorado* (1946) in a rodeo performance sequence. After Rogers sings "My Saddle Pals and I" with the Sons of the Pioneers, Randall may be seen handing Little Trigger off to Rogers. *Heldorado* is, by the way, a great example of Rogers' live performance act of the time.

When Ace and Clyde Hudkins retired and decided to sell their stable, Glenn Randall bought them out. He moved to Newhall and renamed his stable business the Randall Ranch. Corky Randall recounted three of the ranches where his family lived: a rented one in Weedpatch in Bakersfield (Little Trigger lived there for a while, but the original Trigger did not as he was still owned by Hudkins); a ranch they owned in Long Ridge in Van Nuys; and the last ranch they purchased (in 1960) in Newhall on Sherman Way not far from Hudkins Stables. Glenn Randall maintained a herd of over 300 horses, mules, burros. He even boarded camels and other more exotic livestock. Like the Fat Jones and Hudkins stables before, Randall also kept an inventory of vintage horse-drawn vehicles including stagecoaches, covered wagons, chariots, buggies, and hundreds of saddles of many different styles.

Glenn Randall was in his retirement years when western films finally started to wane in

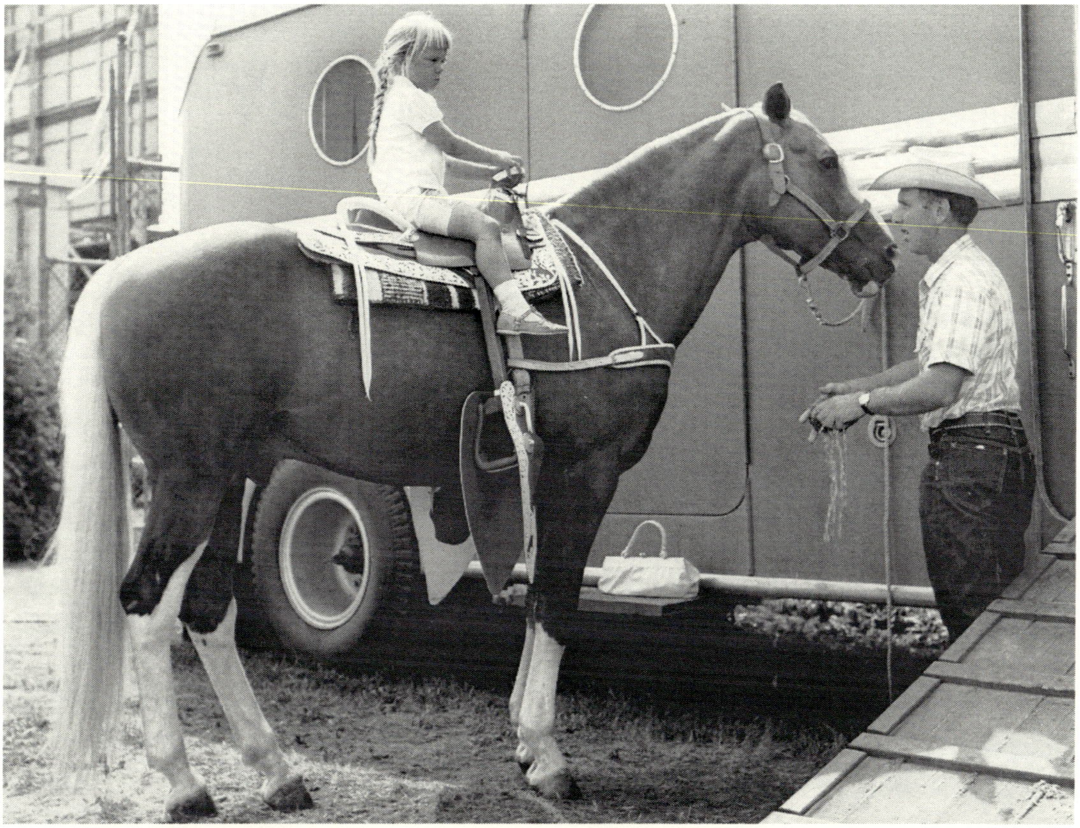

Top: Trigger Jr. on tour in 1958 and being cared for by Corky Randall. That's Randall's daughter Carol, age three, seated in the plastic saddle *(Corky Randall collection). Bottom:* Glenn Randall must have been very pleased when Roy Rogers purchased Trigger Jr. The trainer took a great deal of joy in showing the beautiful stud *(Joel "Dutch" Dortch collection).*

popularity. The old horse trainer sold his ranch and held a public auction to liquidate his holdings. He retired with his wife, Lynn, in a spacious home in the Santa Clarita Valley close to the 50-acre Randall Ranch site.

Glenn Randall was honored on numerous occasions. Honors he won include the Golden Boot Award, the Rodeo Historical Society's Hat's Off Award, and a spot in the prestigious National Cowboy Hall of Fame in Oklahoma City. He was also honored with a dinner dance and reception at the Los Angeles Equestrian Center in Burbank, California, in April 1986. More than 300 friends and admirers from rodeo and movies attended the gala. Lynn and the children, Glenn Jr.,[14] Corky, Pinky, Joan, and Dolores, were present. Dale Evans opened the celebration with a blessing. Former bronc rider Jerry Gatlin acknowledged Randall on behalf of the Hollywood stuntmen for whom he helped train their "falling horses." Roy Rogers thanked and praised Randall for his work with "Trigger."

Randall closed the banquet by saying, "When I go, I visualize myself going off into the sunset driving four white horses to a chariot and leading old Trigger."[15]

Glenn Randall passed away in 1993. Roy Rogers and Dale Evans were asked to give a eulogy at his funeral. Unfortunately, Dale had suffered a heart attack a few days before and the couple was forced to cancel what surely would have been a heartfelt and well-deserved tribute to a great friend and partner.

9

The Smartest Horse in the Movies

"Of all the movie horses I've trained, I've always said Trigger was the smartest and most brilliant. Of all the things you've seen him do on the silver screen, I give a lot of credit to the boss man who rode him and to the director who always got the most out of the story point. Trigger was the 'in Horse' of the motion picture business. In his early pictures, he did the complete picture without the use of doubles. Its hard to express my thoughts of Trigger ... he was a great star."— Glenn Randall[1]

While this book is mostly an equine biography and partial history of a genre, a few words on training horses are in order.

Glenn Randall was constantly asked questions about the training methods he used on "Trigger." Regrettably he never produced a biography, much less a book on how he trained horses. His knowledge was passed along to his son Corky, and it shouldn't be expected of either man to divulge trade secrets gained over years of hard work and experience. Still there have been a number of articles written on the Randalls which include interviews covering their training methods. (Refer to the bibliography.)

When Glenn Randall was in his heyday in Hollywood, the term "horse whisperer" was not in common use, but it would have applied. Randall knew that in order to train a horse successfully he had to understand its true nature and not impose his training methods forcefully. Watching a great horse trainer is like watching a magician. Great trainers work miracles and make it look easy. This is because they speak the language of the horse, through tone of voice, hand gestures, and body language (horses have only a few vocalizations). Horse whisperers, like Monty Roberts, refer to this language as "equus."[2]

Horses are prey animals. Their eyes are on the sides of their heads; they can see almost 350 degrees around with small blind spots directly in front and in back. Horses can hear a hundred times better than humans and also have a very keen sense of smell. They're constantly looking out for danger and will run at an instant.[3] They're also very herd oriented, seeking safety in numbers. Their strong flight response and social nature has kept the species alive for thousands of years. Trainers work within this context and are especially aware of the specific problems they face when engaging horses in front of crowds or in unusual places like movie sets. On a set, the trainer works from a distance, out of camera range, and cannot use voice commands. For this level of training it is imperative that the horse have extraordinary confidence in its trainer. It has to be remembered that training "Trigger" to accept these unusual situations was just as involved and important as training him to perform actual tricks. Roy Rogers had very specific and extraordinary demands of "Trigger." He needed a trainer who could fulfill his needs. Little Trigger went with Rogers on most of his public

Roy Rogers and a seated Little Trigger entertaining townsfolk extras in an outtake scene from Paramount Pictures' color extravaganza *Son of Paleface* (Paramount, 1952).

appearances and often they were indoors—not necessarily in arenas covered in the appropriate turf, but in lobbies or on theatre stages. Little Trigger accompanied Rogers safely and quietly on visits into children's hospital wards and orphanages. The palomino would hold one end of a rope while Rogers and the more able children jumped. "Trigger" was even trained to ride in public elevators. It was because of special circumstances like these that Glenn Randall housebroke Little Trigger. Not an easy thing to do with a horse. It took persistence and patience on Randall's part to teach Little Trigger to relieve himself on command.[4]

The moviegoing public is largely unaware of what it takes to use horses in movies and television shows. Time is money, and directors have little tolerance for animals who compromise a production in any way. It's essential that they hit their marks and tolerate whatever action a story demands. While an audience sees only a horse carrying a rider, the horse sees camera equipment, boom mikes, reflectors, sound trucks, film crews, and more. Such an atmosphere is very stressful for a horse.

Glenn Randall not only had to know the horse training business, but he had to know how to work within the confines of the picture business as well. He had to familiarize himself with directors, and he had to understand completely what kind of horse was needed — not just with respect to breed and color, but in terms of

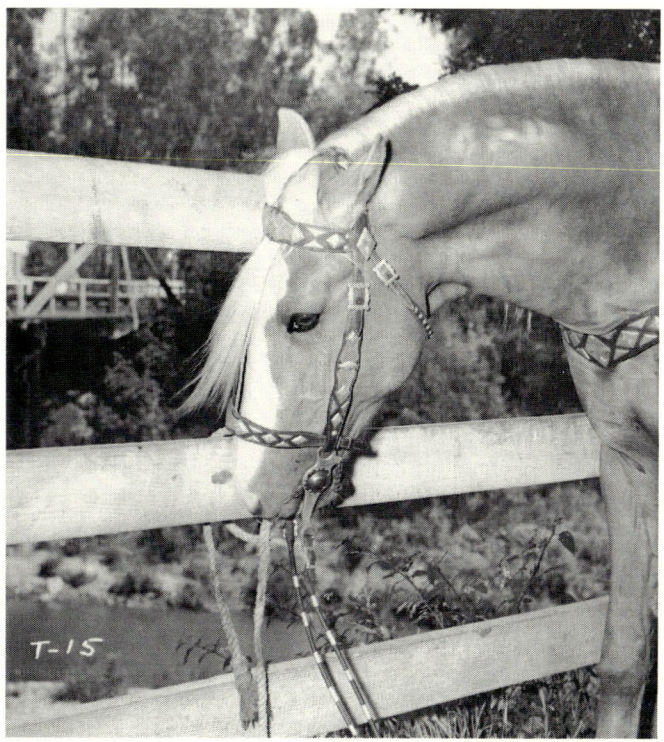

While the original Trigger was not trained to the degree Little Trigger was, he could do some tricks, like untie a knot in a rope *(Roy Dillow collection)*.

what was required of the horse character. Just as important, he also had to educate filmmakers as to what a horse could and could not do.

Training Methods

Glenn Randall generally started training horses to do simple tricks after they were two years of age. By four and five, he would advance them to more strenuous tasks. In order to accomplish all he did with "Trigger," Randall was working in his barn every morning including weekends and holidays. A horse is primarily trained through repetition. Once a horse learns the proper response to a cue, it becomes a habit that is rarely forgotten.

Horses are single-minded and can only focus on one thing at a time. If a horse has no confidence or even fears a trainer, it will not concentrate, much less respond properly to cues. The way to build confidence in a horse (or any animal for that matter) is by understanding the difference between punishment and brutality. "Trigger" respected Glenn Randall, but he was not afraid of him.[5]

Glenn Randall's horses performed at liberty, a type of training referred to as "managed." Little Trigger was a managed horse. He was taught to respond to voice cues, whip cues, and hand signals.[6]

Randall disciplined and corrected with a simple reward-punishment method: for punishment he would take a whip and sting the subject on the leg like a fly. For a reward, kindness and a soft voice went a long way towards getting horses to perform.[7]

Glenn Randall and Little Trigger bid farewell to two young fans before boarding a plane for their next appearance.

"Whip breaking" was the process by which Glenn Randall produced a managed horse. It sounds worse than it was. It began with the animal at liberty in a small square pen. Randall would tap the horse on the rump with a long whip until it turned and faced him. The horse was tapped again on the same place till it walked up to Randall. Randall then gently rubbed the whip over the horse's body, even before a petting reward, as a way to reinforce the idea that the whip was an aid and extension of Randall's arm. After such a foundation, a managed horse was taught rudimentary conduct in front of movie cameras, then minor dramatics when cued: stop, pose, look right or left. After such basics it was taught more demanding tricks: to paw on the ground, charge with ears pinned back, whinny, take a bow, rear up, pretend to be in pain or play dead.

It's easy to understand why a managed horse was essential on a movie set. A trainer and director had to be assured that the animal would obey, not misbehave, and not revert to its strong flight instinct and run away (some filmmaking took place in open spaces). Whip training had to be completely impressed on a movie horse.

Writer Sam Henderson said of Glenn Randall, "People close to him have stated that he always had the horse's confidence. He praised the horse when he did well and scolded him when he miscued. But he only scolded him immediately after a mistake. He knew that if he waited until later to correct the animal, the horse would not realize why he was being disciplined."[8]

Top: Pal and Little Trigger bowing with Dale Evans and Roy Rogers on board. *Bottom:* The original Trigger bowing at liberty.

The Movie Star Horse

Only a very few horses have the potential to succeed in motion pictures (some estimates are one in five hundred). Some manage a movie or two but eventually falter from boredom and routine. A horse that's consistently focused to perform, as Little Trigger was, is rare.

Celebrity horses had a small staff who looked after their needs: a groom who constantly combed, brushed, and trimmed manes and tails; a veterinarian; and even a make-up person to enhance horse's eyes with mascara for close-up shots. Star horses even required stand-ins for the lengthy lighting and technical preparations required before shooting scenes. Without stand-ins, lead horses could become fidgety by the time cameras were ready to roll. It was essential that a star horse had to be fresh and willing to work when it was brought onto a set.

"Trigger" as Student

Glenn Randall often referred to "Trigger" as an exceptional learner. We can assume that he was referring to Little Trigger. He pointed out that the horse was especially good at mouth work: untying ropes, retrieving articles, and so on. Randall said that eventually the palomino had a repertoire of well over one hundred tricks, some never before asked of a horse.

Little Trigger blows a kiss to an audience after a subtle cue from Roy Rogers (*Janey Miller collection*).

"He's the smartest horse I've ever known," Rogers said. "He almost knows when you are talking to him. I have had people ask me if Trigger ever talked to me. That's because he does all his tricks as simply as a trained acrobat."[9]

Rogers once said that when he wanted Trigger to count or to tell his age, he would turn one foot toward the horse, who would start tapping his hoof. When he had tapped enough, Rogers would pull his toe back, and the horse would stop tapping.

One of the attributes that sets cast horses apart from the supporting ones is their ability to calm down quickly after a hard run. The original Trigger was a pro at this. He could slide to a stop and hardly moved out of his tracks even after Rogers dismounted and dropped the reins. Movie horses had to be trained to tolerate hobbles, checking their flight instinct. They had to stand quietly, no matter what was going on around them. In some instances Randall was out of camera range, keeping a horse in place by holding onto its leg with his hand or with a little wire that wouldn't photograph.

Trigger was anything but shy when cameras were rolling. Not only would the palomino stand steady with his ears up and alert; given the slightest chance, he would steal the limelight from Rogers by hamming it up for the camera. It's been suggested that the high frequency hum of the motion picture camera, a sound the human ear cannot pick up, was a cue for Trigger to be on his best behavior. It has even been suggested that the hum would wake him from a sound sleep. Legend has it that Trigger liked to know what was going on at all times. The minute an assistant director yelled, "Quiet on the set!" and noises ceased, the palomino's ears would perk up and he would check to see where Rogers and Randall were.[10]

Trigger the Fearless

The original Trigger had a reputation on movie sets for doing stunts other horses refused. One of the most legendary was recounted in director William Witney's book *Trigger Remembered*. Witney says that in *Far Frontier* (1948), Trigger actually dodged a barrel thrown from a truck by bad guy Roy Barcroft (the barrel was rolling while the truck was moving at high speed). Witney discussed the same sequence in the 1992 Tys Ockersen documentary *Roy Rogers — King of the Cowboys*.

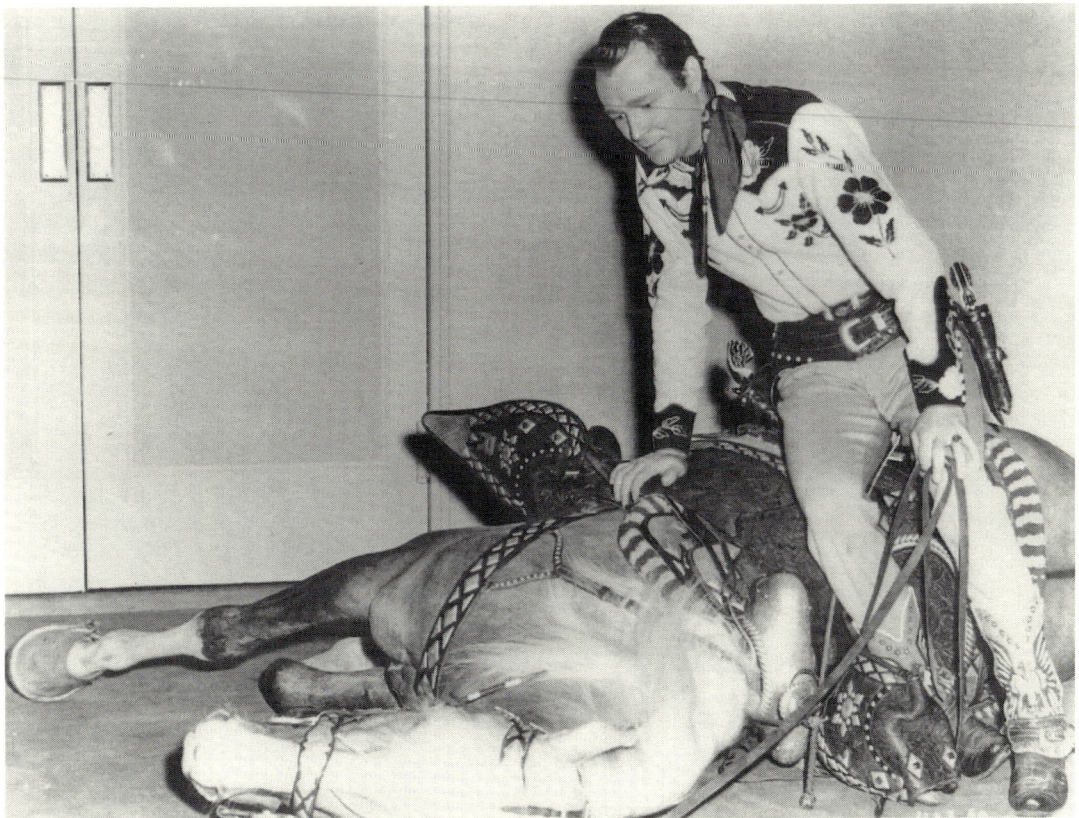

Roy Rogers and Little Trigger demonstrate "the lie down" trick backstage *(Roy Dillow collection)*.

During the filming of *Sunset in the West* (1950), the script called for a stuntman to jump from a running horse onto a train with lots of steam coming out of the wheels. After going through five palomino doubles who balked, director Witney and stuntman Joe Yrigoyen settled on the original Trigger to accomplish the feat.

Joe Yrigoyen said, "Trigger was like a beautiful Mercedes and rode like one as well. It was exhilarating. Being a horseman, he gave me inspiration and much confidence. Trigger would do anything I asked him and would deliver every time. He was the king."[11]

Care and Equipment

Some times a horse's hooves were shod with soft rubber shoes to soften kicks and his teeth covered in gauze to prevent serious bites if an equine fight was being staged. Many times Little Trigger wore rubber boots to prevent slipping on waxed floors. At times cotton was stuffed down a horse's ears when gunfire was part of a scene. Cardboard stirrups were used when a horse was expected to fall on its side. If a horse were to roll on a hard standard stirrup and get injured it would be hard to get it to perform the same stunt again. In the television episode "Phantom Rustlers," Roy Rogers asked Little Trigger to lie on his side. As the palomino performed the stunt, Rogers moved the stirrup and cover (tapadero) out of the way so the horse wouldn't poke himself in the belly. Dale Evans performed the same stunt with her horse Pal in the pilot for her *Dale Evans Queen of the West* show. She too was careful to keep Pal from lying on his stirrup.

According to Corky Randall, Roy Rogers bought Trigger just in time. Randall maintained that his father Glenn had become concerned over Trigger's welfare while he was still being rented out. Apparently the palomino was long overdue for a good trimming and new shoes. One would think that a glamorous horse for hire like Trigger would have been better taken care of. Unfortunately rental horses were sometimes neglected perhaps due to busy schedules and poor record keeping. After Rogers bought the horse outright, Glenn Randall had the palomino's shoes removed and hooves trimmed. Trigger went without shoes till his hooves grew out. Corky Randall claimed Trigger made at least one movie without shoes (he couldn't recall which). Doubles were used for long running shots and over rocky terrain till Trigger could be shod again.

Movie People and Television Commercials

After a time Glenn Randall became somewhat disenchanted with the movie business. While he still trained horses for Hollywood productions, eventually it was his son Corky who actually worked horses in front of cameras once a film went into production.

Both Glenn and Corky gained a reputation in Hollywood for their directness towards movie action directors. They were adamant as to which horse stunts were possible and which weren't. Corky did not mince words when it came to his disgust with movie people. With typical outspokenness he said, "They don't understand livestock, and they'll look at you and say, 'Well, you're a trainer, make him do it.' You get a director that doesn't understand horses, you have to have the power or fortitude to tell him it can't be done." Glenn Randall said, "Livestock people know you don't make a horse, or any animal, do anything. You coax and you train, but to step right up there and make him do it — you can't."[12]

10

Roy Rogers, Horseman

"A man gets to know a lot about a people watching the way they act with horses. Roy Rogers isn't a range cowboy, and he had never pretended to be one. Yet, put to the test, he could put in a day's work with the best. He has a natural seat on a horse that plenty of Texas line-riders world envy. Roy got it from riding bareback. He has kept himself in better shape than most men his age, partly because he has to in order to do the things he does in movies, but mostly because he has a personal pride in good health that's more important."— Glenn Randall[1]

Rogers had great luck and timing, but they would have meant very little if he hadn't had the talent and ambition to seize opportunities that come once in a lifetime. When his career began to take off, Republic Pictures increased the budgets of his movies and started promoting him as the "King of the Cowboys." This laid a challenge before him. He already had the right look and the singing voice. However, as much as anything else, he had to refine his equestrian skills.

Action cowboys were usually much better horsemen than their singing cowboy counterparts, but Rogers was the exception. Beyond his charisma on screen and talents as an entertainer, he was a great rider. While he did not enter into show business from a rodeo background, he rode effortlessly and with great style. His hands were soft on Trigger's reins and his body language flexible and smooth. As a natural rider, all Rogers needed, at the beginning of his screen career, was a little refinement, the right horse, and a great trainer.

B-western movie stars, including singing cowboys who made the transition from radio, had to ride horses as part of their job. If an actor was going to play a cowboy he'd better have some riding skills. Good editing and stunt doubles helped, but only up to a point. Cowboy stars on tour were often expected to ride horses in abnormal situations such as parades or on visits to hospitals and orphanages in front of noisy and unpredictable fans. They needed to be prepared for awkward situations that only a skilled rider should attempt.

A horse trainer teaches not only a horse but its owner as well. Besides rating Little Trigger as one of his finest pupils, Glenn Randall also rated Roy Rogers as a great student. He acknowledged that Rogers was a quick study and often got results that were as good as his own. If the King of the Cowboys had been able to schedule the time necessary to become a horse trainer, there's little doubt he would have been up to the challenge.

Director William Witney was correct when he assessed Rogers' skills on a horse: "Roy was a perfect 10." Rodeo veterans Ken Maynard, Yakima Canutt, and Hoot Gibson may have been better riders, but Roy Rogers was more charismatic in the saddle.

It's been said that the best riders begin learning when they're children. A person who

Roy Rogers and Little Trigger were a great dressage team and proved it in countless live performances *(Roy Dillow collection).*

starts riding as an adult will never be as natural. Roy Rogers started riding when he was a kid. He told Thys Ockerson in the documentary *Roy Rogers King of the Cowboys* (1992) that he learned to ride at about age eight, riding bareback. He used to look at his shadow to keep his head level. "Out on location when the sun would be coming up, I used to practice to see how steady I could make my head go, by watching my shadow. You could get the rhythm of the gait between your ankles, your knees and your hips. Good riding is all a matter of practice."

Tonight Show guest host Burt Reynolds once introduced Roy Rogers by saying, "This man

Roy Rogers and Trigger Jr. The palomino was accomplished in certain dance routines and could perform a number of tricks.

is silk on a horse." Amen to that. In his prime, Rogers mounted, rode, and dismounted Trigger effortlessly. His skill as a rider and "Trigger's" aptitude as a highly trained horse were demonstrated spectacularly in a chase sequence in *Robin Hood of the Pecos* (1941). In order to hide from a posse, Rogers removed Trigger's bridle as they galloped towards a herd of loose horses. He removed Trigger's saddle as they came to a stop. The palomino was let loose among the herd and Rogers hid with the tack behind a rock. After the posse passed through, Rogers whistled for Trigger and saddled him, and they made their escape.

Said Cheryl Rogers-Barnett in her autobiography *Cowboy Princess*: "Dad had never done any serious riding before he got into the movies, but he was a truly gifted athlete, who caught onto the basic principles very quickly. Dad worked with great wranglers and stunt men. He was what they called a quick study and it didn't take him long to pick out the horsemen who he thought rode best and then figure out the mechanics of what they were doing that he liked."

It's been widely rumored that before William Boyd became Hopalong Cassidy, he was afraid of horses. Whether that's true or not, he became a decent rider by the end of his career after years in the saddle. While one would not equate him with horsemen like Wild Bill Elliot, Dick Jones, or Clayton Moore, Boyd was okay. On a subliminal level, the horsemanship skills of his screen persona were played down. He was hardly ever doubled by a stunt man doing fancy riding, quick dismounts or Pony Express mounts. Amazingly, Hopalong Cassidy hardly

Bird's eye view of Roy Rogers on Trigger. It didn't matter from what angle one saw them, no B-western horse and rider looked better at a full gallop than these two *(George Coan collection).*

ever referred to his horse, Topper, by name. The animal was strictly just beautiful transportation and didn't even receive screen billing.

Spurs

Roy Rogers didn't use a whip or spurs in a way that would hurt his horses. Both he and Glenn Randall used them to cue their mounts. Rogers wore spurs all the time. Called cookie spurs, they were smooth and round, not pointed like most spurs. He used his spurs along with leg pressure and voice commands.

Step Mount

Rogers' natural athletic ability enabled him to ride and fight almost on a par with professional stuntmen. Nevertheless, studios are always cautious when it comes to stars doing stunts, and they didn't give Rogers free rein. One of the few stunts they did allow him to do on film was a step mount. It was executed by running at a stationary horse, jumping on the stirrup with his left foot and letting his momentum carry him onto the saddle as he swung his right leg over, at the same time reaching for the saddle horn and reins as Trigger took off. He seemed to hop onto the stirrup and pull himself up at the same time. It was so smooth it seemed he did not so much jump as levitate. Other cowboys did the hop, but there was always a hitch somewhere in their motion. Not Roy Rogers. From the time he started towards Trigger until he was in the saddle it was one continuous, fluid movement. More poetry in motion.[2]

In *On the Old Spanish Trail* (1947) Rogers did a step mount onto Trigger (after his first encounter with adversary Tito "the Gypsy" Guizar) that was smooth and natural, like any experienced cowboy would execute. In *Red River Valley* (1941) Rogers did an easy step mount in front of leading lady Gale Storm. She commented on it and Rogers asked her if she'd like to give it a try. She did, successfully, and rode off on Trigger. At the beginning of *Down Dakota Way* (1949), after a scuffle with a couple of bad guys, Rogers did a running step mount onto Trigger. He did the same thing a little while later in front of a country school house.

Riding Bareback

A rider not using stirrups must have near perfect balance on a horse, especially in the faster gaits. Note contemporary films like *Troy* (Warner Bros., 2004) and *Alexander* (Warner Bros., 2004) where actors, for historical accuracy, had to ride without stirrups.[3] Brad Pitt in *Troy* and Ian McKellen as Gandalf in *The Lord of the Rings: The Return of the King* (New Line Cinema, 2003) rode bareback but were only shown while their mounts were standing

still. Lead players are rarely shown engaging horses at a trot or canter; a couple of exceptions are little Kelly Reno in *The Black Stallion* (1979) and Kevin Costner in *Silverado* (Columbia Pictures, 1985).

After the cinch on Trigger's saddle gave way from a cut, Roy Rogers took a spill during a fox hunting sequence in *Bells of San Angelo* (1947). After a brief inspection of the sabotage, a stuntman (probably Joe Yrigoyen) made a quick croup mount (vaulting onto the saddle over Trigger's croup, the highest part of a horse's hindquarters) and sped down the trail. Rogers was seen in the next cut riding Trigger bareback at a full gallop, a stunt seldom executed by other singing cowboy stars. (Rogers also rode bareback at full gallop in *Trigger Jr.* [1950] and *South of Caliente* [1951].)

Roy Rogers could mount and dismount Trigger flawlessly. Here he demonstrates the step mount (*Roy Dillow collection*).

Riding Mishaps

Sooner or later even the most experienced rider may have a mishap with a horse. Rogers certainly had his share and, in some cases, in front of an arena full of people.

According to Art Rush, towards the end of a Madison Square Garden engagement, as Roy Rogers was entering the arena on "Trigger" at a dead gallop, the palomino's foot penetrated the very wet turf, hit concrete, and slipped. Rogers was thrown through the air and slammed into a concrete wall with a thud.[4]

On another occasion Rogers had an even more narrow escape from serious injury. As they were rounding the arena "Trigger" slipped, throwing Rogers from the saddle. It was the worst of all scenarios: His spur got hooked in the stirrup. "The crowd was furious when Trigger didn't stop running," Glenn Randall said. "They became almost hysterical watching him drag Roy by one leg. But the truth was that Roy's heel accidentally was giving that horse a cue to run. And poor Trigger was just caught between the devil and the deep sea. Several wranglers and I ran into the arena and stopped Trigger. Luckily Roy wasn't hurt except for scratches and bruises."[5]

Roy Rogers and Little Trigger, who excelled in fancy dance routines *(Roy Dillow collection).*

Joe Yrigoyen

Stuntmen performed the more dangerous mounts for Rogers and his peers, like drops from a porch roof onto a horse, crupper mounts (over a horse's rump) or Pony Express mounts (while an animal was in a full gallop).

Joe Yrigoyen was probably Roy Rogers' best known stunt double and rode Trigger and his look-alikes many times. With his brother Bill, Yrigoyen started in the movie business performing stunts at Nat Levine's Mascot Pictures, which produced serials in the early sound era. The Yrigoyens stayed with the company after it was incorporated into Republic Pictures and doubled for cowboy and serial stars like Gene Autry, Wild Bill Elliott, and many villains too. Joe Yrigoyen also worked on such television shows as *Gunsmoke, Zorro, Bonanza,* and *Davy Crockett*. In Yakima Canutt's autobiography *Stunt Man* he noted that Joe Yrigoyen doubled for actor Stephen Boyd driving Messala's team of four black horses in *Ben-Hur* (*MGM*, 1959).[6] In 1985, Yrigoyen was awarded the prestigious Golden Boot Award, and it was presented by Roy Rogers. Yrigoyen passed away in 1998.

Signature Pose

The classic rearing pose was something B-western cowboy stars were often asked to do, and some were better at it than others. A horse rearing up on its hind legs with a cowboy on its back became a symbol for the B-western genre. It's no coincidence that a cowboy on a rearing palomino was used on the poster of director Mel Brooks' satire of western movies, *Blazing Saddles* (Warner Bros., 1974). Ironically, rearing — which has to look effortless and exuberant — is considered a dangerous habit in horses and is discouraged by horse trainers.

With Roy Rogers and Trigger, the image that comes most often to mind is the rearing pose. During personal appearances and for the closing shot in some movies, Rogers often put his golden palomino up on its hind legs. Rogers would smile and wave with his free hand. Appropriately, the last shot of Roy Rogers and Trigger in their last film for Republic Pictures, *Pals of the Golden West* (1951), is of them riding off, stopping, turning towards the camera and rearing up. The last scene of the last film Rogers and "Trigger" did together, *Son of Paleface*, also featured the rearing pose.

"Patted twice just under the mane, he would back away. Patted just two inches lower than that, he'd rear up in the famous pose which became a trademark."[7]

While Roy Rogers may not have been the first cowboy to strike the rearing pose, he made it his own and is the cowboy most closely associated with it. Rogers spent so much time on "Trigger" in that position that it became his trademark and signature pose. No other cowboy star did it as often or as well. No one looked better on a rearing horse. Roy Rogers and Trigger executed the feat effortlessly, with flair and a grace that was hard to match.

Consider the Roy Rogers film *The Bells of Rosarita* (1945), with guest appearances by all the Republic cowboy stars: Allan "Rocky" Lane, Bob Livingston, Sunset Carson, Wild Bill Elliott, and Don "Red" Barry. During the film's climax at Gabby Hayes' wild west show, they rode into the big top to take a bow, and all went into the rearing pose. Rogers appeared solo in the center ring on Trigger. When he cued the palomino to stand on its hind legs, it was plain to see how much better the stunt was executed by the King of the Cowboys and the Smartest Horse in the Movies.

Rogers didn't use the rearing pose in the opening of his television show, perhaps because that's how the *Lone Ranger* show opened. Rogers instead chose to open with a shot of himself on Trigger at a full gallop. However, he used the rearing pose at the close of each show after he'd delivered "The Cowboy's Prayer." For some episodes Rogers would welcome his fans on Little Trigger, rearing up a couple of times in front of the Double R Bar Ranch sign.

While there are a handful of photos of Gene Autry on Champion in the rearing pose, rather than try to compete with Rogers, Autry opted for the safer "end of the trail pose" and used it during personal appearances. It emulated the well known image of an Indian on his pony, the horse's four legs close together and his head hanging low. Autry's horse stepped up with four feet on a small box when doing the stunt. There are but a few photos that exist of Rogers and "Trigger" in the "end of the trail" pose.

Autry also used the "bowing pose" at the beginning of his television show. Champion

Roy Rogers and Little Trigger demonstrate their signature pose in front of the capital dome while on a tour of the East Coast circa 1941.

bowed on one knee as did the original Trigger. Little Trigger could not only go down on one knee but could stretch both front legs forward for a bow.

After Trigger's death, Rogers had him mounted rearing up, another sign of how much he thought of the pose. Saddle Pals can only imagine the pride and pleasure Roy Rogers took from riding a fine horse like Trigger. Putting the palomino up on its hind legs must have been as great a thrill for Rogers to do as it was for fans to see.

In his prime as a rider, Roy Rogers was so accomplished that he would ask Little Trigger to rear up even while the palomino was not wearing a bridle or saddle. Note how relaxed and confident the King of the Cowboys looks.

Republic Pictures' top cowboy stars made guest appearances in Roy Rogers' 1945 movie the *Bells of Rosarita*. From left to right: Sunset Carson, Allan "Rocky" Lane, Roy Rogers, Don "Red" Barry, and Bob Livingston.

Coda

Roy Rogers loved motorcycles and rode them in his spare time. He probably saw them as a vacation from horses.[8]

Two occasions mark the end of Rogers' career as a horseman: a *Fall Guy* television show guest appearance show in 1984 and the AMC biography special, *Roy Rogers — King of the Cowboys* broadcast in 1992.

The closing shot of the *Fall Guy* episode was of Rogers on "Trigger" riding towards the camera and performing his signature rearing pose. The expression on Rogers' face in a still photo of the sequence shows a little apprehension. This was probably due to his advanced age and his unfamiliarity with the "Trigger" double he was riding. Rearing a horse is dangerous, and one may assume Rogers hadn't performed the stunt in a while. Rogers was hanging on to the saddle horn with his right hand, something he never did as a young man. This occasion in all likelihood was the last time Rogers performed his signature rearing pose in public. He was 73 years of age.

In the closing scene of the AMC biography *Roy Rogers — King of the Cowboys*, Rogers is shown on foot leading a bay horse into the desert. Apparently a palomino was not available. Roy Rogers was 81 when the documentary was filmed and it seemed he couldn't or wouldn't ride anymore. Sadly, there comes a time when every rider realizes his time in the saddle is over — even when that rider is the great Roy Rogers.[9]

The last appearance of the "Trigger" character on television occurred on an episode of *The Fall Guy* television show in 1984. The 73-year-old Roy Rogers rode a gorgeous Trigger look-alike for the occasion and even cued the horse into one last rearing pose.

11

Trigger Collectibles and Memorabilia

"You name it, he was on it. And Roy Rogers the King of the Cowboys became the most widely merchandised personality in the entertainment industry." — Larry Mahan (*Horseworld* television show, circa 1995).

With respect to finances, Roy Rogers was small potatoes compared to Gene Autry. Metaphorically Rogers may have ridden the range in style, but Autry owned it. However, Rogers bested Autry in a few instances, merchandising being one. With the help of agent Art Rush, Roy Rogers licensed hundreds of items featuring his likeness and that of his horse. For that matter, no other B-western horse was merchandised to the extent Trigger was. Only Autry's Champion, the Lone Ranger's Silver, and Hopalong Cassidy's Topper came close. One would be hard pressed to find collectibles related to Rex Allen's Koko or the Durango Kid's Raider.

Horses were true sidekicks in movies, and many fans who collect cowboy character–related toys and memorabilia are interested only in items having to do with a hero's horse. Trigger is gone and baby boomers are getting older, but memorabilia associated with Rogers' palomino is still sought after by collectors who are still willing to spend bundles of money.

If one has the money and time, starting a collection devoted to Trigger is not difficult. On most weeks, one can still get around a thousand hits on eBay when doing a search for "Roy Rogers." Thanks to the Internet, many Trigger items are becoming commonplace, and rare ones appear on occasion. The Web, and eBay especially, have blown the lid off collecting to a large degree, because availability affects value. EBay is also a great resource not only for finding items, but for learning about them and networking with fellow collectors.

Republic Pictures made a classic error of short-sightedness when it ceded merchandising rights to Rogers in lieu of a raise. Rogers and his agent parlayed that concession into almost incalculable gain. Rogers even used his children to promote certain items. For example, Dusty Rogers was featured in a television commercial for a Roy Rogers telephone.[1]

Like Walt Disney, the Rogers empire had many characters whose image could be marketed: his wife Dale Evans, her horse Buttermilk, their German shepherd Bullet, comical sidekick Pat Brady, and Brady's jeep Nellybelle. The majority of items featured Rogers and Trigger, but the palomino had a fair share of solo items.

Serious Trigger collectors appreciate the artists and sculptors who took the time to portray Trigger accurately. Three cases in point: the Breyer plastic Small Champ figure, the plush toy, and the most recent version from Hartland of the Roy Rogers and Trigger set issued in 2005. All accurately bear one white stocking on the left hind leg and not the four prominent white stockings that are usually seen. Obviously four stockings are more striking and marketable, but they're not a true representation of the original Trigger.

The following list of Trigger toys, collectibles, books, and so forth is by no means complete. It is almost impossible to list and describe all the Trigger collectibles produced over the years, as well as Roy Rogers items which featured Trigger prominently. It's doubtful any one collector could own every Roy Rogers item produced. At the peak of his popularity, Trigger was everywhere. Whole books have been dedicated to Roy Rogers memorabilia and collectibles (most are listed in the bibliography of this book).

Ironically, the Roy Rogers and Dale Evans Museum in Victorville didn't have a great collection of manufactured memorabilia and collectibles. Private collectors had them beat by miles.

Fantasy Items

A distinction should be made between genuine vintage Rogers collectibles and those produced for the flea market or antique mall crowd. Fantasy items are new, made to look like vintage pieces. They did not exist in that form during the period that they appear to have come from, but they are not outright forgeries, because they do not attempt to exactly copy a genuine item. Examples of fantasy items featuring Roy Rogers include the marbles in a bag with a theater name on the foldover tag (the marbles and a pocket knife made of the same white material with blue graphics), the brass television charm with various pictures of Roy Rogers and Trigger, some bandanas (produced with the same picture that is on the marbles in a single color screen); fake pocket watches and alarm clocks, tin deputy badges, etc. These items are recent and none are licensed.[2]

Miscellaneous Toys and Books

Alarm clock: As with wrist watches and even a pocket watch that featured Trigger, Ingraham had the license to manufacture the Roy Rogers and Trigger animated alarm clock first around 1951; then, with only minor differences in artwork, the Bradley company assumed production in the mid–1950s. With a desert scene background, this clock came with various colored frames.[3] Trigger's legs move each second. The alarm clock is a very desirable collectible.

Books: Examples include *Roy Rogers' Trigger to the Rescue*, illustrated by John Higgs, 6¾ × 8 inches (Cozy Corner Book, WP #2038–25, 1950) and *Roy Rogers' Trigger and Bullet* in "Wild Horse Roundup" by Elizabeth Beecher and August Lenox, 7⅜ × 8¹⁄₁₆ inches, 28 pages (Whitman and Simon & Schuster; produced by Western Printing & Lithographing Company; a Cozy Corner Book, 1953). These books featured either photographs of Trigger or paintings by artists such as Mel Crawford and Joseph Dreany.

Trigger cup and bowl: China ware; issued by the Universal Company. Ovenproof.

Trigger pin-back button: 1953.

Coloring books: Trigger was featured on several large-sized coloring books. One of the most prized is from 1946 with a painting of Rogers on the rearing palomino. Other examples include *Roy Rogers' Trigger and Bullet Coloring Book*, 1956, 8½ × 11 inches (Whitman Pub-

Roy Rogers' Trigger to the Rescue Cozy Corner book.

lishing Company); *Roy Rogers' Trigger and Bullet Coloring Book,* authorized edition, drawings by Nat Edison, 6½ × 7½ inches (Whitman #1315, 1959); and *Roy Rogers and Dale Evans
with Trigger Coloring Book* drawings by Peter Alvardo, 50 pages ((c)1951 by Roy Rogers Enterprises, Whitman Publishing Company).

    Trigger figures: Breyer Trigger figure based on the Small Champ design, complete with
a *My Pal Trigger* video tape in 2000.

    Some unauthorized figures of Roy Rogers and Trigger have been produced. Take for

Roy Rogers' Trigger coloring book issued by Whitman Publishing Company.

example the scarce 1950s Marx Roy Rogers and Trigger figures in box. Contractual agreements between Marx and Roy Rogers Enterprises broke down before this item was issued; consequently, this toy can be found with and without Rogers' name on the box.

Some of the more popular Trigger collectibles were produced by the Hartland Plastics Co. There are a couple of different versions of large Roy Rogers and Trigger figures, each approximately 3" × 8½" × 5". Hartland also produced smaller plastic Triggers that measure only 7" × 11½" and these were originally sold with a Roy Rogers figure both in a box and attached to a card. Alvar Bäckstrand and Roger Williams sculpted the models for Hartland Plastics.

Hartland produced a number of versions of Trigger, including a Small Champ, a walking palomino with a wavy tail, a walking palomino with a straight tail, a semi-rearing palomino, and a rearing palomino. The semi-rearing palomino was reissued with the Roy Rogers figure in 1992–1994 and 2005. There were six different Trigger saddles issued between 1950 and 1960. They were all dark blue with silver trim and only one version did not say "RR" on the tapaderos. The Hartland Trigger had bridles and martingales painted directly on the figures. Any Hartland palomino without a martingale was not a Trigger figure.

Trigger walking palomino figure manufactured by Hartland Plastics.

A Trigger figure manufactured by Hartland Plastics and sold without Roy Rogers came with a full mane and wavy tail and was complete with saddle, reins, and tag. The box sports a painted portrait of a rearing, rather overweight Trigger, printed in red halftones only. Description on the box cover: "Roy Rogers' Palomino Horse 'Trigger' with Roy's saddle. All parts removable — hand painted — tough. A Hartland Creation; Hartland Plastics Inc. Hartland, Wisconsin; no 800P. Trigger Smartest Horse In The Movies — Official! Exclusive! Exact!"

Buttermilk was also issued in a number of versions, including a Small Champ and a Cubby walking. The Cubby walking version was reissued with a Dale Evans figure in 1993–1994 and in 2005.

Roy Rogers and Dale Evans even appeared in person at a trade show held at the Hotel Pierre in New York City in the mid–1950s to promote their Hartland figures, which were among the most popular. Rogers and Evans never visited the Hartland plant but the head of the company, Paul Champion, visited them in California to secure rights for their figures.

Hartland originally shipped its character sets in generic cardboard boxes. After a time, they produced very colorful and creative boxes for most sets. In some cases, such as the solo Trigger figure, they used the same covers for a Black Beauty figure and Silver, changing the top, bottom, and ends to match the character.

Hair from Trigger's tail and mane: Supposedly from a lady named Connie Brothers. She once toured with Rogers' show with trained cats. One of her jobs was to curry "Trigger" before every show. She saved all the loose hair. After she died, her caregiver found a program from Rogers' show among her possessions. Inside was an old 6" × 6" cellophane envelope that had mane and tail hair rolled up inside. Of course, there is absolutely no way to prove the hair is authentic. It was most likely from a touring "Trigger" at best. As this was a one-time offer it seems credible rather than an item someone was selling weekly.[4]

Hobby horses: Some examples will suffice, starting with Roy Rogers' Trigger hobby horse. The N.N. Hill Brass Company. Philadelphia. 39 inches long. 1955–56.

Roy Rogers' Trigger play horse. The Stern Toy Company. 20" high with 18½" wheel base. Plush toy with plastic seat and metal wheels. 1958.

Roy Rogers' Trigger toddler's riding horse by Suzy Goose. 24" high. Steel frame with plastic head, seat and wheels. 1950s.

Trigger rocking horse by Trane-Rite Molding Products. Approximately 33" long. 1950s.

Roy Rogers' Trigger rocking horse. N.N. Hill Brass Company. 25" long by 17" tall. Paper lithography; plastic rein with four bells. 1950s.

Trigger spring horse by Rich Industries Inc. Approximately 39" long. 1955.

Trigger horseshoe: Mounted on a solid walnut shield base with a gold-plated inscription.

Roy Rogers' Trigger inflatable toy: Ideal Toy Corporation. No. 5274. Rust-colored vinyl. 17" high and 21" tall. 1955–1956.

Roy Rogers "Trigger" leather jacket: Wm. Schwartz and Company. Imported suede with calfskin yoke. Rogers rearing Trigger on yoke. Wool quilt lining. Colors: spice, sand, palomino. Sizes: 2–7, 4–12. 1955–56.

Trigger steel lunch box by American Thermos; 6" × 8½" × 3". No Thermos. Circa 1956. Featuring a very interesting painting of Trigger that was slightly doctored, or meticulously copied, presumably by an illustrator named Ed Wexler. He worked for the American Can Company, who produced these boxes in Brooklyn, New York, for the King Seely/American Thermos Company. The actual source painting was done a few years before by Sam Savitt for *Roy Rogers' Trigger Comics* number 5. In the original Savitt version, Trigger is leading a herd

Top: Trigger hobby horse. *Bottom:* Trigger steel lunch box manufactured by American Thermos.

of horses as they escape a prairie fire. In the Wexler lunch box version, Trigger is shown alone on a grassy plain.

Life *magazine* with Roy Rogers and "Trigger" on the cover dated July 12, 1943. Volume 15, Number 2. The cover article runs from page 47 to page 54 and is titled, "King of the Cowboys— Roy Rogers Kisses the Horse, Not the Heroine" by H. Allen Smith.

Trigger manure tray/bowl: Molded from manure taken from Trigger's stall; manufactured by Apple Valley Creations; 9" square. According to Roy Rogers on *The Tonight Show*, the manure was collected from his ranch in Apple Valley; however, the original Trigger had died before the King of the Cowboys lived there. Consequently, there's no original Trigger poop in the items in question. Rogers told guest host Burt Reynolds about a fellow in Victorville with a thousand-pound press who could mold a variety of items. He would go to Rogers' ranch and collect "used hay" to make ash trays.

Trigger marble: ¾" diameter.

Trigger Post Raisin Bran tin: lithograph medal.

Roy Rogers and Trigger plaques. 29" in diameter. Color on heavy board. Issued by Rogden Company, Chicago. One of Trigger may be seen on page 123 of Gail Fitch's book *Hartland Horsemen* hanging on a wall in the background of a photo with Paul Champion, the marketing manager of Hartland Plastics, and in P. Allan Coyle's *Roy Rogers and Dale Evans Toys & Memorabilia*, page 137. Items as rare as this are highly prized.

Photographs where Trigger is prominent are very popular with collectors. Photos are usually 8 × 10 in size, black and white. Color photos are especially striking. Some very rare portrait shots exist which feature Trigger solo. EBay is a great way of finding obscure one-of-a-kind candid shots taken by fans at Rogers' personal appearances.[5]

Roy Rogers' Trigger pocket knife: Made by the Novelty Knife Co. in the U.S. The knife measures approximately 3½" long. The front of the blade shows Trigger rearing up and also a head view. The back of the knife is black plastic or resin. This was manufactured circa the 1990s and is not a vintage item. There were vintage Roy Rogers pocket knives featuring Rogers on Trigger, and at least one was manufactured with palomino alone.

Poseable plush Trigger with articulated neck, back, legs and tail. 17" tall by 19" long, a newer Breyer item. Unlike many representations of Trigger, the poseable plush toy has pretty accurate markings, including the correct single rear left stocking. Trigger plush toys were issued previously by the Stern Toy Company, and a 17" unlicensed version was issued by Brooklyn Doll and Toy Company in 1982.

Roy Rogers' Trigger animated pull toy: N.N. Hill Company. 1955.

Trigger and Bullet puzzle: Whitman Publishing Company. Circa 1950.

Little Golden record: Roy Rogers, Dale Evans and chorus sing "A Cowboy Needs a Horse" and "Happy Trails to You."

Trigger 10 cent kiddie ride: Model #1. Coin-operated ride by Re-Deo-Kiddieland Corporation. Roy Roger's Trigger; authentic galloping reproduction, down to Rogers' distinctive saddle and trappings in genuine leather. "Ride Trigger—10 cents." One minute ride. Manufactured by Exhibit Supply Company from Chicago, Illinois. Motor driven, with gait regulated by reins. Overall height is 54". Height at saddle is 45". Width is 20". Weight approximately 360 lbs. Color is golden palomino. Fiberglass with metal and wood base measuring 48" × 18" × 13". Has sold for as much as $7000 on eBay, 1950s.

Trigger High Stepper: child's stepping stool (the sort designed to be placed in front of a bathroom sink). 1950s.

Trigger hauler and van trailer. Lie Mar Company. Box: 4" × 6½" × 11". Lithographed toy

Trigger 10 cent coin-operated ride by Re-Deo-Kiddieland Corporation (*Janey Miller collection*).

metal van, metal cab hauler. Patterned after the actual truck and trailer used to transport Rogers' palominos to personal appearances. Accurately produced with "Roy Rogers and Trigger" and "Trigger Jr." written on sides and a lithographed painting of Rogers on a rearing Trigger. It was made with and without a remote control unit. The one without is more common; the appearance of the caps (tractors) is different on the two versions. The doors even open and close. 1957. (Note: The actual Trigger van hauler and trailer was used in the "Lady Killer" episode of *The Roy Rogers Show* on television. Rogers lowered the boarding plank and led Trigger out).

Roy Rogers Trigger horse trailer and jeep. Ideal Toy Company. Plastic. Includes: Nellybelle jeep, Pat Brady, Roy Rogers, and Trigger figures. Total length: 15" 1950s.

Trigger trivet: Black with gold glitter image of Trigger rearing. 5½" diameter. Tag on the back says "Plymptons Genuine Abalone. Originals molded by hand, colored by Nature. Made in California. This item was made later for the museum; it's not a vintage collectible.

Roy Rogers' Trigger Trotter Ride-on Toy: Pogo stick with plastic "Trigger" head, approximately 30" tall. Lareo Company Inc.

Western Horseman Magazine: December 1949 issue with a cover article titled, "Trigger: First Get a Good Horse" by Roy Rogers as told to Aaron Dudley. A *Western Horseman* issue from April 1961 with an article titled "A Horse Named Babe" by Duane Valentry is also very desirable.

Specialty Trigger Items

Specialty items were not mass produced for sale to the general public. Consequently, they are very rare and highly prized. With regards to Trigger, two such items come to mind: the Sears Roy Rogers and Trigger store display, and the Roy Rogers View-Master display poster.

Sears store display: In June 1999 a vintage Roy Rogers and Trigger store display was purchased by an anonymous buyer for $3900.00 on eBay. The Indiana seller offering the item guessed it was from the late 1950s, probably manufactured for Sears. The figure of Roy Rogers on Trigger in the signature rearing pose was made of molded composition material. The base measured 42" long, 12" wide and 7" high; the whole piece measured 46" from floor to the tip of Rogers' fingers; from Trigger's ears to the tip of his tail measured 41". The Rogers figure was separate, and Trigger was screwed to the base and could be removed for shipping. The fact that Sears would manufacture such a unique store display is testimony to Roy Rogers' popularity.

Roy Rogers View-Master display: In the 1950s, stores often had several large View-Master displays that had one or more viewers attached to them so that customers could preview the latest reels.

Tru-Vue and View-Master were competitors through the 1940s. Tru-Vue had years earlier acquired the exclusive rights to show Disney characters in 3D. View-Master saw the potential for Disney sales and bought out Tru-Vue. The Roy Rogers reel is unique because of the selection of photos used, including one great portrait shot of Roy Rogers standing between the original Trigger and Trigger Jr. The store display is even more unusual and features the aforementioned photograph. The photo image on the poster measures 13½" × 16½".

The Trigger Certificate of Honorary Ownership *card* is unique because of the story behind its creation. According to Duane Valentry in *Western Horseman* magazine, "When Trigger was in his prime, J.B. Ferguson, wealthy Texas oil and cattle man, tried to buy him for his ranch near Houston, offering Rogers $200,000 [see *Trigger Trivia* section for details]. Rogers turned down the offer as he did all others, reportedly saying, 'Trigger belongs to all the boys and girls of America — they made stars of Trigger and me.'" Pleas for ownership were typical of the fan mail Trigger would get. To make such kids happy, Trigger *Certificate of Honorary Ownership* cards were sent out. The cards read, "This is to certify that _____ is an Honorary Shareholder in 'Trigger,' 'The Smartest Horse in the Movies.' This Honorary Ownership Certificate is awarded to the children of America in recognition of their years of devotion and loyalty, and for supporting us in our motion pictures, radio and television shows and personal appearances." These plastic cards measure 3½" × 2½". Their white surface is printed in light brown ink including a silhouette of Trigger with the text. The

Roy Rogers and Trigger vintage Sears store display.

Honorary Ownership certificates may have also been printed on some of the Hartland box panels.

Estes Tarter Trigger statues: For many serious Trigger collectors the Holy Grail is the Estes Tarter golden statue. One of the most unusual and beautiful items of Trigger memorabilia, the gold metal statues were produced in association with the National Safety Council and were expertly crafted in the mid–twentieth century by the well-known sculptor Estes Tarter. Most were manufactured through the True Cast products company in California and cast in a metal known as spelter (zinc plus lead).

Established in 1949 by Roy Rogers in cooperation with the National Safety Council, the child safety award program reached 27,000 schools in 1955. Finalist entries were evaluated by 65 safety teachers at the University of Southern California. The gold statuettes of Trigger were awarded annually from 1949 till about 1956 to schools across the country. There were first, second, and third place winners. Roy Rogers and Dale Evans presented the top three winning schools' statues in person. Each of the top three winning schools received a large beautiful golden Trigger statue and complete three-dimensional projection equipment for classroom use. Contributed by Sawyer's View-Master, the equipment included the projector, a screen, polarizing glasses, and educational reels in full color. Best-in-state awards were given the smaller Trigger statues which were contributed by the Farmers Insurance Group Safety Foundation.[6] To participate, school children needed to document their schools' safety program and, most of all, have a clean record for safety throughout the academic year. The statues were usually displayed in a school's trophy case. It's anyone's guess what became of these prized items, especially if a school was closed down. Some have found their way into the collector's marketplace and periodically on to eBay.

Trigger, Roy Rogers, and Trigger Jr. photo used in a Viewmaster reel series and store display poster.

The statues were also awarded as prizes in the Roy Rogers Safety Slogan Contests from the 1950s sponsored by Sears & Roebuck. According to announcements, the grand award winner would "appear on the stage with Roy Rogers" to be "presented with a miniature gold-colored statute of his famous horse Trigger — plus — a photograph of the winner sitting in the saddle on Trigger!" At the bottom of entry blanks, it stated that "the decision of the judges — Roy Rogers, Dale Evans and Gabby Hayes — is final." Some versions may have been sold commercially.

Three different versions of the statue were issued. The first was based on the same mold used for the gold palomino horse clocks popular in the 1940s–50s (the sculptor remains unknown). The bridle, saddle and horse were formed by one complete mold. Some were inscribed, "Official Roy Rogers' Trigger The Wonder Horse." Some were inscribed on their base, with the name of the school. There were versions produced with the clock.

"TRIGGER"
Certificate of Honorary Ownership

This is to certify that_____
is an Honorary Shareholder in "Trigger," "The Smartest Horse in the Movies." This Honorary Ownership Certificate is award-ed to the children of America in recognition of their years of devotion and loyalty, and for supporting us in our motion pic-tures, radio and television shows and personal appearances.

Roy Rogers

"King of the Cowboys"

Top: Trigger Ownership Card. *Bottom:* Roy Rogers with the second version of the Estes Tarter Trigger statue *(Roy Dillow collection).*

The second gold-colored Trigger statue was sculpted by Estes Tarter and came with a removable saddle, tapaderos, and wire reins. The name "Trigger" is impressed in the gold-colored base. The artist's name, Estes Tarter, is impressed on the back of the base. The figure stands 8½" high by 8½" long. (There is a gold metal 6¼" tall version with Western tack molded on, red rhinestones, and chain reins. This version is not inscribed.) In 2005, one of these statues in great condition with a bright patina and red saddle blanket sold on eBay for $610. Some come with a red saddle pad, simply a piece of felt cut to fit under the saddle like a pad would.

The third and most elaborate version of the Trigger statue was also sculpted by Estes Tarter. It also came with a removable

Top: This is the second version of the Estes Tarter Trigger statue. *Bottom:* Large ornate Estes Tarter Trigger statue *(Roy Dillow collection; photographed by Carolyn Martin).*

saddle. Highly detailed and ornate, both the bridle (with chain reins) and breast plate were inset with red stones. The body type of the horse is similar to a Tennessee walker or Standardbred. This figure stands 16½" high by 14" long. This type was on display in the Roy Rogers and Dale Evans Museum in Victorville, California.

It is unknown if Tarter was commissioned to sculpt Trigger specifically or if a pre-existing statue was offered to Rogers and company for these National Safety Council awards. It's likely that the statue with the rhinestones was the one Rogers and Evans presented to the first-place school. The medium-sized statue might be the one sent to the second-place school, in which case the smallest one was likely given to the third-place school.

Stuart Trigger figure: Not rare like the aforementioned items, but the plastic Trigger figure produced by the Stuart Toy Company is a thing of pure beauty.[7] It was sold separately and also found in the Mineral City set. The Stuart Manufacturing Company was based in Cincinnati, Ohio, and produced plastic play set figures and horses from about 1950 through the late 1960s. Stuart Manufacturing made horses in three different poses: rearing, standing and running. The Roy Rogers, Dale Evans, Pat Brady, Bullet and Trigger (60mm) figures were originally produced for the 1953 Roy Rogers RR Bar Ranch set cereal premium but were never labeled as "characters" under the Stuart Banner. C.F. Block and Associates (Chicago, Illinois) originally created the Roy Rogers character figures and horses. Como Plastics (Columbus, Ohio) did the mold castings.[8]

The most beautiful of the Stuart horses, the 60mm rearing figure, came in reddish-brown (and brownish red), white, cream, off-white, black, tan (palomino), and silver/gray marbled. This mini-masterpiece could take a place in a museum as a great example of equine

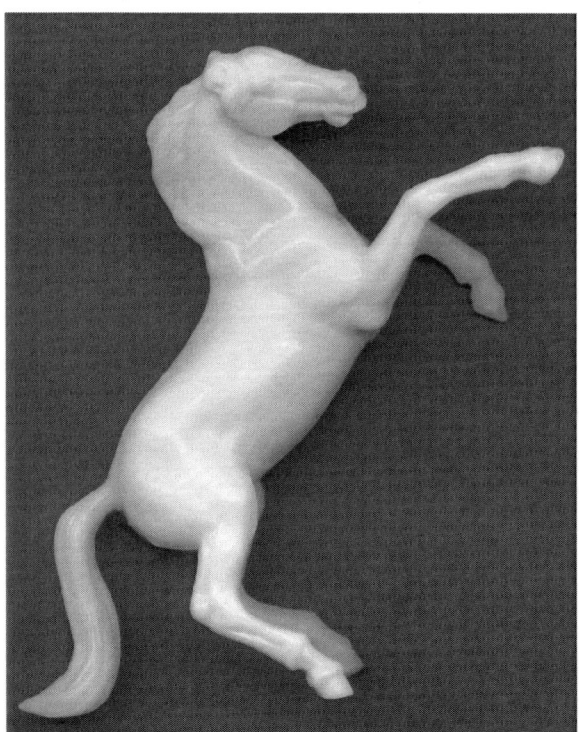

sculpture. Stuart expert Lizabeth West describes the figure as "considered by many to be the most beautiful of the vintage play set horses. This model is like a miniature sculpture. Its head and neck has a well-defined artistry that reflects nobility of the horse."[9]

Auctions

After the deaths of Roy Rogers and Dale Evans and the relocation of their museum from Victorville to Branson, much of their personal memorabilia was sold at auction. Collectors finally got the opportunity to bid not only on rare items that were mass produced but on one-of-a-kind items that the King of the Cowboys actually owned and used.

In January of 2002 the Western Collectables Show and Auction at the Mesa Convention Center in Arizona featured a number of items from the Roy Rogers estate. There was a standing-room audi-

The Stuart rearing Trigger figure **(Lisabeth West collection).**

ence of 1000, including bidders from as far as England, Germany, and Japan. Of special note were custom made parade saddles Rogers used on his beloved Trigger. A McCabe saddle made in 1931 by 16 highly specialized craftsmen during the Depression at a cost of $20,000 was decorated with 136 ounces of gold, 1,400 ounces of silver, and 500 rubies. The maker's mark read: "Gold and silver by John E. McCabe/Leather by J.P. Davis, Hollywood, California." It included a matching martingale and bridle. The final price of $412,500 was more than double the previous price paid for a silver saddle.

Roy Rogers' plastic saddle manufactured by the All Western Plastics Saddle Company in Lusk, Wyoming, sold for $41,250.[10] Constructed in patriotic red, white, and blue sheets of plastic decorated with eagles and the trademark RR Bar brand on the tapaderos, the saddle showed considerable use from public appearances, including the Pasadena Tournament of Roses Parade.

An Olaf Weighorst oil portrait of Trigger that hung in the Rogers study sold for $25,300. Altogether, the Rogers items alone sold for almost one million dollars at the Mesa auction. Auction organizers said the Rogers family offered the items in order to help pay estate taxes as a result of Dale Evans' death in 2001.

The Ultimate B-Western Collectible

The great B-western unique artifacts, like the first Roy Rogers comic book, Champion's bridle with pistol shanks, Lash LaRue's whip, and Clayton Moore's Lone Ranger mask, all take a second seat to Trigger. He is the ultimate B-western artifact and collectible. Trigger may well be to B-western collecting what the Mona Lisa is to fine art. The palomino not only epitomizes the B-western genre but has become, at the same time, a famous heirloom. In the end, after the jokes and differences of opinion fade, Trigger remains, forever in the signature rearing pose he did so often and so well.

In 1976 Trigger's remains were insured for $100,000.[11] When the IRS audited Rogers' estate after he passed away, Trigger alone was valued at between $400,000 and $500,000.

12

Trigger's Peers

"Nothing is exciting as a horse. Planes, cars, trains are okay for speed. But for excitement, there's nothing like a horse." — John Wayne[1]

Trigger wasn't the only special horse working in movies back in the heyday of the western. He was part of a large group of equine stars who entertained millions of fans in genres as diverse as comedy and historical extravaganza. Ask serious B-western fans who their favorite silver screen horse is and you'll get a variety of answers. Certainly Trigger, Champion, and Silver will be the ones most frequently mentioned, but there were a number of great B-western horses and they were as varied as the colors of their coats. Dice and Steel are so well thought of that they've attained cult status among aficionados. Trigger had plenty of competition. However, few screen horses were so well supported by both a studio publicity department and a human co-star with promotional savvy.

Rex Allen rose to fame with a uniquely colored chocolate mount named Koko; Ken Maynard was teamed with a palomino named Tarzan[2]; and Allan "Rocky" Lane rode an ebony stallion named Black Jack. In their heyday, these horses were almost as popular as Trigger. Tom Mix honored his equine partner with a movie titled *Just Tony* (20th Century–Fox, 1922).[3] Ken Maynard used Tarzan in every western he made between 1923 and 1940 except one. Tarzan, who was named after writer Edgar Rice Burroughs' jungle hero, received billing as the "wonder horse" and the "white wonder."[4] A more obscure horse, but very well liked in his day, was Rusty the wonder horse. Actor Jack Randall rode him in a number of westerns. After Randall left Monogram, Rusty was ridden by Tom Keene in a few films for the same studio.

Tom Mix and his chestnut Tony "the wonder horse" built on the image William S. Hart and his great pinto pony Fritz created before him. What Mix added was showmanship with fancy attire and silver show tack.[5] Gene Autry's Champion and the Lone Ranger's Silver also preceded Trigger and set a standard. Rogers was not a pathfinder like Mix and Autry were; he built on a template they refined. However, after a time Trigger eclipsed his equine peers in popularity.

A number of horse hero movies— too many to name them all — were made in the 1940s and 1950s for children. Some were based on books, like *Black Beauty* (20th Century–Fox, 1946), based on Anna Sewell's classic story; *Florian* (MGM, 1940), an A-budget movie about the Lippanzer stallions in Austria in the 1880s; *Smoky* (20th Century–Fox, 1946), based on Will James' classic novel about a wild black stallion who refused to be tamed; and *Gallant Bess* (MGM, 1946), which took place during World War II on an island in the South Pacific.

Hi-Yo Silver. According to Clayton Moore, two Silvers were used in the *Lone Ranger* television show and both feature movies. The first horse, nicknamed Liver Lips, would tongue the copper roller on his bit and consequently his lip would hang down. Moore also noted that the horse had a dark spot on its hindquarters. A second Silver was used when John Hart took over the Lone Ranger role during the 1952–1953 seasons. The only dark spot on Silver #2 was on the left ear *(acquired by Steve Jensen from the Adam Mendoza collection).*

Most horse hero movies were set in the west, like *The Wild Stallion* (Monogram, 1952) with Ben Johnson and a "few-spot leopard" Appaloosa named Top Kick (aka Topkick), and *Snowfire* (Allied Artists, 1958), which starred a Ralph McCutcheon–trained animal named King Cotton. Television continued the horse hero trend with such stars as Fury and Flicka.[6]

Champion the Wonder Horse

The main difference between Trigger and Gene Autry's horse Champion, arguably the palomino's main rival, was in the way their owners related to them publicly. Autry's four-

Gene Autry with the original Champion on the set of *Colorado Sunset* (1939). This Champion, like the original Trigger, came from Hudkins Stables *(Gene Autry and Champion © Autry Qualified Interest Trust and The Autry Foundation).*

legged partner was more of a character than an actual horse. While "Trigger" was played by a number of doubles and stunt horses, Roy Rogers wanted to impress on his fans that "Trigger" was a single real animal. The "one horse illusion" approach could be attributed to Autry with regards to "Champion," but to a far lesser degree than with Rogers and "Trigger."

Autry may be admired for his down-to-earth personality and casual approach to stardom. As famous and rich as he became, as much as he nurtured a clean screen persona, he had his faults and didn't go through great pains trying to hide them. He even acknowledged his drinking problems in his autobiography, *Back in the Saddle Again*. He didn't have Roy Rogers' yodeling ability, Rocky Lane's matinee idol looks, or Wild Bill Elliott's natural horsemanship. Autry was a trail blazer, an entrepreneur. He went into the military service during World War II at the height of his popularity, and from all accounts, he was fair and decent. Gene Autry was foremost a movie star, singer, and composer. He took a more businesslike approach to his mounts. Even though he nurtured a movie ideal of the singing cowboy with a wonder horse and knew "Champion" was important to his success, he still viewed the horse in more practical terms and was more casual towards him then Roy Rogers was to Trigger. Frequently, "Champion" even appeared as a solo attraction with his trainer Johnny Agee and still drew crowds.

Gene Autry on his trick palomino Robin Hood with Champion looking on.

Gene Autry was very candid when he discussed all his "Champions." Again, this was in direct contrast to Rogers, who saw Trigger as the horse who broke the mold. Autry's official Web site carries a detailed history of the different "Champions" who served him. They're even listed with individual names to distinguish one from another: Original Champion, Lindy Champion, Champion Jr., Little Champ, Touring Champion, Television Champion, and Champion Three. That would be unthinkable on the Rogers site. (However, Trigger's most important double was acknowledged officially in 2005 on the Roy Rogers Web site when a glossy color photo was offered for sale; amazingly, it was titled "Roy, Dale & Lil' Trigger Standing.")

Gene Autry and Roy Rogers were different in another important way with regards to their screen mounts: Rogers was in love with one particular palomino, the original Trigger. He also had strong bonds with the two palominos that followed, Little Trigger and Trigger Jr. While Autry no doubt had affection for his equine partners, it seemed his connection never went as deep as Rogers.' The three main horses that Autry rode during his movie and television careers were not even the same color. Autry did not try very hard to give the impression that he was riding the same horse in all his movies and television shows. His first Champion was a dark chestnut; the second, the one referred to as the "strawberry roan" Champion, was a red chestnut; and the third, used for movies and television, was a sorrel with a flaxen mane and tail.[7] According to author David Rothel, Gene Autry owned a palomino named Pal early in his movie career and planned to use the horse later in his color movies. Roy Rogers and Trigger appeared on the scene before Autry had that opportunity.[8] However, Autry did tour with a palomino trick horse named Robin Hood during some of his live appearances.[9] Can you imagine Rogers riding a chestnut for personal appearances? It's common knowledge that real working cowboys use a string of horses in order to avoid riding an animal that is spent. However, in the B-western fantasy, a cowboy was limited to one horse.

In a sense Gene Autry, with his casual approach to all the horses he referred to by one name, was more true to the cowboy life than Roy Rogers.

In *Comin' Round the Mountain* (1936), "Champion" got top billing, but a solid-colored mustang stallion with a star on his forehead was the equine star of the movie. This mustang, Diablo, not only drove the plot but won the climactic race. (Trigger seldom took a subordinate role to another horse in a Roy Rogers movie; exceptions were Trigger Jr., and Frog Milhouse's Ring-eyed Nellie. See the "Golden Stallion" chapter.)

Gene Autry's shrewd business approach was applied to all aspects of his career. When a particular "Champion" got old, Autry simply replaced the animal and made no secret about it. According to Karla Buhlman, vice president of Gene Autry Entertainment, a radio show from 1946 exists where it was suggested that a contest be held asking whether or not Autry should "retire" the old "Champion" and bring on a new one!

Having the "wonder horse" stuffed and mounted would never have occurred to Gene Autry. He was not an outdoorsman or hunter like Rogers. Taxidermy was not something he had a lot of experience with. The story of how Autry reacted to news that Rogers had Trigger mounted has been circulating among fans for years. Allegedly, Autry was somewhat surprised, then mildly amused. When asked if he would have considered doing the same with

Gene Autry and Champion Jr., the "Strawberry Roan," wearing his trademark pistol shanks bit.

"Champion," he asked what it might have cost. When he was told what how expensive it would have been, he was not sympathetic. Cal Thomas reported in *Jewish World Review,* "Gene Autry once told me that when his horse, Champion, died, he was asked if he would like him stuffed and placed in his museum. 'How much would it cost?' asked the multimillionaire. When he was told the price, Autry responded, 'Hell, no, bury the SOB!'"[10]

Champion's Fictional Origins

Fictitious stories having to do with the origins of a cowboy's horse were very popular and went a long way toward establishing an equine star's celebrity. They were also good for business because they added a great deal to a particular animal's value as an icon and marketing tool.

There are a number of fictional accounts of how Gene Autry acquired

Gene Autry rode his sorrel Champion on television and in later movies as well.

"Champion" told in different media: from radio to movies, recordings, and once on television. An episode on the Gene Autry radio show titled "How Gene Found Champion" may have been the first. (Trigger never got his own radio show.) Next came Autry's first color movie feature, *Strawberry Roan* (1948), followed by more airtime in a Mutual Broadcasting System radio serial, *The Adventures of* Champion, which lasted for one season (1949–1950). Then came a *Gene Autry Show* television episode titled "Horse Sense," produced in 1952. A spoken word LP was also released titled "The Story of Champion." "The Story of Little Champ" was also recorded in July 1950; it is a story record (two records with a total of four sides) and was released by Columbia.[11]

When it came to movies having to do with the origins of their mounts, Rogers' was superior to Autry's. By the time Autry got around to filming *Strawberry Roan*—an origin story like Rogers' *My Pal Trigger*—his best work was behind him. Autry produced *Strawberry Roan* in 1948 through his own production company. Although it was filmed in color, the stream-lined budget showed. Gone were the large crowd scenes and big production numbers of his

Republic glory days. Compared to movies like *Back in the Saddle Again* (1941) and *Down Mexico Way* (1941), Strawberry Roan is pretty sparse.[12]

The song *Strawberry Roan* was an old standard written by Curly Fletcher and had been covered by dozens of stars including Marty Robbins and Roy Rogers. It's sometimes referred to as America's greatest horse ballad. Autry and Republic had built movies around songs before, like *South of the Border* and *Mexicali Rose* (both from 1939). It didn't seem to matter that the horse who played the title character was a chestnut and not a strawberry roan. Ironically, Autry never rode a strawberry roan.[13]

Gene Autry's version of the *Strawberry Roan* opened with the title character standing in profile while the credits roll.[14] The story has to do with a boy (played by Dick Jones) who tried to break in a wild stallion and got injured in the process. In a rage the boy's father, played by *My Pal Trigger* villain Jack Holt, tried to shoot the animal. Autry, Holt's ranch foreman, stopped him and freed the stallion. He realized the horse might be just what the boy needed to restore his crushed spirit. The majority of the film involved Autry's attempts to save the strawberry roan and heal Jones. Holt played a role similar to the one Gabby Hayes played in *My Pal Trigger*. Holt was angry with Autry throughout most of the movie because the singing cowboy was protecting Champion.

The "Horse Sense" episode from *The Gene Autry Show* on television was a shorter version of "Champion's" origin in *The Strawberry Roan*. Showcasing his new television screen mount was something Gene Autry was probably more than glad to do, and who could blame him for wanting to show off such a beautiful animal? As it happened, two supporting players were in both versions: Pat Buttram and Dick Jones.

The Adventures of Champion

Through his company Gene Autry managed to do for Champion what Roy Rogers never did for Trigger: give him his own weekly television show. On September 30, 1955, he released *The Adventures of Champion*, a television show that ran for 26 half-hour episodes till March 1956, 7:30 p.m. on Fridays on CBS. For a brief time, Champion eclipsed Trigger in popularity.

The Adventures of Champion was set in the Southwest of the 1880s and told the story of 12-year-old Ricky North, played by actor Barry Curtis, and his stallion, "Champion." Ricky's Uncle Sandy North was played by Jim Bannon (who would also play Red Ryder on television). *The Adventures of Champion* took place in the same setting found in the comics but with a slightly different family: Uncle Smoky became Uncle Sandy, and Ricky West became Ricky North, the only person that "Champion" would allow on his back. The television series apparently gave the impression that the ranch was owned by Uncle Sandy; Autry was seldom (if ever) mentioned.[15]

Champion's Unique Six-gun Bit

The six-gun bit that Champion wore became an Autry trademark and was more unusual than any tack Trigger used. It was not actually made from a real six-shooter, but from a toy gun which was cut in half and from which a mold was cast. After a cleaning, the parts were welded to a stainless steel bit connecting both halves. Adjustments were made for the angle of the mouthpiece and the bridle loop was welded to the end of each half barrel.

The Champs

In 1957 Gene Autry signed a number of rockabilly Texas musicians to record as "The Champs" on his fledgling Challenge Records label in Hollywood. Challenge Records released "Train to Nowhere" as a single on January 15, 1958, with an instrumental titled "Tequila" as the B-side. "Tequila" was written by Daniel Flores, a.k.a. "Chuck Rio," a talented saxophonist, keyboardist and singer from Rankin, Texas. The instrumental B-side not only charted quickly, it shot up the charts and hit number one on March 28 of the same year. A touring band was formed to further promote "Tequila" after it topped the charts. Seals and Crofts, before they became a popular folk duo, joined the Champs at that point and remained for seven years.

The Autry organization (in the person of spokesman Alex Gordon) would neither confirm nor deny when asked if the Champs were named in a gesture to Gene Autry's horse. This writer first heard the story on an oldies radio station in Los Angeles.

Silver, a Fiery Horse with the Speed of Light

More a symbol than an ordinary cowboy, the Lone Ranger was the most fanciful of the B-western heroes. That says a lot. The producers of his television show were more interested in entertainment and family values then realism. Children never questioned what they saw; they accepted and believed. The Lone Ranger was always clean shaven and his hair always cut; he was immaculate though constantly in the saddle. His costume was clean and pressed even after he slept in it, including his mask! The Lone Ranger was also asexual; unlike Roy Rogers and Gene Autry, who both had romantic involvements with their beautiful leading ladies, the Lone Ranger was beyond such nonsense. It was as if he'd also taken an oath of celibacy when he donned his mask and vowed to uphold law and order. The Lone Ranger was pure and true. Symbolically it makes sense he would ride a white horse.

Like "Trigger," Silver was played by many animals over the years in personal appearances, movies, and television. Beautiful though the different white stallions were, it was because they were solid white that there was a generic nature to Silver's screen persona. Because the first Champions were chestnuts with white markings on their faces and legs, fans could see differences in the horses Autry rode. It was virtually impossible to tell all the different Silvers apart.

Not only was the Lone Ranger iconic in nature, but Silver matched his larger-than-life persona. Silver and Scout, Tonto's trusty paint, were well trained, never tired, and were never injured while serving the masked man and his Indian companion. The Lone Ranger and Tonto also traveled light. They did not need pack horses loaded with supplies; it never even rained or snowed on them.

The Lone Ranger's horse came from a context different from that of Trigger or Champion. Silver first existed as a larger-than-life fictional character on radio and in print. Like his masked master, Silver premiered as a character on the radio as voice and sound effects.

On January 30 1933, radio station WXYZ began broadcasting the very successful *The Lone Ranger* show. In the first stories it was revealed that the masked man found his Silver in Wild Horse Canyon. The horse had been fighting a buffalo bull and was about to be gored to death

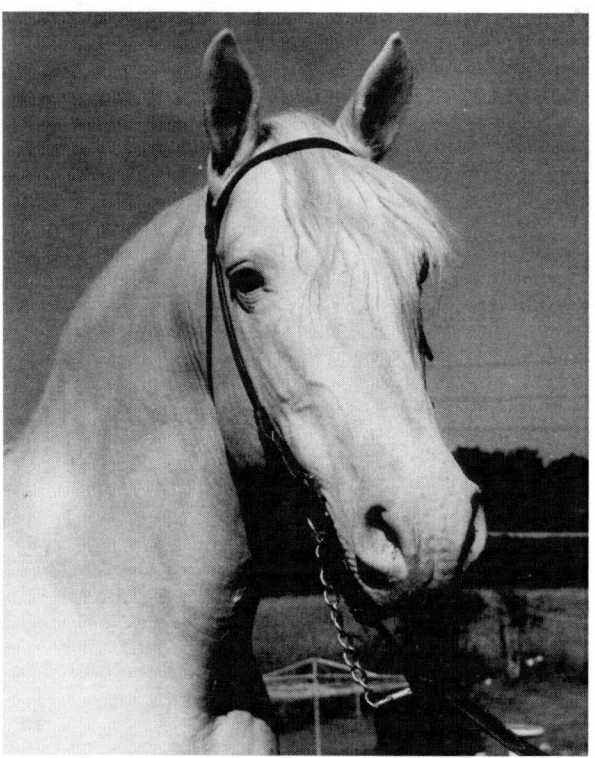

Brace Breemer's own horse, Silver's Pride, was 27 years old at the time this picture was taken. The photo was sent to Lone Ranger fan Frank E. Swain of Pulaski, Virginia, in 1966 by Brace Breemer's widow, Leta *(Dawn Moore collection)*.

when the Lone Ranger intervened and saved its life. The masked man and his Indian companion, Tonto, nursed the stallion back to health.

With the transition into children's books, pulps and comic books it became necessary that the Lone Ranger and Silver characters make personal appearances. The first Silver to appear in public was a rented horse named Hero owned by Carl A. Romig. Hero was used in July 30, 1933, by Brace Beemer who narrated the *Lone Ranger* radio show and was appearing as the Ranger at a school field day hosted by the Detroit Department of Recreation at Belle Isle.[16] Beemer eventually did promotions with his own horse Silver's Pride.

In 1938, "Hi Yo Silver" (DeVaughn and Erickson) was a hit song for the one and only Roy Rogers and reached to number 13 on the charts.[17]

The Lone Ranger became so popular on the radio and in print, it was just a matter of time till he appeared on the silver screen in a series of chapter plays. Lee Powell was the first actor to play the Lone Ranger on screen in the 1938 *Lone Ranger* Republic serial. Silver was portrayed by Silver Chief and listed that way on movie posters.[18] For the follow-up serial, *The Lone Ranger Rides Again* (1939), Bob Livingston assumed the title role and Silver was once again played by Silver Chief.[19]

Enter Clayton Moore

No individual animal was the real Silver in the sense there was an original Trigger. There were two who came close: the Silvers actor Clayton Moore used in the *Lone Ranger* television show which aired in the 1950s. According to Moore, they were of Morgan and Arabian mix — Morabs.[20]

In 1949, after he was cast as the Lone Ranger, Clayton Moore personally chose the Silver he would ride on television. Silver #1 was hand-picked from stock at a San Fernando Valley horse ranch owned by Hugh Hooker. Moore had an eye for horses, and the white stallion he decided on was an impressive 17-plus hands tall. It's no wonder Moore would refer to the animal on screen as "big fella." The stallion was registered as White Cloud and was about 12 years of age at the time. Silver #1 did not know many tricks but was very impressive when he reared and would stand quietly for anyone due to his gentle nature.[21]

In 1945, Silver #2 was born outside Danville, Iowa. He was a stallion from registered

Saddlebred stock and was first named Tarzan's White Banner. He eventually reached 15.2 hands at the withers and weighed 1150 pounds fully grown. The name was derived from his sire, Tarzan, coincidentally the same name as Trigger's sire though not the same horse. Virginia Lee Perry, his first owner and trainer, sold Tarzan's White Banner when he was four years to Charles VanDyke of Peoria, Illinois. That same year George Trendle, owner of the Lone Ranger Radio Broadcasting Company, purchased the stallion from VanDyke for the *Lone Ranger* television series and registered him as Hi-Yo Silver. During his tenure as the Lone Ranger's mount, he would be used only for close-ups and special appearances.

Trendle's Hi-Yo Silver was in California during the 1952–1953 television seasons and took over the role as the Lone Ranger's mount while John Hart played the *Lone Ranger*, Moore having left temporarily over a contract dispute. During the season when the production company was not filming, Hi-Yo Silver was used for Lone Ranger public appearance tours and promotions. The high-strung stallion had a reputation for being skittish on the set if he heard camera motors running. There were those who had trouble riding him. However, Hart had very nice things to say about his four-legged co-star: "He was half American saddle horse and half Arabian — pure white, with big, dark blue eyes, no pink in them. And very, very smart. He was a stallion, a stud, and they're very nervous and jumpy. Nobody had really used him before, and I picked him out and worked him for about a month before we even started shooting. After fifty-two episodes, I really hated to part company with him."[22]

When Clayton Moore returned to *The Lone Ranger* the following year, he too used Hi-Yo Silver almost exclusively and also took the horse on publicity tours. Glenn Randall trained and stabled Hi-Yo Silver at the Randall Ranch in Newhall, California, during the filming seasons.

For the *Lone Ranger* episodes featuring the character Dan Reid, the Lone Ranger's nephew, a third white horse was rented, this one from the Spahn ranch. Dan Reid's horse was named Victor and, in the story line, was supposedly sired by Hi-Yo Silver.

In 1954 Trendle sold the *Lone Ranger* show rights to Jack Wrather. Hi-Yo Silver and the silver-laden saddle and tack were not included in the $3,000,000 deal Trendle and Wrather negotiated. Trendle wanted an additional $25,000 for the horse and tack. An agreement was reached when Wrather suggested splitting the difference instead. Trendle agreed, and Hi-Yo Silver and all copyrights to the Lone Ranger character were sold to the Wrather Corporation of California.

After the motion picture *The Lone Ranger and the Lost City of Gold* was completed in 1956, Hi-Yo Silver and Scout were put in the care of horse wrangler and stuntman Wayne Burson and his wife Louise at their ranch in California. Wayne Burson had appeared in several westerns in the 1940s and 1950s and had been Hi-Yo Silver's wrangler on the Lone Ranger set. He had also doubled for Tonto in the television series. Along with the Bursons, Clayton Moore and Hi-Yo Silver toured the country performing for audiences till 1962. After that the stallion retired to the Bursons' ranch, where he enjoyed a life of leisure till he died in 1974 at the age of 29.

One of best known Silvers was a stand-in stunt and chase double named Traveller. His owner, Bill Ward, in full Lone Ranger costume, rode him exclusively during scenes involving chases and jumps. Whenever a scene demanded that the Lone Ranger unseat a fleeing outlaw by leaping from Silver at full gallop, it was almost always Bill Ward performing the stunt from Traveller. Clayton Moore never rode Traveller during the run of the show, as the horse wouldn't let just anybody ride him. After he was retired from film making, Traveller became Tommy Trojan, the University of Southern California Trojan mascot ridden during football games.

Clayton Moore and Silver in a striking rearing pose like the one used to open *The Lone Ranger* television show.

Silver #1 was pretty much retired after a brief stand-in appearance for Hi-Yo Silver in the 1956 movie *The Lone Ranger* (Warner Bros.) with Clayton Moore. He was sold to the Ace Hudkins stables and, being fairly old, was used only for close-ups and head shots.

In a 1976 *People* magazine interview, Jay Silverheels, who played Tonto, recalled that Silver actually was somewhat of a slow-running horse and Scout had to be reined in "lest he leave the masked rider in that traditional cloud of dust."

Although Silver and Scout were basically beautiful transportation on the *Lone Ranger* tele-

Clayton Moore on Silver #1 with Dale Evans on Buttermilk and Roy Rogers on the original Trigger at the Los Angeles Coliseum in the mid–1950s. (Man and woman at left unidentified.) Silver #1 topped out at 17 hands. Buttermilk, at 15 hands, looked like a pony in comparison *(Dawn Moore collection)*.

vision show, each had a special scene in the two full-length color feature films. In *The Lone Ranger* (Warner Bros., 1956) Scout actually ran to the Lone Ranger for help when an angry crowd threatened to hang Tonto. In *The Lone Ranger and the Lost City of Gold* (Warner Bros., 1958) Silver found an abandoned infant and later rescued it again. In a short comedy sequence Scout was actually sleeping next to Tonto. Both were sharing a blanket which Scout pulled much the same way Little Trigger did in *Son of Paleface* when he shared a bed with comedian Bob Hope.

Clayton Moore's Fate

Unlike Roy Rogers, who had the foresight and opportunity to own his screen name and likeness, and unlike William Boyd, who bought the rights to the Hopalong Cassidy character, Clayton Moore did not have the opportunity to own the Lone Ranger character. Moore was hired to play a role and remained a work-for-hire actor.[23] Nor did Moore own any of the Silvers he rode as the Lone Ranger. The closest he got was to work Silver #1 on the trails around his Tarzana residence.[24]

Silver Coda

If equine B-western celebrity is a long-distance horse race, Silver will win it. He will do so simply because he's a fictional character. It's conceivable the Lone Ranger might be the subject of a movie or television show in the future. If so, Silver, as part of the myth, will be present in his full glory. Fictional characters like Zorro, Robin Hood, and Sherlock Holmes come to life on the screen every now and then in updated versions. It seems a remote possibility at best that bio-pictures will ever be made on the lives of Roy Rogers and Gene Autry.

Trigger may have eclipsed Silver as the premiere B-western horse, but the white stallion's catch phrase, "Hi-Yo Silver, away," endures. The other area where Silver left his palomino rival in the dust was in comic books, one of the most popular entertainments of the day (see the chapter titled "Trigger Horse Hero Comic Books").

Koko, the Miracle Horse of the Movies

Rex Allen was known as "the Arizona Cowboy," and his horse, Koko, was referred to as "the Miracle Horse of the Movies." Koko has the distinction of being the last of the B-western horses to get top billing in a film. *Phantom Stallion* was released by Republic Pictures in 1954 and Koko, as always, was given screen credit under Allen.

Rex Allen wrote in his autobiography *Arizona Cowboy*:

Glenn Randall, Trigger's trainer, one day said, "You know, I've got a chocolate colored horse with a white mane and tail that I bought in St. Louis. I thought Dale Evans might like him, but he's a stud and a little too much horse for a woman."

So I bought him.

Glenn said, "You'll have to ask Roy if it's all right for me to train him."

Roy said, "You bet. Glad you're getting Glenn to do it."

I stabled him at Glenn Randall's while he was being trained, and kept him there for several years while I lived in Tarzana. At Randall's ranch, he was well taken care of and always shiny and ready to go on the road. Of course, when I bought my ranch, I kept him out there until he died.

Rex Allen often lamented that he almost wore Koko out while filming and touring because the stallion was so hard to match with its unique chocolate coat and flaxen mane and tail. Koko had the same kind of blaze as the original Trigger, with a sharp turn towards the lip, but it was further up on the muzzle. Allen also confirmed that the horse was a stallion. When asked in a 1995 interview, Allen claimed that Koko sired two foals. Corky Randall maintained that the stud was never considered as a mount for Dale Evans, contradicting the story Rex Allen often repeated. Koko was too big a horse for Dale Evans. In Corky's words, "It just wouldn't have looked right." Koko was about 15 hands with a "bulldog" type build like Little Trigger." Corky Randall described him as "chunky."

Rex Allen wanted to ride Koko in his first Republic movie, *The Arizona Cowboy* (1950), but Glenn Randall suggested he not use the stallion till his second movie, *Hills of Oklahoma* (1950). According to Allen, the horse was still green and hadn't been completely trained to work on a movie set.[25]

The Rex Allen movie *Rodeo King and the Senorita* (1951) was sort of a remake of Roy Rogers' *My Pal Trigger*. Koko performed a few tricks in this outing. The stallion nudged a barrel, causing it to roll. Later, Allen asked him if he wanted to say his prayers. Koko nodded yes, knelt on the ground, and tucked his head beside his leg. When villain Roy Barcroft caused Koko to crash into a fence, the chocolate stallion lay still on the ground as if his leg were injured. In a later sequence, Koko also took the peg out of the latch and opened the stall door.

Rex Allen on Koko, the world's wonder horse. The chocolate colored stallion had a blaze similar, but not identical, to the original Trigger's.

Like his cowboy master, Koko simply arrived on the B-western scene as it was winding down and was not showcased in movies like some of his peers.[26] According to Glenn Randall, Koko could have been trained to the same degree as Little Trigger, but it wasn't necessary. Allen's movies were limited in their budgets and did not often lend themselves to horse tricks, which required a little more time to prepare and shoot.

Dice: Beauty and Brains

Dice was a flashy black and white overo (pronounced oh-VAIR-oh) owned by Ralph McCutcheon, a man with talents as a trainer on a par with Glenn Randall. The overo paint was descended from horses brought to North America by Spanish Conquistadors, and with its dramatic irregular, scattered markings was revered by Native Americans. A horse described as overo generally has a single-color tail. The overo pattern may be either predominantly dark or white. Paints come in three specific coat patterns: overo, tobiano, and tovero.[27] Tonto's horse, Scout, was a tobiano, and the Cisco Kid's mount, Diablo, was an overo. Viewed together, these two paint types are quite different. The third type, tovero, is rare, and no screen cowboy would use one as it would be difficult to double.[28]

Noel Neill, who would become Lois Lane in *The Adventures of Superman* television show from the mid–1950s, got to ride the spectacular Dice while visiting the set of the Paramount film *Arizona* (1940).

Although many well-known stars rode Dice on screen, what he didn't have was a long and permanent career with a cowboy star equal to Roy Rogers. Had Dice been teamed with such a cowboy for the length of his motion picture career, there's no telling what fame he might have achieved. It could be said that Dice was a match for Trigger and Little Trigger together. He had Trigger's striking looks and camera presence combined with Little Trigger's endurance and talent.

Colorado native and outdoors man Ralph McCutcheon's lifelong dream of a career as a horse trainer was realized when he acquired Dice. Born around 1928, Dice was quick to learn

Many well-known stars rode Dice on screen, including Arthur Lake, best known as Dagwood Bumstead in 28 "Blondie" pictures from 1938 through 1950 *(Petrine Day Mitchum collection)*.

under McCutcheon's direction, and as soon as the animal was ready, they began making appearances at local rodeos. It was at a horse show in Colorado that the head of livestock procurement for MGM Studios noticed him and asked McCutcheon if Dice could be screen-tested for a western film. Dice passed with flying colors and beat out eight other horses for a role in the Richard Dix movie *It Happened in Hollywood*. McCutcheon was hired as trainer and went on to enjoy a successful career in both movies and television.

Dice was a hard horse to forget once you saw him on screen. He earned a reputation among filmmakers as a great performer with a repertoire tailor-made for the movie business. Dice was especially valuable to movie-makers because of his extraordinary ability to "track"—

that is, he was able to follow a predetermined path on cue. This is difficult for horses and very important for a filmmaker who positioned cameras and lighted set. Tracking was a tremendous asset while working under a deadline and, especially, a tight budget. In rehearsals, human actors blocked scenes so they knew when and how to hit certain marks after cameras started rolling. In rehearsals Dice would work at liberty. McCutcheon would walk him at the desired speed along a predetermined path. When the director, actors, and crew were ready to film a scene, Dice was turned loose and cued. He did not veer from the original walk-through.

Many Western stars rode Dice. Wild Bill Elliott used Dice when Columbia cast him as the lead in its 15-chapter serial *The Great Adventures of Wild Bill Hickok* (1938) and again in *Frontiers of '49* (1940). Dice was even cast as an Arabian (true Arabs do not come as paints) in *Tarzan's Desert Mystery* (studio, 1943) with the one and only Johnny Weissmuller. Columbia Pictures hired Dice extensively, which secured McCutcheon the position of head horse trainer and handler for the studio.

Dice was also featured in *Cowboy from Brooklyn*. About 35 minutes into the movie, star Dick Powell arrived at Grand Central Station in the heart of New York City. He serenaded a waiting crowd of fans in the grand ballroom. After he finished, co-stars Pat O'Brien and Ronald Reagan presented him with Dice as a gift. The overo appeared from behind a curtain, fully tacked. He was cued by a handler (probably Ralph McCutcheon) to rear up. Powell, whose character was afraid of animals, ran away, leaving Dice standing in a corner. The scene was quick but, with a frame by frame inspection, the black and white markings confirm the horse as Dice.

Dice has often been confused with other overo paints working in Hollywood at the same time. He did not appear with Gene Autry in *Comin' Round the Mountain* (1936) as a renegade Mustang stallion. It has also been reported that Autry rode Dice in *Strawberry Roan* (1948) when in fact the flashy paint was the same animal who would become Duncan Renaldo's mount, Diablo, in *The Cisco Kid* television series. Dice has also been confused with another overo named Domino who was ridden by Charlton Heston in *The Big Country* (United Artists, 1958).

The high point of Dice's career occurred in 1946 when he was cast as the lead horse with Gregory Peck and Jennifer Jones in director King Vidor's epic Western *Duel in the Sun* (Selznick International, 1946). Ralph McCutcheon was hired as technical advisor and horse supplier. *Duel in the Sun* was produced by none other than David O. Selznick, who saw it as a way of duplicating his success seven years earlier with *Gone with the Wind* (MGM, 1939). *Duel in the Sun* featured an all-star cast including the great Lionel Barrymore, silent film star Lillian Gish, and, as the film's narrator, the legendary Orson Welles. Dice was at his peak, in great company, and up to the challenge of such an important movie.

Based on the novel by Niven Busch, *Duel in the Sun* was a huge money-maker. As much a supporting character as any human on the set, Dice was featured in key scenes along with the two lead actors. Gregory Peck even referred to the overo by name on screen. The producer saw Dice as such an asset that after *Duel in the Sun* was completed his contract was extended to participate in a cross-country promotional tour. The studio did not allow Dice to be used in any other motion picture while *Duel in the Sun* was playing the national circuit.

Dice's last film was *Thunderhoof* (Columbia, 1948), the story of a wild stallion. Reportedly McCutcheon had difficulty with Dice during the production as the horse was growing old and showing signs of senility. After *Thunderhoof*, Dice was retired and put out to pasture at the McCutcheon stables in Van Nuys, California. In 1958 when Dice's health started to fade, he was humanely put to sleep. He was 30 years of age.

With Dice's career earnings Ralph McCutcheon bought and developed a large stable of horses for movie work. A standout in his herd was Highland Dale, a black stallion from Missouri. The horse came to be called Beaut but would go on to even greater fame as Fury.

Like Dice before him, Beaut combined the beauty and talent of Trigger and Little Trigger. He was never teamed with a particular cowboy star. Instead he was used in a variety of movie roles and would eventually build quite a resume: *Black Beauty* (20th Century–Fox, 1946); *Gypsy Colt* (MGM, 1954); *Johnny Guitar* (Republic, 1954); *Outlaw Stallion* (Columbia, 1954); and *Giant* (Warner Bros., 1956).

Even with all his appearances in A-list movies, Beaut found his greatest fame in a contemporary western television show titled *Fury*. It ran an astounding 116 episodes from 1955 till 1960.[29] The show was later syndicated under the title *Brave Stallion* from 1960 until 1966.

After Beaut retired from his life as a Hollywood star he remained with McCutcheon. The ebony stallion eventually developed a breathing disorder. He died in 1972 at age 29.

Bays in the Background

Beyond a fabulous star like Trigger, there were dozens of horses on movie sets during the heyday of the western. There were the extras, the anonymous beasts of burden who pulled stagecoaches, buckboards, and covered wagons. There were the old reliables who carried supporting players and posses on their backs in hundreds of A- and B-western features. Equine extras came in a variety of colors, but 90 percent of the time, they were bay. These anonymous horses were the ones that villains like Roy Barcroft or Leroy Mason rode. Sidekick Gabby Hayes' regular mount Eddie was a bay. As a rule, only star players or Indians rode more colorful mounts.

The bays in the background were loyal, sturdy and dependable. They ran their hearts out, took many a tumble, endured the sound of gunfire, worked long hours, and tolerated heavy-handed novice riders. Although extra horses were looked upon as atmosphere, like the stars, they had to be well schooled with even tempered dispositions. According to Anthony Amaral's book *Movie Horses — Their Treatment and Training*, in the 1950s studios were paying $10 a day for the use of a background horse.[30]

"Trigger" got lots of well deserved attention, but it was the bays in the background who added atmosphere and context.

Highland Dale, aka Beaut, aka Fury.

13

Horse Hero Comic Books

Comic books were instrumental in furthering the celebrity of cowboys and their horses. In the 1940s and 1950s, before the onslaught of television and the invention of video games, the major forms of entertainment for kids were movies, radio, and comic books. The cowboy was king in all three. It was the Golden Age of comics, and they sold in the millions. Almost every movie cowboy (along with a few cowgirls) was featured within the pages of comic books published by such companies as Fawcett, Magazine Enterprises (ME) and Dell. When the Saturday matinee was over, youngsters left the movie theater and headed straight for the local drugstore to spend what was left of their allowance on comic books. Coincidentally, they cost the same as a movie.

Comic books were first seen as throwaway kiddy entertainment. Parents and even publishers assumed that after a few readings, they would be trashed. However, because the stories and characters were so entertaining and engaging, children started collecting them. Some fans stayed loyal and, in some cases, continued that way into adulthood.

The talented writers and artists were the backbone of the industry. Not only were they prolific, but the quality of their work remained consistently high. Some of the best stories related to Trigger and his peers are found in comic books. The history of horse heroes and the B-western genre would not be complete without discussing comics and the talented people who produced them.

Horse Hero Comic Books

Roy Rogers' Trigger, Gene Autry's Champion, and *The Lone Ranger's Famous Horse Hi-Yo Silver* were among the most popular comic books Dell published in the 1950s.[1] Some of the greatest talents in the comic book industry worked on these titles. An amazing powerhouse of creativity — and all for the cost of one dime! Although some illustrations and scripts remain uncredited to this day, it has been determined that Gaylord Du Bois (pronounced Du Boyce, like "voice") and, later Paul S. Newman, wrote most of the story lines; Sam Savitt painted striking covers for all three titles; and Tom Gill rendered the great interior art in the *Hi-Yo Silver* comics.

While Dell dominated horse hero comic books, other companies produced their own titles. Charlton Comics Group published two of note: *Rocky Lane's Black Jack* and *Black Fury. Rocky Lane's Black Jack* started with issue number 20; it ran from November 1957 till November 1959, ending with issue number 28, and included work by Steve Ditko, who would go on to Marvel and draw the first Spiderman comics. *Black Fury* was published from May 1955 till

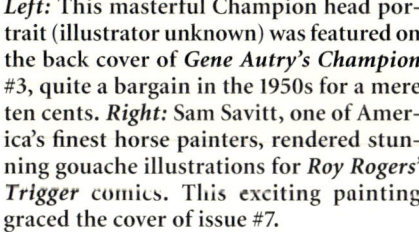

Left: This masterful Champion head portrait (illustrator unknown) was featured on the back cover of *Gene Autry's Champion* #3, quite a bargain in the 1950s for a mere ten cents. *Right:* Sam Savitt, one of America's finest horse painters, rendered stunning gouache illustrations for *Roy Rogers' Trigger* comics. This exciting painting graced the cover of issue #7.

March–April 1966, an impressive 57 issues, more than any other equine title. Steve Ditko also penned one *Black Fury* story. By far the best illustrator associated with *Black Fury* was the late Ernest Huntley Hart, who also went by the pseudonym E.H. Huntley. His dramatic and well-muscled depictions of the ebony stallion are prized by collectors to this day.[2]

Pound for pound, DC and Fawcett artists did more dynamic and accomplished interior work than what was done at Dell. Tom Gill was the exception. While his work did not have the flourish of a Gil Kane, it was refined and solid.[3]

Roy Rogers Comics

In 1939 Dell Publishing took over a "one-shot" comic book series from United Features Syndicate (UFS) called *Single Series* and renamed it *Four-Color Comics.* This was a test market venue; if a title was well received, it would be published on a regular basis under its own title. The first western title Dell published in this line was *Roy Rogers Comics* #38, issued April 1944. It came complete with a Western character full-color photo cover (a first), two inside black and white (or sepia) full-sized photos, and a color photo back. Due to its significance in the history of Western comic books, it's considered the "daddy of them all" and as such has become a highly sought after piece of Roy Rogers paper memorabilia and a prized comic book collectible.[4]

Gene Autry's Champion #9 gouache cover by Sam Savitt. Dell horse hero comic covers were done independently from interior stories and did not reflect plot lines. Savitt and his editors discussed cover ideas till the best concept was agreed on.

In point of fact Dell comics remain one of the best resources for quality photos of Roy Rogers and Trigger in their prime. They were a great showcase for the ornate cowboy outfits for which Rogers became famous. One also sees "Trigger" in his spectacular show tack. Little Trigger graced a few covers and was featured in many interior cover shots. Even Trigger Jr. showed up a couple of times on inside cover shots. Every now and then, Rogers was pictured with an anonymous palomino double. In all probability, the casual use of the original Trigger on the covers had more to do with frequency and availability than accuracy; doubles on covers were not given a second thought. The original Trigger appeared on the covers of five of the *Four-Color* issues: 117, 124, 144, 153, and 177. Issue 86 sported a cover with Rogers and an unidentified Trigger look-alike.

Although many of the photos of Roy Rogers appeared to be candid, most were Republic Studios publicity shots that were not used in any other medium. They can be found only in comic books and, with rare exceptions, only in original issues. Noted photographers such as Republic's Ramon Freulich took some of the photos. Like most vintage western comics, Roy Rogers issues are either difficult to locate in nice condition, or, when they are found, very expensive. *The Official Overstreet Comic Book Price Guide* lists them with a hefty market price in near-mint condition.

When *Roy Rogers* became a monthly comics title on its own, "Trigger" occasionally shared a cover with his master. The original Trigger may be seen on issues 7, 9, 13, 15, 19, 21, 23, 27, 30, 36, 41, 43, 51, 92 (*Roy Rogers Comics* became *Roy Rogers and Trigger Comics* with this issue), 97, 102, 105, 106, 112, 118, 125, 128, 129, and 131. Little Trigger is pictured with Rogers on the covers of issues 2, 5, 71, 76, 77, and 100. Pal was featured on the covers of issues 4, 5, and 9 of *Dale Evans Queen of the Westerns Comics*. The photos were printed so darkly that Pal sometimes looks more chestnut colored than palomino. As one might expect, Buttermilk was pictured with Evans on a number of later covers.

Roy Rogers Comics were eventually reissued as *Roy Rogers and Trigger Comics* in 1967 under the Gold Key imprint. There were many Western titles through the 1970s and beyond; *Roy Rogers Comics* alone ran for 159 issues and was fairly representative of the cowboy genre. The high production values, especially the photographs used, remained consistent throughout the years.

Roy Rogers' Trigger Comics

Trigger appeared in every Roy Rogers comic book, of course. He had always been used by writers of books, comics, and radio as a sounding board for Rogers when he was riding alone. This was a way to move a story forward and to humanize Trigger. Through comic books, writers and artists could embellish and broaden a character's legend further than in movies because any scenario could be realized. Trigger rated his own story in Rogers' *Four-Color Comics*. A regular Trigger solo backup feature began in *Roy Rogers Comics* number 20 (August 1949) and continued until number 46 (1951). They returned from issues 100 to 131.[5] Trigger was even allotted a story in the initial issue of Dell's *Western Roundup* series in 1952.

Giving the palomino his own comic book was a logical move, and he got his own series in Dell's *Four-Color* line. The first appeared in issue 329 (May 1951). The series got its own title for the second issue (November 1951) complete with a photo of the original Trigger gracing the cover. Published on a bi-monthly basis, fifteen more issues of *Roy Rogers' Trigger Comics* appeared from December 1952 till June 1955 (copyrighted by Roy Rogers Enterprises). Taken

Roy Rogers' Trigger comics #15. Sam Savitt was not provided with photo reference when he painted Trigger or Champion and consequently had to improvise their markings.

together, *Roy Rogers' Trigger* accounts for approximately 50 separate Trigger adventures. All the covers included a small photo of Rogers in the upper right-hand corner.

Gaylord Du Bois established a context for horse heroes in comic books by keeping the animal's owner out of the stories lest human overshadow horse. Roy Rogers did not appear in Trigger stories, although his name came up occasionally. Likewise, Gene Autry took a back seat to his horse in *Gene Autry's Champion*. Silver was handled differently: The Lone Ranger was present, narrating the adventures of the stallion when he was wild.

The first Champion comic book featured a photo cover, as had the second Trigger comic. Periodically photos were used to grace interior and back covers. Photos were not used in the Silver comics. This practice of using photos did not last long. Drawings were almost mandatory with horse hero comics because covers necessitated exciting scenes to draw potential buyers—scenes that would have been almost impossible to recreate with live action and too expensive to photograph anyway.

Not only did the creative talents in the comic book field work anonymously, rarely getting credit for their text or images; they also worked independently from each other.[6] Anonymity was company policy and the norm. A few of the talents preferred it that way, seeing comics as a vehicle towards a career in illustration or, better yet, as gallery painters. It's interesting to note with regards to western comics that writers seemed to stay for the duration of their careers, while artists moved in and out of the field.

According to author and Roy Rogers expert Ray White, "To get around the 'no signing' policy of comic book publishers, artists often placed their names or initials in conspicuous places within a story, just as famed caricaturist Al Hirschfield hid his daughter Nina's name in every drawing he did. Comic book artists placed their names on grave stones, signs on country stores, etc."[7]

John Buscema, who would later make a name for himself at Marvel comics drawing the Silver Surfer and Conan characters, drew nine Trigger stories featured in *Roy Rogers* comics 100–108. Morris Gollub might have painted the first cover (*Four-Color* #329, May 1951); Rafael DeSoto signed a portrait of Trigger and a palomino colt used on the back cover of the same issue. *Roy Rogers' Trigger* interior stories were illustrated in part by Al Savitt and Til Goodan.

Robert W. Phillips credited western painter and historian Randy Steffens as one of the men who illustrated interior stories for *Roy Rogers' Trigger* comics. During an interview at his home in North Salem, New York, Sam Savitt confirmed that his own younger brother Al had illustrated some interior stories in the same issues. Al Savitt kept a list of all the Trigger stories he illustrated.[8]

Both Savitt brothers were living in the New York City vicinity, close to the Dell offices, when these comics were produced. By 1950 Randy Steffens was in his home state of Texas editing a local magazine. He even accepted a number of freelance assignments, including many from *Western Horseman* magazine. With all due respect to Robert W. Phillips, there is no evidence to suggest that Steffens worked for Dell. When comparing a handwritten list Al Savitt provided with a list of stories Phillips thought were attributed to Steffens (to my knowledge Phillips never interviewed Steffens), one finds they are practically identical. This confusion is understandable because Al Savitt and Randy Steffens had similar drawing styles, especially with respect to the representation of horses. Phillips noted that Steffens did interior stories in issues 3, 4, 5, 6, 7, 8, 9, 10, 12, 13, 14, 15, and 16. Al Savitt claimed to have illustrated stories in all but two of the same issues, numbers 6 and 15. Given that the illustrations in these stories look like the work of one man, it is easy to conclude that Al Savitt did them all.

Both Randy Steffens and Al Savitt depicted horses with slight features particularly in the head, often "dished" (concave profile with prominent eyes) like Arabians. But the two depicted humans differently. Steffens' were very generic and very white Anglo-Saxon protestant, while Al Savitt's looked almost native American.[9]

When *Roy Rogers' Trigger Comics* ended with issue 17, it merged with *Roy Rogers Comics*.[10]

Gaylord Du Bois

Gaylord Du Bois had a long, diverse and prolific career in comic books. He was the major — perhaps the only — writer on the *Roy Rogers' Trigger Comics* from 1944 to 1960. He produced approximately 250 separate adventures.[11]

Du Bois' first Trigger story was published in 1946 in *Roy Rogers Comics* and titled "Trigger Trails the Herd." From July to December 1956, Du Bois' Trigger stories appeared in the re-christened *Roy Rogers and Trigger Comics*.

A deeply religious man, Du Bois refused assignments having to do with sex, horror, or the occult. His scripts were known for the moral and emotional values they portrayed and that made him partial to his Roy Rogers stories because the King of the Cowboy's Christian ideals where similar to his own.

Around 1938 Du Bois met Oskar Lebeck, who was on the editorial staff of Whitman. Through that connection, Du Bois began writing comic book scripts full time.

Sam Savitt

Dell cover artist Sam Savitt worked apart from writers and interior artists; it wasn't imperative that his paintings relate to the stories inside. Savitt's gouache covers were dramatic and eye-catching, powerful images that could stop a potential buyer in their tracks. Savitt's job was to get a kid's attention, and he did it. Once seen on newsstands and comic book racks, his dynamic covers were hard to pass up.

Sam Savitt's travels provided him with the opportunity to observe, ride, and train horses of all breeds and temperaments. He became accomplished in both English and western riding styles. These disciplines, needless to say, served his paintings.

Savitt's first significant comic book work came right out of art school when he was hired by Western Printing to paint a series of Dell comic book covers beginning with *Gene Autry's Champion*. At the same time, Dell was premiering *The Lone Ranger's Famous Horse Hi-Yo Silver* and *Roy Roger's Trigger*. By the time he finished working for Western Printing in 1960, he had produced covers and interior material for Dell's *Four-Color Comics* line and a variety of miscellaneous titles such as *Ben Bowie and his Mountain Men, Red Ryder Ranch Magazine, King of the Royal Mounted, Indian Chief, The Cisco Kid, Ben-Hur,* and *Zane Grey's Stories of the West*. He painted 15 of the 17 *Roy Rogers' Trigger* covers; 27 of the *Gene Autry's Champion* covers; and all 36 *Hi-Yo Silver* covers. The list of Savitt covers now stands at about 150.[12]

Al Savitt

Al Savitt was about five years younger than his brother Sam. Beyond his illustrations for Western Printing in the *Roy Rogers' Trigger* and *Gene Autry's Champion* comics, records of

Interior pen and ink illustration by Al Savitt, Sam Savitt's younger brother, for *Roy Rogers' Trigger* #17 (June–August 1955) for a story titled "Trigger Comes Home."

his professional work are vague. According to Al Savitt's sister-in-law Bette Orkin, during the comic book years he did a lot of interior illustrations for books and magazines. Many were not necessarily horse stories.[13]

In 1956 Al Savitt received the Thomas Alva Edison Foundation National Mass Media Award for artwork in *A Treasury of Dogs* (published by Western Printing) as the best comic book aimed at children over eight years of age.

Till Goodan

According to western comics expert Bill Black in his *Golden Age Greats Volume II: Roy Rogers and the Silver Screen Cowboys — An Illustrated History of the Matinee Western*, Till Goodan (or Goodman as it's also been spelled) illustrated some of the interior Trigger stories. Author Tim Lasiuta believes Till Goodan illustrated *Gene Autry* comics.[14]

Stories

The comic book version of Trigger was given human characteristics and allowed to think on the same level. Trigger was wise beyond animal norms. Although Du Bois also humanized the Lone Ranger's stallion Silver, his stories were never silly or unnecessarily violent. Du Bois' writings were warm and heartfelt and stand as some of the best of this type.

In the Trigger comic stories, the palomino was in the care of the Hanford family, and many of the stories took place while he was living on their Circle H ranch. While Trigger was established as Roy Rogers's horse, for unknown reasons he was cared for by Uncle Mike, Aunt Martha, and their ranch foreman, Curly. Also on hand were the Hanford nephew and niece twins, Pete and Pat. A particular action of Trigger's would draw the attention of the children, prompting one of his caretakers to recount the palomino's deeds of heroism. These stories were told in retrospect almost completely without dialogue balloons, much like the great *Prince Valiant* Sunday comic strips by Hal Foster — more illustrated short stories than comic books.

In other stories Trigger roamed the open range with a pony named Pinto Jack and a band of mares, protecting them from humans and animal predators and the forces of nature. With issue 109, Trigger resided on Rogers' ranch in the care of a young Mexican boy named Chico.

Hi-Yo Silver Comics

Although Silver's presence was strong in print and on the radio, and although he was referred to by name at all times, his role on the big and little screens was limited mostly to beautiful transportation. His spectacular feats were relegated to books and comic books, and it was in the latter that Silver outdistanced Trigger and Champion. The Dell issues collectively are far superior to anything else published in the horse hero genre. They had the highest consistency of craftsmanship, the strongest narrative, and contained the most interesting characters. *The Lone Ranger's Famous Horse Hi-Yo Silver Comics* also had the longest run of the Dell equine titles, 36 issues.[15]

While Paul S. Newman produced a handful of key stories for *The Lone Ranger's Famous Horse Hi-Yo Silver* and his work on those comics is considered his best work in the genre, Gaylord Du Bois contributed the lion's share of the text for the series. He was first to translate the stories to comics, embellishing and enhancing the bygone western settings, and he greatly refined the cast of characters, endearing them to readers. Gaylord Du Bois wrote *The Lone Ranger* from 1948 till 1962 and *Hi-Yo Silver* from 1952 till 1960.

Illustrator Tom Gill defined the Lone Ranger's world, giving form to Paul S. Newman's and Gaylord Du Bois's words. With his clean, crisp, stylized work, he brought their stories to life, and fans believed. His version of the Lone Ranger also closely mirrored the character Clayton Moore played on television.

Interior pen and ink illustration by the prolific Tom Gill for *The Lone Ranger's Hi-Yo Silver* #13 (January–March 1955), story titled "Silver and the Dry Water Hole."

Cover artist Sam Savitt was a fan of Will James, and the legendary western painter's influence is obvious in Savitt's dynamic gouache cover for *The Lone Ranger's Hi-Yo Silver* #16.

In 1949 Tom Gill was hired to draw the Gene Autry comic strip. Sadly, by the time he was done, the market for the western genre was saturated and Gill's strips were never published. Luckily he took the strips to Oscar LeBeck, an editor at Western Printing. Gill noted, "Roy Rogers indirectly got me started doing westerns when Gene Autry approached me to do a comic strip to compete with Roy. Once my editors at Dell saw it they took me off other subjects I was doing for them and put me forever more doing westerns."[16]

Gill was offered a half-year run on a western strip, *The Lone Ranger*, an association with a character that would last for 20 years, into the 1970s. His straightforward style became synonymous with the character, bringing a powerful visual continuity to the entire series. At one time or another, Tom Gill worked on all the major titles associated with the Lone Ranger character — *The Lone Ranger, The Lone Ranger's Famous Horse Hi-Yo Silver* (his pencils began with issue #7 and ran through every issue), and some of the *Tonto* comic book interiors.[17]

Silver Stories

The Silver comic book stories were usually narrated by the Lone Ranger. In the first comic book tale, "Birth of a Prince," readers met Silver's sire, the wild horse leader King Sylvan, and his favorite mare, Moussa, Silver's mother. Silver even had a sidekick, the mischievous Black Scamper, a black colt with a white blaze.

By far the most interesting character in the Silver myth, one who added a symbolic aspect to the stories, was an Indian named Keenay. The cleverest of the Apache horse hunters, he swore he would catch Silver or die trying. Keenay would speak in grandiose terms during his quest: "O medicine horse! O silver colt! Great is your wisdom and power! But old Keenay will yet be your master!"

Always traveling alone, Keenay tirelessly pursued Silver. The old horse hunter learned to respect the white stallion, for not only would the animal take flight to keep his freedom, but he would fight if necessary. Keenay was almost a tragic figure with his obsession for the great white stallion he would never have. Keenay became Silver's shadow from one adventure and narrow escape to another. To the stallion, the old Apache was his enemy trying to end his freedom; to readers, Keenay was a guardian angel rescuing Silver from others who also had designs on him. In the end and after years of failed attempts, Keenay realized Silver would not be his. The magic horse would be ridden by another.

A *Complete List of* Roy Roger's Trigger Comics

Roy Rogers' Trigger (Four-Color Comics #329), May 1951: Cover: While it's not known for sure, Morris Gollub may have painted the first one. Inside cover: photo of original Trigger at liberty and rearing up. Inside back cover: photo of the original Trigger in full show tack, bowing. Back cover: illustration by Rafael DeSoto (signed) of Trigger and a foal. Story: "Trigger" by Gaylord Du Bois, illustrator unknown.

Roy Rogers' Trigger #2, September–November 1951. Cover: a heavily doctored photo of a Trigger look-alike. Back cover: painting of Trigger wading in a stream, illustrator unknown. Stories: "Trigger and the Drygulcher of Gunsight Notch" by Gaylord Du Bois, illustrated by A. Moore; "Trigger Junior Meets the Test" by Gaylord Du Bois, illustrated by A. Moore.

Roy Rogers' Trigger #3, December 1951–February 1952. Cover: Sam Savitt gouache painting. Stories: "Trigger Tackles a Sidewinder" by Gaylord Du Bois, illustrator unknown; "Trigger and the Underground Railway" by Gaylord Du Bois, illustrated by Al Savitt.

Roy Rogers' Trigger #4, March–May 1952. Cover: Sam Savitt gouache painting. Stories: "Trigger Fights for Life" by Gaylord Du Bois, illustrated by Al Savitt; "Weetamah's Bridle," author unknown, illustrator unknown but probably Al Savitt; "Trigger Trails the Lost" by Gaylord Du Bois, possibly illustrated by Moore.

Roy Rogers' Trigger #5, June–August 1952. Cover: Sam Savitt gouache painting. Stories: "Trigger Wins a Warrior's Plume" by Gaylord Du Bois, possibly illustrated by Moore; "Trigger Shares Danger on the Dark Continent" by Gaylord Du Bois, illustrated by Al Savitt.

Roy Rogers' Trigger #6, September–November 1952. Cover: Sam Savitt gouache painting. Stories: "Trigger Beats the Gun" by Gaylord Du Bois, possibly illustrated by Moore; "Trigger Runs the Gantlet" by Gaylord Du Bois, probably illustrated by Al Savitt.

Roy Rogers' Trigger #7, December 1952–February 1953. Cover: Sam Savitt gouache painting. Stories: "Trigger Takes to the Wild" by Gaylord Du Bois, illustrated by Al Savitt; "Trigger Outruns a Robber" by Gaylord Du Bois, illustrated by Al Savitt.

Roy Rogers' Trigger #8, March–May 1953. Cover: Sam Savitt gouache painting. Stories: "Trigger in Horse Thief Cove" by Gaylord Du Bois, possibly illustrated by Joe Russo; "Trigger and the Red Renegade" by Gaylord Du Bois, illustrated by Al Savitt.

Roy Rogers' Trigger #9, June–August 1953. Cover: Sam Savitt gouache painting. Stories: "Trigger Fights for Two" by Gaylord Du Bois, possibly illustrated by Joe Russo; "Trigger and the River's Secret" by Gaylord Du Bois, illustrated by Al Savitt.

Roy Rogers' Trigger #10, September–November 1953. Cover: Sam Savitt gouache painting. Stories: "Trigger in Killer Cat," author unknown, illustrated by Al Savitt; "Trigger Turns Detective," author unknown, illustrated by Al Savitt.

Roy Rogers' Trigger #11, December 1953–February 1954. Cover: Sam Savitt gouache painting. Stories: "Trigger and the Carnival Killer," author and artist unknown; "Trigger and the Milk Run," author and artist unknown.[18]

Roy Rogers' Trigger #12, March–May 1954. Cover: Sam Savitt gouache painting. Stories: "Trigger in Peril Rides the Storm," author unknown, illustrated by Al Savitt; "Trigger in Deep-Water Rustlers," author unknown, illustrated by Al Savitt.

Roy Rogers' Trigger #13, June–August 1954. Cover: Sam Savitt gouache painting. Stories: "Trigger in Timberland Terror," author unknown, illustrated by Al Savitt; "Trigger to the Rescue," author unknown, illustrated by Al Savitt.

Roy Rogers' Trigger #14, September–November 1954. Cover: Sam Savitt gouache painting. Stories: "Trigger in Tide of Peril," author unknown, illustrated by Al Savitt; "Trigger and the Moaning Cave," author unknown, illustrated by Al Savitt.

Roy Rogers' Trigger #15, December 1954–February 1955. Cover: Sam Savitt gouache painting. Stories: "Trigger in Challenge of the Wolf Pack," author unknown, probably illustrated by Al Savitt; "Trigger in Journey of Peril," author unknown, probably illustrated by Al Savitt.

Roy Rogers' Trigger #16, March/May 1955: Cover: Sam Savitt gouache painting. Stories: "Trigger King of the Herd," author unknown, illustrated by Al Savitt; "Trigger and the Morongo Roundup," author unknown, illustrated by Al Savitt.

Roy Rogers' Trigger #17, June–August 1955. Cover: Sam Savitt gouache painting. Stories: "Trigger in Rangeland Rescue," author unknown, illustrated by Al Savitt; "Trigger Comes Home," author unknown, illustrated by Al Savitt.

14

The Last Ride

"I can't say enough for him. I can't hardly go into the museum without getting tears in my eyes." — Roy Rogers[1]

The last motion picture in which the original Trigger appeared was *Pals of the Golden West,* released in December of 1951. Since the palomino was not in *Son of Paleface* (Paramount, 1952) or in any of the countless television variety shows Rogers and Evans did well into the 1970s, the *Roy Rogers Show* television episodes completed in 1957 are among his last filmed appearances.[2]

When *The Roy Rogers Show* came to an end, Rogers and Dale Evans appeared from 1958 to 1960 in fourteen NBC variety hours sponsored by Chevrolet called *The Chevy Show.* It was during one of these broadcasts that "Trigger" was officially retired. The "last ride" presentation took place at a rodeo performance with "Trigger" entering on the back of a flatbed truck. Little Trigger doubled for Trigger on this occasion (how oddly appropriate). Trigger Jr. was present and introduced as the original Trigger's replacement. Roy Rogers and Dale Evans continued to appear at fairs and such into the 1970s, but most of the time without horses.

The last time the "Trigger" character was portrayed on television was by a look-alike in a third season episode of *The Fall Guy* (February of 1984) titled "King of the Cowboys."

Rare straight-on solo shot of the original Trigger.

A beautiful shot of the original Trigger from the color movie *The Golden Stallion.*

One of Rogers' last appearances on a palomino was during the *Randy Travis — Happy Trails* television special shown on the Nashville Network in October of 1990.

In 1957, after 19 years in show business, the original Trigger was retired at age 23 to the Rogers' Chatsworth, California ranch. In 1963 Trigger was moved by Corky Randall to Hidden Valley, California. On June 27, 1965, Rogers sold his ranch and moved to Apple Valley. According to Corky, Trigger was not moved with the rest of the stock because of his age and blindness. It was thought that the stress of moving to unfamiliar surroundings would be difficult on the aged horse.

One of Trigger's greatest admirers, director William Witney, gave a description of Trigger in his final years in his booklet *Trigger Remembered.* Witney was directing a television show in the vicinity of the ranch where the palomino was stabled and made a point to visit him. According to Witney, Trigger's appearance was so altered that he was not even sure the horse he was looking at was indeed "the Old Man." Trigger was shrunken and his color was dull. His golden coat had grayed. He was gray around his eyes and ears. Witney didn't know he was with the right horse until he looked in his eye.[3]

Trigger lived an easy life until the day he took his final breath, July 3, 1965, almost exactly 31 years after he was born.[4]

Roy Rogers recalled one of the saddest phone calls he'd ever received. It was from one of Trigger's caregivers.[5] "I picked up the phone, and before anything was said, I said, 'Old Trigger died, didn't he?' I just had a feeling.... Danny said, 'Just a few minutes ago.' Danny had turned Trigger out after he'd fed him. He was feeding the other horses and he went and got a cup of coffee. Trigger was lying out there in the field but Danny thought he'd just laid down after he played around a little bit, so he went back out to finish feeding the horses. Then he said, 'I went back out there again, and he was just lying there. So I thought maybe I'd better check him.' He went out there and 'phht (Roy's voice cracks) ... he was gone.'"[6]

Bischoff's Taxidermy

Unable to face burying his close friend Trigger, Rogers decided to have him mounted by Bischoff's Taxidermy and Studio Prop Rental of Burbank, California.[7] An avid outdoorsman, Rogers hunted a variety of animals from North America to Africa. He kept taxidermists busy for years, and having Trigger mounted probably seemed normal. "So I came up with a plan to preserve Trigger for myself and for all the other people who loved him. I thought about the hunting trophies I had collected over the years and I contacted Mr. Bischoff, the famous taxidermist in Los Angeles, to see what he could do."[8]

Dale Evans and Dusty Rogers protested the plan, arguing for a funeral and a final resting place with a monument at a pet cemetery, but Rogers' mind was set. According to one source, Dale Evans "once said, 'All right. But when you go, I'm gonna have YOU stuffed and put on top of Trigger!' Roy said, 'Fine. Just make sure I'm smiling.'"[9]

Rogers ordered that Trigger be mounted in a rearing position in full regalia: bridle, saddle, and martingale. He always referred to Trigger as having been "mounted," not "stuffed" and would correct anyone if they used the latter term. An animal whose hide has been filled with sawdust is stuffed. An animal whose hide is stretched over a cast is mounted. After a taxidermist takes an animal's measurements, a Styrofoam mold is made, over which a fiberglass frame is created. The Styrofoam is removed after the fiberglass hardens. Finally, the animal hide is stretched over the fiberglass mold.

After Trigger was mounted, the Smithsonian Institution asked for him, but Rogers politely turned them down. For a time Trigger was in the living room of Rogers' home in Apple Valley, California. However, Roy Rogers had a very special place in mind for his four-legged co-star. Trigger was placed on display at the Roy Rogers and Dale Evans Museum in Victorville, California, where he stood until he was moved with the museum to Branson, Missouri, in 2003.

In 2005 the Branson Hollywood Wax Museum gave a Roy Rogers wax figure to Rogers' new museum by to be placed next to Trigger. Rogers always said in jest that he wanted to be stuffed and put on old Trigger; this is as close as he came.

More than once, Rogers said that he had Trigger mounted because he couldn't bear the thought of putting the horse in the ground. This statement suggests that the horse was preserved in his entirety, which of course is untrue — possibly the most untrue or erroneous statement Rogers ever made about Trigger. In actuality, all that was preserved of Trigger was his hide, mane, and tail. Everything else that made up the fabulous animal — his heart, brain, internal organs, eyes, and so on — were disposed of.[10] What was preserved was a facade, an illusion, if you will. There are those who find that ironic, and in some ways, appropriate.

Animals, like humans, grey as they age. According to Dusty Rogers in his autobiography, "Trigger lived to be 33 years old — more than 100 years in human terms. His golden hair had grayed considerably, and he was gray around his eyes and ears." It's entirely possible the taxidermist "enhanced" the markings on Trigger's face and put some makeup on his near side. One wonders how much cosmetic work was involved in his mounting process, especially since

The original Trigger in his last pose, compliments of Bischoff's Taxidermy. The wax figure of the King of the Cowboys was donated to the Roy Rogers and Dale Evans Museum by the Branson Hollywood Wax Museum (*Janey Miller collection*).

One of the last known photographs of Roy Rogers and the original Trigger together. Rogers was 52 at the time and Trigger was near 31. Trigger's mane had thinned out, but he had more hair than usual on his coat. Within a year after this photo was taken, the great palomino was dead *(Roy Dillow collection).*

Trigger now looks very plain. The subtlety of his features is missing, along with much of his musculature. He doesn't even have the definition of a carousel horse. His thick mane and forelock, much of what gave Trigger his beauty, are devoid of shape and sheen. If the eyes are truly the windows to the soul, the effect of glass substitutes is that of an empty stare. Like all mounted animals, Trigger looks vacuous, without personality. Trigger was truly an "old man" when he died, and that's what the taxidermist had to work with: an aged horse.[11]

There is little doubt that Roy Rogers loved the original Trigger. There is also little doubt that Rogers' humble beginning had a huge impact, and he was reluctant to part with material things as demonstrated by what was on display at the Victorville museum. However, Rogers would have done his beloved horse and his fans a greater service had he let Trigger remain a beautiful memory, rather than turn him into a generic substitute for past glory. The life-size bronze De L'Esprie sculpted for the plaza of the Autry National Center in Los Angeles is a far better tribute to Gene Autry and his Champion(s) than the mounted morbid remains of poor old Trigger. It's almost too bad the technology did not exist to freeze-dry Trigger. This eliminates most of the procedure used in traditional taxidermy. The results are much closer to the actual look of a particular subject.[12]

In his final form, Trigger requires regular upkeep. An exterminator is called in to make sure bugs and parasites do not damage his hide. His glass eyes are polished with window spray. His coat, mane and tail still require brushing.[13]

After a while, the mounted Trigger came to be treated like an inanimate object. During an appearance on the *American Rifleman Show*,[14] Rogers was interviewed in front of Trigger and Buttermilk (also mounted) in his Victorville museum. Trigger not only served as a backdrop, but also as a prop for Rogers and the *American Rifleman* host to lean against.

Unfortunately Rogers' decision to have Trigger mounted did not sit well with most fans and the poor old horse became the butt of jokes. "More hay, Trigger?" "No thanks, Roy, I'm stuffed!"[15]

As mentioned above, Trigger was not the only animal connected to Roy Rogers who ended up at the taxidermist's. Dale Evans may have originally protested Trigger's fate, but her quarter horse gelding, Buttermilk, ended up the same way. Penny Edwards remarked, "I started doing Roy's pictures when Dale was having a baby. I rode Buttermilk first. Years later, when I went to the Roy Rogers Museum, I almost fainted. I knew Roy had Trigger stuffed, but I did not realize that Buttermilk was there too; I loved that horse. I used to go out to Glenn Randall's ranch and practice on Buttermilk while mother rode Trigger."[16]

Even Rogers' German shepherd, Bullet, was mounted and joined the others on display at the museum. Trigger Jr. also suffered the same fate and ended up on open display mounted and fully tacked. Unfortunately he was positioned in a very unflattering, dancing pose. To make matters worse, his head and neck were placed in such a way that he looks ewe-necked, a neck bowed instead of arched. It is surprising that an experienced horseman like Rogers allowed such a basic fault in conformation, especially since Trigger Jr. wasn't ewe-necked when he was alive.

Little Trigger was not mounted. Perhaps that was his best reward for contributing so much to Roy Rogers' career. Nevertheless, Joel "Dutch" Dortch, member of the Happy Trails Foundation, stated, "Roy told me he sure regretted not having Little Trigger mounted and placed in the museum as he did Trigger and Trigger Jr."

The Roy Rogers and Dale Evans Museum in Victorville

The Roy Rogers and Dale Evans Museum was located in the high desert city of Victorville, about two hours northeast of Los Angeles. Once described as romantically picturesque, Victorville became a generic retirement area best described as typical of contemporary America with strip malls, industrial blight, and condos everywhere.

Out in front of its "Fort Apache" styled structure, the Roy Rogers and Dale Evans Museum featured a huge statue of Trigger in the classic rearing pose. Inside was the mounted Trigger. At the museum's peak of popularity it was estimated some 200,000 visitors attended each year, and most of them went to see Trigger. Dusty Rogers said, "We close at five and stop selling tickets at 4:30. But people come after that and beg to get in for a few minutes. They drove 3,000 miles just to see Trigger. We let them in — and they go away, happy."[17]

On October 31, 1995, vandals struck at the Roy Rogers and Dale Evans Museum and sprayed graffiti on the pedestal supporting the statue of Trigger, the nearby sidewalk, and a sign near the monument. A portion of the statue's anatomy was also painted blue over the same weekend. The following Monday the statue had been restored.[18]

Trigger III

At the end of Roy Rogers' life, "Trigger" took the form of a grey motorized cart with handle bars. The aged King of the Cowboys used it to get around the huge Victorville museum. Painted in a white script font on the side of the diminutive vehicle was the name "Trigger III."

Trigger's Final Home

In 2003 Graebel Los Angeles Movers, Inc., moved nine truckloads of memorabilia and household goods from Victorville, California, to Branson, Missouri. The load included the entire Roy Rogers and Dale Evans collection including Trigger, Trigger Jr., Buttermilk, and Bullet.

The new Roy Rogers and Dale Evans Museum in Branson is 26,000 square feet and occupies four acres. The building, located at 3950 Green Mountain Drive, includes a 300-seat theatre which is home base to Dusty Rogers and his band, the High Riders. Dusty's son Dustin was appointed general manager, a job that includes running the museum, theater, and gift shop with the help of other family members.

The museum displays are arranged on both sides of a horseshoe-shaped walk which resembles an old western town. The centerpiece behind glass is Trigger. In April of 2003 a seven-man crew took almost two hours to install the 23½-foot-tall fiberglass Trigger statue outside.

Even with a move to Branson, the Roy Rogers and Dale Evans Museum may not exist beyond the next two decades. It's critical that Roy Rogers' children have the celebrity to draw fans to their theatre on a regular basis. Their audience may shrink as baby boomers age and cannot travel as much. Dusty Rogers will be past normal retirement age in 2011.

Gene Autry will probably be the only B-western star whose name will endure and carry the legacy of the B-western cowboy into the future. This will be done through the Autry National Center. This great resource will remain viable for learning and entertainment for decades to come. Some B-western elements will probably also survive: the fancy Nudie Cohen–styled clothes; Bohlin-styled tack; the influence of the stunt work in films; some of the music ("Don't Fence Me In," "Back in the Saddle Again," "Happy Trails," and "Tumbling Tumble Weeds"); the "Hi Yo Silver" catch-phrase; and possibly the image of a Roy Rogers–type hero on a rearing horse.

Unfortunately, the Roy Rogers and Dale Evans Museum, everything in it and the land it sat on, was not put into a trust. Apparently it wasn't thought to be necessary because the museum was already a tax exempt institution. After Roy Rogers died, however, the IRS gave his estate a bill and one year to pay it. The bill was in the amount of one half of the IRS's assessed value of the museum, contents, and land. The values were apparently based on the overblown prices people were willing to pay at an estate sale for Roy Rogers memorabilia. At that point, the mounted Trigger was valued at $400,000. It took months to straighten the situation out.[19]

During a Museum Board of Directors meeting in Apple Valley in 2004, Dusty Rogers was asked about the possibility of the Smithsonian owning Trigger and the other horses. He denied there was any truth to the rumor. Dusty said that Trigger, Trigger, Jr., Buttermilk,

Roy Rogers and Trigger: truly a team.

their saddles, and Nellybelle are all owned by the Roy Rogers and Dale Evans Museum itself. Dale Evans, he said, made an outright gift of them to the museum shortly before her death in December 2000. Dusty Rogers said that if and when the Roy Rogers and Dale Evans Museum ceased to do business, being organized as a charitable organization under the IRS Code section 501(c)(3), the museum had to distribute its assets (including Trigger) to another non-profit organization like the Buffalo Bill Museum in Cody, Wyoming, or the National Cowboy Hall of Fame and Museum. It is not believed that Trigger will ever end up in the Autry Museum. In the end, Trigger will never be owned by a collector, fan, or private individual.

Despite what Dusty Rogers says, it's been rumored that Trigger, Buttermilk, et al., are currently on loan to the Roy Rogers and Dale Evans Museum for 15 years. The deal was made as part of the tax settlement; their value was deducted from the tax bill, and they were loaned to the museum for display. The official word is that "Trigger, Trigger Jr., Bullet and Butter-milk were donated to the Roy Rogers–Dale Evans Museum by Dale. In turn, we can only donate them to another non-profit 501(c)(3) foundation. The Smithsonian has expressed interest in Trigger, and it will be his last stop when we are done. Nellybelle belongs to the Rogers family."[20]

Roy Rogers' Funeral

Appearing on *A&E Biography* toward the end of his life, Rogers remarked, "The sad part about getting up in years, I think, most of all my sidekicks are gone. It's sad. My horse's gone. But it's life." On July 6, 1998, Rogers, too, passed away.

Roy Rogers' family intended that he go out with the same flair with which he lived; that was obvious from his funeral with its honor guard, horse-drawn caisson, and such. However, given all the "Triggers" Rogers used throughout his career, one wonders why there wasn't a palomino look-alike present. As a very important part of Rogers' image, "Trigger" in his fancy show saddle should have been part of the funeral procession. Rogers' trademark white hat could have hung off the right side of the saddle horn, one of his colorful neckerchiefs on the other side, and reversed boots in the stirrups. A riderless palomino would have been a memorable and powerful statement.[21]

When it came to his career, Roy Rogers often cited three lucky breaks: Gene Autry going into the army; being able to sneak on to the Republic Pictures lot for an audition after he learned (almost by accident) that the studio was looking for a singing cowboy; and finding Trigger. Rogers said, "Without those three incidents, there wouldn't have been a Roy Rogers."[22] The golden palomino helped make the King of the Cowboys, and, to that degree, Trigger is not only a bittersweet memory of days gone by; he was the best friend Roy Rogers ever had.[23]

15

My Pal Trigger

"He's not for sale at any price. I couldn't part with him. But more important than that, he's not really mine — he belongs to children everywhere." — Roy Rogers[1]

I last visited the Roy Rogers and Dale Evans Museum in the summer of 1998 when it was still in Victorville, California. I went fully aware that Roy Rogers was in poor health and would not be around much longer. I wanted to see him once more.

Fittingly, it was right after I'd left the Trigger display that I heard someone say, "There's Roy!" I looked down a dimly lit hallway and saw a distinctive silhouette — a figure in a familiar flat-topped styled cowboy hat with the "Denton Pinch" creased crown. Rogers was driving a grey motorized cart in my direction and stopped directly in front of me. A crowd gathered and flashbulbs began to go off. Although I was speechless as I stared into his familiar eyes I managed to extend my hand. The King of the Cowboys' grip was weak.

Roy Rogers was dressed as one would expect: western dress pants, black boots, a bolo tie, a western shirt, and a jacket. Between heart attacks, angina, and diabetes, he looked every bit of 86 years. Decades of touring and making movies showed on the old cowboy's face. He was a little slouched over, looked a little heavy, and his thinning hair was grey. Age spots dotted his face, his breathing was irregular, and he was hard of hearing — probably due to all the gunfire he'd been exposed to on movie sets and on hunting trips.

Roy Rogers was accompanied by a bodyguard, obviously there to make sure enthusiastic fans did not overwhelm their cowboy hero. In his fragile state, Rogers could not tolerate a strong hug. A woman gently put her arm around him while another told Rogers what joy he'd brought to everyone's lives. Women teared up and men became little boys.

As fans continued to take pictures I discreetly asked the bodyguard how Rogers' health was. He candidly replied, "He's not going to be around much longer." My mood went from wonder to bittersweet. Seeing my boyhood hero old and frail was difficult. Everyone present could see he was close to the end.

I will always regret that I could not have a long private conversation with Roy Rogers. I had many questions to ask about his horses, but the time for interviewing him had past. Rogers had only minutes to reciprocate his fans' greetings individually; no one could feel he owed more after a lifetime of entertaining them. Rogers was a hero and father figure to the generation who grew up on his movies. Still, I felt like he belonged only to me.

Fantasy and illusion were Roy Rogers' art, and the line between that art and reality blurred. He may have started out merely as an entertainer creating a celebrity persona for himself and his horse, but he represented much more.

While B-westerns may have been conceived as cheap entertainment and simple moral-ity plays, they too became more. They directed and nurtured young fans. Roy Rogers' movies were made with sublime innocence and breathtaking artistry (especially with regards to horse-manship) at a time when their simple values rang straight and true. In these cynical times with antiheroes as the norm, Rogers' glorious black and white movies exist in an eternal state of hope and as cinematic anachronisms. Devoted fans require no mature plot lines, no revi-sionist analysis; it's enough that Rogers and Trigger weren't afraid to meet injustice head on and fight it with great style no matter the odds. Optimism is at their core.

It's a common misconception to assume that B-westerns were only popular with chil-dren. That could not be further from the truth. Not everyone, especially in the thirties, identified with gangsters and wealthy socialites. The migration that took place at that time from the farm to the city was massive and those involved saw themselves much more read-ily in Gene Autry and Roy Rogers than they did in William Powell. People could really iden-tify with cowboys and their fight against crooked bankers and corrupt businessmen who wanted to chase them off their land.

Peter Stanfield makes a great case for how popular B-westerns were with adults in his scholarly work *Horse Opera: The Strange History of the 1930s Singing Cowboy* (University of Illinois Press, 2002).

In a press release from the official Gene Autry site, the thesis of Stanfield's book is described as follows. "In this innovative take on a neglected chapter of film history, Peter Stanfield challenges the commonly held view of the singing cowboy as an ephemeral figure of fun and argues instead that he was one of the most important cultural figures to emerge out of the Great Depression. The rural or newly urban working-class families who flocked to see the latest exploits of Gene Autry, Roy Rogers, Tex Ritter, and other singing cowboys were an audience largely ignored by mainstream Hollywood film. Hard hit by the depression, faced with the threat — and often the reality — of dispossession and dislocation, pressured to adapt to new ways of living, these small-town film goers saw their ambitions, fantasies, and desires embodied in the singing cowboy and their social and political circumstances dramatized in 'B' Westerns."

Loyal fans could never be angry with Roy Rogers for his dogged adherence to his own public relations. We all have too much affection and respect for him as an entertainer and as a man. Roy Rogers had a career plan and knew public relations were vital to his success. Beyond that, he gave his fans a moral code and the promise of better things, not to mention great entertainment and a wonderful fantasy. As a storyteller he created and nurtured two of the best characters of all time: the King of the Cowboys and the Smartest Horse in the Movies. Rogers may have embellished the truth, but he did it for all the right reasons and no one was lesser for it.

While many continue to take Rogers at face value and believe everything he said, there are those of us who temper our affection and respect with experience. We remain devoted to his legend — Trigger's too — and all the wonderful things the legends stood for. Roy Rogers' and Trigger's public personas were an unspoken agreement between them and their fans. We were all playing make-believe together. Trigger belonged to us all; he was our pal, too.

16

Trigger Time Line

*Only a few key films are included in this chronology. For a complete list
of Trigger's film appearances, see the Filmography.*

1934: A palomino colt is born in San Ysidro, California, on a ranch managed by horse breeder Roy Cloud. The colt is named the Golden Cloud.

1936: The Golden Cloud started under saddle.[1]

1937: The Golden Cloud is registered with the Palomino Horse Association. • Although there is no documentation of a sale, it's during these years that the Golden Cloud was most likely acquired by Hudkins Stables. The stock farm in San Diego where the Golden Cloud was born is purchased by Ace Hudkins of North Hollywood. • Little Trigger may have been born in this year, though again there is no documentation to prove it.

1938: The Golden Cloud is ridden by actresses Priscilla Lane in *Cowboy from Brooklyn* and Olivia De Havilland in *The Adventures of Robin Hood.* • *Under Western Stars* marks the first B-western movie appearance by Roy Rogers and the Golden Cloud, whose name is changed to Trigger. • The first fictional account of how Rogers came to own Trigger is told at the beginning of *Come On, Rangers.*

1939: Trigger is ridden by actor Gilbert Roland in the film *Juarez.* • Roy Rogers hires horse trainer Jimmy Griffin.

1940: Roy Rogers acquires another palomino, Little Trigger, to use in personal appearances. • Rogers appears without Trigger in supporting role to John Wayne in the movie *Dark Command.*

1941: According to writer David Rothel, trainer Glenn Randall claimed to have started working with "Trigger," replacing Jimmy Griffin. • Trigger Jr. (registered name Allen's Gold Zephyr) is born May 11; his owner is Paul K. Fisher of Souderton, Pennsylvania. • Buttermilk, Dale Evans' horse, is born.

1942: Roy Rogers and "Trigger" debut at the 17th annual Madison Square Garden Rodeo in October. During the show's run, "Trigger's" birthday is celebrated. • Trigger is ridden by Victor Jory in *Shut My Big Mouth.* • Trigger appears in the Charles Starrett movie *Bad Men of the Hills* as Russell Hayden's horse.

1943: Trigger is ridden by Russell Hayden in *Silver City Raiders.* • The original Trigger is purchased by Roy Rogers from the Hudkins Brothers with a final payment completing the total purchase price of $2,500. The Hudkins Stables Bill of Sale is dated September 18. By this time Rogers has made 40 movies with the palomino. • Roy Rogers and Little Trigger appear on the cover of *Life* magazine. • *Hands Across the Border* is released. It's the first movie story where "Trigger" is central to the plot, and the second fictional version of how Rogers met

Roy Rogers and Trigger in their classic signature rearing pose.

and came to own him. • "Trigger" first gets screen credit and is billed as "the Smartest Horse in the Movies" for the first time in *Silver Spurs*. • Little Trigger debuts in *Song of Texas*.

1944: Roy Rogers and Trigger make their debut in *Four-Color Comics* (April). • Roy Rogers and Little Trigger appear in *Hollywood Canteen*. • *Lights of Old Santa Fe* is released, and "Trigger" drives the plot to a large degree. In the film, he is part of a package deal with Rogers that's being fought over by two rival rodeos. • Rogers rides "Trigger" on a war bond drive on the Paul Revere trail from Boston to Concord, Massachusetts.

1946: *My Pal Trigger* is released, the definitive fictional account of "Trigger's" beginnings. • According to *Screen Guide* magazine (October) Trigger is valued at $20,000.

1947: During a rodeo appearance at Chicago Stadium Roy Rogers (astride "Trigger")

Roy Rogers and Dale Evans accept a trophy during a personal appearance as the ever handsome Trigger looks on *(Roy Dillow collection).*

proposes to Dale Evans (riding Pal) while waiting to make their arena entrance. (This story is disputed by some who believe that Rogers probably proposed over breakfast.)

1948: *Roy Rogers Comics* makes its first appearance on newsstands in January. "Trigger," of course, is part of the cast of characters. • *Under California Stars* is released in Trucolor. The plot centers around the kidnapping of "Trigger." • Rogers buys the Hitching Post Theatre in Beverly Hills. He and Little Trigger place their footprints in cement.[2]

1949: In April 21, Roy Rogers and the original Trigger place their prints in cement at Grauman's Chinese Theatre in Hollywood. Dale Evans, Pat Brady, the Riders of the Purple Sage, Eddie Dean (master of ceremonies), and Hoot Gibson are in attendance.[3] • *The Golden Stallion* is released in Trucolor. • Rogers and Trigger appear on the cover of *Western Horseman* magazine in December. The lead feature is titled, "Trigger: First Get A Good Horse." • In December, King Features begins syndicating the Roy Rogers comic strip featuring Trigger to newspapers all across America. • *The Palomino Horse* by Doreen M. Norton is published. Trigger is referred to as "the best known Palomino in America." • Trigger's canine pal Bullet, a German shepherd, is born.

1950: *Trigger, Jr.* is released in Trucolor. • *Trigger Tricks,* a weekly television show, is

An enormous crowd has turned out to see Roy Rogers and Little Trigger, visible left of the center circle. This photograph was taken by a fan during the County Sheriff's Annual Rodeo at the Los Angeles Memorial Coliseum in August of 1950.

proposed. The series is intended to showcase all of his famous rodeo and personal appearance stunts. • Buttermilk first appears in *Twilight in the Sierras* ridden by Dale Evans.

1951: *Pals of the Golden West* is released and marks the last movie appearance by the original Trigger. • *The Roy Rogers Show* premieres along with a 30-minute special that promos both the television show and the *Son of Paleface* movie with Bob Hope. • *Roy Rogers' Trigger Comics* makes its debut in the Dell *Four-Color* series (May) and reportedly accounts for earnings of $10,000. • The third *Roy Rogers' Trigger Comics* (December) appears, sporting a cover by renowned equine illustrator Sam Savitt. • Businessman John Fergeson offers Roy Rogers $200,000 for Trigger in the fall (*Open Road* magazine 1952). • Roy Rogers pays $50,000 for a ruby-studded Crown Jewel saddle originally created by Edward H. Bohlin (Hollywood's foremost saddle maker and silversmith) for Mrs. H.L. Musick, a millionaire sportswoman of Los Angeles.

1952: In Los Angeles, actress Mabel Smeyne (aka Mable Smaney) files a lawsuit against Roy Rogers Enterprises. She alleges that Rogers and others recklessly failed to control "Trigger" on the movie set of *Son of Paleface*, allowing him to kick her. The trial does not begin till October of 1954. The jury renders a verdict in favor of Rogers and "Trigger."

1953: Little Trigger is among the guests who surprise Roy Rogers on the television show *This Is Your Life.* • "Trigger" wins a Patsy award (animal equivalent for the Oscar) for his role in *Son of Paleface.*

1955: *Roy Rogers Comics* becomes *Roy Rogers and Trigger Comics* in August. • The last issue of *Roy Rogers' Trigger Comics* (#17) is published. • Two biographies on Roy Rogers are published: *The Answer Is God* by Elise Miller Davis and *Roy Rogers: King of the Cowboys* by Frank Rasky. Both discuss "Trigger."

1957: The last of *The Roy Rogers Show* television episodes are completed. These half-hour black and white programs are the last filmed appearances of the original Trigger. • The original Trigger is retired at age 25 to the Rogers' ranch in Chatsworth, California.

1958: Roy and "Trigger" receive the Richard Craven Award from the American Humane Society. The award is presented annually for outstanding feats performed by animals before a live audience.

1960: From 1958 to 1960 Roy Rogers and Dale Evans appeared in fourteen NBC variety shows sponsored by Chevrolet called *The Chevy Show*. It is during one of these broadcasts that Trigger was officially retired.

1963: Trigger is moved to Hidden Valley, California.

1965: Trigger dies on July 3 at age thirty-one. Rogers decides to have him mounted by Bischoff's Taxidermy and Studio Prop Rental in Burbank, California. • Rogers contacts Fiber Glass Menagerie of Alpine, Colorado, to make a larger-than-life fiberglass likeness (23½ feet tall) of his equine co-star.

1966: Bischoff's Taxidermy completes work on Trigger, and the horse is put on display in Roy Rogers' home.

1967: The first Roy Rogers museum is built in Apple Valley. Trigger is put on display. The fiberglass rearing Trigger statue is placed at the entrance. • *Movie Horses: Their Treatment and Training* by Anthony Amaral is published; it includes a chapter on "Trigger."

1969: Trigger Jr. dies at the age of 28.

1972: Buttermilk dies at age 31.

1976: The new museum, renamed the Roy Rogers and Dale Evans Museum, is completed in Victorville, California. • The *It's Showtime* movie documentary appears showcasing "Trigger" and a number of other Hollywood animal celebrities.

1979: *Happy Trails: The Story of Roy Rogers and Dale Evans*, by Roy Rogers with Carlton Stowers, is published. It includes a chapter on "Trigger."

1980: *The Great Show Business Animals* by Dave Rothel is published, including a chapter on Trigger.

1984: The "Trigger" character makes a final appearance on television in an episode of *The Fall Guy*.

1987: *The Roy Rogers Book* by David Rothel is published with comments on Trigger by Roy Rogers.

1989: *Trigger Remembered*, a booklet by director William Witney, is published. It mentions Little Trigger publicly for the first time.

1990: The last appearance on television of Roy Rogers riding a palomino happens on the *Randy Travis: Happy Trails* television special broadcast on TNN. The horse is never referred to as "Trigger."

1993: In October Roy Rogers auctions the last of his horses, which includes grandsons and granddaughters of Trigger Jr.[4] • Trigger's trainer, Glenn Randall, passes away on May 5.

1995: *Roy Rogers* by Robert W. Phillips is published. It's the first serious and detailed study of Trigger and his doubles. Phillips follows up with essays in *The Southwest Horse Trader* ("Trigger — Known Around the World," parts one and two) and *The Western Horse* ("Trigger: the Smartest Horse in the World").

1996: *Oaktree Express* publishes "The Legend of 'Trigger,' the Smartest Horse in the Movies," another serious essay by Robert W. Phillips on Trigger.

1998: Roy Rogers, Trigger's owner, partner, and best friend, dies on July 6. • Joe Yrigoyen, Roy Rogers' longtime stunt double and a man who rode the original Trigger and a number of Trigger doubles, dies.

1999: B-western cowboys are honored during the Academy Awards show in March. Actor Val Kilmer leads a grandson of Trigger Jr. on stage as a tribute to Roy Rogers, Gene Autry, and their cowboy peers.

2000: George Coan's newsletter *The Old Cowboy Picture Show* (volume 4, number 12) devotes an entire issue to "Trigger," with updated and comprehensive work by Robert W. Phillips and Leo Pando.

2001: Dale Evans dies on February 7. • Estate taxes become a problem between the Roy Rogers and Dale Evans Museum and the IRS. The original mounted Trigger is valued at $400,000. • The first estate sale is held from March 31 to April 1 at the Roy Rogers and Dale Evans Museum; many Trigger items go on the auction block. • *Silent Hoofbeats* by Bobby J. Copeland is published. It includes a section on Trigger.

2002: The Roy Rogers and Dale Evans Museum announces that it will close and relocate to Branson, Missouri. • The History Channel program *America's Lost and Found* presents a ten-minute segment on "Trigger." • *The Encyclopedia of TV Pets* by Ken Beck and Jim Clark is published. It includes a section on Trigger and mentions Little Trigger.

2003: The grand opening of the new 26,000-square-foot Roy Rogers and Dale Evans Museum and Happy Trails Theater is set for Memorial Day weekend, May 24, with the original mounted Trigger as the centerpiece. • Trigger places 32nd on an Animal Planet two-hour cable television show titled *50 Greatest Movie Animals.* • *Cowboy Princess* by Cheryl Rogers-Barnett and Frank Thompson is published. It includes a chapter on Trigger and Little Trigger.

2005: *Hollywood Hoofbeats* by Petrine Day Mitchum and Audry Pavia is published. It includes a section on Trigger and an acknowledgment of Little Trigger.

2006: The mounted Trigger is featured in a Santa Monica Press book titled *The Ruby Slippers, Madonna's Bra, and Einstein's Brain: The Locations of America's Pop Culture Artifacts* by Chris Epting.

17

A Dictionary of Trigger Trivia

Accidents: Dusty Rogers has claimed that "Trigger" once fell through a stage during a performance. "Yes, one time when Dad, Dale and Trigger were in England, Roy and Trigger were performin' their act on a big stage, and the stage collapsed! Trigger fell down through the stage. Everyone rushed over to get to Trigger and get him out. When they got him out on a solid surface, he scrambled to his feet without bein' hurt; just displayin' a few minor scratches here and there. It could have been a lot worse!"[1]

In a 1952 article called "A Slice of My Life" (published in a magazine called *Who's Who in Western Stars*) Rogers wrote about things that happened in his life that year. According to the article, he and Trigger were rehearsing a scene for the TV show on the set of Mineral City on August 11, 1952. A blustery wind was throwing dust in everyone's face and making the other horses nervous. Rogers tied Trigger behind a portable wall that was made to be moved from set to set. Rogers said that he hadn't taken 20 steps when a gust of wind blew the wall over on Trigger's back, knocking him to the ground. Naturally, everyone ran to help the horse. Rogers said that Trigger got up shaking his head, something that he would do when he was mad for whatever reason. Rogers ran his hands over Trigger's hide, looking for breaks or cuts. A vet checked the horse, too, and gave him a clean bill of health — though all agreed his disposition had suffered temporarily. That was a small price to pay considering that the wall could have killed or seriously injured Trigger.

Another accident was reported in Frank Rasky's biography *Roy Rogers: King of the Cowboys.* Rogers was driving to a movie location in Lone Pine, California. The trailer he was hauling Trigger in broke away from his car and turned over down a hillside bank. The trailer ended up on its side. Trigger was unharmed. Rogers seemed more shaken up than his horse.[2]

The Adelphi Hotel: While on tour in Great Britain in March of 1954, Roy Rogers and Dale Evans came down with influenza and ended up secluded in the Adelphi Hotel in Liverpool. Some 4,000 fans crowded Lime Street outside and kept up the chant, "We want Roy Rogers." A publicity stunt had been planned for Rogers and "Trigger" to make a grand entrance from the mezzanine floor to the main lounge. As that opportunity was lost, it was decided to have Little Trigger deliver a bouquet of flowers to Rogers and Evans as they lay in bed.

Little Trigger reared up, took a bow or two outside the Adelphi Hotel and entered, becoming the first horse to set a hoof inside. The palomino took more bows from a first floor window as hundreds of fans watched. He also made his mark at the registration desk with a pencil clutched between his teeth, something he'd done before in Glasgow, Edinburgh, and Birmingham. Little Trigger climbed upstairs till he made it into his lady's and master's chamber and delivered his flowers. Followed by an entourage of guests, young admirers, and reporters, the palomino finally went into the residents' lounge for a very unique press reception.[3]

Allen, Woody: In Woody Allen's Oscar-winning comedy *Annie Hall* (United Artists, 1977) the comedian delivers a retort to musician Paul Simon, who plays a Hollywood record producer. As Simon shows off his Beverly Hills mansion to Allen and actress Diane Keaton (the title character), he tells them that the previous owners were singer Nelson Eddie and gangster Legs Diamond. The quintessential New Yorker, Allen sarcastically added another celebrity to the list: "Trigger."

American Humane Association: The AHA presented a Trigger with a special award to honor his Silver Anniversary in show business

Band of Brothers: In the HBO World War II television mini-series *Band of Brothers*, the GI's named their German shepherd mascot "Trigger."

Care: Trigger was fed a flake of the choicest fifty-five-dollar-a-ton hay each morning. Twice a day he got specially prepared grain (a blend of bran, corn, and mineral salt).

Dr. Charles Reid, a Hollywood veterinarian, checked Rogers' remuda of palominos' health at least three times a year. They were wormed regularly and had their teeth examined periodically.

Frank Carrol, a San Fernando Valley blacksmith, shoed Trigger every six weeks. When Trigger was performing on a smooth concrete surface, he wore iron shoes. On the waxed floors of theater stages, rubber shoes were used for safety.

Craven, Richard, Award: In 1958 Roy Rogers and Trigger received the Richard Craven Award from the American Humane Society. The award was presented annually for outstanding feats performed by animals before a live audience in theatre, rodeo, or other live entertainment venues (television and film feats were not eligible).

CSI: The last *CSI* show of the 2005 season, titled "Grave Danger," included a scene where agent Sara Sidle (Jorja Fox) walks into the office of Gil Grissom (William Peterson), picks up something framed on his desk and asks, "What's this?" He explains that it's an honorary certificate of ownership for Trigger that children used to get when they wrote to Roy Rogers. He had one as a child and lost it. He found one at the Roy Rogers Museum that used to be in California but is now in Branson, Missouri. Grissom talks for quite some time about Roy Rogers, Trigger, and the recent move. Sara asks, "Roy Rogers the cowboy?" Grissom says that would be "Roy Rogers, King of the Cowboys!" She looks at him funny and says, "You framed it?" The look on his face seems to say, "What's so unusual about that?" She sets the certificate down and they continue with the show. The episode was directed by Roy Rogers fan Quentin Tarantino.

Fan Mail: Trigger had his own fan club and received an enormous amount of mail. Doreen M. Norton, in her book *The Palomino Horse*, wrote, "Trigger is a motion picture star in his own right. He gets an average of two hundred fan letters a month, addressed to him!" Responses to fan letters sent to "Trigger" were answered on paper autographed with a hoof print.

Said Norton, "When a boy in Liverpool, England, wrote a letter, addressed simply, 'Trigger,' it was delivered to Roy Rogers."

Ferguson, J.B.: Roy Rogers had been booked for twelve days at the Houston Fat Stock Show when he received a telegram from wealthy Texas oilman J.B. Ferguson, who already owned an impressive stable of Thoroughbreds and quarter horses. Ferguson offered Rogers $200,000 for Trigger. Ferguson indicated that he wished to buy Trigger as a birthday gift for his son. Rogers had received numerous offers to buy Trigger in past years but never considered them.[4] He didn't get around to answering the telegram and continued on tour. At the same time, the story broke in the Houston paper. The paper quoted Ferguson as being deadly serious and furthermore gave the impression that Rogers, too, was seriously considering the offer. By then the original Trigger was almost nineteen and Trigger Jr. had already been acquired.

When Rogers arrived in Texas, hundreds of children greeted his train. They were all concerned over the possibility that he might sell Trigger. When Rogers reached the Samrock Hotel where he was staying, there were stacks of telegrams and telephone messages urging him not to consider Ferguson's offer.

The story took on a momentum of its own and continued under its own power even after Rogers tried to make it clear that Trigger was not for sale at any price. Rumors started circulating that Rogers was in such a financial bind that it was necessary to sell his beloved palomino. Back in California, letters were arriving from kids all over the country who'd broken their piggy banks and sent pennies, nickels, and dimes to the King of the Cowboys hoping to provide the needed financial assistance.

Rogers was finally able to put the issue to rest by calling a giant press conference at the Samrock Hotel. Ferguson was also on hand. Rogers thanked him for his offer but told him he would not sell Trigger for all the money in Texas. After the crisis passed, secretaries back in California were faced with the task of returning money to thousands of loyal Trigger fans.[5]

It's been rumored that Ferguson loaned Rogers a sorrel which he bred with Trigger at his Valley Ranch, the foal going to Ferguson as a consolation. Nevertheless, as noted earlier, Rogers stated definitively that Trigger never sired a foal.

Grauman's Chinese Theatre: The original Trigger was one of a rare few animals who was immortalized at Grauman's Chinese Theatre in Hollywood, California. Trigger and Roy Rogers were honored in 1949. Sid Grauman was the host. Gene Autry's Champion, Tom Mix's Tony and Lassie were some of the other four-legged stars who had been honored. Little Trigger placed his hoof prints in cement at the Hitching Post Theater in Los Angeles.

Injury Avoided: In the documentary *Roy Rogers King of the Cowboys*, William Witney spoke of an incident that almost injured Trigger. While filming a running insert, Rogers and Trigger were alongside a truck loaded with camera equipment and a crew. As they reached a full gallop, a large reflector that hadn't been secured fell off. It landed right in front of Trigger, who managed to jump over it. Luckily, Rogers was able to stay with him. Witney stopped the scene, dreading what he would find. Rogers had already dismounted and was checking Trigger's legs. The horse was fine.

Jeopardy: Trigger's appearance in the 1938 Warner Bros. color film *The Adventures of Robin Hood* is common knowledge, so much so that it was once a question on the ABC network game show *Jeopardy*. On another episode of *Jeopardy* (January 10, 2007), the category "Hollywood Rides" offered the answer "Nellybelle, Buttermilk, Trigger" to provoke the question, "What was *The Roy Rogers Show*?"

Junk Food: According to Cheryl Rogers-Barnett, the original Trigger liked mayonnaise sandwiches and Coca-Cola. She described Trigger as being like a goat when it came to eating habits: he would eat anything. He even shared coffee with Roy Rogers on occasion.

The original Trigger set his hoof prints in cement at Grauman's Chinese Theatre in Hollywood on April 21, 1949. Dale Evans, Glenn Randall (squatting), and the Riders of the Purple Sage were among those in attendance. Note the expressions of joy and pride on Roy Rogers' face *(Roy Dillow collection).*

Nelson, Willie: Like B.B. King's guitar Lucille, country legend Willie Nelson's old Martin N-20 acoustic is very well known. It's been signed by some of Nelson's musician friends, and the front is so worn that it has an extra hole next to the actual sound hole. Nelson named the instrument "Trigger Jr." A 13 × 17 poster of the guitar was issued by Martin Guitar captioned "This Is My Guitar — on naming his model n-20 'Trigger'"

Only Fools and Horses: According to the web source Wikipedia, Trigger, a character in a British sitcom titled *Only Fools and Horses*, is named after Roy Rogers' palomino because the actor, Roger Lloyd Pack, looks like a horse.

Pioneer Town Race: Western character actor Dick Curtis opened a ranch used as a Western movie location and tourist trap. The *American Movie Classics* network has, from time to time, run a short filler on this ranch, called Pioneer Town. The *AMC* short features early color footage of Dale Evans on Trigger in a mini-parade; Roy Rogers and his daughter on Little Trigger; and brief footage of Roy Rogers on Trigger racing a group of ranch hands.

On one occasion a group of local cowboys were at Pioneer Town with their horses. They decided to confront Rogers and the original Trigger and challenged them to a race. Rogers politely told them Trigger was not a race horse, but a schooled picture horse. Not satisfied, they heckled the King of the Cowboys to the point where their remarks got a little personal and nasty towards Trigger. Rogers could tolerate unkind remarks towards himself but not towards his horse. When he'd had enough, he pulled out a wad of greenbacks, placed them on the ground, covered them with a rock and said, "Cover it (meaning the total amount of the money) and you've got a race for a quarter mile." The cowboys managed to cover Rogers' bet and the race was on. After a quarter mile course was laid out on main street in Pioneer Town, the cowboys saddled up and approached the starting line. Roger joined them and sat calmly on Trigger, studying his opponents and their mounts. All were riding quarter horses, and Rogers was pretty sure some had run professionally. Without giving much of a thought to backing out, Rogers soon found himself and Trigger in the middle of the pack, surrounded on both sides. He leaned forward and hissed in Trigger's ear as he'd done often in running inserts when he needed a little more speed. Trigger went into third gear, laid his ears back and jolted forward. Trigger loved competition and wasn't about to lose. After winning, Rogers returned to the finish line and picked up his winnings. With a little grin he looked at his competitors and said, "Thanks fellows. Trigger and I'll oblige anytime."[6]

Reportedly a similar incident occurred on the set of *My Pal Trigger*. Republic had fired professional jockeys for the race scene at the end of the movie, and they, too, wanted to find out if Trigger was as fast as claimed. The outcome was the same as that of the Pioneer Town Race.[7]

Police Horses: In the 1980s Rogers donated horses to the mounted police patrols of Boston, New York City, and Philadelphia. "Trigger" was the name he suggested for each animal.

Reader's Poll: In May of 2002 *The Old Cowboy Picture Show* newsletter (volume 6, number 5) conducted a reader's poll. As with a real general election, only about a quarter of those eligible participated, but the results were a good representation of fan preferences as the readers were serious and knowledgeable.

Trigger won easily for best horse. He not only dominated as the favorite horse, but received more votes than any other category winner. Only bad guy Roy Barcroft came close to Trigger in overall votes. Another palomino, Ken Maynard's wonder horse Tarzan, came in a very distant second. Gene Autry's four "Champions" were third.

Ringling Brothers and Barnum and Bailey Circus: Where's Trigger when you need him? Roy Rogers and Dale Evans hosted the 1966 edition of Ringling Brothers and Barnum and Bailey Circus. Apparently the King of the Cowboys was loaned a horse for the occasion. *Reminisce Magazine* reported on that occasion with a photo caption reading, "Roy Rogers gives a crowd of 6000 in Greensboro, North Carolina, a scare when he takes a bad fall after being thrown off a white stallion while performing with the Ringling Brothers and Barnum and Bailey Circus. Fortunately, the 55 year old cowboy singer isn't seriously hurt."[8]

Eleanor Roosevelt: On his sixty-first birthday President Franklin D. Roosevelt invited Roy Rogers to the White House for a March of Dimes Ball. The cowboy felt out of place among the other Hollywood celebrities present. Mrs. Roosevelt invited him to the kitchen where they ate hamburgers and talked about one of her favorite subjects: Trigger![9]

Super Password: This game show differed from its predecessor, *Password*, in that each word acted out was one of four clues for a specific person or thing. A broadcast in 1975 offered the clues "Roy Rogers," "museum," "partner," and "stuffed." The answer was "Trigger."

Sixteenth American Air Squadron: During the war years, a Sixteenth American Air Squadron bomber was named after Trigger.

Tack: Trigger appeared in fancy show tack in his first film with Rogers, *Under Western Stars* (1938). In the movies that followed, his tack is changed from production to production for aesthetic reasons or because of upkeep and use. This is normal given the wear and tear saddles go through over time. The original silver saddle was modified throughout Rogers' career. The breast plate changed, and some silver was added to the front of the leg straps which hold the stirrups and the tapaderos which fit around them. The silver pieces were smaller than those used on the original tapaderos.

It's doubtful Roy Rogers owned the saddle he used in *Under Western Stars*; he didn't own Trigger then, so why would he own the saddle? It was probably rented from Hudkins Stables along with Trigger. It was also used on the palomino in the movie *Shut My Big Mouth*, made at Columbia at around the same time.[10]

On occasions when Rogers was playing an out-of-work cowboy or an historical figure like Billy the Kid or Bill Hickok, Trigger was in plain brown leather tack. In *Young Buffalo Bill* (1940), Trigger was ridden in show tack. After a while Trigger was filmed only in show tack. In *Sunset in El Dorado* (1945), Trigger first appears in fancy show tack. In a later dream sequence, he's in plain leather tack. In *My Pal Trigger* (1946), Trigger plays his own father, the Golden Sovereign, and is ridden by Dale Evans in English tack. This was the only time he was ever seen in anything other than a western gear. Finally, in the *Son of Paleface* (Paramount, 1952), Little Trigger may be seen in special custom-made red, white, and blue plastic western tack.

Rogers sported jockey attire and rode a Thoroughbred in an English racing saddle during a steeplechase sequence in *Wall Street Cowboy* (1939). In *Spoilers of the Plains* (1951) Rogers, playing an oil company worker, used a protective suit to stop a pipeline fire. Trigger also got to wear protective gear.

It's been rumored that Rogers used a saddle sized for a woman. The filming techniques and camera angles usually made the actors and actresses appear taller than they actually were. Circa 1995 Robert W. Phillips received a letter from one Art Grigg of Huntington Beach, California, with a photo of Roy Rogers and two unidentified people standing in front of a fancy show saddle. Mr. Grigg had read an article by Phillips in *Western Horseman* and noted an error: apparently Phillips referred to a saddle at the Roy Rogers and Dale Evans Museum as made by Edward H. Bohlin.

Mr. Grigg wrote,

> I believe the ruby studded saddle that you refer to in your article is the one in the enclosed picture, which is the one under plastic cover at the RR museum. If in fact it is, then it is almost certainly not a Bohlin saddle.
> The saddle in the picture was made around 1931 by Davis and McGabe of McGabe Silversmiths, and their names appear on the saddle. It was made for a Mrs. Musik who owned a championship horse named Diamond, which she kept in Palm Springs.

Roy Rogers with his fabulous McCabe saddle, which was decorated in gold, silver, and rubies. It was worn by Trigger in a Pasadena Tournament of Roses Parade. Trigger Jr. may be seen wearing it in the Roy Rogers Viewmaster reel *(Larry Roe collection; Roy Dillow, information source).*

An interesting fact is that the saddle shown in your article was also intended for a woman, being a Bohlin model designated the Miss Dickson. There also were other saddles with the Dickson name. The largest of these was the Dick Dickson, named after the Fox West Coast Director. There was a Dick Dickson Jr. saddle which was a size in between the others mentioned. There also was a Dickson Jr. Special which had a Cheyenne roll cantle. I assume the Miss Dickson model may have been named after the daughter of Dick Dickson.

So Roy being of slight stature compared to some of the cowboys, used a smaller size saddle and in these two cases ones intended for women.[11]

Rogers said that he got his fancy Bohlin show saddle some time around 1943. Actually it was used for first time in *Heart of the Golden West*, released November 16, 1942. One has to have the uncut version to verify this, because Trigger does not wear it till the last scene. The saddle was not used in the next Roy Rogers feature, *Ridin' Down the Canyon*, which was released December 30 of the same year. In the next movie, *Idaho*, released March 10, 1943, the saddle is used only in one scene. About halfway through the movie, Rogers rides up, dismounts, reads a letter, and talks with actor Harry Shannon. In *King of the Cowboys*, released on April 9 of the following year, the Bohlin saddle is used for almost the entire production and would remain a prominent fixture for the rest of movies Rogers and Trigger made at Republic Pictures. Roy Rogers used a model similar to the "Dick Dickson" style on Trigger. He paid $50,000 for a ruby studded Crown Jewel Bohlin saddle in 1950.[12]

Rogers even owned a saddle that belonged to Buck Jones. One of Rogers' silver saddles with Double R brand on the tapaderos was made by Nudie Cohen. This was the saddle Trigger Jr. was wearing in the museum. Rogers even had a silver saddle with no Double R brands on the tapaderos; early on it was used on Trigger in the museum for a time. Rogers was probably having the Bohlin saddle restored.

Rogers had eight plastic saddles. Two were on a base color of white with red eagles and blue stripes, with the Double R brand on the tapaderos which were blue with red eagles. Two more were the same as previous except the tapaderos were a blue base color with white Double R brand and red eagles. A plastic Rose Parade saddle, cream to white in color, had green leaves and yellow roses. Two additional matching saddles were blue, white, and red with no brands, made by All Western Plastics. One dark pink and white saddle was made for Buttermilk.[13]

The Tail Waggers Club: After covering fifty thousand miles in one year on personal appearance tours, "Trigger" was admitted to the Tail Waggers Club, a company for illustrious equine travelers. Famous race horses were also among the members.[14]

Trailer Deluxe: When "Trigger" made personal appearances with Roy Rogers at such places as the Cow Palace in San Francisco, stock shows in Ft. Worth, Texas, or Madison Square Garden in New York City, he traveled in comfort and safety in a custom-built trailer pulled by a three and one-half ton Burma Road Dodge truck. The vehicle was the result of the practical experience and ideas gathered over years by Rogers while touring. The construction took three months and required ten sets of blueprints before Rogers was satisfied with the design. The truck required high-test gasoline, stored in two 40-gallon fuel tanks. It came with a two-speed axle and was capable of 50 mph on the highway, averaging seven miles to the gallon. Both truck and trailer were equipped with air and hydraulic brakes. As a backup safety measure, there was an extra set of brakes on the tractor. The combined rig sat on 10 wheels with puncture-proof tubes in all tires. The overall weight of the entire outfit was 12 tons; it measured 35 feet in length and was 11 feet high. There was also a separate generator

Roy Rogers with Trigger Jr. in front of their custom-made hauler and trailer (*Joel "Dutch" Dortch collection*).

on board for the 110-volt lighting system which supported both DC and AC electric currents for the trailer. Both vehicles were fully insulated. The stalls of the trailer were air conditioned.

The trailer included air-conditioned living quarters for the driver and trainer or groom. The horse compartment sported three fully padded stalls with feed bins for "Trigger" and his equine company and even kennels for Rogers' hunting hounds, which he transported on occasional hunting trips. Each side of the trailer featured loading ramps and rungs on the outside to tie "Trigger" while he was being groomed and tacked. A tack room not only accommodated "Trigger's" saddles, bridles, and miscellaneous riding equipment, but also bunk beds for the driver and trainer or groom. The modest but stylish living quarters consisted of a stainless steel kitchen complete with refrigerator, butane cooking stove, and a small table for meals. Other creature comforts included indirect lighting, electric heater, hot and cold running water, wardrobe closets, and bedroom.

The trailer interior was paneled throughout in combed mahogany. The floor was of a composition material and fully carpeted. The exterior of the trailer was a streamlined design, finished in blue and cream colors with chrome trim. All the windows were copper screened, and screen doors were included inside of the living quarters.

Trigger Burgers: After Roy Rogers licensed his name to a chain of restaurants, a joke started circulating about "Trigger burgers." The joke may have originated in *Cracked* magazine.[15]

Trigger Statue: When Trigger died in 1965, Rogers contacted Fiber Glass Menagerie of Alpine, Colorado, to make a larger-than-life fiberglass likeness. It was 23½ feet tall and featured Trigger in the signature rearing pose. It was placed at the front of the Roy Rogers and Dale Evans Museum in Victorville and later moved to the museum's new location in Branson, Missouri. Ironically, the statue, with its four white socks, resembled Little Trigger more than the original Trigger.

Trigger Street and Trigger Place: There are streets in Chatsworth, California, in the San Fernando Valley, named to reflect the fact that Roy Rogers and family had a home and ranch there: Trigger Street, Trigger Place (which probably came later, after the subdividing of lots on Trigger Street), and Dale Court. Trigger Place is not far from Trigger Street, heading in a southwesterly direction on Valley Circle Boulevard, past the Oakwood Cemetery on the right; after Cactus Avenue and Dale Court, the road eventually intersects with Trigger Place. Trigger Street is another right turn.

Trigger Street Productions: Actor Val Kilmer grew up in the San Fernando Valley, California, and lived next to Roy Rogers and Dale Evans. In a 2004 *Biography* channel interview

The Trigger statue as it appears in front of the Roy Rogers and Dale Evans Museum in Branson, Missouri *(Hunter Hampton collection).*

Kilmer reminisced about how he would knock on their door and ask if Rogers could come out and play. The Kilmer family eventually owned the Roy Rogers ranch in Chatsworth. "That was great fun," Kilmer said. Not to mention surreal. "Trigger was stuffed in the recreation room, where you could see him through the curtains."[16]

Kilmer met Kevin Spacey at the Chatsworth High School in the San Fernando Valley. The two friends shared early dreams of becoming famous actors. At one point they envisioned their own theatre to be named after one of the local streets in the area, the Trigger Street Theatre. Spacey later named his movie production company Trigger Street Productions. He and producer Dana Brunetti of Trigger Street Productions and TriggerStreet.com, as well as writers and directors Adam Kassen and Mark Kassen, joined forces to form Trigger Street Independent, a fully funded production company headquartered in New York.

Trigger Teaser: For a time in the 1950s there was a popular saying, "What a face, what a figure, two more legs and she'll look like Trigger."

18

Trigger Filmography

The following filmography lists all the movies "Trigger" made at Republic Pictures with Roy Rogers. It also includes movies the palomino made "solo," i.e., without Rogers and cameo appearances they made together.

1. *The Adventures of Robin Hood* (Warner Bros., 1938) (**solo no. 1**)
2. *Cowboy from Brooklyn* (Warner Bros., 1938) (**solo no. 2**)
3. *Under Western Stars* (Republic, 1938)
4. *Billy the Kid Returns* (Republic, 1938)
5. *Come On, Rangers* (Republic, 1938)
6. *Shine On, Harvest Moon* (Republic, 1938)
7. *Juarez* (Warner Bros., 1939) (**solo no. 3**)
8. *The Arizona Kid* (Republic, 1939)
9. *Rough Riders' Roundup* (Republic, 1939)
10. *Frontier Pony Express* (Republic, 1939)
11. *Southward Ho!* (Republic, 1939)
12. *In Old Caliente* (Republic, 1939)
13. *Wall Street Cowboy* (Republic, 1939)
14. *Saga of Death Valley* (Republic, 1939)
15. *Days of Jesse James* (Republic, 1939)
16. *Young Buffalo Bill* (Republic, 1940)
17. *The Carson City Kid* (Republic, 1940)
18. *The Ranger and the Lady* (Republic, 1940)
19. *Colorado (Republic*, 1940)
20. *Young Bill Hickok* (Republic, 1940)
21. *The Border Legion* aka *West of the Badlands* (Republic, 1940)
22. *Robin Hood of the Pecos* (Republic, 1941)
23. *In Old Cheyenne* (Republic, 1941)
24. *Sheriff of Tombstone* (Republic, 1941)
25. *Nevada City* (Republic, 1941)
26. *Badman of Deadwood* (Republic, 1941)
27. *Jesse James at Bay* (Republic, 1941)
28. *Red River Valley* (Republic, 1941)
29. *Shut My Big Mouth* (Columbia, 1942) (**solo no. 4**)
30. *Bad Men of the Hills* (Columbia, 1942) (**solo no. 5**)
31. *Man from Cheyenne* (Republic, 1942)
32. *South of Santa Fe* (Republic, 1942)

33. *Sunset on the Desert* (Republic, 1942)
34. *Romance on the Range* (Republic, 1942)
35. *Sons of the Pioneers* (Republic, 1942)
36. *Sunset Serenade* (Republic, 1942)
37. *Heart of the Golden West* (Republic, 1942)
38. *Ridin' Down the Canyon* (Republic, 1942)
39. *Idaho* (Republic, 1943)
40. *King of the Cowboys* (Republic, 1943)
41. *Song of Texas* (Republic, 1943)
42. *Silver Spurs* (Republic, 1943)
43. *Man from Music Mountain* aka *Texas Legionnaires* (Republic, 1943)
44. *Hands Across the Border* (Republic, 1943)
45. *Silver City Raiders* (Columbia, 1943) (**solo no. 6**)
46. *The Cowboy and the Senorita* (Republic, 1944)
47. *The Yellow Rose of Texas* (Republic, 1944)
48. *Song of Nevada* (Republic, 1944)
49. *San Fernando Valley* (Republic, 1944)
50. *Lights of Old Santa Fe* (Republic, 1944)
51. *Hollywood Canteen* (Warner Bros., 1944) (**cameo no. 1**)
52. *Utah* (Republic, 1945)
53. *Bells of Rosarita* (Republic, 1945)
54. *The Man from Oklahoma* (Republic, 1945)
55. *Sunset in El Dorado* (Republic, 1945)
56. *Don't Fence Me In* (Republic, 1945)
57. *Along the Navajo Trail* (Republic, 1945)
58. *Song of Arizona* (Republic, 1946)
59. *Rainbow Over Texas* (Republic, 1946)
60. *My Pal Trigger* (Republic, 1946)
61. *Under Nevada Skies* (Republic, 1946)
62. *Roll On Texas Moon* (Republic, 1946)
63. *Home in Oklahoma* (Republic, 1946)
64. *Out California Way* (Republic, 1946) (**cameo no. 2**)
65. *Heldorado* (Republic, 1946)
66. *Apache Rose* (Republic, 1947)
67. *Hit Parade of 1947* (Republic, 1947) (**cameo no. 3**)
68. *The Kid from Gower Gulch* (Friedgen/Aster, 1950) (**cameo no. 4**)
69. *Bells of San Angelo* (Republic, 1947)
70. *Springtime in the Sierras* (Republic, 1947)
71. *On the Old Spanish Trail* (Republic, 1947)
72. *The Gay Ranchero* (Republic, 1948)
73. *Under California Stars* (Republic, 1948)
74. *Eyes of Texas* (Republic, 1948)
75. *Melody Time* (RKO Radio Pictures, 1948) (**cameo no. 5**)
76. *Night Time in Nevada* (Republic, 1948)
77. *Grand Canyon Trail* (Republic, 1948)
78. *The Far Frontier* (Republic, 1948)
79. *Susanna Pass* (Republic, 1949)
80. *Down Dakota Way* (Republic, 1949)
81. *The Golden Stallion* (Republic, 1949)

82. *Bells of Coronado* (Republic, 1950)
83. *Twilight in the Sierras* (Republic, 1950)
84. *Trigger, Jr.* (Republic, 1950)
85. *Sunset in the West* (Republic, 1950)
86. *North of the Great Divide* (Republic, 1950)
87. *The Trail of Robin Hood* (Republic, 1950)
88. *Spoilers of the Plains* (Republic, 1951)
89. *Heart of the Rockies* (Republic, 1951)
90. *In Old Amarillo* (Republic, 1951)
91. *South of Caliente* (Republic, 1951)
92. *Pals of the Golden West* (Republic, 1951)
93. *Son of Paleface* (Paramount, 1952)
94. *Jamboree* (Exploitation Productions, 1954) (**cameo no. 6**)
95. *It's Showtime* (United Artists, 1976) (**cameo no. 7,** a rerun of old footage)

Chapter Notes

Preface

1. Serious Roy Rogers and Trigger fans feel the same way and are reminded of their parents when they reflect on the King of the Cowboys and the Smartest Horse in the Movies. Says Roy Rogers collector and researcher Jerry Dean, "I know that my love of the old movie cowboys stems entirely from the love I have for the life I remember having as a child. Roy et al. remind me of that. It was my parents who provided that life for me as I was growing up, and it is the two of them who are really the ones I am remembering as I recall Roy and Trigger."

2. From e-mail correspondence circa 1999.

3. Spoken during a 1998 broadcast of *Siskel & Ebert at the Movies* (Buena Vista Entertainment).

4. Some actors—for example, Jack Nicholson—refuse to do promotional tours for their films. There are a number of reasons for this refusal, but the one relevant here has to do with the creation of characters on screen. The more familiarity an audience has with an actor, the harder it is for that actor to disappear into a character. Rock legend Bob Dylan maintains a mysterious persona that's been very alluring for decades; he does so by not discussing his lyrics or himself in detail. Even when he finally chose to write a memoir (*Chronicles*, 2005), he did not discuss his lyrics in any great depth. Artists don't like being tagged with labels that narrow and restrict their work.

5. E-mail dated May 13, 2005.

6. The literal translation of Tír na nÓg (from Irish Gaelic) is "Land of the Young." It is used to refer to the afterlife.

7. "Aye, we all see it, but that doesn't mean it's real necessarily." From the motion picture *Moby Dick* (Warner Bros., 1956).

8. "He Wishes for the Cloths of Heaven" by William Butler Yeats: "Had I the heavens' embroidered cloths, / Enwrought with golden and silver light, / The blue and the dim and the dark cloths / Of night and light and the half-light, / I would spread the cloths under your feet; / But I, being poor, have only my dreams; / I have spread my dreams under your feet; / Tread softly, because you tread on my dreams."

Introduction: The Horse Prances

1. From *Apocalypse*, 1931.

2. Gary A. Yoggy, ed., *Back in the Saddle: Essays on Western Film and Television Actors* (Jefferson, NC: McFarland, 1998), p. 182.

3 Quoted in David Rothel, *The Great Show Business Animals* (La Jolla, CA: A.S. Barnes, 1980), p. 214.

Chapter 1

1. Dusty Rogers told Thys Ockersen in his documentary *Roy Rogers, King of the Cowboys* that he and his siblings have a duty to carry on his dad and mother's legacy.

2. On March 30, 1966, a UPI Telephoto/Files report read, "Hollywood: Cowboy star Roy Rogers revealed 3/30 that his trusty steed, Trigger, died at age of 33 almost a year ago. Rogers kept the loss to himself for fear fans across the country would go into shock on learning that the gallant horse had died." Rogers and Trigger were shown in a 1954 file photo that was suggested for use with story by Vernon Scott. (Source: Janey Miller.)

3. For a time Dusty Rogers became his father's manager.

4. Joe Curreri, "Forget the Girl — Kiss the Horse," *Persimmon Hill*, Vol. 13, no. 2, 1990.

5. Vol. 12, no. 3, April 2004.

6. Author Dana Cain also recognized Little Trigger in her book *Film and TV Animal Star Collectables* (Norfolk, VA: Antique Trader, 1998), p. 76: "'Little Trigger' was used as Trigger's stand-in, and frequently traveled to promotional appearances, allowing the 'real' Trigger to relax."

7. "Corky is no do-it-yourself fan. He served a long apprenticeship to his father." Joan Fry, "Training the Black Stallion, Part II," *Horse and Rider*, January 1982.

8. October 24, 2005; February 16, April 8, May 21, and June 24, 2006.

Chapter 2

1. Spoken by reporter Maxwell Scott (Carleton Young) in *The Man Who Shot Liberty Valance* (Paramount, 1962).

2. Roy Rogers and Dale Evans with Jane and Michael Stern, *Happy Trails: Our Life Story* (New York: Simon & Schuster, 1994).

3. "This tour brought out 168,000 people for a total of $278,000 in Madison Square Garden, New York. The engagement grossed $1.1 million in a little over a month; the Houston Fat Stock Show and Rodeo played to 171,000 spectators and a $468,000 gate in 12 days." Duane Valentry, "A Horse Named Babe," *The Western Horseman*, April 1961, p. 58.

4. Todd McCarthy and Charles Flynn, eds., *Kings of the Bs* (New York: E.P. Dutton, 1975).

5. In *The Roy Rogers Book* by David Rothel (Madison, NC: Empire, 1987), Rogers says just enough about Trigger to imply that one horse did the majority of the work and look-alikes were brought in for minor tasks. "I have always owned four or five extra palomino horses in case anything should happen to Trigger. So in long-distance

shots where they weren't identifiable, we would use one of the other horses to give Trigger a break." It was noted by Sam Henderson in "Leonard Slye: The King of the Cowboys" (*The Western Horse,* December 1989, pp. 40–41) that Rogers had several "Triggers": one to ride in parades, one for rodeo appearances, one to stand in for the more dangerous roles, another for fast-paced action scenes, and the original Trigger for the close-ups.

6. I saw the Roy Rogers Rodeo show at the state fair in Albuquerque in 1957 and, as far as I was concerned, the palomino he was riding at the time was *the* Trigger. In retrospect I recall the palomino as being quite stocky. Now I'm inclined to believe it was Little Trigger.

A photograph of Roy Rogers riding the original Trigger during a personal appearance was published in *Happy Trails: A Pictorial Celebration of the Life and Times of Roy Rogers and Dale Evans* by Howard Kazanjian and Chris Enss (Guilford, CT: Globe Pequot, 2005). The photograph was most likely taken in Southern California — judging by the type of hat Rogers was using, sometime around 1946.

7. Cowboys were always changing their names. Mostly they took on nicknames. This goes back to the days of William Bonny, aka Billy the Kid. When individuals were groomed as movie stars by major studios, a name change was almost the first thing they underwent.

8. A similar and shorter piece by Trigger Jr. titled "Rock 'n' Roll" was also published; again, the publisher is unknown.

9. There are no movie cowboys anymore in the tradition of Roy Rogers, Gene Autry, and William S. Hart. What we have today are actors who occasionally appear in westerns, like Kevin Costner, Clint Eastwood, Robert Duvall, and Tommy Lee Jones.

10. *The Roy Rogers Story,* http://petcaretips.net/roy_rogers.html.

Chapter 3

1. On *The Merv Griffin Show,* filmed at Snuff Garrett's ranch; with guests Gene Autry, Rex Allen, Yakima Canutt. NBC, 1982.

2. *All Politics,* July 6, 1998.

3. In November of 1937 Crosby and Lindsay Howard founded Binglin Breeding Stables. Their first equine purchases were made by Lindsay Howard in Argentina. Howard's father, Charles S. Howard, transported them to California on the same train as his famous horse Seabiscuit. The Crosby's fourth son was named after Lindsay Howard. Bing Crosby was one of the founders of Delmar Raceway in San Diego. (Source: Crosby expert Malcolm Macfarlane, editor of *BING* magazine, published by the International Club Crosby.)

4. In Thoroughbred racing circles every horse shares a "birthday" of January first. A horse becomes one year old on the first of January after he or she is born, and turns two one year later, regardless the actual date of his or her birth.

5. Georgia Morris and Mark Pollard, *Roy Rogers: King of the Cowboys* (San Francisco: Collins, 1994).

6. There is no biological difference between a "warm-blooded" or a "cold-blooded" horse. (All horses are, of course, warm-blooded mammals.) Horses descended from the smaller Arabian or Barb are considered "warm-blooded." Thoroughbreds are descended from Arabs or Barbs. All other horses are considered "cold-blooded," including modern day draft horses descended from the type of large horses ridden by knights of old. (Source: The International Museum of the Horse, Kentucky Horse Park, Lexington, KY.)

7. Registered Thoroughbred stallions were used to upgrade the remount horses who were generally grade and draft horses.

8. Grace Larson, "Roy Rogers and Gene Autry and Their Tennessee Walkers," *Walking Horse News,* September-October 2000.

9. Jones not only rented horses, he also made money as a rider. Because he weighed over 250 pounds, he once doubled for the equally rotund comedian Fatty Arbuckle.

10. Fat Jones was one of the last of the old-timers who witnessed the birth and rise of the motion picture industry. He passed away in 1963.

11. In the winter of 1916, James left Nevada range country to find work in the warmer southern California climate and ended up at the Fat Jones stable. For a time he worked in motion pictures, doubling actors and, in true cowboy fashion, even breaking a few horses. James departed the following spring and went on to write the classic western horse story *Smoky,* which would eventually be turned into a Hollywood film on three different occasions, in 1933, 1946, and 1966.

12. Roy Rogers with Carlton Stowers, *Happy Trails: The Story of Roy Rogers and Dale Evans* (New York: Bantam, 1981), p. 64.

13. In *The Palomino Horse* (Los Angeles: Borden, 1949), author Doreen M. Norton stated that the original Trigger was bought at auction in 1937.

14. Herbert Yates of Consolidated Film Laboratories, Inc., and Trem Carr of Monogram joined their companies to form Republic Pictures, taking over the old Mack Sennett Studios in Studio City.

15. B-westerns generally took from eight days to two weeks to film.

16. "Roy's birth name was Leonard Franklin Sly," said Phillips. Actually, to complicate matters even further, Roy Rogers was born Leonard Frank Sly. He was later referred to as "Leonard Franklin Sly," and he also added the "e" at the end of Slye, although never filed a formal name change. He did sign his first marriage certificate "Slye." Phillips went on: "The way I have always handled that 'Sly' and 'Slye' situation is the context and situation in which it is being used. If I am referring to hard, biographical name, then to me he is 'Sly.' But if I were mentioning a film credit, then I would have to show 'Slye.' Apparently Roy did some checking into the family history (and his birth record as well as that of his sisters) and learned I was right, for one of the last published interviews he gave, he set the record straight and admitted that he was born Leonard Frank Sly. I often, when using the Sly spelling, attach an asterisk and show in a footnote 'actual birth name, without the "e" added later.' That way folks will not only become educated, they will know that the writer didn't accidentally misspell the name."

17. When the Roy Rogers and Dale Evans Museum was still in California, the first promotional brochure Republic produced to introduce him was on display. It was done so early that he was riding a dark bay.

18. Rogers with Stowers, p. 56.

19. "The Man Who Makes Horses Say Yes," *Western Stars,* July 9, 1950.

20. Dana Cain, *Film and TV Animal Star Collectables* (Norfolk, VA: Antique Trader, 1998), p. 76.

21. *The Republic Pictures Story,* AMC, 1991.

22. Elise Miller Davis, *The Answer Is God* (New York: McGraw-Hill, 1955), p. 42.

23. Provided by Joel "Dutch" Dortch, executive director of the Happy Trails Children's Foundation.

24. Bobby Copeland.

25. Rogers' initial salary was $75.00 weekly, and at the

end of the contract, his pay had escalated to $1000 weekly. Rogers then signed a term picture arrangement which included a $10,000 bonus and pay of $21,000 plus a $500 clothing allowance for each of 11 films over a two-year period. In February 1950, Republic exercised their option to extend that contract for six more films at $21,667 each. Republic and Roy agreed to another extension for his final two Westerns at $25,000 each. (Source: Bobby Copeland.)

26. Monte Hale, in David Rothel's book *The Singing Cowboys* (San Diego: A.S. Barnes, 1978), said, "They wrote a picture for me called *Don't Fence Me In*. It was to have all of Roy's cast in it: Gabby Hayes, Dale Evans, the Sons of the Pioneers—the whole bunch. This was when they thought Roy was going into the Army. They wrote it for me and gave me the script. I learned every part in it. I studied that script day and night. Then one day they called me up to the front office and told me Roy was not going into the service and that I was not going to make the movie, that Roy wanted to make it. It broke my heart a little bit."

27. Joel Dortch, "Roy Rogers—A Man's Man!" *Shoot!* Vol. 22, May–June 2003.

28. Many of the cowboys were ashamed they'd participated in B-westerns. With a few exceptions, most would have rather been stars in A-features and making big bucks with the likes of Errol Flynn, Clark Gable, Jimmy Stewart, et al. It would be unfair to blame them. The possible exception would be Gene Autry, who didn't have any delusions about his acting abilities and whose business acumen put him right up there with Bing Crosby, Bob Hope and Frank Sinatra. Roy Rogers may have considered himself lucky, but unlike Autry, he placed family and hobbies above business. While he obviously did very well, especially in merchandising and personal appearances, he was never a businessman on a par with Autry. It's not far-fetched to assume even Rogers would have been tempted to move from Republic had some studio like Columbia approached him. Unlike Bob Steele or Don Barry, Rogers never had any acting ambition; he accepted children as his audience.

29. Roy Rogers told this story about *The Front Page* for decades, but he probably meant *Behind the News*, made in 1940 (remade by Republic as *Headline Hunters* in 1955). It's a newsroom story set in a big-city with actor Lloyd Nolan as a cynical reporter with a penchant for sticking his neck out. The description is right, and the star is right, as well as the time period. Once again, we see the lax attitude toward a little thing like facts. Two are wrong here: Rogers got the title of the movie wrong, and despite what he claims to have said to Yates, he did not own Trigger yet.

"'To get me in line, he threatened to take away my upcoming cowboy roles as well, and to put a point on his threat, he said he would replace me with another actor who could ride Trigger in my place.' The horse would make a star of anyone who rode him, he argued. 'Trigger is the one who's earning the paycheck, not you, Rogers,' he said." Roy Rogers and Dale Evans with Jane and Michael Stern, *Happy Trails: Our Life Story* (New York: Simon & Schuster, 1994) p. 106.

30. Jack Mathis, *Republic Confidential: The Players* (Barrington, IL: Jack Mathis Advertising, 1992), p. 2.

31. Rogers and Evans with Stern and Stern.

32. Schedules varied from studio to studio, from production to production, with regard to how much time there was between the completion of a B-western film and its release. Today, the time between completion and release of a film might stretch to a year or more. In contrast, B-westerns were probably more like today's TV shows, with just days of shooting, and only months between the end of filming and broadcasting.

33. Smoke died tragically when he ate some wire that was mistakenly left in with his feed.

34. "One story goes that 'Pistol' was the horse's nickname at this time." Robert W. Phillips, "Trigger: the Smartest Horse in the World," *The Western Horse*, Vol. 19, no. 1, issue 1, January 1995.

35. "His Palomino registered name was Golden Cloud, but the Golden Cloud name went the way of Leonard Slye. I had already decided to name him Trigger." *Mountain Broadcast and Prairie Recorder,* March 1946.

36. Todd McCarthy and Charles Flynn, eds., *King of the Bs* (New York: E.P. Dutton, 1975).

37. Morris and Pollard.

38. Robert W. Phillips believed that Rogers had acquired two main identical palominos. This theory could be argued from here to eternity without a resolution. This writer does not agree with Phillips.

39. A contest to name these fictional colts offered one thousand dollars in cash prizes.

40. According to George Mudryj, member of the Palomino Horse Association, the horse owned by Randy Travis came from Pennsylvania breeder Paul K. Fisher, who sold Rogers Trigger Jr.

41. Len Simpson, "Trigger Man" *Movie Land*, October 1946.

42. Don Allen, "Trigger and His Doubles," *Pic*, July 1946, p. 65.

43. Allen, p. 66.

44. It also has to be remembered that mares sometimes injure stallions while they're being bred, and consequently some owners do not want to risk a prized stallion.

45. Sam Henderson, "Leonard Slye: The King of the Cowboys," *The Western Horse*, December 1989, pp. 40–41.

46. Cain, p. 76.

47. In 1955 Post sponsored a "Name the Pony" contest. "Boys! Girls! Give me a name for this pony," Roy said in advertisements. "Names like Beauty, Dandy, and Flash are all good, but you can do better. So get along, buckaroos! Send in your names today!" Each entry had to be accompanied by a Post Cereal box top. Rogers and Evans with Stern and Stern, p. 141.

48. Rogers and Evans with Stern and Stern, p. 149.

49. Rogers and Evans with Stern and Stern, p. 143.

Chapter 4

1. Quoted by Ken Beck and Jim Clark, *The Encyclopedia of TV Pets* (Nashville: Rutledge Hill, 2002); p. 263.

2. Quote from 1986 appearing in Dan Gagliasso, "Remembering Roy," *Cowboy & Country*, Fall 1998.

3. When administrator@royrogers.com was asked in 2005 about Little Trigger's background the reply was, "Little Trigger could have been purchased from Ray Corrigan, but we don't have any lineage or ownership papers here on that particular horse. Sorry."

4. Little Trigger didn't really require registration papers (they just say an animal is a purebred) as he was not bred. The only papers necessary were current health certificates for traveling from state to state and parts of Europe.

5. Don Allen, "Trigger and His Doubles," *Pic*, July 1946, p. 66.

6. Republic Pictures paid rental on Trigger for movies, but Rogers had to pay rental for the personal appearances before he owned the palomino.

7. Carol R. Johnson, letter to Bobby J. Copeland.

8. (New York: Julian Messner, 1955). Chapters 13 and 15 discuss "Trigger."

9. Bobby J. Copeland, "Early Roy Rogers— Two Versions," *Westerns and Serials*, number 40 (no month posted), 1993.

10. Copeland, "Early Roy Rogers."

11. He also believed Little Trigger might have been acquired from the Fischer Farms in Pennsylvania where Trigger Jr. was purchased. No evidence has ever surfaced to prove the Fischer connection. Robert W. Phillips, *Roy Rogers* (Jefferson, NC: McFarland, 1995), p. 20.

12. In an article titled "Who Was the Smartest Horse in the Movies?" published in the July 1992 issue of *Classic Images*, Mike Newton claimed that Roy Rogers "found the horse at Corriganville, owned by Ray 'Crash' Corrigan, who was also a Republic cowboy star." It is worth noting, however, that Corky Randall, in interviews for this book, did not confirm that Rogers bought Little Trigger from Corrigan; nor did he offer an alternative seller.

13. Merrill T. McCord, *Brothers of the West* (Bethesda MD: Alhambra, 2003), p. 112.

14. McCord, p. 112.

15. "The event will be celebrated this morning at a party in the Plantation Room of the Hotel Dixie. On hand with Mr. Rogers will be the Sons of the Pioneers, the singing group, who appear with the actor and the horse in Republic westerns. Trigger, Mr. Rogers and the Pioneers opened last night in the rodeo at Madison Square Garden."

16. "He has flown in a plane and traveled by ship, and at one time was given a birthday party at one of New York's most exclusive hotels— a party attended by various other film horses and at which raw carrots were the treat of the evening." From a Roy Rogers comic book special section titled, "Trigger! Smartest Horse in the Movies!" Reprinted in *Roy Rogers Western Classics* (AC Collector Classics number 3, 1990).

17. Reprinted in *Roy Rogers Western Classics* number 3, 1990.

18. Beck and Clark, p. 262.

19. (Madison, NC: Empire, 1987), p. 66.

20. (Madison, NC: Empire, 2001), p. 102.

21. Frank Rasky, *Roy Rogers: King of the Cowboys* (New York: Julian Messner, 1955), p. 117.

22. Larry Roe.

23. There are many movie sequences where Trigger and Little Trigger's facial markings may be scrutinized with great accuracy. This is especially true with the frame-by-frame and pause options on most DVD players. Luckily movies like *Son of Pale Face* and *Trigger Jr.* are both available on DVD. In the latter Trigger's blaze may be seen very closely after he loses a fight with the rogue stallion, the Phantom. When Rogers first notices the palomino has been blinded and when a vet examines him in the following sequence, one may see his blaze clearly on both sides. An even better view is provided after a second fight with the Phantom and Trigger is knocked on the ground. He's wearing protective goggles and a mask but it slips off and the blaze is clear.

24. Larry Roe.

Chapter 5

1. William Roper, *Roy Rogers: King of the Cowboys* (T.S. Denison, 1971).

2. Dusty Rogers says that his father was always on the lookout for good palominos and would put them in training with Glenn Randall. Some just didn't take to training or did not have suitable dispositions. These horses were sent to a working cattle ranch in the San Joaquin Valley in which Rogers had an interest.

3. TWHBA record #931975 states that Allen's Gold Zephyr was foaled on January 1, 1941. The Palomino Horse Breeders Association record #4055 states that Rogers bought Trigger Jr. in 1948. (Source: Larry Roe.)

4. David Rothel, *The Roy Rogers Book* (Madison, NC: Empire, 1987), p. 33.

5. Three of the breeding stallions used by Fisher were offspring of one of Gene Autry's Champions.

6. Ken Beck and Jim Clark, *Encyclopedia of TV Pets* (Nashville: Rutledge Hill, 2002).

7. Johnny D. Boggs, "Val Kilmer — Playing Cowboy," *Cowboy & Country Magazine,* summer 1999.

8. Joel "Dutch" Dortch.

9. After winning the Triple Crown in 1933 Sir Barton was purchased by the U.S. Remount and was sent to Wyoming Remount Station, where he stayed until his death in 1937.

10. Duane Valentry, "A Horse Named Babe," *Western Horseman,* April 1961.

11. Naomi K. Chesky, "In Search of a Palomino," *The Fence Post,* January 3, 1994.

12. In her book *Cowboy Princess,* Cheryl Rogers-Barnett claimed that Pal was eventually given to her.

13. As heard by Larry Roe during a *Happy Trails Theater* taping session at the Cintel studios in the mid to late 1980s for later broadcast on the Nashville Network.

Chapter 6

1. Roy Rogers, "Trigger and Me," publisher and date unknown.

2. Experts have said that a well-conditioned horse can run about two miles full out before it's spent. However, an experienced rider can get much more distance from his mount by alternating gaits. A horse can replenish oxygen in a trot and go on for about 50 miles.

3. *Cowboy from Brooklyn* was released in the United Kingdom as *Romance and Rhythm.*

4. Larry Roe was the first to discover Trigger in *Shut My Big Mouth.*

5. Released in the United Kingdom as *Wrongly Accused.*

6. It was George Coan of Lugoff, South Carolina, who first discovered Trigger in *Bad Men of the Hills.*

7. Russ Hayden was Lucky Jenkins in the Hopalong Cassidy movies. He kept the nickname — unlike Windy Hayes, who was not allowed to— but changed the last name. He may have had a better relationship with the powers at Paramount, because they didn't stop him.

8. Larry Roe was the first to identify Trigger in this lobby card photo, which was published in Bobby J. Copeland's book *Silent Hoofbeats* (Madison, NC: Empire, 2001, page 60). This unique photo was taken with actor Russell Hayden. Oddly, Trigger was identified as "Banjo," even though Trigger at one point in *Silver City Raiders* was called "Comanche." The lobby card was discovered by saddle pal Derwood Harris. The caption beneath the photo read, "Hold it ... or I'll let you have it."

9. Trigger was first discovered in *Silver City Raiders* by Larry Roe. The film was screened in 1989 by Harold Smith at a Riders of the Silver Screen club meeting.

10. For *Saddles and Sagebrush* Hayden rode a beautiful chestnut. By the time he starred in *Riders of the Northwest Mounted,* he was riding a sorrel.

11. It's reasonable to suggest that Trigger may have been used in other Columbia movies with Hayden, since Hayden made seven other movies for the studio: *The Royal Mounted* (1941), *West of Tombstone* (1942), *Lawless Plainsmen* (1942), *Down Rio Grande Way* (1942), *Riders of the Northland* (1942), and *Overland to Deadwood* (1942). In *Riders of the Badlands* (1941), Hayden rides two different palominos, neither of them Trigger.

12. William Roper, *Roy Rogers: King of the Cowboys* (T.S. Denison, 1971).

13. Monarch is also seen in the "Trigger's Doubles" photograph.

14. A cremello is a cream-colored horse with pink skin and blue eyes; the mane and tail are white. A cremello is born a light cream or gold color. Although this color may fade to nearly white in adulthood, a cremello is not a white horse; white horses are born white.

15. The Double R "Bar" name did not apply until the television series. The ranch gate showed a circle with an RR inside a circle with the word "Ranch" on the bottom of it. The ranch was referred to, several times, as the "Double R Ranch." Rogers apparently hadn't added the bar yet. He was interested in a clean-cut image, after all. (Source: Jerry Dean.)

16. Coincidentally, in the film, Rogers' ranch was located in Victorville—17 years before he moved there in real life.

17. "Bell Mare" is akin to "bell wether," a castrated ram, usually wearing a bell around its neck, that is used to lead sheep and lambs to the slaughter. Since the bad guys were using this mare to lead a wild horse herd where they wanted it to go, it would be natural for them to have called her the Bell Mare. What is odd, though, was that Rogers and the others started calling her by that same name long before they figured out what the bad guys were doing. A mistake on the part of the writers, because the leader of a wild horse herd is not a bell horse but simply the leader, and that is how they would probably refer to her.

18. Rick Lyman, "Whoa, Trigger! Auteur Alert!" *The New York Times*, September 15, 2000.

19. Quentin Tarantino helped sponsor a Saturday Morning Film Club kiddie-matinee double bill which included William Witney's *The Golden Stallion*. In his introduction, Tarantino noted that there was a resemblance between Trigger and Uma Thurman. Louis Black, *Austin Chronicle*, August 24, 2001.

20. William Witney, *In a Door, Into a Fight, Out a Door, Into a Chase* (Jefferson, NC: McFarland, 1996), p. 94.

21. The Hatton phrase is "Hi Ho" as opposed to the Lone Ranger's "Hi Yo."

22. It was actually Trigger who jumped over the barrel, as William Witney said—not some stunt horse.

23. "Bullet Von Berge" was the AKA registration name of the German shepherd called "Bullet." He was later billed as a "wonder dog." (*Happy Trails Forever* Web site, www.ourchurch.com/view/?pageID=157671.)

24. Early in this exciting sequence two stuntmen make the initial jump from one wagon to the next. The first stuntman makes the leap without a problem. As the second makes the leap, the wagon swerves slightly and he loses his hold, sliding off the wagon and under the rear wheel! As it goes over his chest, the scene is cut.

25. Smiley Burnette's horse was first known as Black-eyed Nellie, then Ring-eyed Nellie and finally just Nellie.

26. Republic Pictures directors added stock footage or scenes from other westerns to save money and time. This was a common practice and later heavily employed in television. On rare occasions, footage with Rogers and Trigger slipped by an editor and made it into another cowboy's movie. With their striking looks, an ordinary scene was not the generic view it was supposed to have been.

27. Where possible, composers, release dates, labels, and album titles are noted. In a career as long as Roy Rogers', many of the songs were recorded more than once and released on different compilations and in a variety of formats, from 78 LPs to CDs.

Chapter 7

1. From a preface written by Roy Rogers for the book *A Pictorial History of Performing Horses* by Charles Phillip Fox (New York: Bramhall House, 1971).

2. Most likely a money-saving move by Republic.

3. Autry opened his show with a voice-over: "Hello, folks. Say, I've got a swell story I want to tell you today. Champ and I are ready for action."

4. Source: Larry Roe.

5. Roy Rogers and Dale Evans with Jane and Michael Stern, *Happy Trails: Our Life Story* (New York: Simon & Schuster; 1994), p. 164.

6. "Val Kilmer led Triggerson, Trigger Jr.'s grandson, on stage." Johnny D. Boggs, "Val Kilmer—Playing Cowboy," *Cowboy & Country*, Summer 1999.

Chapter 8

1. Roy Rogers' television show stunt double, quoted in Ken Beck and Jim Clark, *The Encyclopedia of TV Pets* (Nashville: Rutledge Hill, 2002), p. 260.

2. Cheryl Rogers-Barnett with Frank Thompson, *Cowboy Princess: Life with My Parents Roy Rogers and Dale Evans* (Boulder, CO: Taylor Trade, 2003).

3. According to Bobby J. Copeland's *Silent Hoofbeats* (Madison, NC: Empire, 2001), p. 54, Johnny Goodwin trained Dick Foran's horse, Smoke (aka Smokey, Smoky), an almost dirty looking palomino. Corky Randall also recalled that Goodwin trained one of the Silvers Clayton Moore used on the *Lone Ranger* television show.

4. Len Simpson, "Trigger Man," *Movie Land*, October 1946, page 70.

5. Mario DeMarco, *Gene Autry and Roy Rogers*, Vol. 1 (West Boylston, MA: Published by the author, n.d.).

6. Elise Miller Davis, *The Answer Is God* (New York: McGraw-Hill, 1955), p. 42.

7. Davis, p. 42.

8. Beck and Clark.

9. *Movie Fan* magazine article, March 1953. In an article titled "Trigger's Tricks," which appeared in *Movie Life* magazine in 1943, it was claimed, "Most 'high schooled' horses do not learn advanced tricks until they are four or five years old, but Roy started coaching Trigger when he was a year old to kneel, bow, and pick things up."

10. From an article titled "Roy and Trigger" by Glenn Randall, source unknown. This article was excerpted in DeMarco.

11. Ken Maynard's palomino, Tarzan, was most likely as smart as "Trigger." Tarzan was often showcased in his master's films; he was even the centerpiece of the movie *Come On Tarzan* (KBS/World Wide Studios, 1932). Although the assumption has never been substantiated, most experts agree that when one saw Tarzan or Tom Mix's horse, Tony, performing a special trick on film, it was really that horse and not a double.

12. Rogers quoted in *Horseworld*, a television show aired around 1995. He said the same in print: "During all those hard rides for pictures and television, he never fell once. We had to do more retakes for human actors than for Trigger." (*Persimmon Hill*, Vol. 13, no. 2, 1970.) And again: "How that boy loved to run! All I had to do was shift my weight forward and he was off like a streak of lightning. Sit deep in the saddle and he'd shutter right down like the best roping horse there ever was." Roy Rogers and Dale Evans with Jane and Michael Stern, *Happy Trails: Our Life Story* (New York: Simon & Schuster, 1994).

13. Davis, p. 42.

14. Glenn Randall Jr. also worked in motion pictures. As a stunts coordinator and second unit director, he has contributed to such films as *Ben-Hur* (1959), *Harum Scarum* (1965), *Planet of the Apes* (1968), *Little Big Man* (1970), *Diamonds Are Forever* (1971), *Blazing Saddles* (1974), *Earthquake* (1974), *The Towering Inferno* (1974), *The Black Stallion* (1979), *Return of the Jedi* (1982), *E.T. The Extra-Terrestrial* (1982), *Indiana Jones and the Temple of Doom* (1983), *Species* (1995), and *The Mask of Zorro* (1997).

15. *Western Horseman*, Vol. 51, no. 9, September 1986.

Chapter 9

1. *Western Clippings*, number 36, July–August 2000. (Source: Bobby Copeland.)

2. On *The Pat Sajak Show*, Sajak interviewed Roy Rogers and made reference to the *Life* magazine issue with Rogers and Little Trigger on the cover. Sajak read a passage which mentioned the palomino's repertoire of tricks. Rogers acknowledged that horses aren't as smart as dogs and noted how they require hand gestures to perform.

3. Known as a "flight or fight response" — if threatened, a horse's first instinct is to take flight. If it cannot flee, it will defend itself.

4. Allegedly Randall did it by poking the palomino, just when he should want to go, in the ribs right in front of his hind legs. At first he'd be poked repeatedly with the thumb. Little Trigger would flinch every time, but eventually he'd do his business. After some practice he required only a shorter cue.

5. A horse is a reflection of the person who trains and handles it. If it's lazy and ill mannered, one only has to look at who's managing it to see the source of the problems. Likewise, a gentle and confident horse reflects a gentle and confident trainer.

6. "The Randalls' movie horses are what's known as 'managed' horses in that they perform at liberty, without restraint, in response to Randall's voice and whip cues. A seasoned movie horse ... is trained to come to the trainer, then go out away from him. He'll circle at a trot or hand gallop, do figure-eights, rear and paw, back, play dead, pin his ears and charge, whinny, and bow." Joan Fry, "Training the Black Stallion — Part I," *Horse and Rider*, December 1981.

7. Roy Rogers: "Unlike so many trainers who rewarded horses with cubes of sugar after they have properly followed their cue, Glenn explained to me that a pat, a kind word, and perhaps an occasional carrot would get the trick done just as well. He would later tell me he was amazed at the quickness with which Trigger learned." Roy Rogers with Carlton Stowers, *Happy Trails: The Story of Roy Rogers and Dale Evans* (New York: Bantam, 1979), page 64.

8. Sam Henderson, "Leonard Slye: The King of the Cowboys," *The Western Horse*, December 1989, pp. 40–41.

9. Duane Valentry, "A Horse Named Babe," *The Western Horseman*, April 1961, p. 56.

10. There are trainers who maintain that some horses eventually become camera-wise. When they detect the red light on a camera, they know a scene is being shot and it's time to focus. When the light shuts off and the camera stops, they relax.

11. *Western Clippings*, number 22, March-April 1998.

12. Fry.

Chapter 10

1. From an article titled "Roy and Trigger" by Glenn Randall excerpted in *Gene Autry and Roy Rogers: Kings of the Movie Cowboys*, Vol. 1, by Mario DeMarco (published by the author; no date).

2. Clayton Moore explained in his autobiography, "In a running-start mount, you run, leap towards the horse, put your foot in the stirrup, and mount — you do the whole thing on the run." Clayton Moore with Frank Thompson, *I Was That Masked Man* (Boulder, CO: Taylor Trade, 1996).

3. Most experts agree that stirrups were invented in China around 322. They were not used in Europe till the eighth century.

4. Elise Miller Davis, *The Answer Is God*, p. 52.

5. Davis, p. 52.

6. Yakima Canutt with Oliver Drake, *Stunt Man* (New York: Walker, 1979).

7. Duane Valentry, "A Horse Named Babe," *The Western Horseman*, April 1961, p. 57.

8. "As much as people believed Roy enjoyed riding horses, it wasn't known publicly until the early 1970s that his true love was motorcycles." Sam Henderson, "Leonard Slye: The King of the Cowboys," *The Western Horse*, December 1989, pp. 40–41.

9. Larry Roe met screen legend Ben Johnson March 31, 1989 at a film festival in Knoxville, Tennessee. When Johnson, a professional cowboy and expert horseman, was asked to name a half dozen movie cowboys who he thought rode really well, the first he mentioned was Roy Rogers. He was also quick to say that Rogers usually rode stallions.

Chapter 11

1. On a *Tonight Show* appearance with guest host Burt Reynolds, Rogers said that at one time he had as many as 400 items out and he was second only to Disney in merchandising.

2. They are sold by people producing fakes for the antique market.

3. The same clock was sold in Canada with a background mountain scene and sometimes shows up on eBay.

4. According to collector Jerry Dean.

5. On January 21, 2006, a professional 4 × 5 inch photo negative dated June 20, 1947, of Roy Rogers and Little Trigger closed on eBay for $713.75. Item number: 62442 62841.

6. *Double R Bar Ranch News*, November/December 1955.

7. Were I to play out a *Citizen Kane* scenario and pick a toy that is my own "Rosebud," the last words on my lips would be "Silver." This is a reference to the white Stuart rearing horse I got as a child. It came with a red cowboy figure, a black saddle and bridle. I remember my grandmother buying the set for me at Woolworth's when I was about five or six. I honestly do not recall if these figures were sold as Roy Rogers and Trigger. Because the figure came with a fringed shirt, I named him Bill after Guy Madison, who played Wild Bill Hickok on television. I called the horse Silver after the Lone Ranger's horse simply because it was white. I still have them, mint and complete.

8. Lizabeth West, "Unraveling the Stuart Mystery," *Plastic Figures & Play Set Collector*, number 68, October 2000.

9. Lizabeth West narrowed the designer of the premium/Stuart rearing horse down to two possibilities: C.F. Block and Associates with Kirk Melzer, or Melzer with the assistance of an ad agency Block brought in to help (he couldn't remember which agency). West was unable to locate Kirk Melzer; however, Block said that they used a

photo of a rearing horse and strived for accuracy and that the project was a group effort. West also offers the following speculation: Perhaps Melzer did the drawing, as he worked on other projects for Block as well. Possibly Block hired an ad agency to polish the idea or provide input regarding the design, then come up with the advertising.

10. The All Western Plastics Saddle Company, later of Scottsbluff, Nebraska, was also the company that made the plastic yo-yos that were to be used in the Roy Rogers and Trigger contest that never happened. Apparently the yo-yos were stored and only within the last 20 years have appeared on the collectible market.

11. David Rothel, *The Roy Rogers Book* (Madison, NC: Empire, 1987).

Chapter 12

1. Joe Curreri, "Forget the Girl — Kiss the Horse," *Persimmon Hill*, Vol. 13, no. 2, 1970.

2. Maynard certainly didn't have the same kind of love and respect for his mounts that Roy Rogers did. Consider the following quote from *The Vanishing Legion* by Jon Tuska: "Maynard's drinking kept him permanently surly. Maynard would also, to the horror of the cast and crew, take out his frustrations by beating his palomino horses. One of his more violent sessions was recorded by the sound engineers and played back for [Nat] Levine. How could this man, this cowboy hero who supposedly loves horses and Tarzan above all, whip his horses mercilessly, the animals screaming in torment? The answer, of course, was very simple. Hollywood had made Ken Maynard a movie hero. Those who were horrified were horrified because they were believing the illusion they themselves were responsible for creating." From Jon Tuska, *The Vanishing Legion: A History of Mascot Pictures 1927–1935* (Jefferson, NC: McFarland, 1999), p. 136. Director William Witney reported an even more heartless episode involving Maynard: "One day in a fit of temper, he ran one of Tarzan's doubles at a tree with his spurs dug deep into the horse's flanks. As the horse tried to shy away from the tree, Maynard stepped off the horse, jerking the reins with him, thereby pulling the horse's head into the tree with a sickening thud that knocked the poor animal to the ground." From William Witney, *In a Door, Into a Fight, Out a Door, Into a Chase* (Jefferson, NC: McFarland, 1996), p. 32.

3. *Horse Illustrated*, Vol. 9, no. 6, June 1985.

4. Raymond E. White, "B-western Horses," *Western Horseman*, Vol. 66, no. 6, June 2001.

5. Tom Mix's wonder horse, Tony, was put to sleep at age 39, two years after his master was killed in a car wreck. Mix died October 12, 1940 and Tony died October 10, 1942. — Bobby Copeland.

6. *Fury* had 116 episodes that ran 1955–1960; *My Friend Flicka*, 39 episodes on CBS from September 1955 until June 1956.

7. People use "chestnut" and "sorrel" for horses that are red in color. There are those who refer to the redder versions as sorrel; some refer to the redder versions as chestnut. Horses with flaxen manes and tails are generally called sorrel by some people, but not by all. There are even some who consider sorrel a term only for horses who are ridden in a western saddle and use the term chestnut for horses ridden in English tack. To complicate matters more, some breed registries use only one term, either chestnut or sorrel; some use both.

8. David Rothel, *The Gene Autry Book* (Madison, NC: Empire, 1988), p. 87.

9. Whitman Publishing produced a children's book titled *Gene Autry and the Golden Stallion*, something Autry may have even approved of.

10. Cal Thomas, "My Lunch with Roy Rogers," *Jewish World Review*, July 8, 1998.

11. A Little Golden Record 78 based on the 1950s television show *Champion The Wonder Horse* was released as a 78 RPM 6-inch yellow vinyl disk. The Little Golden Record was numbered 226 and included two songs: "Champion the Wonder Horse" and "Bridle and Saddle." The tunes were sung by Mike Stewart and the Sandpipers, accompanied by Mitch Miller and His Orchestra.

12. *The Strawberry Roan* was almost derivative. In point of fact two other *Strawberry Roan* films were made before Autry's — one in the United Kingdom by the British Film Corporation in 1945 and one in 1933 by none other than Autry's old pal Ken Maynard. It was released by Universal and filmed around Lone Pine, California. This version went a long way towards popularizing singing cowboys.

13. Roan is a coat color that comes from a mix of white hairs with a base coat of another color. It gives the horse a lightened appearance, while the mane, tail and head remain the original color. A red base, or chestnut, plus roan produces a strawberry roan. Since roan can occur combined with any color, the appearance of roan horses varies greatly. Roan horses are born roan and stay the same color throughout their lives. Autry's "Champion" in this instance had no white hairs in his coat; he was a solid chestnut.

14. Roy Rogers' film *The Golden Stallion* would open the same way a year later.

15. Episode titles include "Calhoun Rides Again," "Renegade Stallion," "Mystery Mountain," "Lost River," "A Bugle for Ricky," "Canyon of Wanted Men," "Medicine Man Mystery," "King of the Rodeo," "Hangman's Noose," "Outlaw's Secret," "Stone Heart," "Badmen of the Valley," "Return of Red Cloud," "Saddle Tramp," "Diehards," "Rails West," "Andrew and the Deadly Double," "Salted Ground," "Deerhunters," "Cross-road "Trail," "Brand of Lawless" and "Real Unfriendly Ghost."

16. The *Lone Ranger* radio show lasted until September 1954, a staggering 2,596 episodes.

17. The color feature *The Lone Ranger and the Lost City of Gold* (Warner Bros., 1958) opened with a theme song titled, "Hi-Yo Silver." This newer version was written by Lenny Adelson and Les Baxter and encapsulated the Lone Ranger legend.

18. In this first serial, Tonto, played by Victor Daniels (aka Chief Thunder Cloud), rode a horse named White Feller (White Fellah), not Scout.

19. Silver Chief was the white horse actor Thomas Mitchell rode as Scarlett O'Hara's father in *Gone with the Wind* (MGM, 1939).

20. Wranglers and owners described Silver #1 as a Tennessee walking horse and Silver #2 as equal parts Arabian and Saddlebred.

21. Apparently Moore was introduced to Hugh Hooker by Bill Ward, his stand-in and stunt double as well as one of the *Lone Ranger* television show's wranglers (1949 through 1954). In an interview with author Ken Beck, Ward acknowledged that he bought White Cloud from Hooker, who was starting a Hollywood rental facility, Studio Stables, shortly after the series began.

22. *Persimmon Hill*, Vol. 13, no. 2, 1970.

23. Clayton Moore's dedication to the Lone Ranger character was misunderstood by some fans; many assumed he did not relinquish the character even in his private life. In a July 2006 letter Moore's daughter Dawn wrote, "While dad embraced the character, he absolutely was 'Clay' at home — not the Lone Ranger. Over the years,

there have been suggestions that he became a little wacky thinking he was this fictional character. He didn't. He indeed loved the character, but I would say that 'obsessed' might be a little misleading."

24. Moore actually owned a buckskin horse named Buck.

25. Rex Allen at a western film festival in Knoxville April 27, 1990. Source: Larry Roe.

26. "Actually I came in a little too late. Yeah, I didn't know it and they forgot to tell me the whole thing was over when I started." Rex Allen on *The Merv Griffin Show*, NBC, 1982.

27. "Each paint horse has a particular combination of white and any color of the equine spectrum: black, bay, brown, chestnut, dun, grullo, sorrel, palomino, buckskin, gray or roan. Markings can be any shape or size, and located virtually anywhere on the paint's body." — American Paint Horse Association Web site, http://www.apha.com/breed/index.html.

28. With the tobiano type the spots are generally "regular and distinct as ovals or round patterns that extend down over the neck and chest, giving the appearance of a shield." In overo types "the white is irregular, and is rather scattered or splashy." American Paint Horse Association Web site, http://www.apha.com/breed/tobiano.html and http://www.apha.com/breed/overo.html.

29. Some claim there were well over 150 episodes.

30. B-westerns generally cost around $90,000 to make. Rogers' more elaborate productions topped the $100,000 mark.

Chapter 13

1. Dell also produced two equine titles in conjunction with popular television shows, *Fury* and *My Friend Flicka*.

2. Little is known about him. He had a long career at Timely during the 1940s as a funny-animal artist and worked at Charlton from about 1959 to 1962. He worked on and off for Stan Lee at Marvel Comics through the 1950s, mostly as a writer, and even came back in the early 1960s during the Silver Age superhero revival. Information on illustrator Ernest Huntley Hart is from Michael Ambrose, editor of *Charlton Spotlight*.

3. Both Hopalong Cassidy and his horse, Topper, got an artistic boost when Gil Kane took over the artwork of the *Hopalong Cassidy* comics produced by DC in the 1950s. Kane started with issue 118, and Cassidy and Topper were never the same. When the series was cancelled, Kane shifted gears and went on to even greater glory when he drew the Silver Age *Green Lantern* and *Atom* titles.

4. Before *Roy Rogers Comics* became a monthly title, 13 issues were published as part of Dell's *Four-Color* line.

5. To note the change, issue 100 featured a cover shot of Rogers on Little Trigger with three small gouache portraits of a palomino, each painted by Sam Savitt.

6. Much to my amazement, during my first interview with cover artist Sam Savitt in 1995, Savitt said he did not know Tom Gill had done the interior work on *The Lone Ranger's Famous Horse Hi-Yo Silver* or that Paul S. Newman and Gaylord Du Bois had written the stories. When Gill and Newman contacted me a few years later on separate occasions, they said they had not known Savitt was the cover artist. As a youngster, reading and collecting these comics in the 1950s, I never dreamed I would identify these men to each other!

7. Ray White, "Quick Draw: The Comics of Roy Rogers, Dale Evans and Trigger," conference paper ca. 1990. Robert W. Phillips claimed that many of the artist's signatures are not visible to the naked eye and were buried in the artwork on some covers and interior splash pages. He accidentally discovered this while studying pages with a magnifying glass. Phillips may have documented his findings with letters or phone calls to these men and their families or through some official resource like the Grand Comic Book Database.

8. His work may also be found in three issues of *Gene Autry's Champion Comics*. In number 7, August–October 1952, "Champion and the Ghosts of Red Dog" and "Champion in Waterfall Hide-out"; in number 10, May–July 1953, "The Sure Real Deal" and "The Fugitive Bank Robber"; and in number 12, November–January 1954, "Champion Roundup Trouble" and "Champion Proves His Point."

9. It would be thrilling to say that a man like Steffens, with his impressive resume, contributed to the Trigger comics. After all, he was an authority on the dress, tack, weaponry, and equipment horsemen used worldwide. He specialized in the American West and spent a lifetime documenting it. Steffens illustrated and wrote a regular column for *Western Horseman* magazine that was eventually collected into a series of books: *Hints for Horsemen*, *Horseman's Scrapbook* and *Handy Hints*. Steffens even worked as a stuntman on *The Adventures of the Cisco Kid* show on television, often doubling for star Duncan Renaldo.

10. Refer to the list of *Roy Rogers' Trigger Comics* at the end of this chapter.

11. In excess of 8 percent of his total literary output, rivaled only by his greatest achievement in comics, a 20-year run on *Tarzan Comics*.

12. After seeing an article in *Equus* magazine #150 in 1990, titled "The Mustangs of the West," with accompanying paintings by Sam Savitt, I suspected that he might have painted the covers for *Roy Rogers' Trigger*, *Gene Autry's Champion* and *The Lone Ranger's Famous Horse Hi-Yo Silver*. I wrote him in care of *Equus* asking if he'd painted covers for Dell Comics. A few weeks later a letter of confirmation arrived from Savitt himself. Bette Orkin, his wife, had kept records of his work. When I met them in 1995, I'd already accounted for more than double the Savitt covers on her list. Savitt was eventually able to confirm even more covers for a variety of Dell titles that Robert W. Phillips and I discovered together in the following years.

13. Only three books with Al Savitt's illustrations are known: *History in Harness: The Story of Horses* by Mildred Boyd (Criterion, 1965); *Heroic Horses and Their Riders* by Kate Klimo (Platt & Munk, 1974); and *What Goes On in Horses' Heads* by Eric Hatch (Putnam, 1970). Orkin confirmed that on occasion, Sam helped Al finish illustration jobs when deadlines were tight.

14. Robert W. Phillips attributed some interior Trigger stories to "A. Moore" and some remained unknown. Tim Lasiuta also theorizes that "A Moore" may be a ghost name like "Manyhands."

15. Many American comics were published in other countries, such as Australia, by a British company called World Distribution, Ltd. It is likely that Western Printing sold reproduction rights in other markets like France, Spain, Ireland, Scotland, and Mexico. The Dell Western Printing line was no exception. Interior stories were mixed with other covers to create unique foreign issues, which also carried their own issue numbers (*Hi-Yo Silver* number 10 was published outside the United States as number 3). World Distribution comics are different from their American counterparts, especially when it comes to production values: the covers are more flat, washed out in appearance, with little gloss due to the low-grade cover stock and newsprint pages.

16. Phone conversation with the author.

17. Jose Delbo finished *The Lone Ranger* series off at Gold Key when the Tom Gill reprints ended. (Source: Tim Lasiuta.)

18. The "unknown" artist here may very well be Til Goodan, according to the essay "Cowboy Stars and their Comic Books" which appeared in *Golden-Age Greats Volume II: Roy Rogers and the Silver Screen Cowboys* by Bill Black.

Chapter 14

1. Dan Gagliasso, "Remembering Roy," *Cowboy & Country*, fall 1998.

2. The last broadcast episode of *The Roy Rogers Show* was titled "Johnny Rover" (June 9, 1957). Four were produced but not aired at the time: "Fishing for Finger Prints," "Phantom Rustlers," "Doc Steven's Traveling Store," and "Born Fugitive."

3. *Roy Rogers: King of the Cowboys*, documentary by Thys Ockersen, Holland, 1992.

4. Wrote Beverly Olsen of Thousand Oaks, Ca.: "Roy Rogers' golden palomino died suddenly on July 3, 1965. He had been active and very alert for an old boy of 34 years. Trigger was being cared for here on Hidden Valley Ranch, formerly Rogers' Frontier Ranch. A special vehicle and trailer was being built to transport him in comfort to Rogers' new ranch in Apple Valley, Ca." Beverly Olsen, "Trigger Dies" (Letter to the Editor), *Western Horseman*, 1965.

5. The year 1965 was a hard one for Roy Rogers. Not only did he lose his beloved Trigger, but his son Sandy died while in the service and stationed in Frankfurt, Germany.

6. Rebekah Ferran Witter, *Living with Horse Power!* (North Pomfret, VT: Trafalgar Square, 1998). Trigger was born on the Fourth of July and died on July 3, 1965. Roy Rogers died on July 6, 1998. The King of the Cowboys and the Smartest Horse in the Movies passed away in different years, of course, but still within days of each other.

7. Bischoff's Taxidermy and Studio Prop Rental has been in business since 1922. They were located at 54 East Magnolia Blvd., Burbank, California 91502.

8. Roy Rogers and Dale Evans with Jane and Michael Stern, *Happy Trails: Our Life Story* (New York: Simon & Schuster; 1994). "Too many people loved him, I just couldn't bury him," Roy Rogers said to Thys Ockerson in the documentary *Roy Rogers: King of the Cowboys*, 1992.

9. Stan Freberg on radio's *The Stan Freberg Show*, 1998.

10. According to the Internet Movie Database (http://www.imdb.com/name/nm1022326/bio), after an investigation revealed that Trigger's meat had been sold to several small eateries in the Southwest (contrary to the Prevention of Food Adulteration Act of 1954), butcher John L. Jones was sentenced to five years in prison. Even if one had access to local newspapers and police records, proving the meat in question came from Bischoff's Taxidermy of California and the original Trigger would be extremely difficult after 40 years. Consequently this writer cannot take this claim seriously.

11. "The horses, remarkably enough, look exactly like huge toys; there's little or no sense that they were ever real animals." Comments on Trigger and company from Michael Barrier, "What's New," Archives: October 2004; http://www.michaelbarrier.com.

12. "Taxidermy," episode of *Modern Marvels*, broadcast on the History Channel in 2005.

13. Rogers and Evans with Stern and Stern.

14. Circa 1980; sponsored by the National Rifle Association.

15. Joel Achenbach, "Achenblog: Daily Humor and Observations," *The Washington Post*, December 9, 2005.

16. *Wrangler's Roost* newsletter; source: Bobby Copeland.

17. *Roadside America* Web site, http://www.roadsideamerica.com/pet/trigger.html.

18. *The Daily Press*, Victorville, California, October 31, 1995, page A4.

19. According to an October 1946 issue of *Screen Guide* magazine, Trigger was valued at $20,000. Of course, that was more than 50 years before the IRS made its assessment; inflation must be taken into consideration.

20. Response by Dave Koch, the Internet administrator for the museum and Dusty Rogers' son-in-law, in response to an inquiry made by Joel Dortch in May of 2006.

21. A Silver look-alike was present at Clayton Moore's memorial service complete with his saddle on loan by the Wrather Corporation.

22. As heard by Larry Roe during a *Happy Trails Theater* taping session at the Cintel studios in the mid to late 1980s for later broadcast on the Nashville Network (TNN).

23. "But if there's a heaven for horses, that's where Trigger is." Roy Rogers quoted by Joe Curreri in "Forget the Girl — Kiss the Horse," *Persimmon Hill*, Vol. 13, no. 2, 1970.

Chapter 15

1. Roy Rogers, "Trigger and Me"; publication and date unknown.

Chapter 16

1. Inferred. Horse trainers agree that a horse is not started under saddle before two years of age.

2. "The Life of Dale Evans and Roy Rogers," *Movie Life Yearbook* (Bilabra, 1946).

3. The audio of this event may be found on *The Roy Rogers Collection (1937–1990)*, released by Rhino Records in 1999.

4. According to Joel "Dutch" Dortch, board member of the Happy Trails Foundation.

Chapter 17

1. "Triggers, Buttermilk, Bullet and Nellybelle," *Happy Trails Forever* Web site, www.ourchurch.com/view/?pageID=157671.

2. *Evening Express*, Monday, March 8, 1954.

3. Frank Rasky, *Roy Rogers: King of the Cowboys* (New York: Julian Messner, 1955).

4. In 1942 a wealthy Baltimore sportsman offered Rogers $15,000 for "Trigger." *Junior Rodeo Fans*, May 1943.

5. Roy Rogers with Carlton Stowers, *Happy Trails: The Story of Roy Rogers and Dale Evans* (New York: Bantam, 1981), p. 151.

6. Roy "leaned forward and hissed in Trigger's ear. He always used this in the running inserts when he needed a little more speed. The big stallion laid his ears back and jolted forward, nearly putting Roy behind in the saddle." William Witney, *Trigger Remembered* (Toney, AL: Earl Blair Enterprises, 1989), p. 65.

7. Both stories are told by Witney in *Trigger Remembered*.

8. *Reminisce Magazine*, July–August 2001. (Source: Jerry Dean.)

9. Rasky.

10. Source: Larry Roe.

11. The Grigg letter was not dated. I received it in August of 1996. Mr. Grigg has since moved to Wilcox, Arizona.

12. Research compiled by Roy Dillow and Larry Roe.

13. Bernard Thon started making leather saddles in an apprentice program sponsored by the Veterans Administration in a small shop in Lusk, Wyoming, just after World War II. Leather and saddletrees were scarce when the U.S. government appropriated beef and leather for the war effort. After the war T.C. "Tommy" Nielson, owner of the saddle shop, made a deal for the Lusk facility. He and Thon set up plastic riding tack business and produced 60 plastic saddles.

"Although the saddles were built on regular rawhide-covered trees, the ground seat was made of and shaped with leather, while the seat, fenders and 3-inch stirrup straps were made of quarter-inch plastic. Also of plastic were the fork covers, jockeys and horn coverings made from eighth-inch plastic. Padded seats were sewn and glued in place. All straps and decorations were welded in place with a hot iron. Unlike leather, which is soaked in water and cured for shaping, the plastic had to be heated or warmed in an oven and glued to the saddle while still hot."

As luck would have it Roy Rogers ordered two cream-colored plastic saddles trimmed in blue and red, one for himself and another for Dale Evans. Trigger and Buttermilk were not pleased; the saddles were cold and stiff in inclement weather, hot and sweaty when the temperature rose. (Anna Koch, "Synthetic Saddlery," *Star-Tribune*, September 26, 2005).

14. Rasky.

15. The East Coast Roy Rogers fast food restaurants numbered 800 in their heyday in the late 1980s. At one time the company names Roy Rogers and McDonald's were used interchangeably on the East Coast to signify fast food. Some Roy Rogers restaurants still exist. CKE Restaurants bought and converted most. There was no actual "Trigger Burger" offered.

16. Johnny D. Boggs, "Val Kilmer — Playing Cowboy," *Cowboy & Country Magazine*, Summer 1999.

Bibliography

Information pertaining to "Trigger" came from a variety of sources. Autobiographies of the figures involved were obviously one such source. It should be noted, however, that in their autobiographies, Roy Rogers, Dale Evans, and their son Dusty all mentioned Trigger in general public relations terms; daughter Cheryl Rogers-Barnett went into more detail. When being interviewed for biographies, articles, and the like, all four family members stayed within the framework of public relations. A few comments about the accuracy of certain works may therefore be worthwhile.

The Cowboy and the Señorita by Chris Enss and Howard Kazanjian (foreword by Roy "Dusty" Rogers), published in 2004, correctly states that Trigger "appeared in a few other small-budget pictures before teaming up with the King of the Cowboys in *Under Western Stars*." This book's refers to Glenn Randall thus: "Roy and another trainer taught the horse self-restraint." Every photo of a palomino in this book is captioned as Trigger, never drawing the distinction between the original and Little Trigger.

The same authors also compiled a picture book, *Happy Trails: A Pictorial Celebration of the Life and Times of Roy Rogers and Dale Evans* (2005). While many of the photos are unique and rare, the text is laced with errors (the first three photos in the chapter on Trigger are captioned as being "Trigger" but they are of Trigger Jr.) and stays well within the usual public relations.

In his *Roy Rogers: A Biography, Radio History, Television Career Chronicle, Discography, Filmography, Comicography, Merchandising and Advertising History, Collectibles Description, Bibliography and Index* (1995), Robert W. Phillips devoted an entire chapter to Trigger, discussing and analyzing him as he'd had never been scrutinized before. Some objected to this treatment of "Trigger," but many of those who were initially critical have since acknowledged Phillips' research and discoveries.

King of the Cowboys and Queen of the West: Roy Rogers and Dale Evans, A Career Biography by Raymond E. White is the only biography on Roy Rogers since Robert W. Phillips' book that makes a serious attempt to cut through the usual public relations. In contrast to the Phillips book, it says very little about Trigger.

Finally, there is the loving tribute *Trigger Remembered* by William Witney, who directed Roy Rogers' films from 1946 to 1951. Witney got to know the animals very well. Loaded with anecdotes and reminiscences, this book was printed in a small print run and sells for a very high price today.

Text on "Trigger" generated by the national media (newspapers, magazine articles, books, etc) was by and large cut from a public relations template. Exceptions are two articles by Robert W. Phillips: "The Legend of 'Trigger' the Smartest Horse in the Movies" (*Oaktree Express*, Vol. 3, no. 2, 1996), and the two-part article "Trigger—Known Around the World" (*The Southwest Horse Trader*, January 1995 and February-March 1995). Also commendable are articles published in the *Old Cowboy Picture Show* newsletter: Vol. 4, no. 12 (December 2000); Vol. 7, no. 2 (March/April 2003); and Vol. 8, no. 4 (July/August 2004.

These things said, here is a complete list of the sources used in researching this book.

Glenn and Corky Randall

As the man who trained "Trigger" from 1941 till the mid–1950s, Glenn Randall was the primary source for all things "Trigger." Fortunately, he gave interviews into the 1980s, and I have been able to draw on that material. Buford "Corky" Randall, Glenn's son, assisted his father and went on to become a well-respected horse trainer in his own right. Corky very graciously allowed me to interview him for this book and was most generous with his time in all respects, even providing a foreword.

Books

Adams, Les, and Buck Rainey. *Shoot-Em-Ups: The Complete Reference Guide to Westerns of the*

Sound Era. Waynesville, NC: World of Yesterday, 1986.

Adams, Richard. *Traveller.* New York: Dell, 1988.

Adler, Larry. *Famous Horses of America.* New York:
David McKay, 1979.

Allen, Rex, as told to Paula Simpson. *The Arizona
Cowboy: "My Life — Sunrise to Sunset."* Scotts-
dale, AZ: RexGarRus, 1989.

Amaral, Anthony. *Movie Horses: Their Treatment
and Training.* Indianapolis: Bobbs-Merrill, 1967.

Autry, Gene, with Mickey Herskowitz. *Back in the
Saddle Again.* Garden City, NY: Doubleday, 1978.

Beck, Ken, and Jim Clark. *The Encyclopedia of TV
Pets.* Nashville: Rutledge Hill, 2002.

Black, Bill. *Golden-Age Greats Volume II: Roy Rogers
and the Silver Screen Cowboys: An Illustrated History of the Matinee Western.* Publisher unknown.

Burt, Don. *Horses and Other Heroes: Reflections of a
Life with Horses.* Guilford, CT: Lyons, 2002.

Cain, Dana. *Film and TV Animal Star Collectables.*
Norfolk, VA: Antique Trader, 1998.

Canutt, Yakima, with Oliver Drake. *Stunt Man.*
New York: Walker, 1979.

Carman, Bob, and Dan Scapperotti. *Roy Rogers,
King of the Cowboys: A Film Guide.* Robert C.
Carman, 1979.

Copeland, Bobby J. *Silent Hoofbeats: A Salute to
the Horses and Riders of the Bygone B-Western
Era.* Foreword by William "Buck" Rainey. Madison, NC: Empire, 2001.

Coyle, P. Allan. *Roy Rogers and Dale Evans Toys &
Memorabilia: Identification & Values.* Paducah,
KY: Collector Books, 2000.

Cunningham, Eugene. *Triggernometry: Gallery of
Gunfighters.* Caldwell, OH: Caxton, 1956.

Davis, Elise Miller. *The Answer Is God: The Inspiring Personal Story of Dale Evans and Roy Rogers
and the Miracle That Changed Their Lives.* New
York: McGraw-Hill, 1955.

DeMarco, Mario. *Gene Autry and Roy Rogers: Kings
of the Movie Cowboys.* Vol. 1. W. Boylston, MA:
Published by the author, n.d.

_____. *Horse Bits from the B-Western Movies and
Television.* West Boylston, MA: published by the
author, 1995.

_____. *The Lone Rangers of the Silver Screen and
Television.* W. Boylston, MA: Published by the
author, n.d.

Enss, Chris, and Howard Kazanjian. *The Cowboy
and the Señorita: A Biography of Roy Rogers and
Dale Evans.* Foreword by Roy "Dusty" Rogers,
Jr. Guilford, CT: Globe Pequot, 2004.

_____, and _____. *Happy Trails: A Pictorial Cele-
bration of the Life and Times of Roy Rogers and
Dale Evans.* Guilford, CT: Globe Pequot, 2005.

Epting, Chris. *The Ruby Slippers, Madonna's Bra,
and Einstein's Brain: The Locations of America's
Pop Culture Artifacts.* Santa Monica, CA: Santa
Monica, 2006.

Fitch, Gail. *Hartland Horsemen: With Price Guide.*
Altglen, PA: Schiffer, 1999.

Fox, Charles Phillips. *A Pictorial History of Performing Horses.* Preface by Roy Rogers. New
York: Bramhall House, 1960.

Green, Ben K. *The Color of Horses.* Flagstaff, AZ:
Northland, 1983.

Hake, Ted. *Hake's Guide to Cowboy Character Col-
lectables: An Illustrated Price Guide Covering 50
Years of Movie & TV Cowboy Heroes.* New York:
Wallace-Homestead, 1994.

_____. *Hake's Price Guide to Character Toy Premi-
ums.* York, PA: Gemstone, 1996.

Hake, Theodore L., and Robert D. Cauler. *Six-gun
Heroes: A Price Guide to Movie Cowboy Collectables.* New York: Wallace-Homestead,1976.

Heide, Robert, and John Gilman. *Box Office Buckaroos: The Cowboy Hero from the Wild West Show
to the Silver Screen.* New York: Abbeville, 1982.

Hintz, H. F. *Horses in the Movies.* Cranbury, NJ: A.
S. Barnes, 1979.

Holland, Dave. *From Out of the Past: The Pictorial
History of the Lone Ranger.* Granada Hills, CA:
Holland House, 1989.

Horn, Maurice. *Comics of the American West.*
North Hackensack, NJ: Stoeger, 1977.

Horwitz, James. *They Went Thataway: From Tom
Mix to Tonto, the Cowboy Movies and the Men
Who Made Them. Where Are They Now?* New
York: Ballantine, 1976.

Kazanjian, Howard, and Chris Enss. *Happy Trails:
A Pictorial Celebration of the Life and Times of
Roy Rogers and Dale Evans.* Guilford, CT: Globe
Pequot, 2005.

Lenius, Ron. *The Ultimate Roy Rogers Collection:
Identification and Price Guide.* Iola, WI: Krause,
2001.

Lindenberger, Jan, with Dana Cain. *501 Collectible
Horses: A Handbook and Price Guide.* Altglen,
PA: Schiffer, 1995.

Martin, Carolyn. *Metal Horse Figurines.* 2004.

McCarthy, Todd, and Charles Flynn, eds. *King of
the Bs: Working Within the Hollywood System.*
New York: Dutton, 1975.

McCord, Merrill T. *Brothers of the West.* Bethesda,
MD: Alhambra, 2003.

Mitchum, Petrine Day, with Audry Pavia. *Hollywood Hoofbeats: Trails Blazed Across the Silver
Screen.* Irvine, CA: BowTie, 2005.

Moore, Clayton, with Frank Thompson. *I Was That
Masked Man.* Boulder, CO: Taylor Trade, 1996.

Morris, Georgia, and Mark Pollard. *Roy Rogers:
King of the Cowboys.* San Francisco: Collins,
1994. 1998.

Norton, Doreen M. *The Palomino Horse.* Los Angeles: Borden, 1949.

Overstreet, Robert M. *The Overstreet Comic Book
Price Guide.* 34th ed. York, PA: Gemstone,
2004.

Petty, Kate. *Horse Heroes: True Stories of Amazing Horses*. New York: Dorling Kindersley, 1999.

Phillips, Robert W. *Roy Rogers: A Biography, Radio History, Television Career Chronicle, Discography, Filmography, Comicography, Merchandising and Advertising History, Collectibles Description, Bibliography and Index*. Jefferson, NC: McFarland, 1995.

Rasky, Frank. *Roy Rogers: King of the Cowboys*. New York: Julian Messner, 1955.

Rogers, Roy, and Dale Evans, with Jane and Michael Stern. *Happy Trails: Our Life Story*. New York: Simon & Schuster, 1994.

Rogers, Roy, with Carlton Stowers. *Happy Trails: The Story of Roy Rogers and Dale Evans*. New York: Bantam, 1981.

Rogers, Roy "Dusty," Jr., with Karen Ann Wojahn. *Growing Up with Roy and Dale*. Ventura, CA: Regal, 1986.

Rogers-Barnett, Cheryl, and Frank Thompson. *Cowboy Princess: Life with My Parents Roy Rogers and Dale Evans*. Boulder, CO: Taylor Trade, 2003.

Roper, William L. *Roy Rogers: King of the Cowboys*. Denison, 1971.

Rothel, David. *The Gene Autry Book*. Rev. ed. Madison, NC: Empire, 1988.

_____. *The Great Show Business Animals*. La Jolla, CA: A.S. Barnes, 1980.

_____. *The Roy Rogers Book*. Madison, NC: Empire, 1987.

_____. *The Singing Cowboys*. San Diego: A.S. Barnes, 1978.

_____. *Who Was That Masked Man? The Story of the Lone Ranger*. San Diego: A.S. Barnes, 1976.

Seggerman, Sheri, and Mary Tiegrenn. *1001 Reasons to Love Horses*. New York: Stewart, Tabori and Chang, 2005.

Spitz, Bob. *The Beatles: The Biography*. Boston: Little, Brown, 2005.

Stanfield, Peter. *Horse Opera — The Strange History of the 1930s Singing Cowboys*. Champaign: University of Illinois Press, 2002.

Sullivan, George, and Sullivan, Tim. *Stunt People*. New York: Beaufort, 1983.

White, Raymond E. *King of the Cowboys and Queen of the West: Roy Rogers and Dale Evans, A Career Biography*. Madison: University of Wisconsin Press/ Popular Press, 2005.

Witney, William. *Trigger Remembered*. Foreword by Alan G. Barbour. Toney, AL: Earl Blair Enterprises, 1989.

Witter, Rebekah Ferran. *Living with Horse Power!* North Pomfret, VT: Trafalgar Square, 1998.

Yoggy, Gary A. *Back in the Saddle: Essays on Western Film and Television Actors*. Jefferson, NC: McFarland, 1998.

Periodicals

Allen, Don, with photos by Bob Wallace. "Trigger and His Doubles." *Pic*, July 1946, p. 65.

Big Reel, March 1997.

Bird, Allen. "A Horse Fit for a King." *Horseman*, May 1978.

"Bob Hope a Cowboy? Trigger Had a Horse Laugh." *New York Herald Tribune Magazine*, June 1, 1952.

Boggs, Johnny D. "Val Kilmer — Playing Cowboy." *Cowboy & Country Magazine*, Summer 1999.

Chesky, Naomi K. "In Search of a Palomino." *Fence Post*, January 1994.

Curreri, Joe. "Forget the Girl — Kiss the Horse." *Persimmon Hill*, Vol. 13, no. 2, 1970.

Curreri, Joseph. "Movie Horses Who Make Their Marks." *Horse Illustrated*, Vol. 9, no. 6, June, 1985.

The Daily Press [Victorville, California], October 31, 1995, p. A4.

Fry, Joan. "Training the Black Stallion, Part I." *Horse and Rider*, December 1981.

_____. "Training the Black Stallion, Part II." *Horse and Rider*, January 1982.

Gagliasso, Dan. "Remembering Roy." *Cowboy & Country* magazine, Fall 1998.

Goodman, Mark. "The Singing Cowboy." *Esquire*, December 1975.

Henderson, Sam. "Leonard Slye: The King of the Cowboys." *The Western Horse*, December 1989.

_____ "The Singing Cowboys of Yesterday." *The Western Horse*, Vol. 8, no. 1, issue 30, Spring 1989.

Lasiuta, Tim. "A Tribute to Tom Gill." *Illustration*, Vol. 3, no. 10, June 2004.

Lyman, Rick. "Watching Movies with Quentin Tarantino." *The New York Times*, September 15, 2000.

"The Man Who Makes Horses Say Yes." *Western Stars*, July 9, 1950.

Manns, William. "A Saddle Fit for a King." *American Cowboy*, March/April 2002.

Newton, Mike. "Who Was the Smartest Horse in the Movies?" *Classic Images*, July 1992.

Norris, Monty. "For Movie Trainer Randall, the Horseplay's the Thing." *Friends*, December 1982.

Ol' Waddy. "Trailer Deluxe." *The Western Horse*, October 1959.

Olsen, Beverly. "Trigger Dies." (Letter to the Editor.) *Western Horseman*, 1965.

Pando, Leo. [Sam Savitt biography.] "Oh So" (Letters to the Editor), *The Comic Buyer's Guide*, #1499, January 26, 2001.

_____. "Sam Savitt: Horse Painter from a Golden Age." *Oaktree Express*, Vol. 3, no. 3, 1996.

_____. "Sam Savitt: Painter, Author, Teacher and Horseman." *Illustration*, Vol. 1, no. 4, August 2002.

Phillips, Robert W. "Champion — Gene Autry's Equine Star and Related Collectables." Phillips, Robert W. "Collecting Western Comics." *Antique Trader*, August 1994.

Phillips, Robert W. "Horses are Heroes, Too!" by Robert W. Phillips. Date and publication unknown.

Phillips, Robert W. "The Roy Rogers Show—Happy Trails and Western Tales." *Television Chronicles*, no. 5, April 1996.

Phillips, Robert W. "Trigger: the Smartest Horse in the Movies." *The Western Horse*, Vol. 19, no. 1, issue 1, January 1995.

Randall, Glenn. "Roy and Trigger: I'll Match Roy Against Any Texas Line-rider!" *Western Stars*, October 12, 1949.

Rogers, Roy. "Trigger and Me." Publication and date unknown.

_____, as told to Aaron Dudley. "Trigger: First Get a Good Horse." *Western Horseman*, Vol. 14, no. 12, December 1949.

_____, as told to Adrienne Ames. "How I Trained Trigger." *Motion Picture*, February 1944, pp. 55 and 86.

Rogers-Barnett, Cheryl. "Roy Rogers and Trigger: An Affectionate Remembrance." *Cowboys & Indians*, Vol. 12, no. 3, April 2004.

Ross, Carol Ann. "Honoring Glenn Randall, Hollywood Horse Trainer." *Western Horseman*, Vol. 51, no. 9, September 1986.

"Roy Rogers: Trigger Man." *Movie Land,* October 1946.

Saunders, David. "The Art of Rafael M. DeSoto." *Illustration*, Vol. 3, no. 10, June 2004.

Sifaki, Carl. "Trigger, Roy Rogers' Boss." *Movie Fan,* March 1953.

Smith, H. Allen. "King of the Cowboys—Roy Rogers Kisses the Horse, Not the Heroine." *Life,* Vol. 15, no. 2, July 12, 1943.

Smith, Lewis. "Steel: The Horse the Stars Rode." *Horse Illustrated*, Vol. 9, no. 6, June, 1985.

Spangenberger, Phil. "He Spoke Horse." *Cowboy Magazine,* Summer 1992.

Strassberg, Stephen. "That Horse, Trigger." *Pageant,* February, 1947, pp. 68 and 69.

Sullivan, John Jeremiah. "Horseman, Pass By—the Glory, Grief, and the Race for the Triple Crown." *Harpers*, October 2002.

Thomas, Cal. "My Lunch with Roy Rogers." *Jewish World Reviews*, July 8, 1998.

Trigger. "My Life with Roy." *Movie Thrills*, July 1950.

Trigger Jr. "Rock 'n Roll." Publication and date unknown.

"Trigger's Tricks." *Movie Life*, 1943, p. 44.

Valentry, Duane. "A Horse Named Babe." *Western Horseman*, April 1961.

West, Lizabeth. "Unraveling the Stuart Mystery." *Plastic Figures & Playset Collector*, no. 68, October 2000.

White, Ray. "Quick Draw: The Comics of Roy Rogers, Dale Evans and Trigger" Paper presented at a conference of the American Popular Culture Association, ca. 1990.

White, Raymond E. "B-western Horses." *Western Horseman*, Vol. 66, no. 6, June 2001.

"Win a Wee Trigger!" *Movie Star Parade,* November 1947.

Ziemann, Irvin H. "Gaylord Du Bois—King of the Comic Writers." *The Comic Buyer's Guide*, November 1989.

Zimmer, Steve. "The Art of the Horseman." *Western Horseman*, Vol. 70, no. 1, January 2005.

Newsletters

The Old Cowboy Picture Show. Miscellaneous articles from Vol. 2, no. 1 (August 1998) through Vol. 8, no. 6 (December 2004).

Western Clippings, no. 22, March/April 1998.

Western Clippings, no. 36, July/August 2000.

Web Pages

Bart Kooker's Web page. www.iowalink.com/users/kbar/silver.htm

The Broken Wheel. brokenwheelranch.com/. Everything one would want to know about television's favorite black stallion, Fury.

Clayton Moore, The Lone Ranger. members.tripod.com/~ClaytonMoore/index.html. Host Steve Jensen has done a masterful job chronicling the history of the Lone Ranger and keeps fans up to date with current news.

The Grand Comic Book Data Base. www.comics.org/. Details and history of comic books. Membership is required and well worth it.

Happy Trails Forever. Maintained by ourchurch.com via the Christian Web Site Services. Contains a page titled "Triggers, Buttermilk, Bullet, and Nellybelle" at www.ourchurch.com/view/?pageID=157671.

Horse Fame. members.tripod.com/~horsefame/index.htm. More of a chat room than a history site per se. Some interesting information has been posted and it's a great way to meet other fans who love movie horses.

Illustration. www.illustration-magazine.com *Illustration* editor Dan Zimmer maintains this fine site where he even offers FTP downloads of past issues.

The Official Roy Rogers and Dale Evans Web Site. www.royrogers.com/. Mostly devoted to sales of merchandise and promotion of current events. Offers a good filmography, but if you're looking for information on Trigger, you won't find much. For members of the Roy Rogers Riders Club, questions are answered online at administrator@royrogers.com by Dave Koch, the Internet administrator for the museum and Dusty Rogers' son-in-law.

The Official Web Site of Gene Autry, America's Favorite Singing Cowboy. http://www.autry.com/. As usual, those responsible for maintaining the legacy of Gene Autry have done a first class job. This Web site is friendly, nice to look at, and chock full of great information, including a detailed history of the various Champions at www.geneautry.com/html/geneautry/champion/index.html.

The Old Corral. www.surfnetinc.com/chuck/trio.htm. By far the best site on the Web for B-westerns. Chuck Anderson's magnificent site is well networked and updated regularly.

Palomino Horse Association Home Page. www.palominohorseassoc.com/. Registry founded in 1936 for palomino horses and ponies in all breeds. Includes history and membership information.

The Roy Rogers Show. petcaretips.net/roy_rogers_trigger.html. All about Trigger, Buttermilk, Bullet, Pat Brady, and Nellybelle.

Those Elusive Stuarts. dkmoon.tripod.com/. Toy collectors owe Web master and Stuart figures expert Liz West a debt for publishing the history behind these beautiful figures on this fabulous site.

DVDs

Researching Trigger is often complicated by problems with still photographs and film footage. Pictures are often out of focus, cropped or doctored to create a desired illusion or to produce an eye-appealing effect. Lighting conditions and camera angles can also cause problems. An animal may be posed in a way that makes its markings hard to determine. When lighting is diffuse or contrast is high, subtleties are difficult to determine.

Film presents a still greater challenge. The freeze-frame option on VCRs can be helpful, but images are often blurred or out of focus. DVDs are better for freezing individual film frames but cannot account for motion blur. Even nature gets in the way. A horse may have a thick forelock that obscures the top part of its blaze.

Still, one appreciates the power of DVD players to move frame by frame and freeze an image precisely. This power is a great aid for studying the markings from one "Trigger" to another. Case in point: the musical number "Singin' Down the Road" from the 1945 movie *Bells of Rosarita*. The original Trigger was used for his good looks, and Little Trigger was used in the scene for his dancing ability. With a DVD player, it's clear that Trigger and Little Trigger were switched in and out of the sequence to create the illusion of one horse.

The DVD of *Seabiscuit* (Universal, 2003) comes with a documentary on the making of the film. At one point the director talks about all the horses required to play Seabiscuit. Articles on the great film *The Black Stallion* (United Artists, 1979) usually mentioned Cass Olé, the horse who played the title character, and acknowledged the other horses required for filming. The same could be said of the equine epic *Hidalgo* (Buena Vista/Touchstone Pictures/Walt Disney Pictures, 2004). Film and horse magazines candidly mentioned the string of overo paints used for the movie. In a documentary included on the DVD of the film, an equine makeup artist may be seen using an airbrush loaded with food coloring to match the markings of one horse to another. While some airbrush-doctored photos of the original Trigger exist, to my knowledge, palominos were not touched up on film sets or personal appearances, although it was a possibility.

Index

Numbers in **bold italics** indicate pages with photographs.